ESENT!

CHAPTER ONE
"IT'S A BIRD"

WRITER - CHRISTIAN COOPER

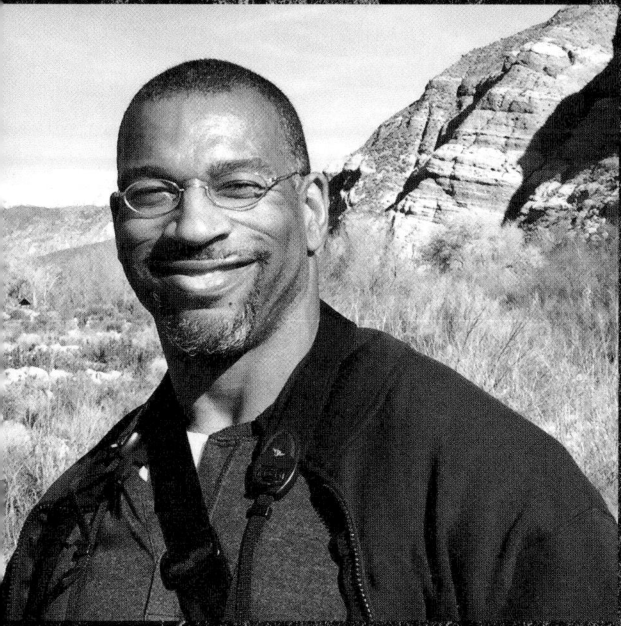

per is a writer and editor, a longtime birder, and a
r of New York City Audubon. Upon graduating from
vorked in the comic book industry through the 1990s.
nat time and into the present, he has been active in
Black rights and progressive political movements.

PENCILLER - ALITHA E. MARTINEZ
INKER - MARK MORALES
COLORIST - EMILIO LOPEZ
LETTERER - ROBERT CLARK

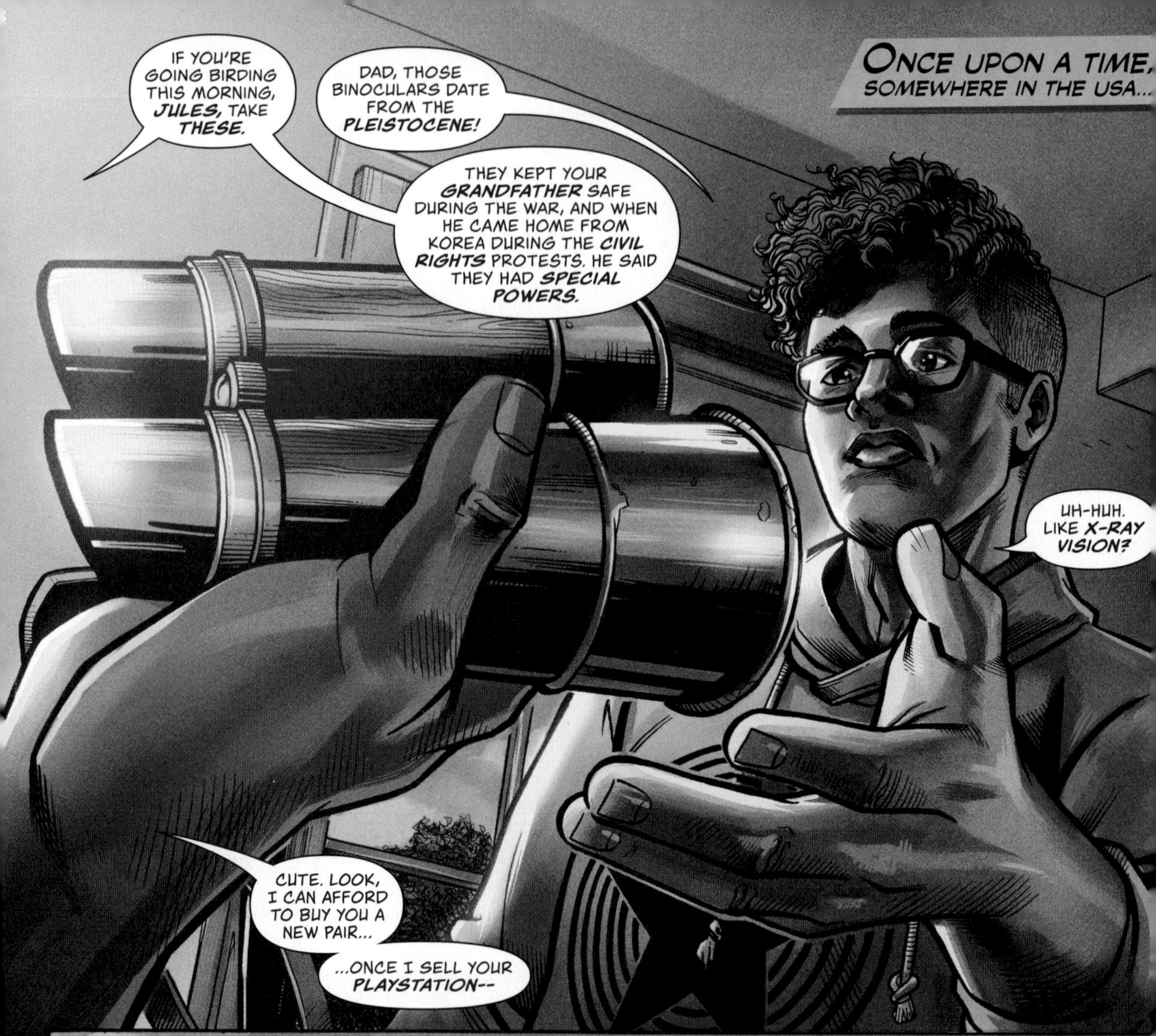
ONCE UPON A TIME, SOMEWHERE IN THE USA...
IF YOU'RE GOING BIRDING THIS MORNING, *JULES,* TAKE *THESE.*
DAD, THOSE BINOCULARS DATE FROM THE *PLEISTOCENE!*
THEY KEPT YOUR *GRANDFATHER* SAFE DURING THE WAR, AND WHEN HE CAME HOME FROM KOREA DURING THE *CIVIL RIGHTS* PROTESTS, HE SAID THEY HAD *SPECIAL POWERS.*
UH-HUH. LIKE *X-RAY VISION?*
CUTE. LOOK, I CAN AFFORD TO BUY YOU A NEW PAIR...
...ONCE I SELL YOUR *PLAYSTATION--*

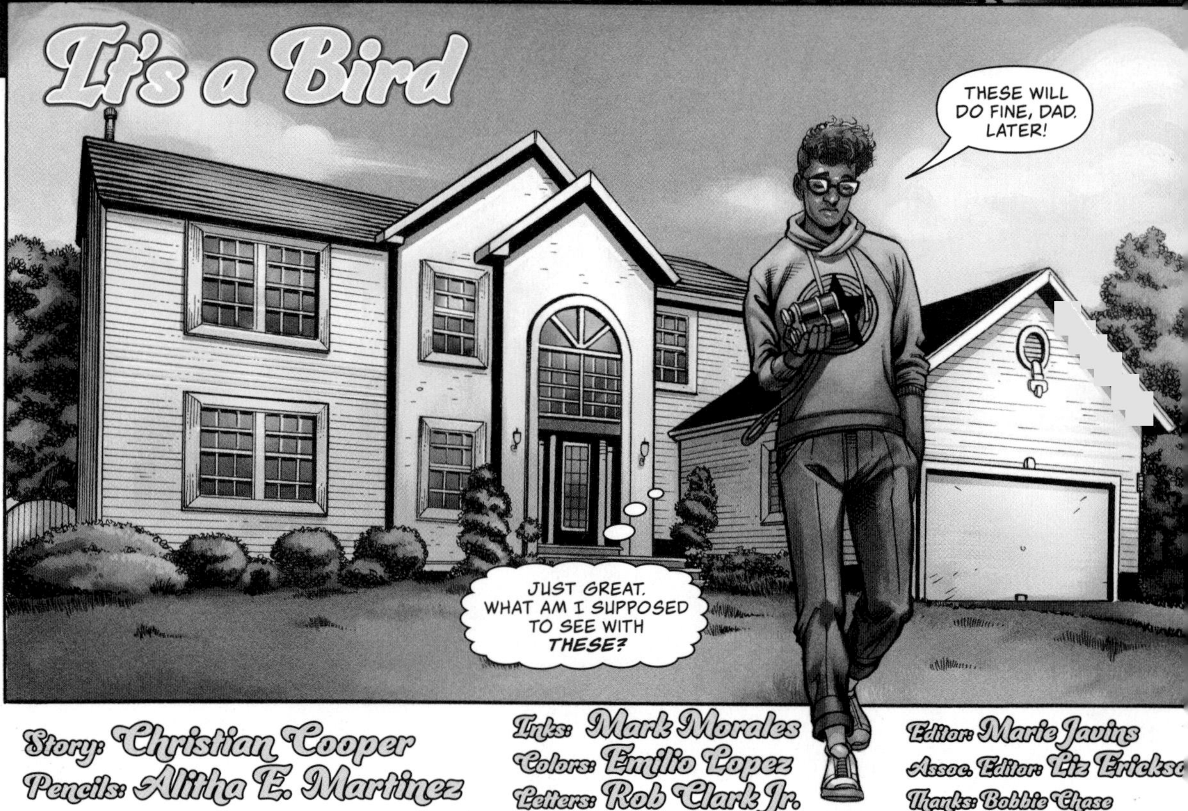
It's a Bird
THESE WILL DO FINE, DAD. LATER!
JUST GREAT. WHAT AM I SUPPOSED TO SEE WITH *THESE?*

Story: Christian Cooper
Pencils: Alitha E. Martinez
Inks: Mark Morales
Colors: Emilio Lopez
Letters: Rob Clark Jr.
Editor: Marie Javins
Assoc. Editor: Liz Erickson
Thanks: Bobbie Chase

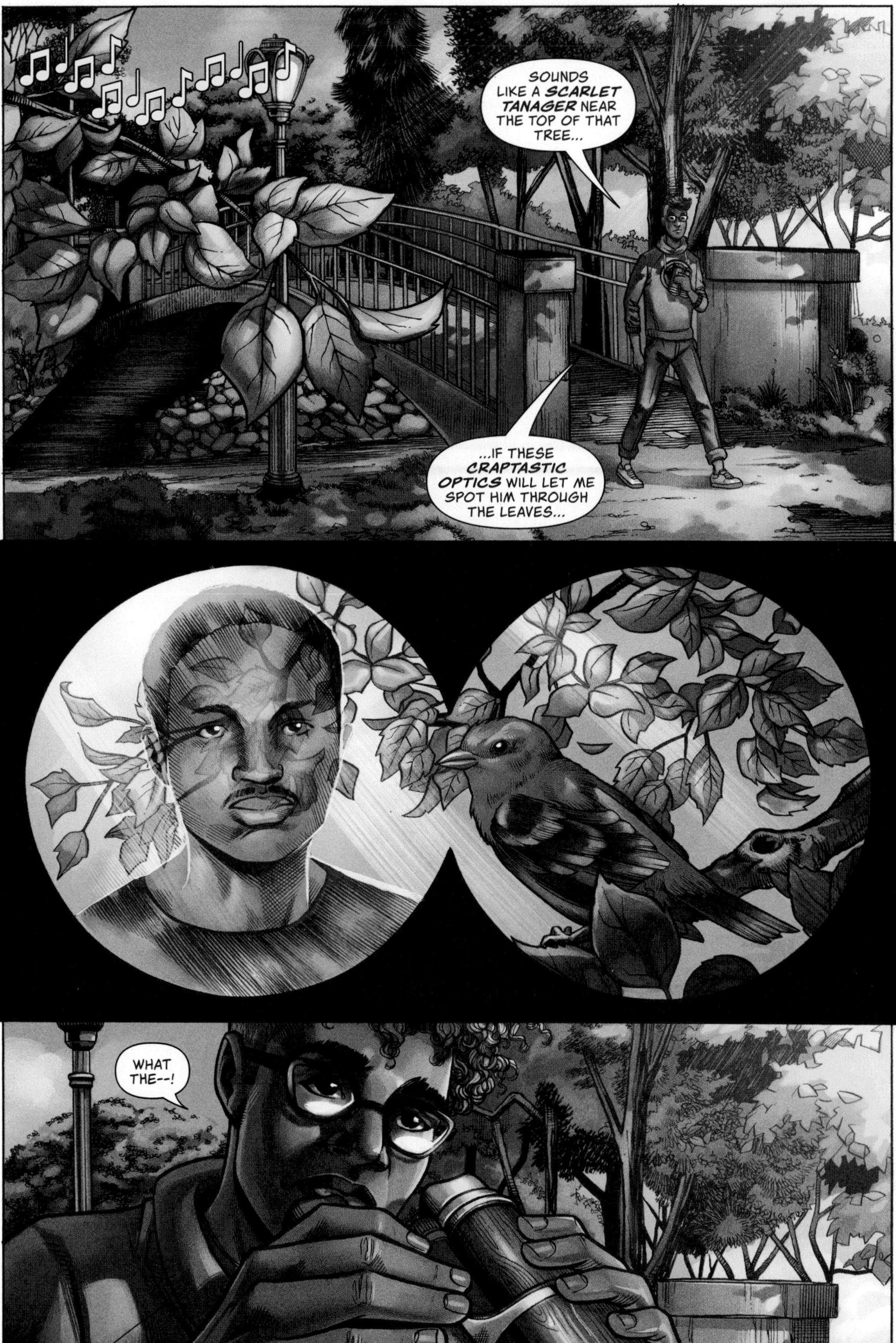
SOUNDS LIKE A **SCARLET TANAGER** NEAR THE TOP OF THAT TREE...
...IF THESE **CRAPTASTIC OPTICS** WILL LET ME SPOT HIM THROUGH THE LEAVES...
WHAT THE--!

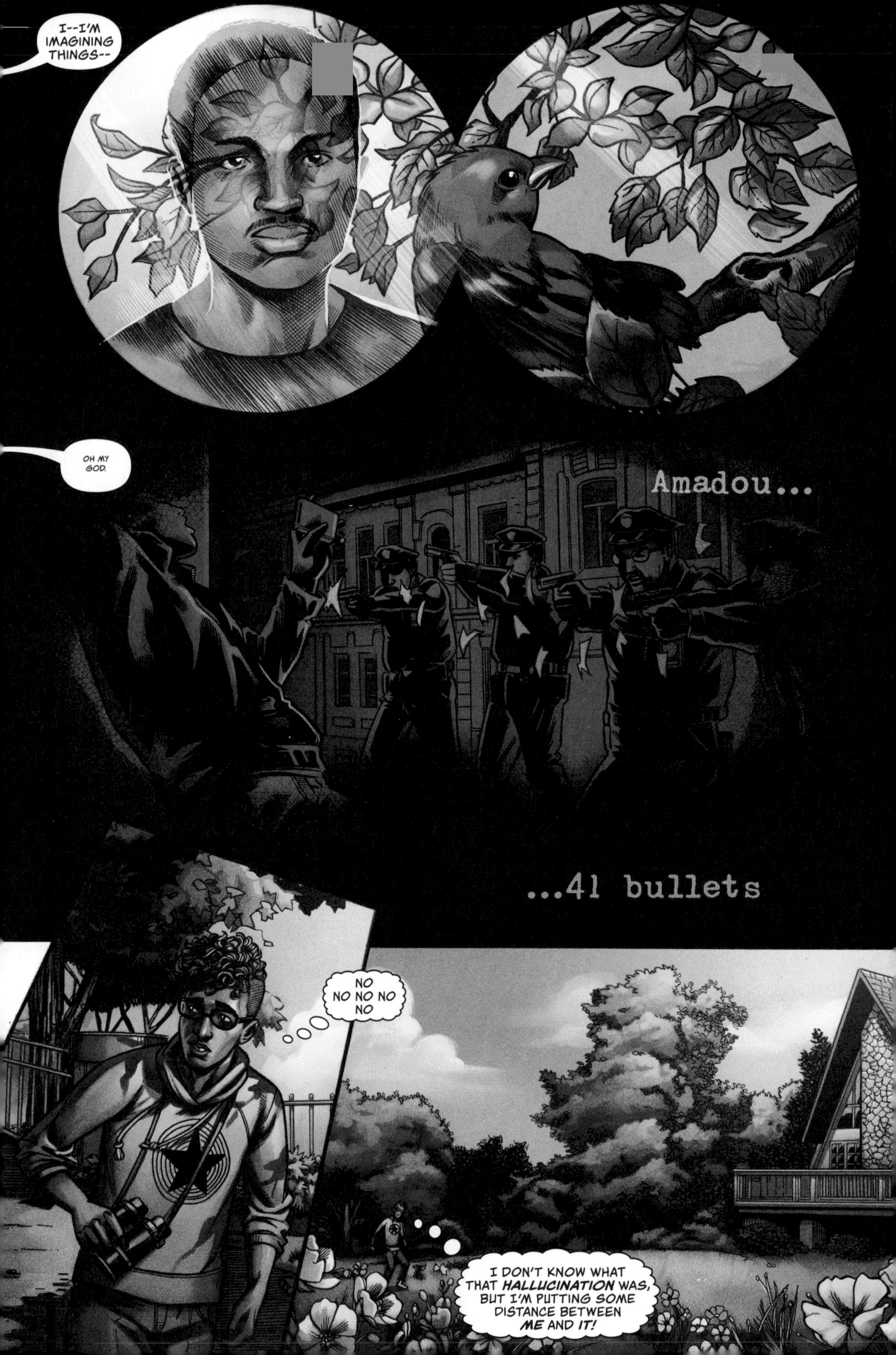
I--I'M IMAGINING THINGS--
OH MY GOD.
Amadou...
...41 bullets
NO NO NO NO NO
I DON'T KNOW WHAT THAT ***HALLUCINATION*** WAS, BUT I'M PUTTING SOME DISTANCE BETWEEN ***ME*** AND ***IT!***

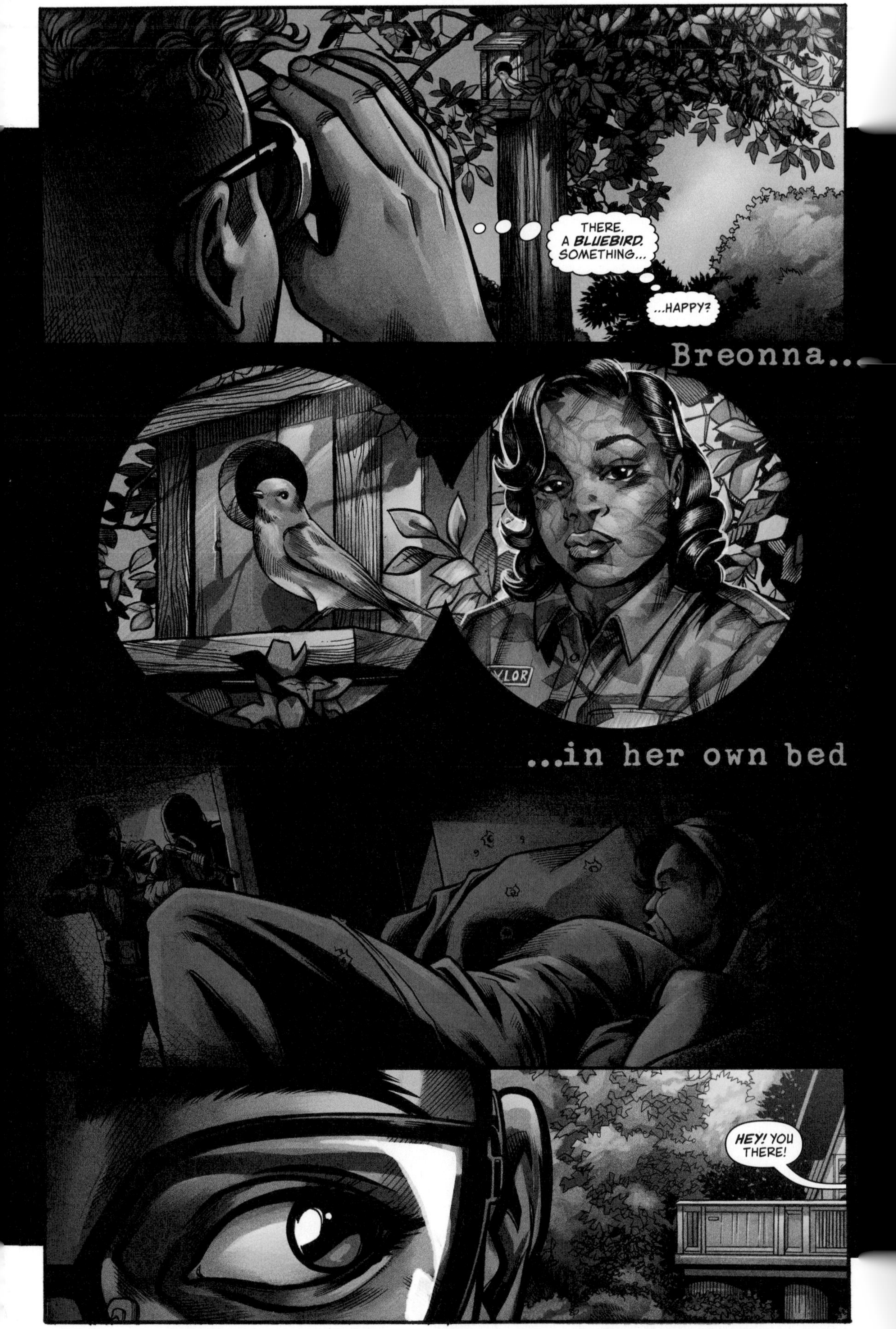
THERE. A **BLUEBIRD.** SOMETHING...
...HAPPY?
Breonna...
...in her own bed
HEY! YOU THERE!

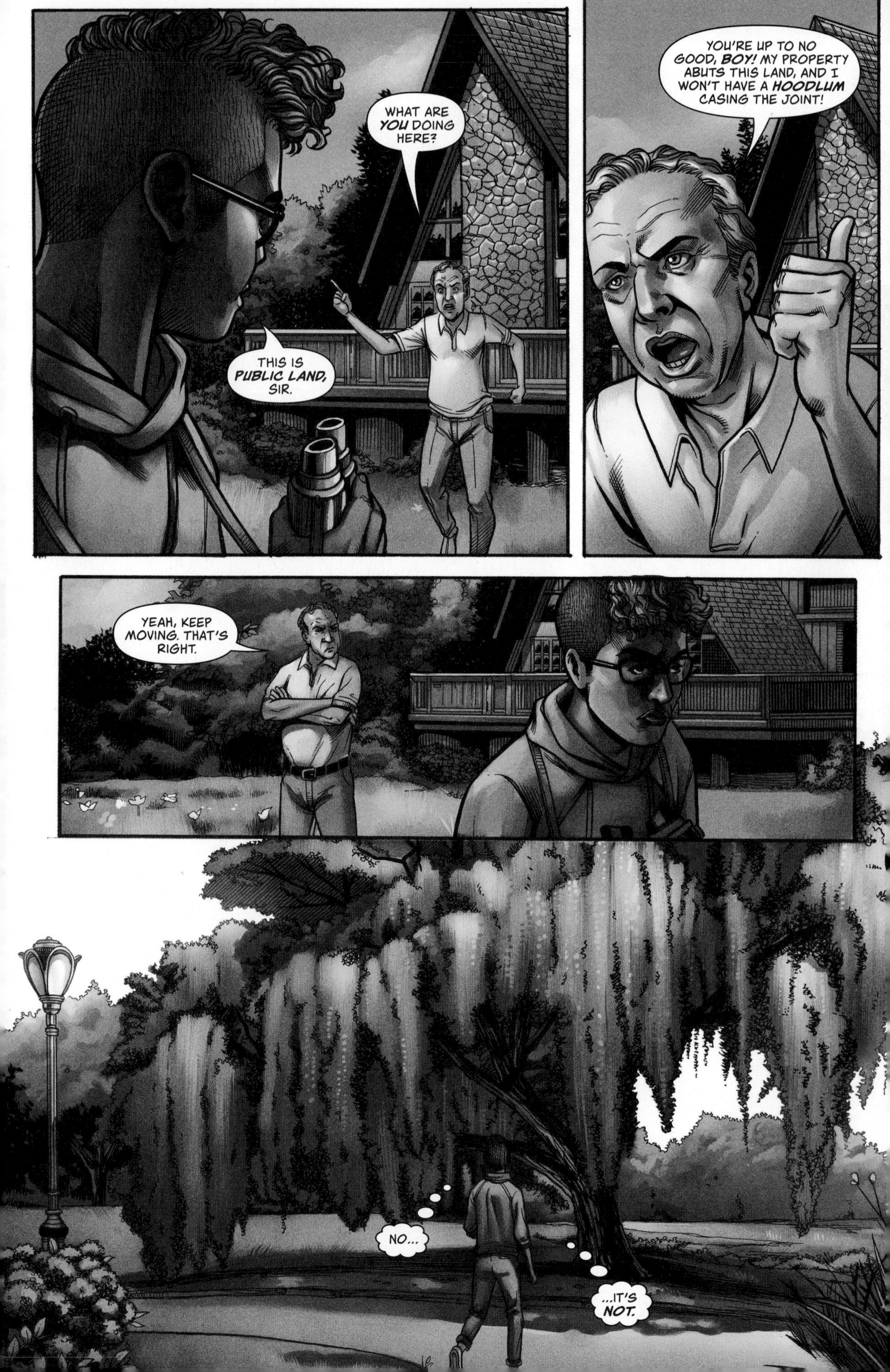
WHAT ARE YOU DOING HERE?
THIS IS PUBLIC LAND, SIR.
YOU'RE UP TO NO GOOD, BOY! MY PROPERTY ABUTS THIS LAND, AND I WON'T HAVE A HOODLUM CASING THE JOINT!
YEAH, KEEP MOVING. THAT'S RIGHT.
NO...
...IT'S NOT.

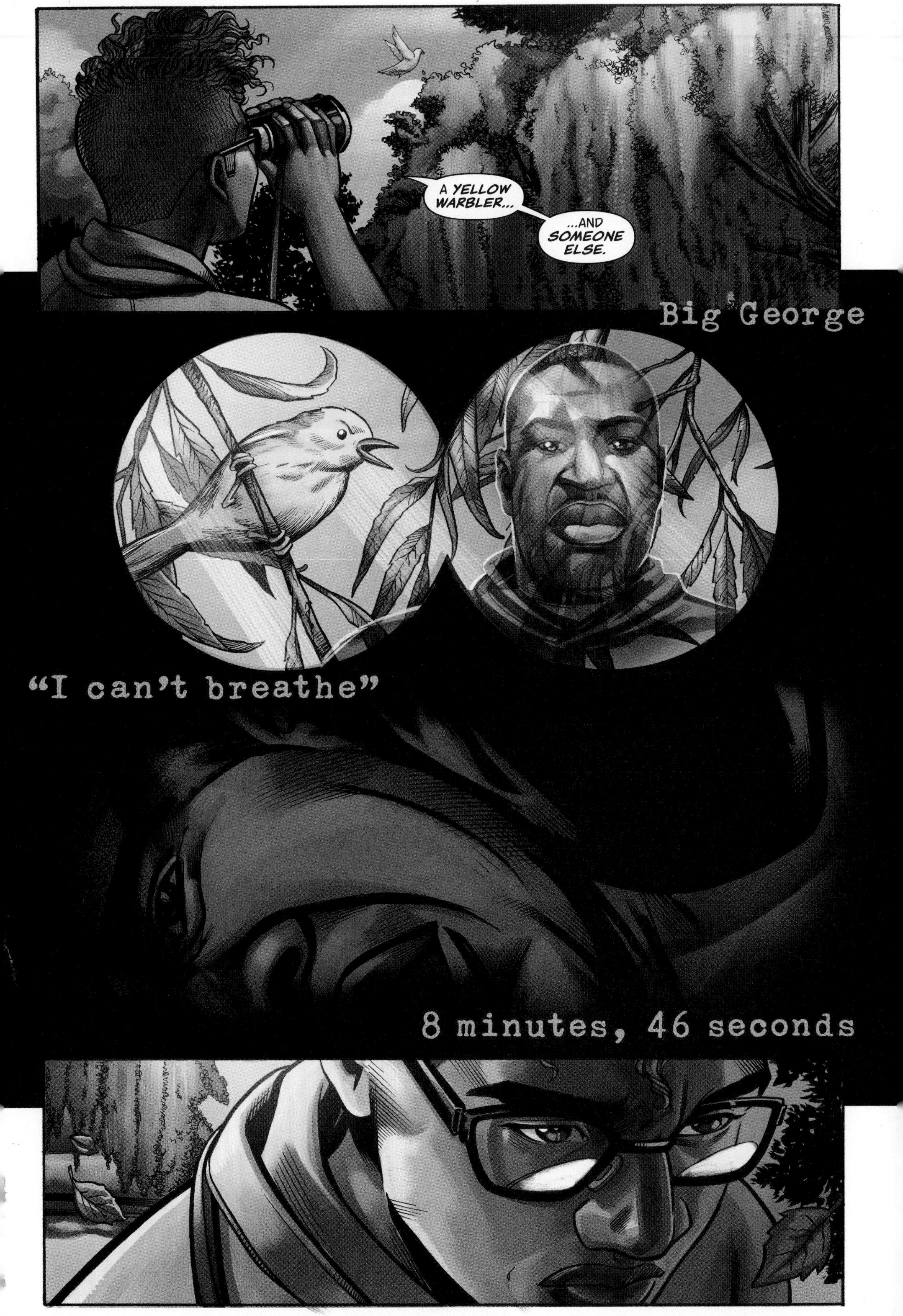
A YELLOW WARBLER...
...AND SOMEONE ELSE.
Big George
"I can't breathe"
8 minutes, 46 seconds

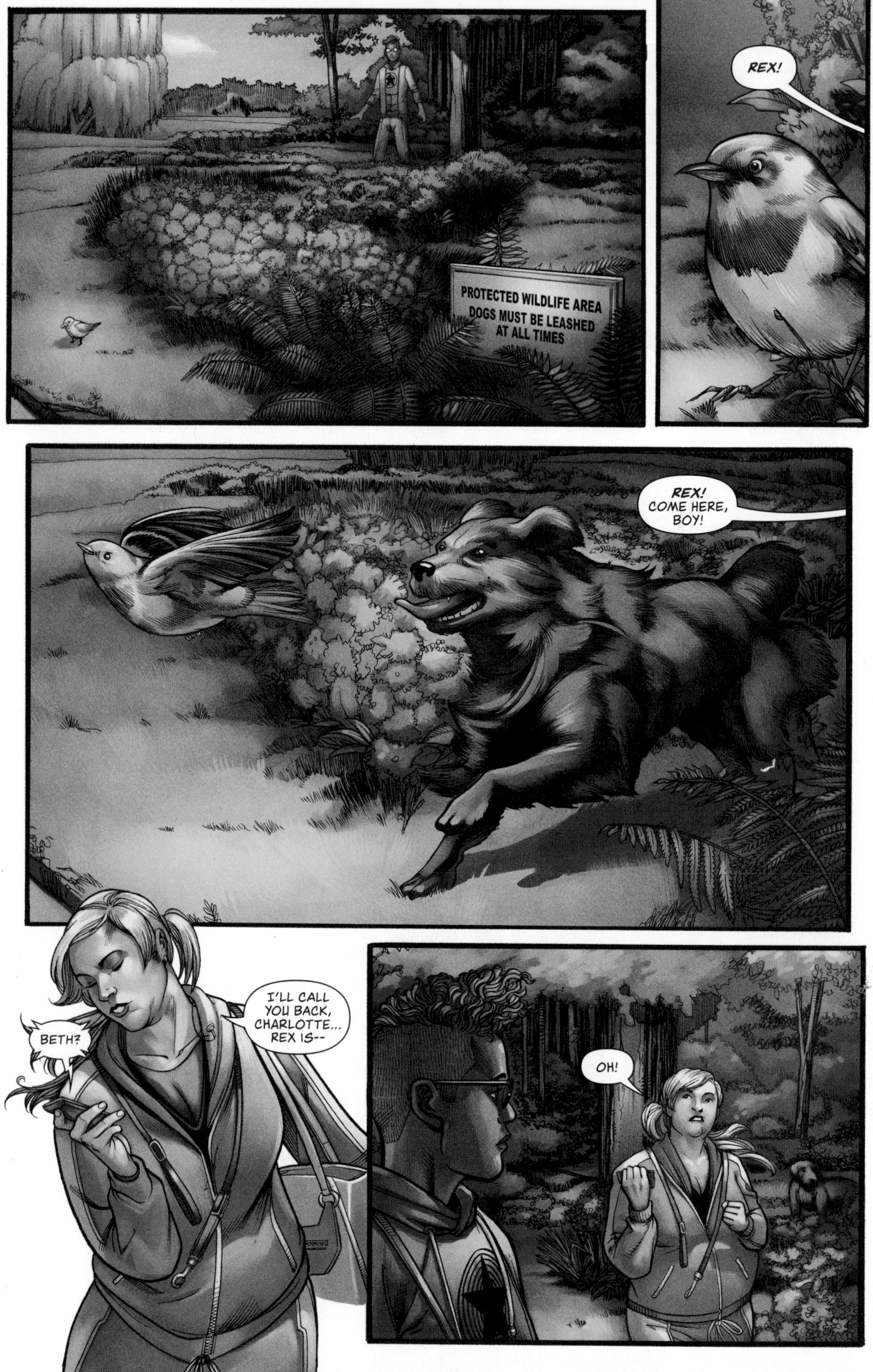
PROTECTED WILDLIFE AREA
DOGS MUST BE LEASHED
AT ALL TIMES
REX!
REX! COME HERE, BOY!
BETH?
I'LL CALL YOU BACK, CHARLOTTE... REX IS--
OH!

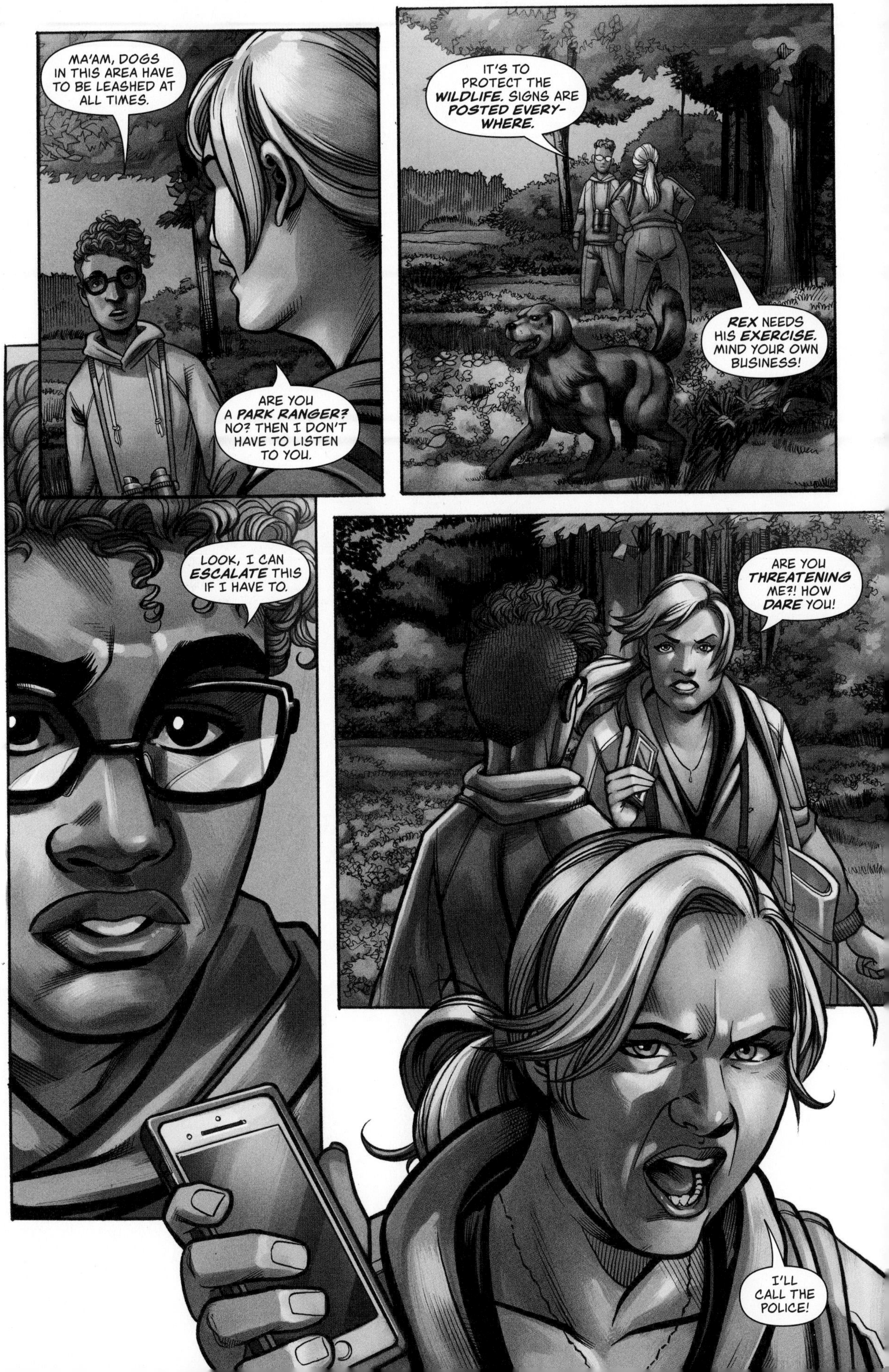
MA'AM, DOGS IN THIS AREA HAVE TO BE LEASHED AT ALL TIMES.
ARE YOU A PARK RANGER? NO? THEN I DON'T HAVE TO LISTEN TO YOU.
IT'S TO PROTECT THE WILDLIFE. SIGNS ARE POSTED EVERY-WHERE.
REX NEEDS HIS EXERCISE. MIND YOUR OWN BUSINESS!
LOOK, I CAN ESCALATE THIS IF I HAVE TO.
ARE YOU THREATENING ME?! HOW DARE YOU!
I'LL CALL THE POLICE!

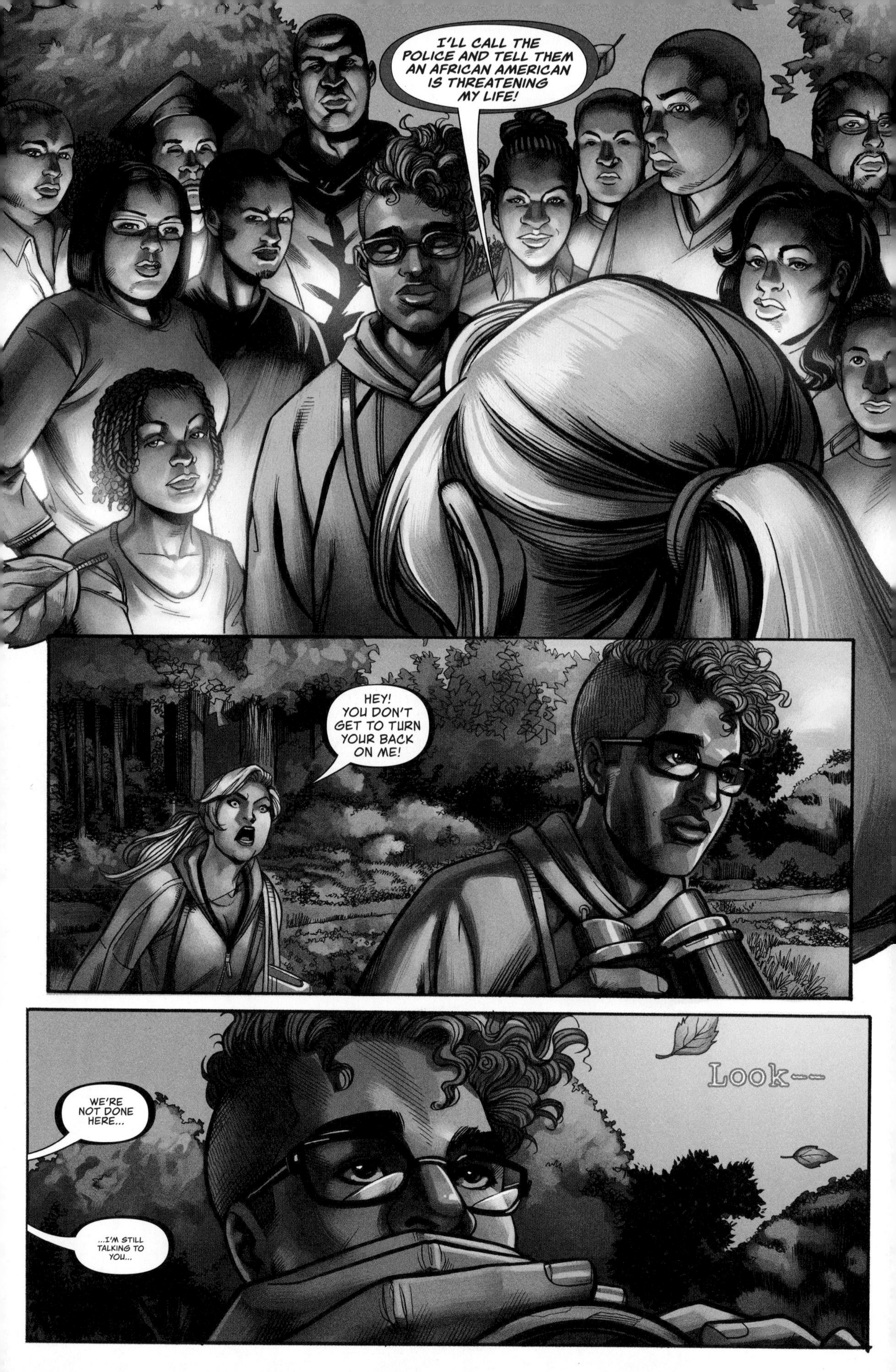
I'LL CALL THE POLICE AND TELL THEM AN AFRICAN AMERICAN IS THREATENING MY LIFE!
HEY! YOU DON'T GET TO TURN YOUR BACK ON ME!
Look---
WE'RE NOT DONE HERE...
...I'M STILL TALKING TO YOU...

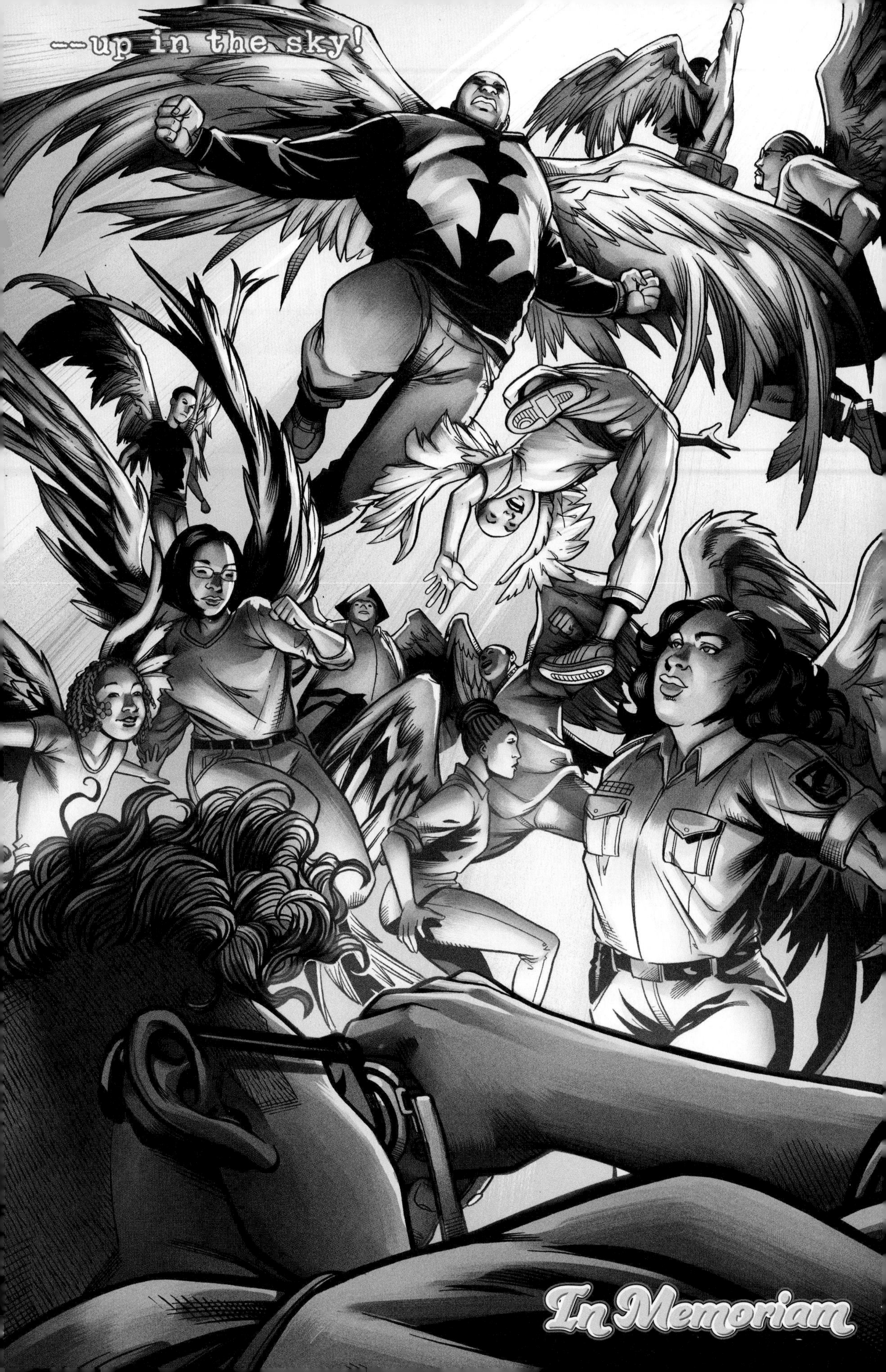
--up in the sky!
In Memoriam

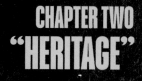

DC REPRESENT!

CHAPTER TWO
"HERITAGE"

WRITER - JESSE J. HOLLAND

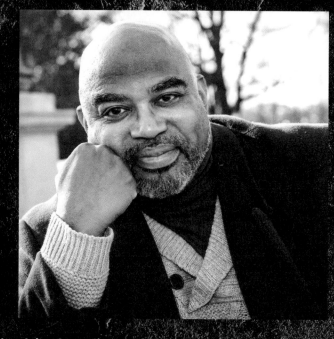

Jesse J. Holland is the editor of the *Black Panther: Tales of Wakanda* prose anthology and the author of the *Black Panther: Who Is the Black Panther?* prose novel, which was nominated for an NAACP Image Award in 2019. Jesse is also the author of *Star Wars: The Force Awakens–Finn's Story*, a young adult novel, as well as the nonfiction books *The Invisibles: The Untold Story of African American Slaves in the White House* and *Black Men Built the Capitol: Discovering African American History in and around Washington, D.C.* Jesse is currently serving as the Saturday host for C-Span's *Washington Journal* and as an assistant professor of media and public affairs at George Washington University.

ARTIST - DOUG BRAITHWAITE
COLORIST - TRISH MULVIHILL
LETTERER - DERON BENNETT

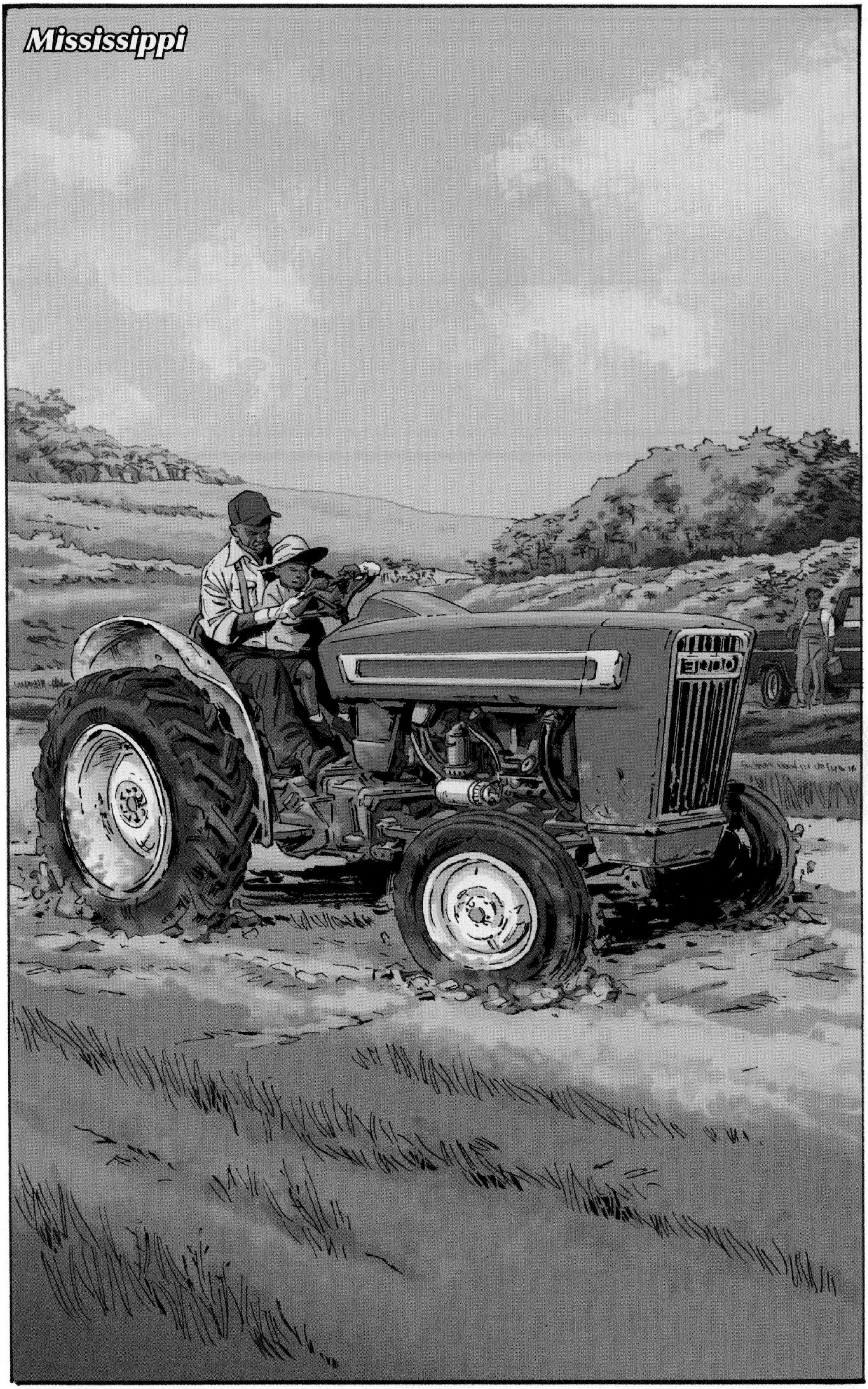
Mississippi
3000

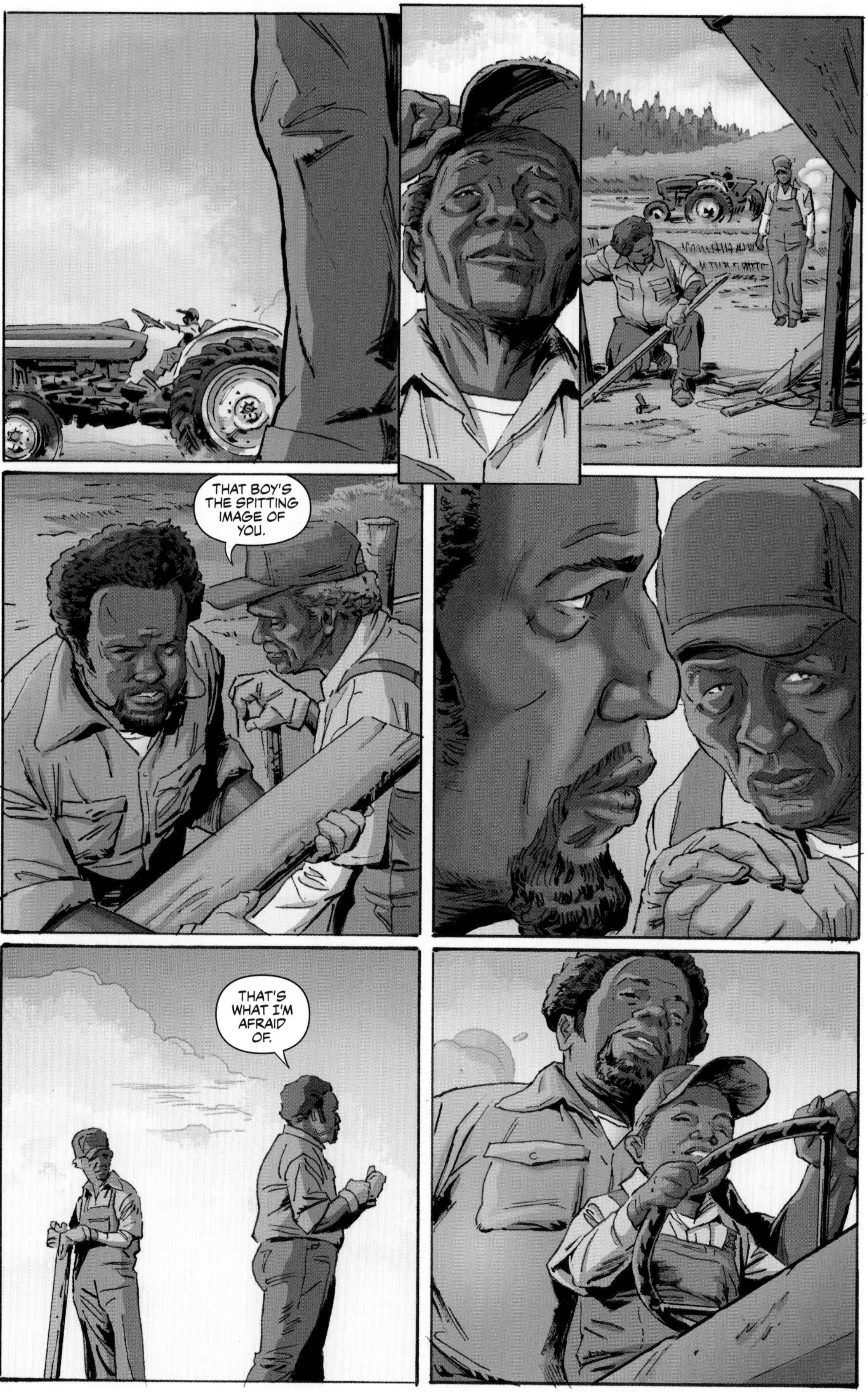
THAT BOY'S THE SPITTING IMAGE OF YOU.
THAT'S WHAT I'M AFRAID OF.

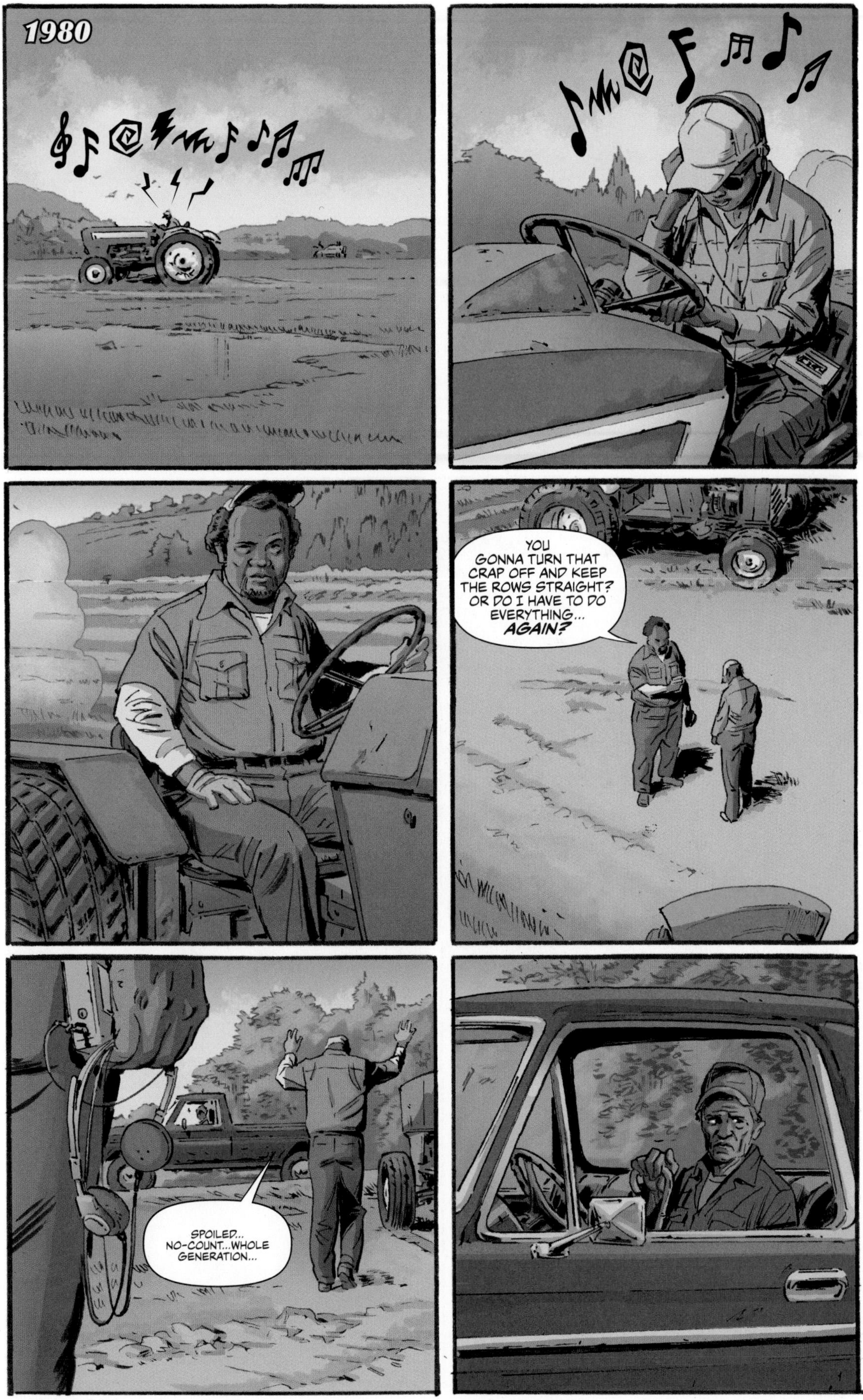
1980
YOU GONNA TURN THAT CRAP OFF AND KEEP THE ROWS STRAIGHT? OR DO I HAVE TO DO EVERYTHING... AGAIN?
SPOILED... NO-COUNT...WHOLE GENERATION...

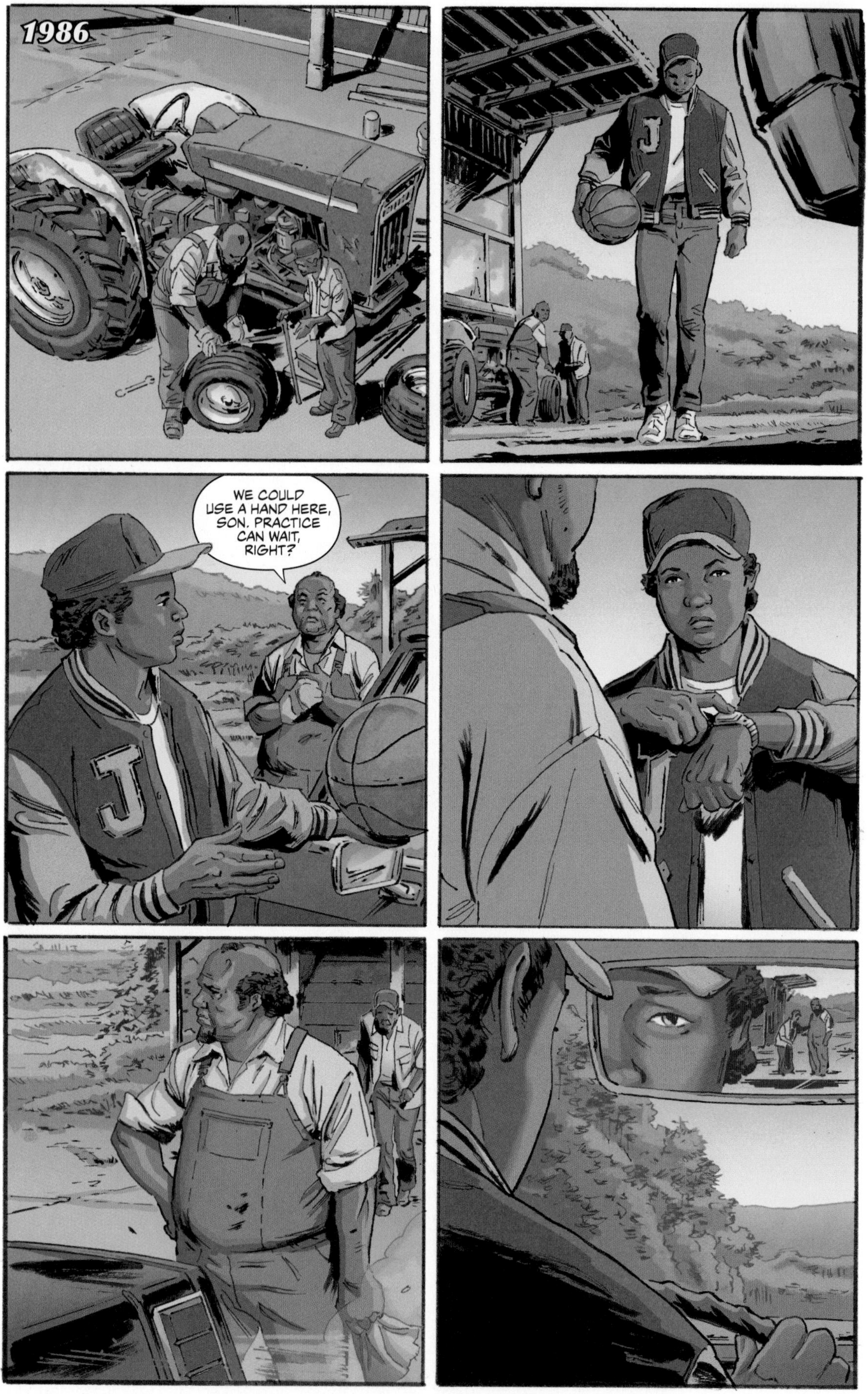
1986
WE COULD USE A HAND HERE, SON. PRACTICE CAN WAIT, RIGHT?

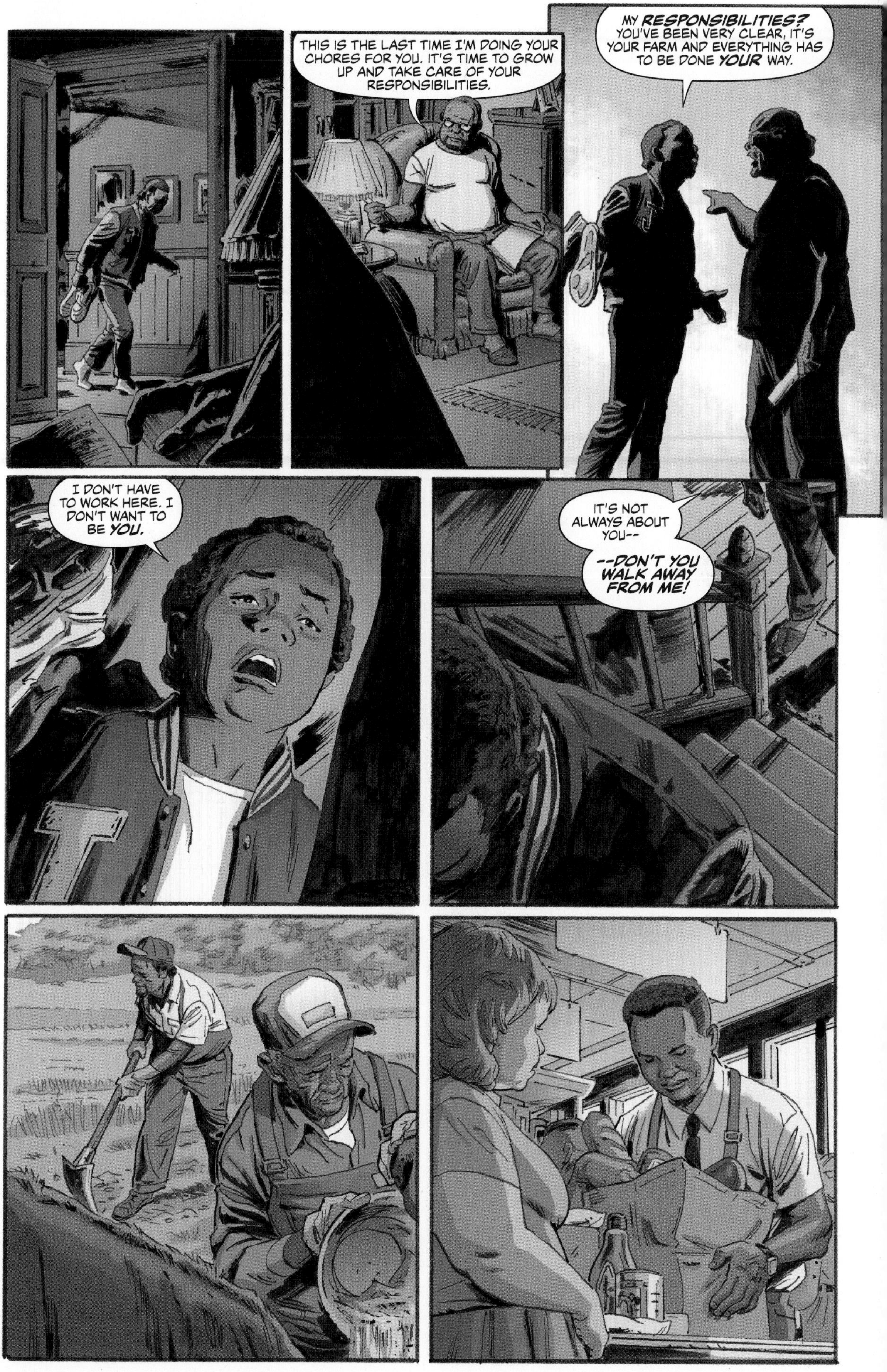
THIS IS THE LAST TIME I'M DOING YOUR CHORES FOR YOU. IT'S TIME TO GROW UP AND TAKE CARE OF YOUR RESPONSIBILITIES.
MY RESPONSIBILITIES? YOU'VE BEEN VERY CLEAR, IT'S YOUR FARM AND EVERYTHING HAS TO BE DONE YOUR WAY.
I DON'T HAVE TO WORK HERE. I DON'T WANT TO BE YOU.
IT'S NOT ALWAYS ABOUT YOU--
--DON'T YOU WALK AWAY FROM ME!

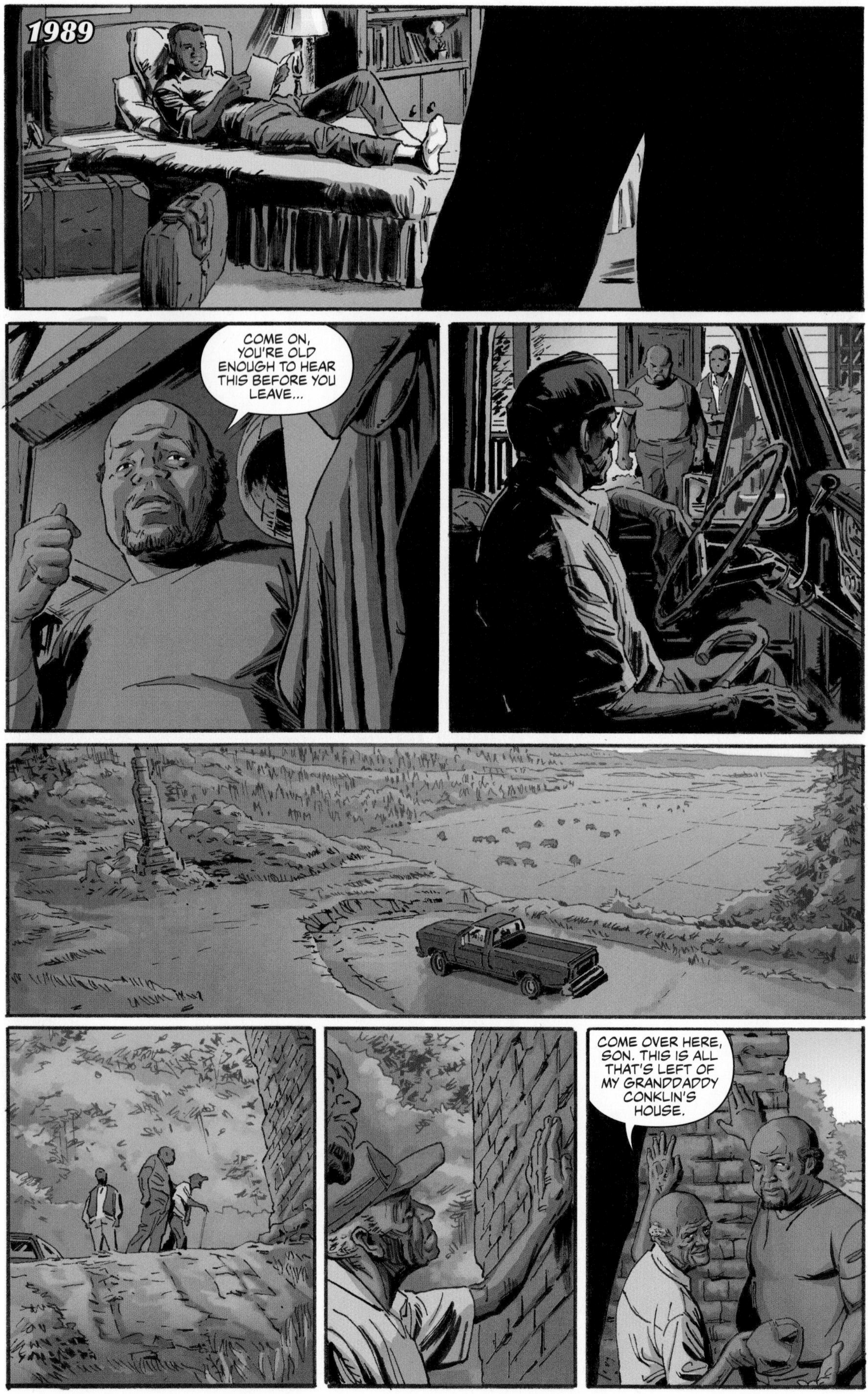
1989
COME ON, YOU'RE OLD ENOUGH TO HEAR THIS BEFORE YOU LEAVE...
COME OVER HERE, SON. THIS IS ALL THAT'S LEFT OF MY GRANDDADDY CONKLIN'S HOUSE.

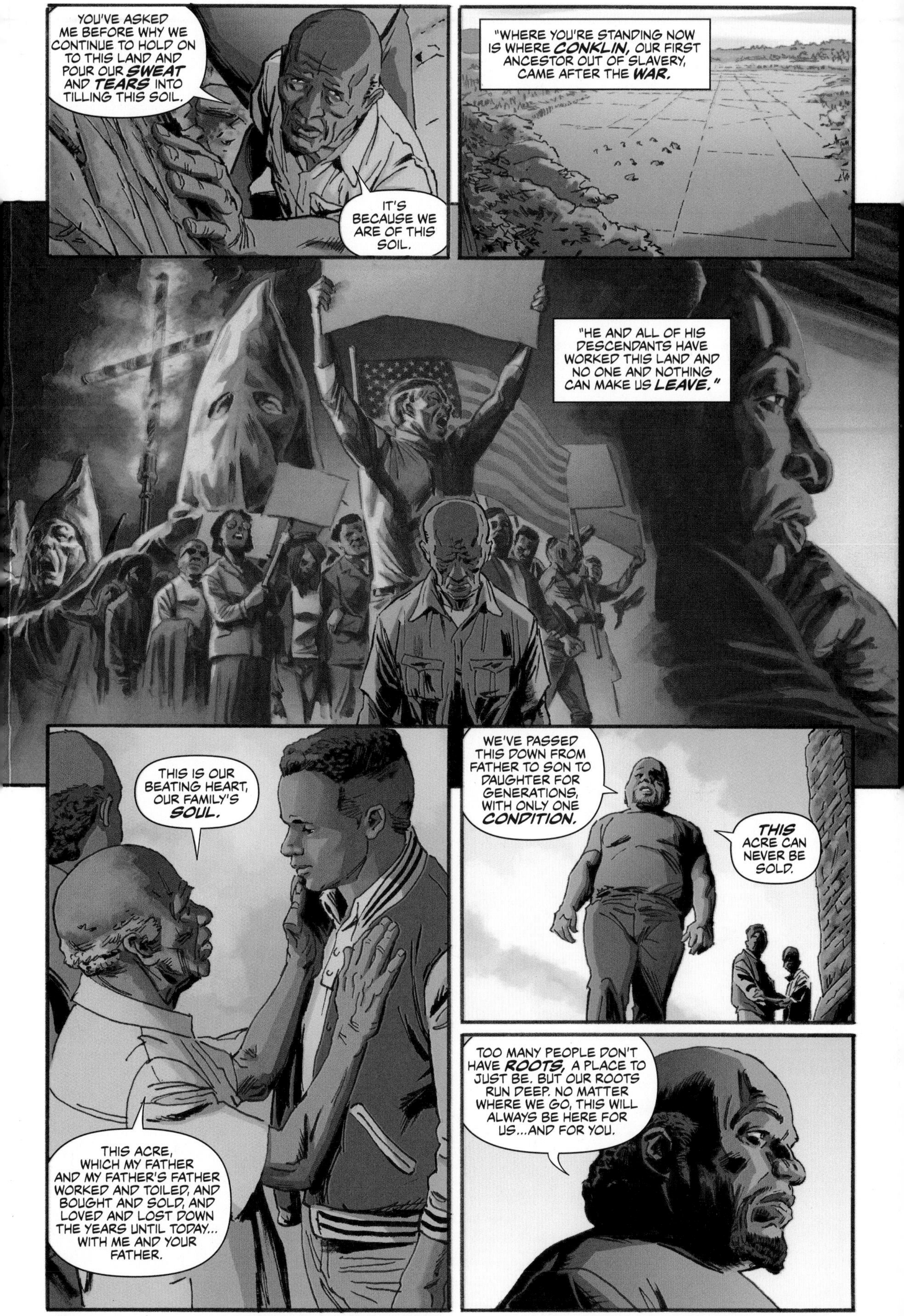
YOU'VE ASKED ME BEFORE WHY WE CONTINUE TO HOLD ON TO THIS LAND AND POUR OUR SWEAT AND TEARS INTO TILLING THIS SOIL.
IT'S BECAUSE WE ARE OF THIS SOIL.
"WHERE YOU'RE STANDING NOW IS WHERE CONKLIN, OUR FIRST ANCESTOR OUT OF SLAVERY, CAME AFTER THE WAR.
"HE AND ALL OF HIS DESCENDANTS HAVE WORKED THIS LAND AND NO ONE AND NOTHING CAN MAKE US LEAVE."
THIS IS OUR BEATING HEART, OUR FAMILY'S SOUL.
THIS ACRE, WHICH MY FATHER AND MY FATHER'S FATHER WORKED AND TOILED, AND BOUGHT AND SOLD, AND LOVED AND LOST DOWN THE YEARS UNTIL TODAY... WITH ME AND YOUR FATHER.
WE'VE PASSED THIS DOWN FROM FATHER TO SON TO DAUGHTER FOR GENERATIONS, WITH ONLY ONE CONDITION.
THIS ACRE CAN NEVER BE SOLD.
TOO MANY PEOPLE DON'T HAVE ROOTS, A PLACE TO JUST BE. BUT OUR ROOTS RUN DEEP. NO MATTER WHERE WE GO, THIS WILL ALWAYS BE HERE FOR US...AND FOR YOU.

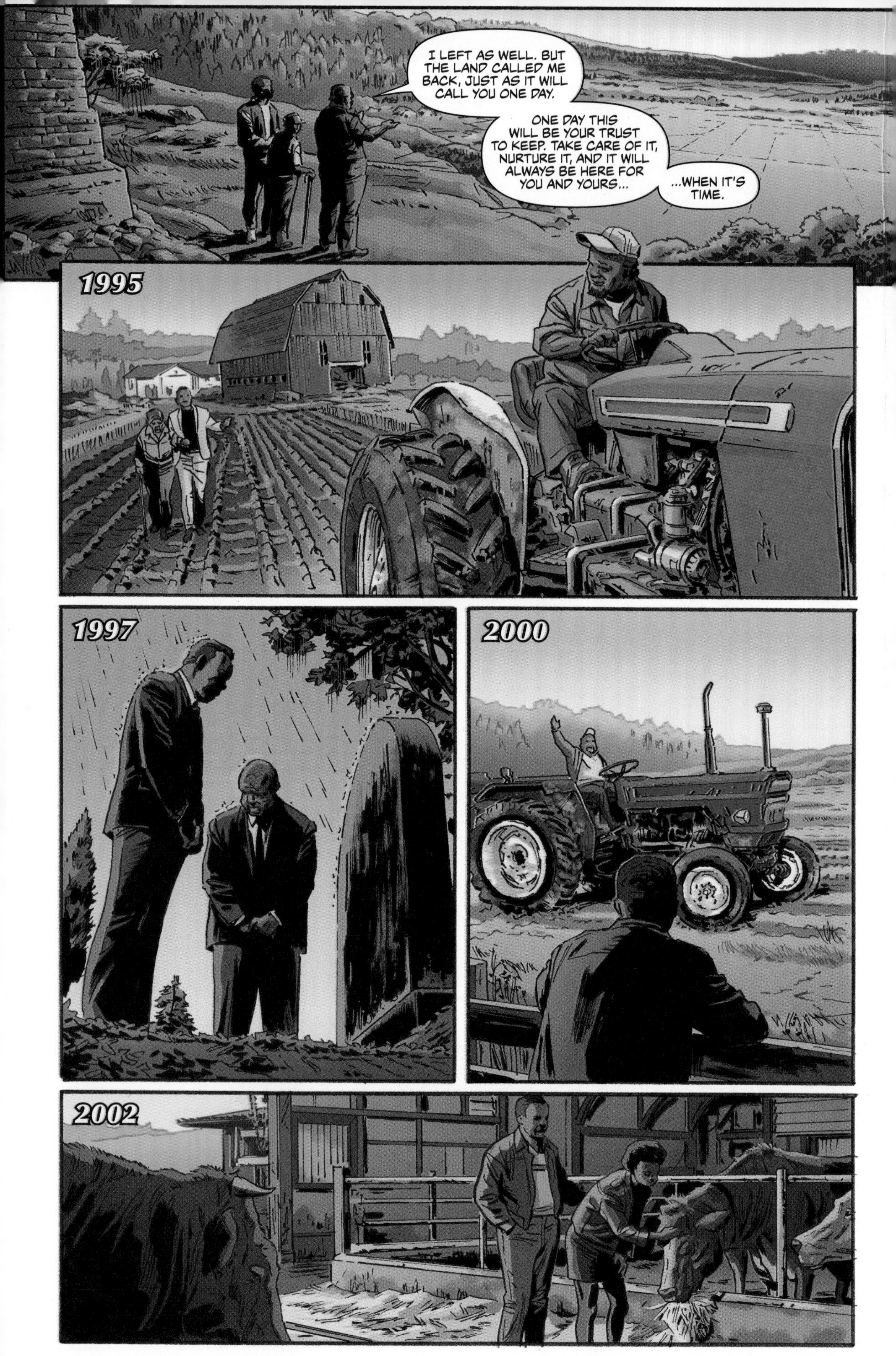
I LEFT AS WELL. BUT THE LAND CALLED ME BACK, JUST AS IT WILL CALL YOU ONE DAY.
ONE DAY THIS WILL BE YOUR TRUST TO KEEP. TAKE CARE OF IT, NURTURE IT, AND IT WILL ALWAYS BE HERE FOR YOU AND YOURS...
...WHEN IT'S TIME.
1995
1997
2000
2002

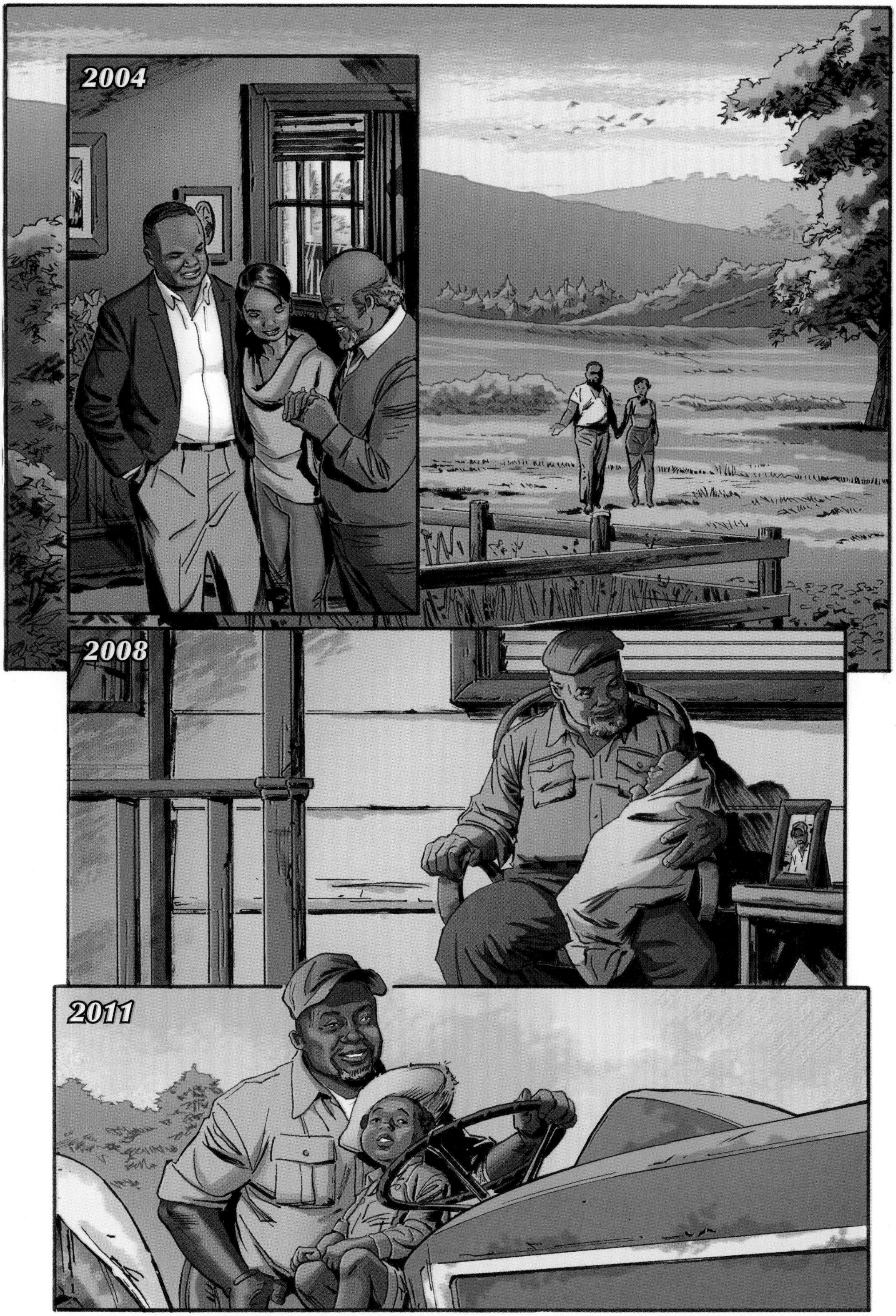
2004
2008
2011

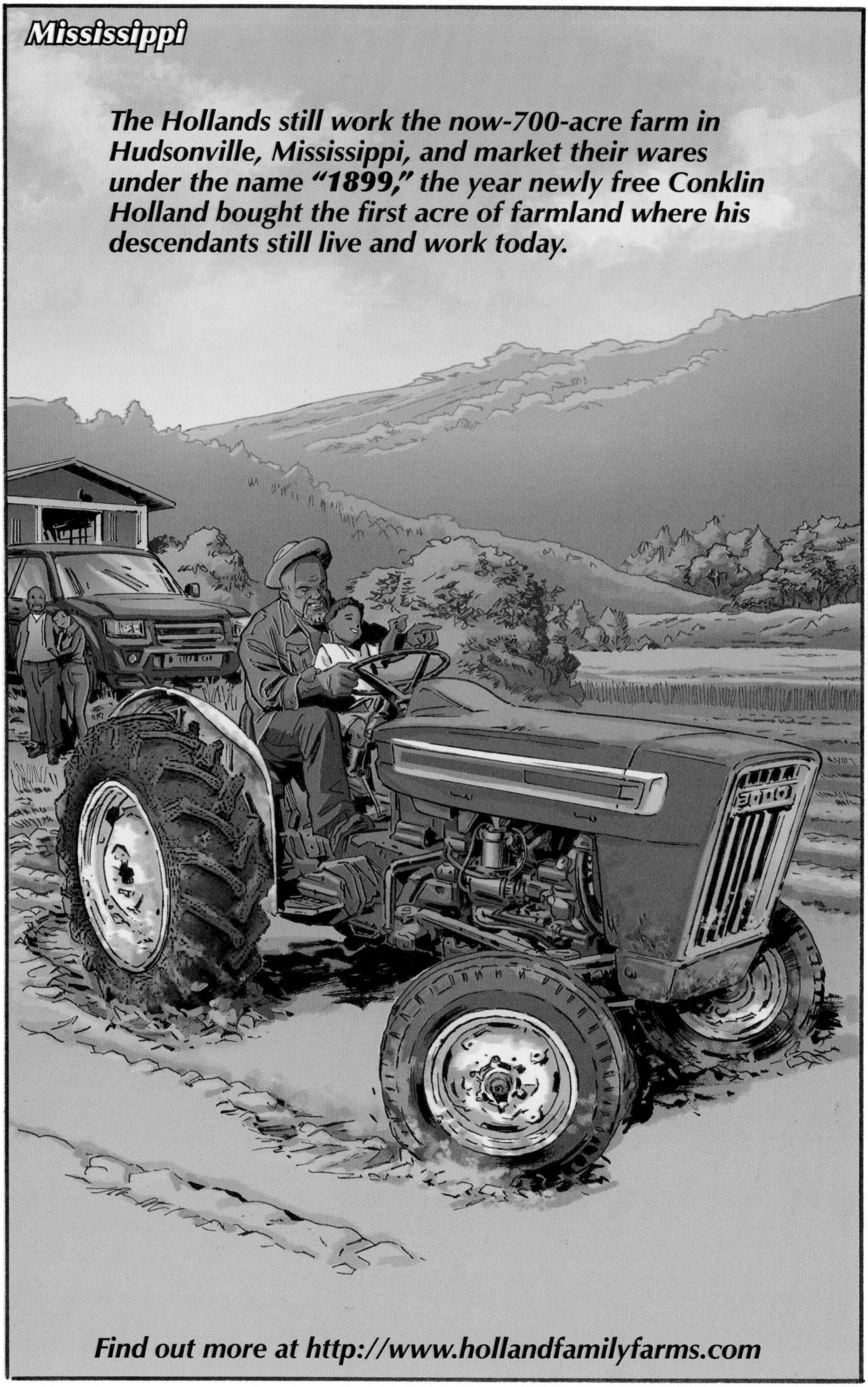
Mississippi
The Hollands still work the now-700-acre farm in Hudsonville, Mississippi, and market their wares under the name "1899," the year newly free Conklin Holland bought the first acre of farmland where his descendants still live and work today.
Find out more at http://www.hollandfamilyfarms.com

DC REPRESENT!

CHAPTER THREE
"FOOD FOR THOUGHT"

WRITER - REGINE SAWYER

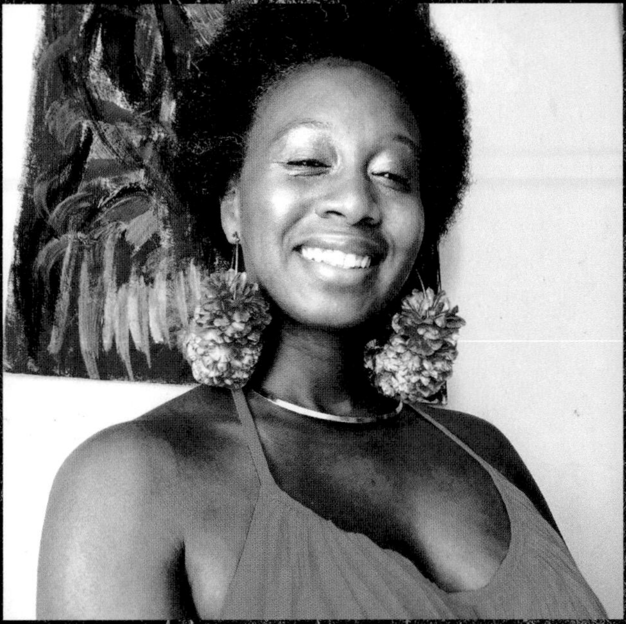

Regine L. Sawyer is a Queens-based comic book writer and small press publisher. She's also the founder of Women in Comics Collective International, an organization that recognizes the work of BIPOC creators in the comic book industry. Regine is a four-time Glyph Award judge, a 2019 Glyph Lifetime Achievement Award recipient, a National Book Foundation Writing Camp Fellow, and a Kickstarter Creator-in-Residence alum. In addition, she has written articles and essays discussing race, culture, and gender in comics via DC and Marvel Comics, *Blerd Galaxy* magazine, Lion Forge, Graphic Policy, the Freelancer's Union, Comic Book Resources, and *Time* magazine.

ARTIST - ERIC BATTLE
COLORIST - BRYAN VALENZA
LETTERER - DERON BENNETT

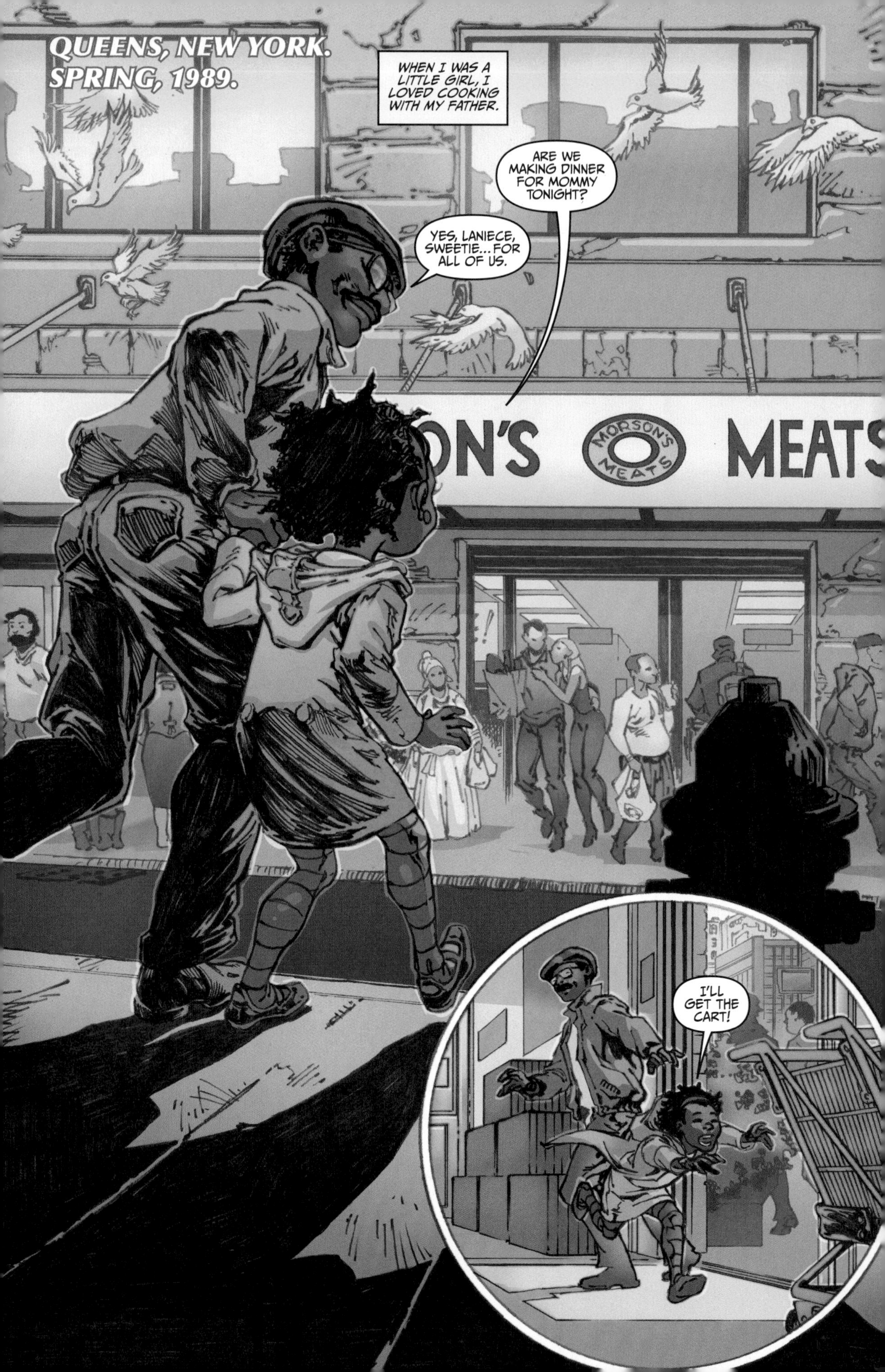
QUEENS, NEW YORK. SPRING, 1989.
WHEN I WAS A LITTLE GIRL, I LOVED COOKING WITH MY FATHER.
ARE WE MAKING DINNER FOR MOMMY TONIGHT?
YES, LANIECE, SWEETIE...FOR ALL OF US.
ON'S
MORSON'S MEATS
MEATS
I'LL GET THE CART!

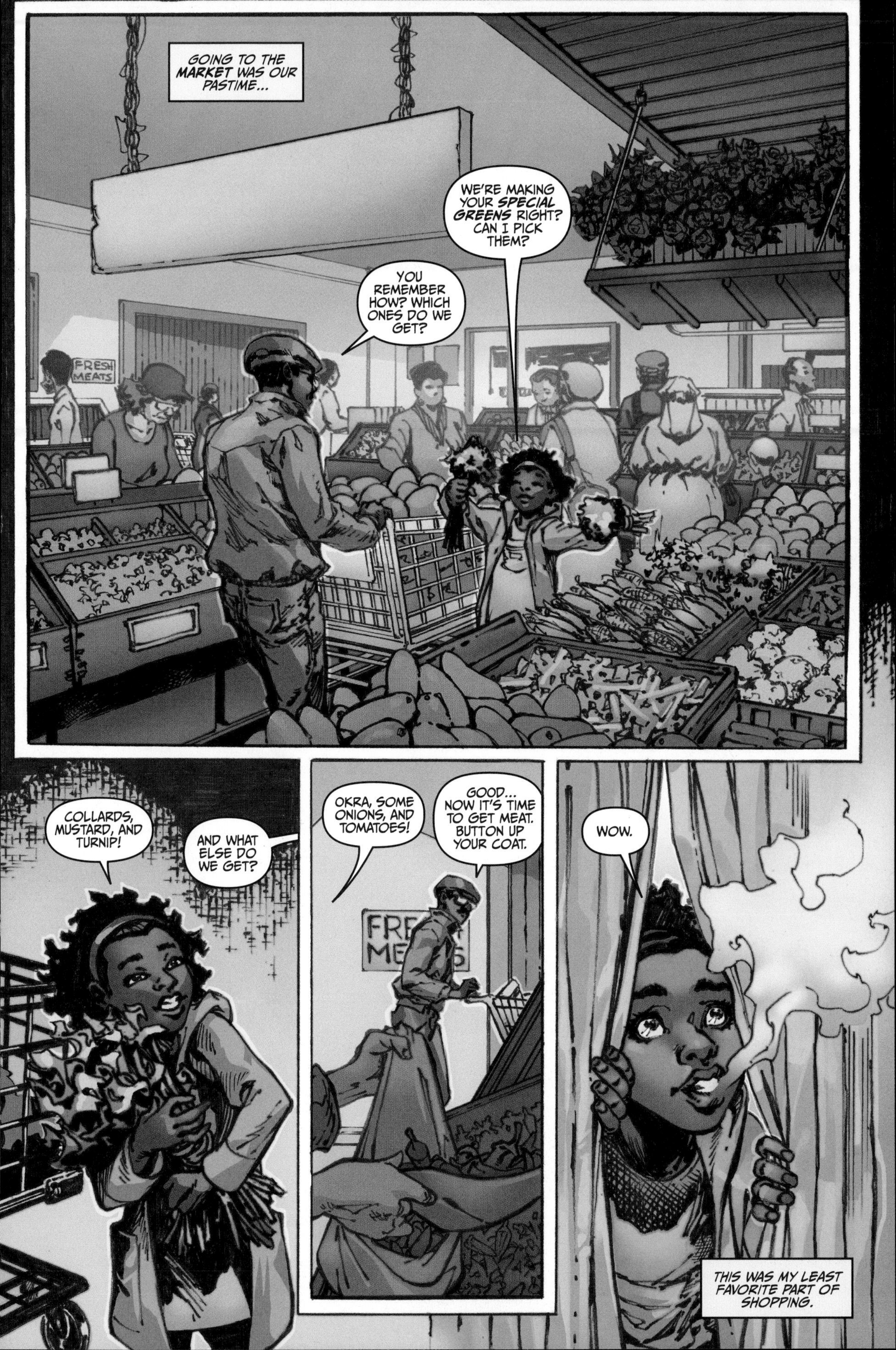
GOING TO THE MARKET WAS OUR PASTIME...
YOU REMEMBER HOW? WHICH ONES DO WE GET?
WE'RE MAKING YOUR SPECIAL GREENS RIGHT? CAN I PICK THEM?
FRESH MEATS
COLLARDS, MUSTARD, AND TURNIP!
AND WHAT ELSE DO WE GET?
OKRA, SOME ONIONS, AND TOMATOES!
GOOD... NOW IT'S TIME TO GET MEAT. BUTTON UP YOUR COAT.
WOW.
THIS WAS MY LEAST FAVORITE PART OF SHOPPING.

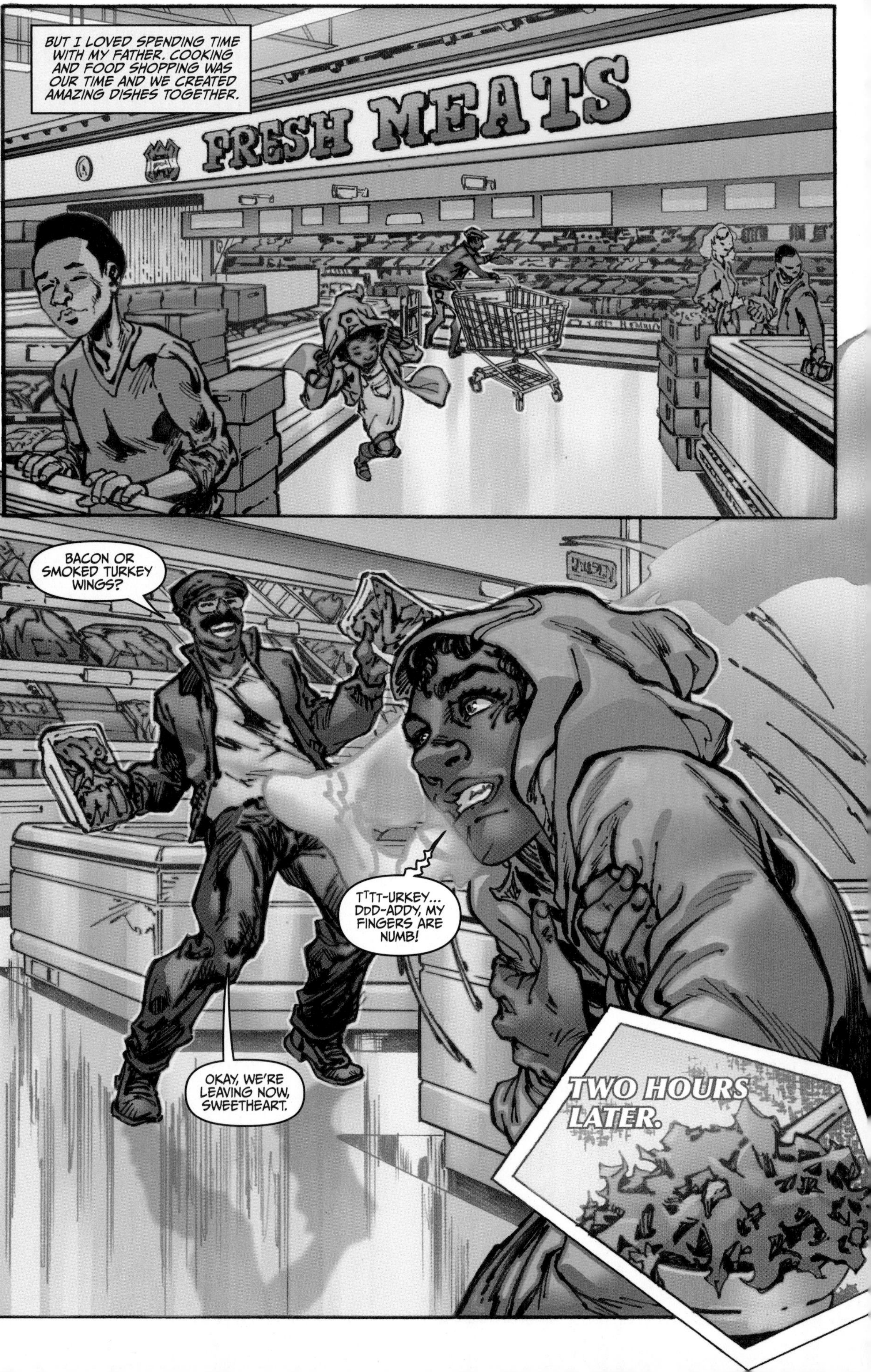
BUT I LOVED SPENDING TIME WITH MY FATHER. COOKING AND FOOD SHOPPING WAS OUR TIME AND WE CREATED AMAZING DISHES TOGETHER.
FRESH MEATS
BACON OR SMOKED TURKEY WINGS?
TTTT-URKEY... DDD-ADDY, MY FINGERS ARE NUMB!
OKAY, WE'RE LEAVING NOW, SWEETHEART.
TWO HOURS LATER.

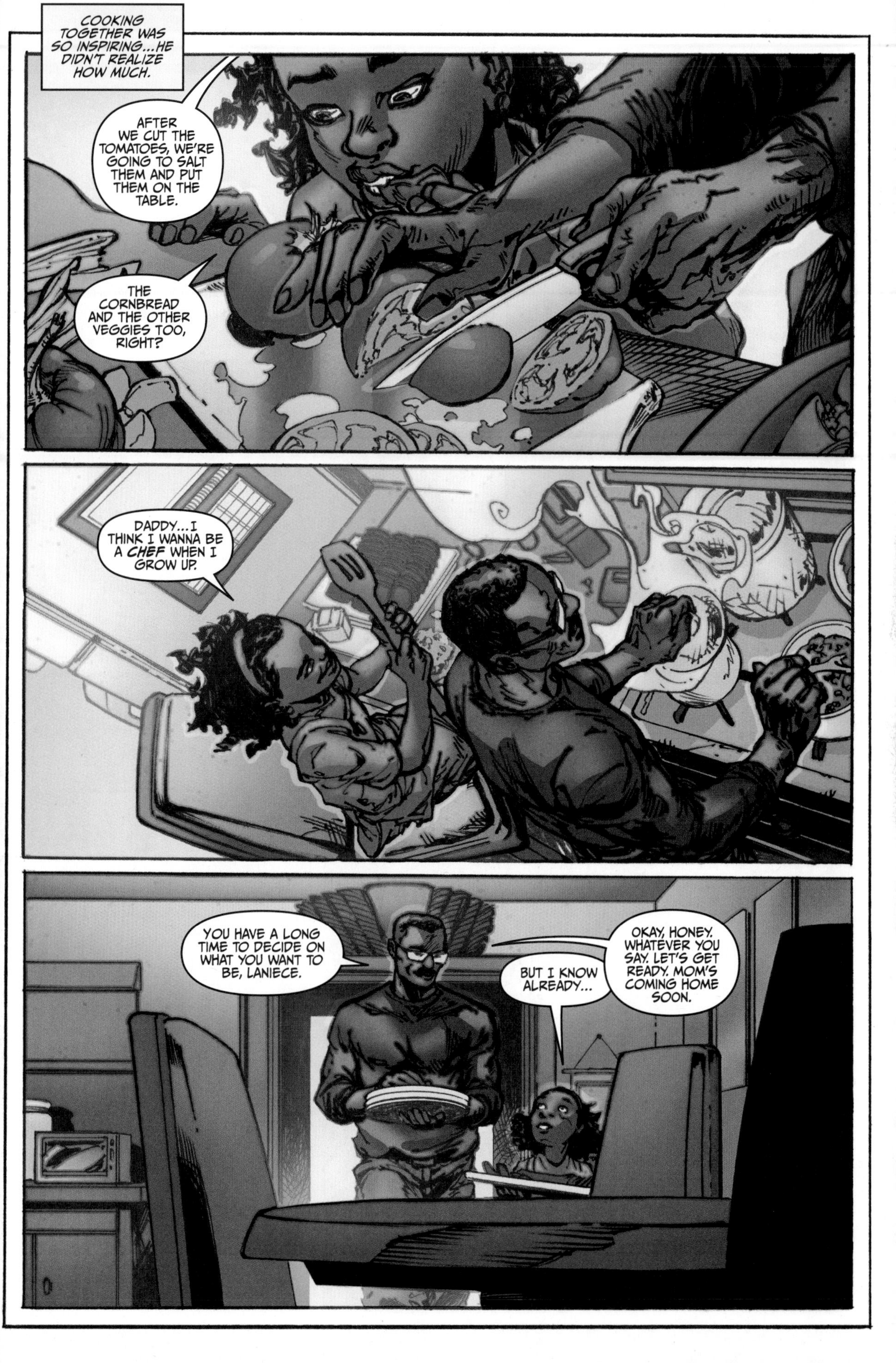
COOKING TOGETHER WAS SO INSPIRING...HE DIDN'T REALIZE HOW MUCH.
AFTER WE CUT THE TOMATOES, WE'RE GOING TO SALT THEM AND PUT THEM ON THE TABLE.
THE CORNBREAD AND THE OTHER VEGGIES TOO, RIGHT?
DADDY...I THINK I WANNA BE A *CHEF* WHEN I GROW UP.
YOU HAVE A LONG TIME TO DECIDE ON WHAT YOU WANT TO BE, LANIECE.
BUT I KNOW ALREADY...
OKAY, HONEY. WHATEVER YOU SAY. LET'S GET READY. MOM'S COMING HOME SOON.

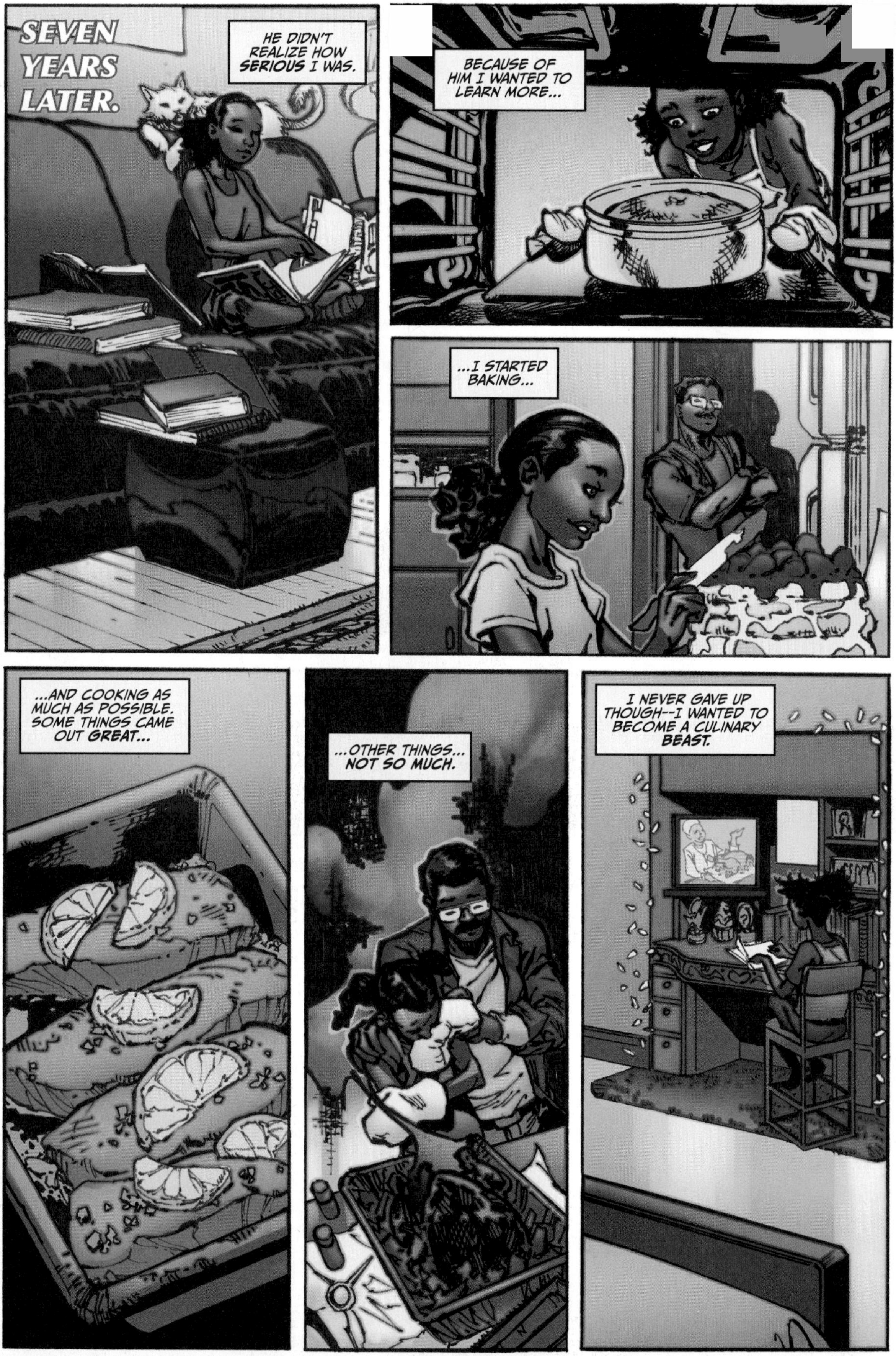

SEVEN YEARS LATER.
HE DIDN'T REALIZE HOW SERIOUS I WAS.
BECAUSE OF HIM I WANTED TO LEARN MORE...
...I STARTED BAKING...
...AND COOKING AS MUCH AS POSSIBLE. SOME THINGS CAME OUT GREAT...
...OTHER THINGS... NOT SO MUCH.
I NEVER GAVE UP THOUGH--I WANTED TO BECOME A CULINARY BEAST.

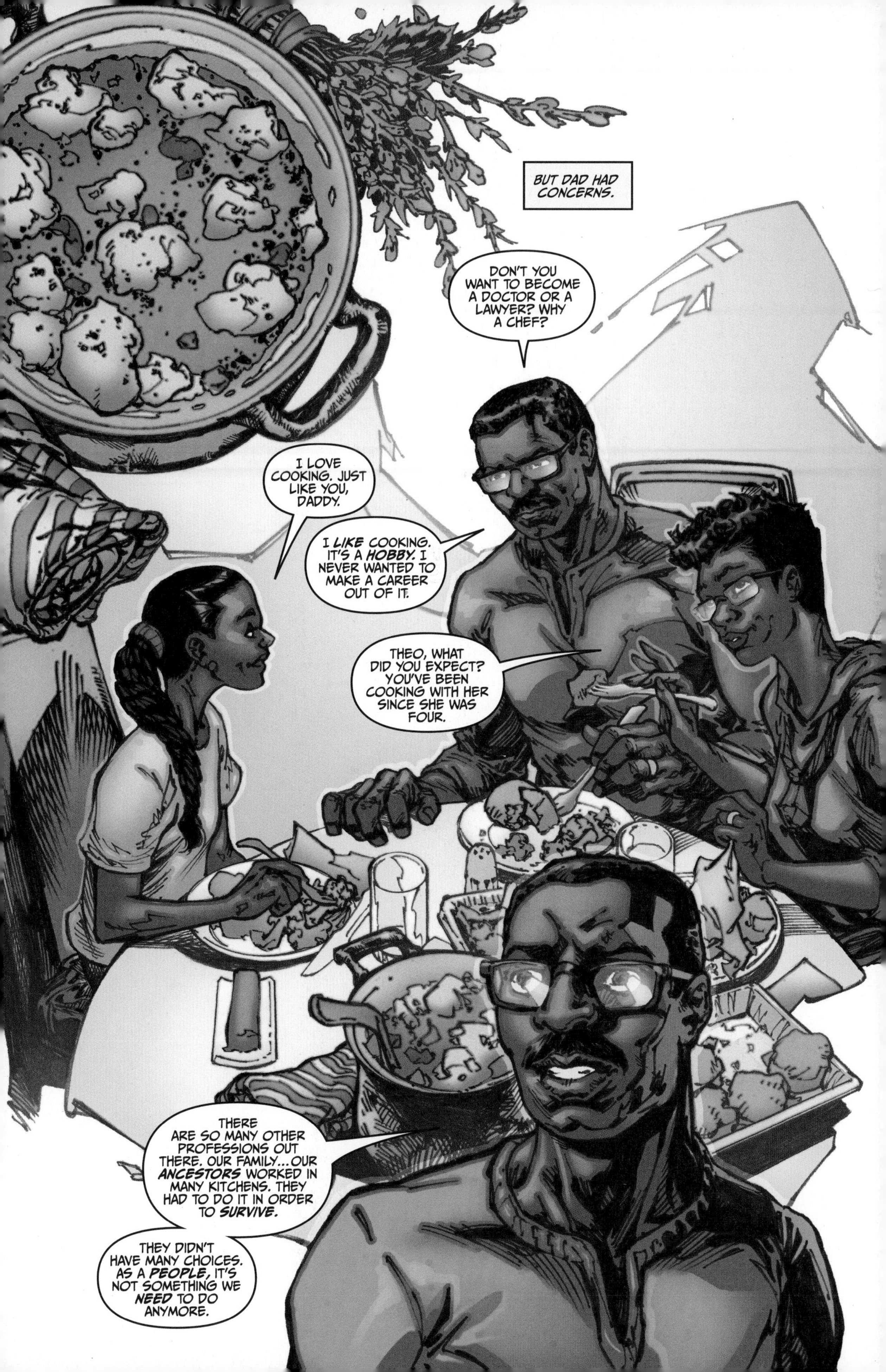
BUT DAD HAD CONCERNS.
DON'T YOU WANT TO BECOME A DOCTOR OR A LAWYER? WHY A CHEF?
I LOVE COOKING. JUST LIKE YOU, DADDY.
I LIKE COOKING. IT'S A HOBBY. I NEVER WANTED TO MAKE A CAREER OUT OF IT.
THEO, WHAT DID YOU EXPECT? YOU'VE BEEN COOKING WITH HER SINCE SHE WAS FOUR.
THERE ARE SO MANY OTHER PROFESSIONS OUT THERE. OUR FAMILY...OUR ANCESTORS WORKED IN MANY KITCHENS. THEY HAD TO DO IT IN ORDER TO SURVIVE.
THEY DIDN'T HAVE MANY CHOICES. AS A PEOPLE, IT'S NOT SOMETHING WE NEED TO DO ANYMORE.

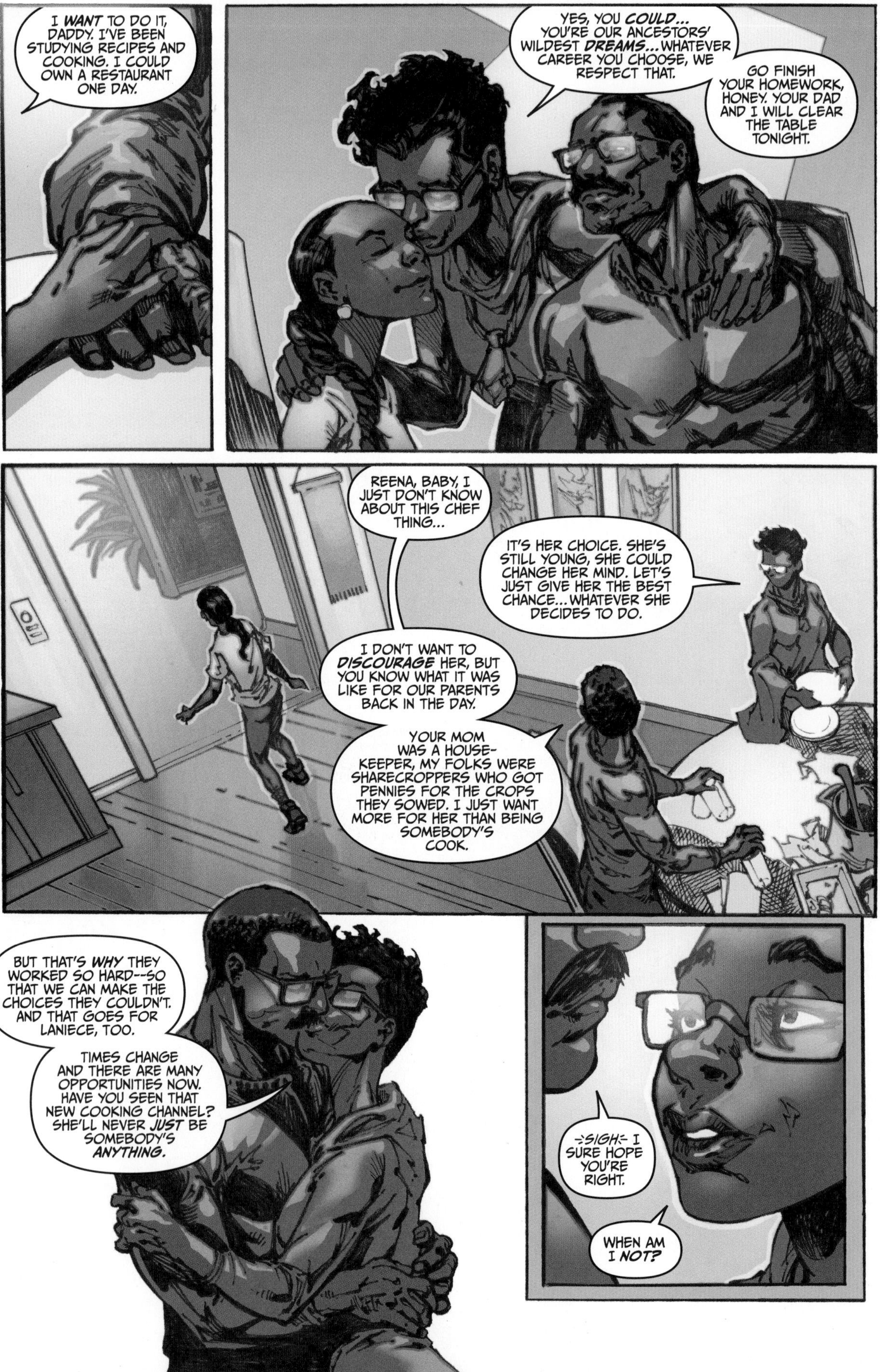
I WANT TO DO IT, DADDY. I'VE BEEN STUDYING RECIPES AND COOKING. I COULD OWN A RESTAURANT ONE DAY.
YES, YOU COULD... YOU'RE OUR ANCESTORS' WILDEST DREAMS... WHATEVER CAREER YOU CHOOSE, WE RESPECT THAT.
GO FINISH YOUR HOMEWORK, HONEY. YOUR DAD AND I WILL CLEAR THE TABLE TONIGHT.
REENA, BABY, I JUST DON'T KNOW ABOUT THIS CHEF THING...
IT'S HER CHOICE. SHE'S STILL YOUNG, SHE COULD CHANGE HER MIND. LET'S JUST GIVE HER THE BEST CHANCE... WHATEVER SHE DECIDES TO DO.
I DON'T WANT TO DISCOURAGE HER, BUT YOU KNOW WHAT IT WAS LIKE FOR OUR PARENTS BACK IN THE DAY.
YOUR MOM WAS A HOUSE-KEEPER, MY FOLKS WERE SHARECROPPERS WHO GOT PENNIES FOR THE CROPS THEY SOWED. I JUST WANT MORE FOR HER THAN BEING SOMEBODY'S COOK.
BUT THAT'S WHY THEY WORKED SO HARD--SO THAT WE CAN MAKE THE CHOICES THEY COULDN'T. AND THAT GOES FOR LANIECE, TOO.
TIMES CHANGE AND THERE ARE MANY OPPORTUNITIES NOW. HAVE YOU SEEN THAT NEW COOKING CHANNEL? SHE'LL NEVER JUST BE SOMEBODY'S ANYTHING.
-SIGH- I SURE HOPE YOU'RE RIGHT.
WHEN AM I NOT?

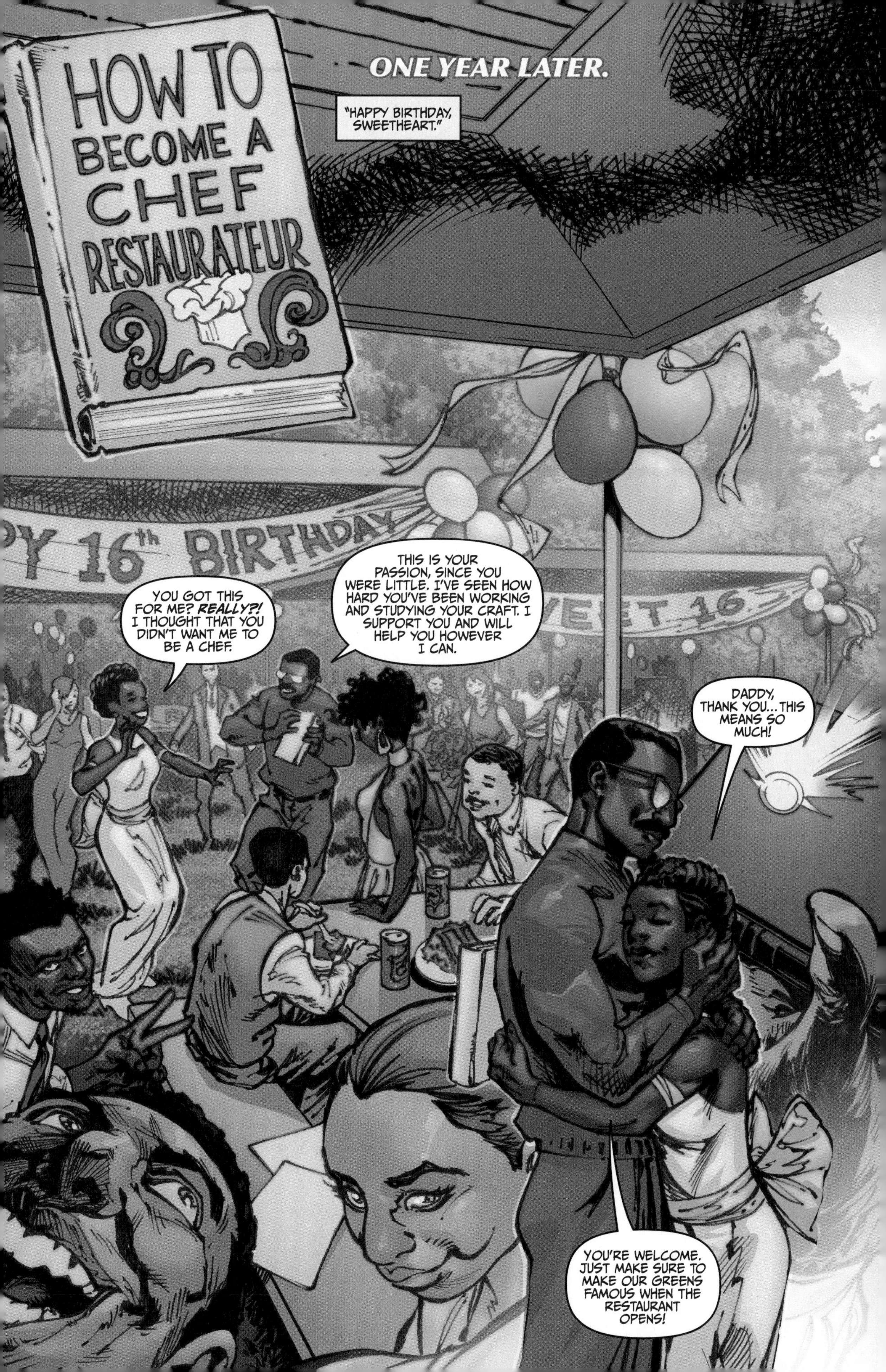

HOW TO BECOME A CHEF RESTAURATEUR
ONE YEAR LATER.
"HAPPY BIRTHDAY, SWEETHEART."
PY 16th BIRTHDAY
VEET 16
YOU GOT THIS FOR ME? REALLY?! I THOUGHT THAT YOU DIDN'T WANT ME TO BE A CHEF.
THIS IS YOUR PASSION, SINCE YOU WERE LITTLE. I'VE SEEN HOW HARD YOU'VE BEEN WORKING AND STUDYING YOUR CRAFT. I SUPPORT YOU AND WILL HELP YOU HOWEVER I CAN.
DADDY, THANK YOU... THIS MEANS SO MUCH!
YOU'RE WELCOME. JUST MAKE SURE TO MAKE OUR GREENS FAMOUS WHEN THE RESTAURANT OPENS!

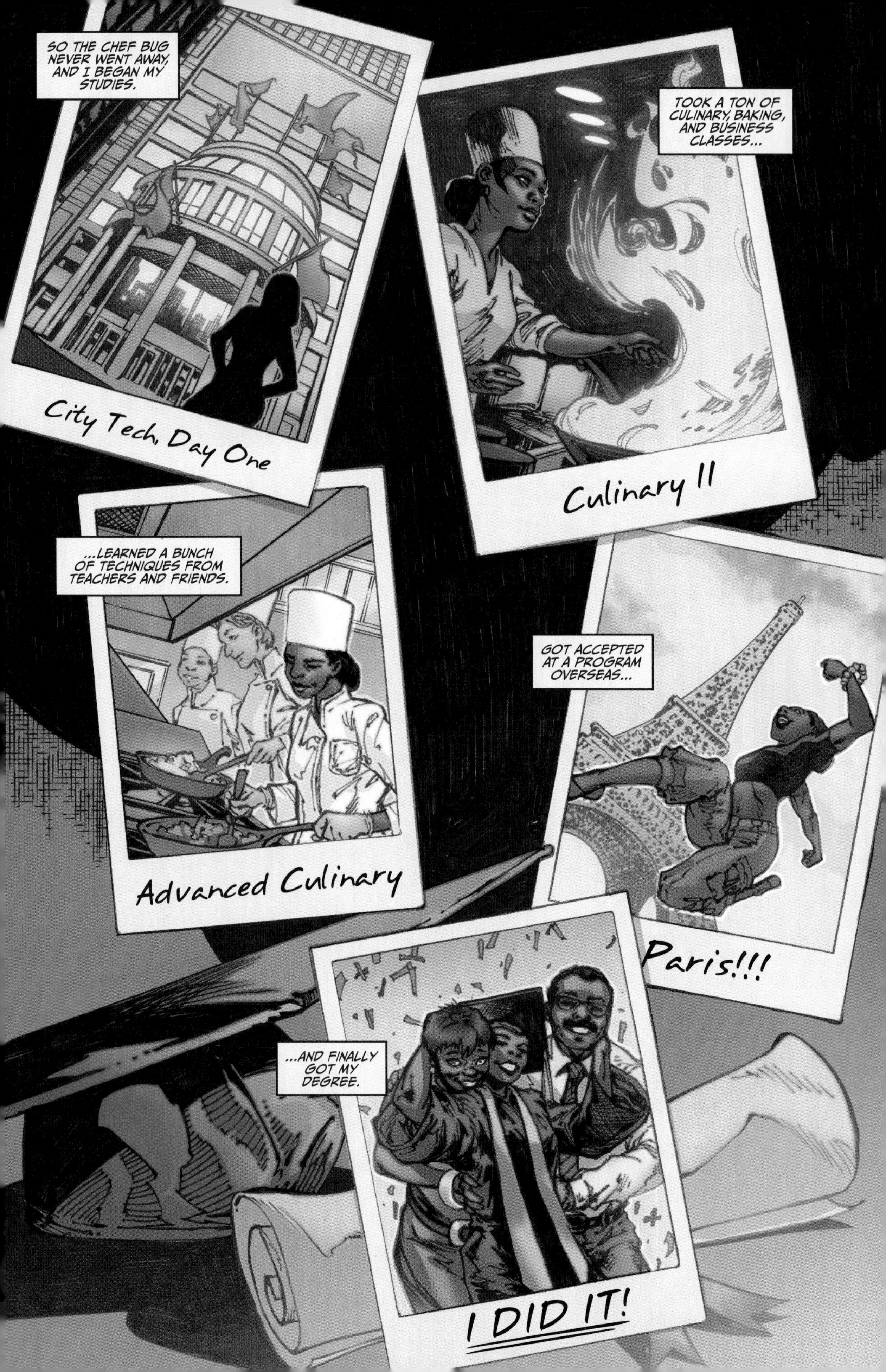

SO THE CHEF BUG NEVER WENT AWAY, AND I BEGAN MY STUDIES.
City Tech, Day One
TOOK A TON OF CULINARY, BAKING, AND BUSINESS CLASSES...
Culinary II
...LEARNED A BUNCH OF TECHNIQUES FROM TEACHERS AND FRIENDS.
Advanced Culinary
GOT ACCEPTED AT A PROGRAM OVERSEAS...
Paris!!!
...AND FINALLY GOT MY DEGREE.
I DID IT!

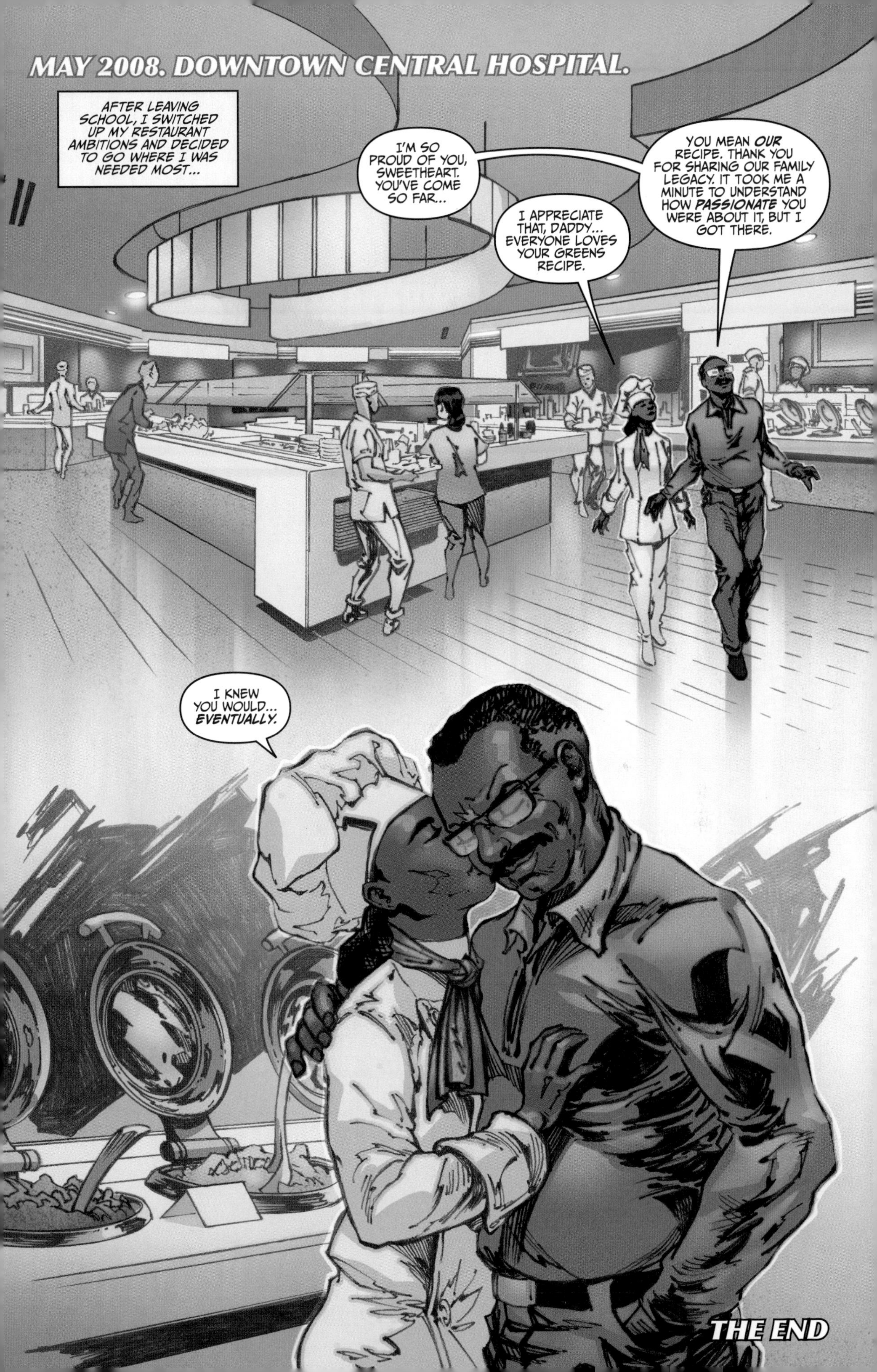
MAY 2008. DOWNTOWN CENTRAL HOSPITAL.
AFTER LEAVING SCHOOL, I SWITCHED UP MY RESTAURANT AMBITIONS AND DECIDED TO GO WHERE I WAS NEEDED MOST...
I'M SO PROUD OF YOU, SWEETHEART. YOU'VE COME SO FAR...
I APPRECIATE THAT, DADDY... EVERYONE LOVES YOUR GREENS RECIPE.
YOU MEAN OUR RECIPE. THANK YOU FOR SHARING OUR FAMILY LEGACY. IT TOOK ME A MINUTE TO UNDERSTAND HOW PASSIONATE YOU WERE ABOUT IT, BUT I GOT THERE.
I KNEW YOU WOULD... EVENTUALLY.
THE END

DC REPRESENT!

CHAPTER FOUR
"BELIEVE YOU"

WRITER - NADIRA JAMERSON

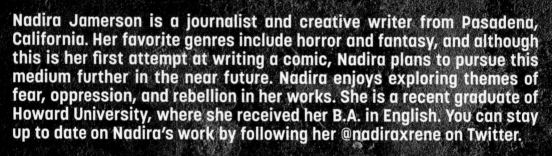

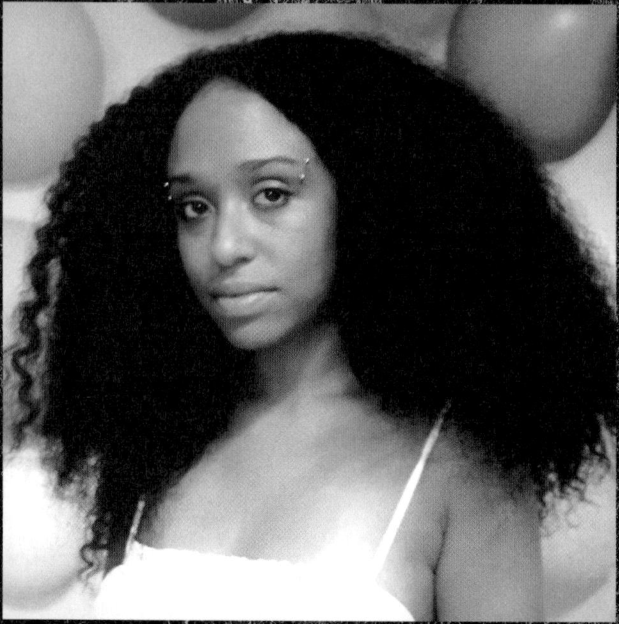

Nadira Jamerson is a journalist and creative writer from Pasadena, California. Her favorite genres include horror and fantasy, and although this is her first attempt at writing a comic, Nadira plans to pursue this medium further in the near future. Nadira enjoys exploring themes of fear, oppression, and rebellion in her works. She is a recent graduate of Howard University, where she received her B.A. in English. You can stay up to date on Nadira's work by following her @nadiraxrene on Twitter.

ARTIST - BRITTNEY WILLIAMS
COLORIST - ANDREW DALHOUSE
LETTERER - DERON BENNETT

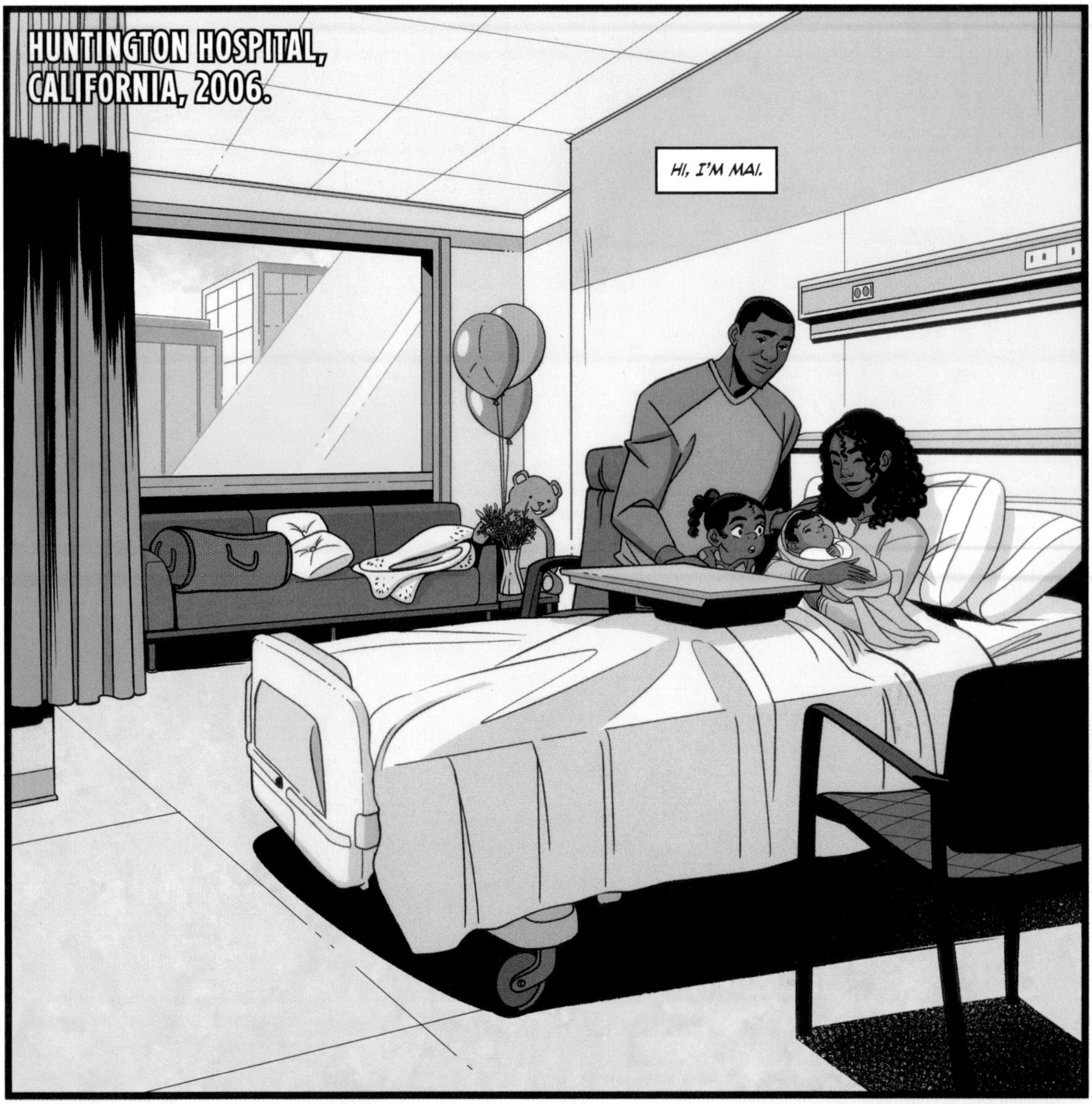
HUNTINGTON HOSPITAL, CALIFORNIA, 2006.
HI, I'M MAI.

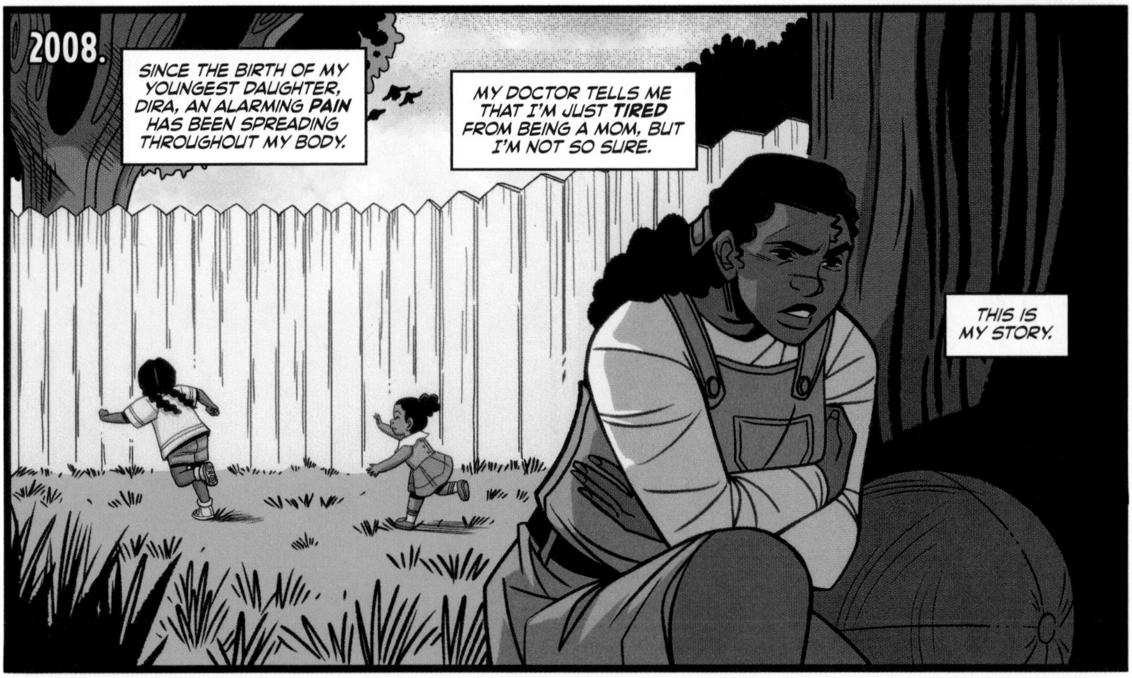
2008.
SINCE THE BIRTH OF MY YOUNGEST DAUGHTER, DIRA, AN ALARMING PAIN HAS BEEN SPREADING THROUGHOUT MY BODY.
MY DOCTOR TELLS ME THAT I'M JUST TIRED FROM BEING A MOM, BUT I'M NOT SO SURE.
THIS IS MY STORY.

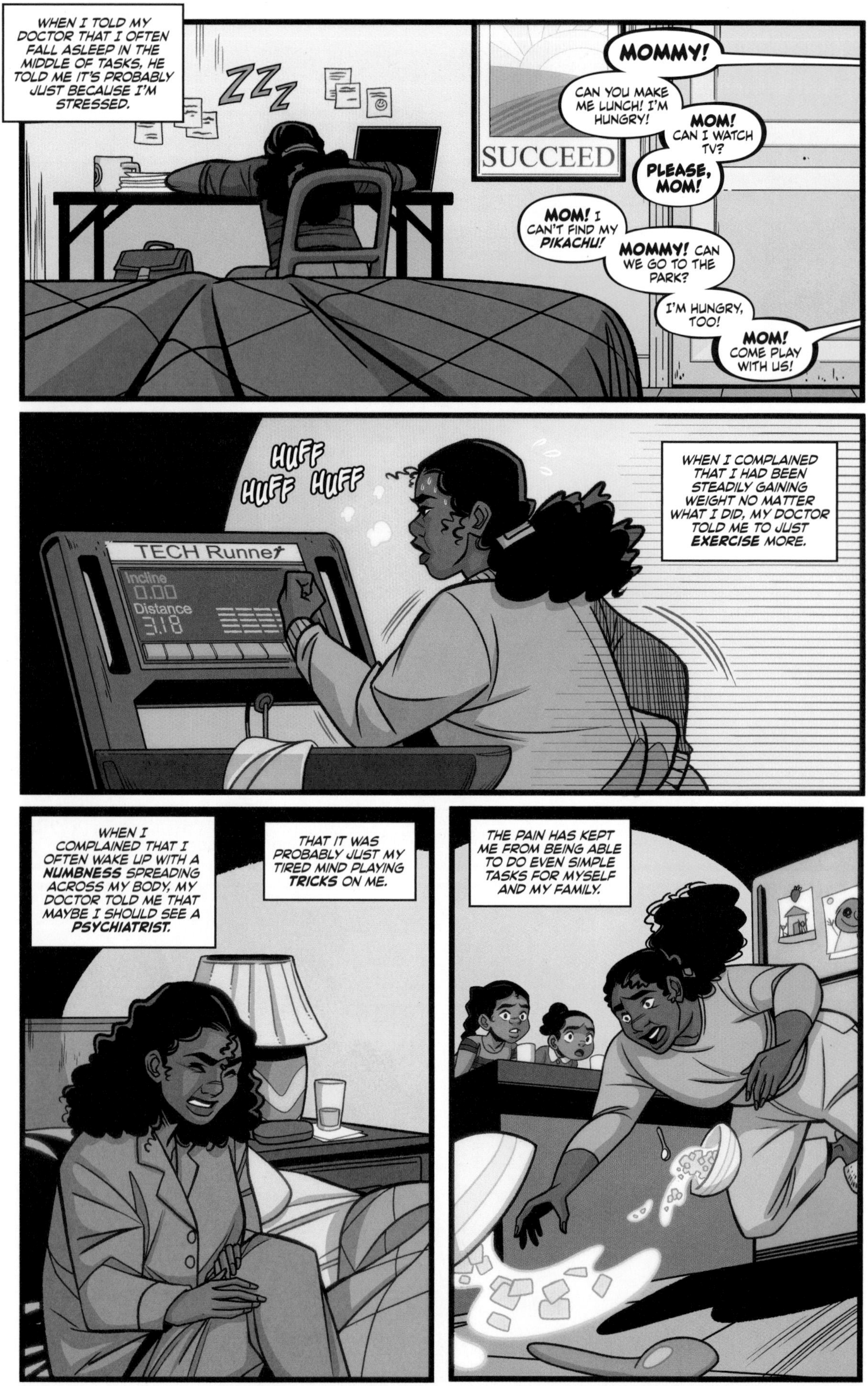
WHEN I TOLD MY DOCTOR THAT I OFTEN FALL ASLEEP IN THE MIDDLE OF TASKS, HE TOLD ME IT'S PROBABLY JUST BECAUSE I'M STRESSED.
ZZZ
SUCCEED
MOMMY!
CAN YOU MAKE ME LUNCH! I'M HUNGRY!
MOM! CAN I WATCH TV?
PLEASE, MOM!
MOM! I CAN'T FIND MY PIKACHU!
MOMMY! CAN WE GO TO THE PARK?
I'M HUNGRY, TOO!
MOM! COME PLAY WITH US!
HUFF HUFF HUFF
TECH Runner
Incline
0.00
Distance
3.18
WHEN I COMPLAINED THAT I HAD BEEN STEADILY GAINING WEIGHT NO MATTER WHAT I DID, MY DOCTOR TOLD ME TO JUST EXERCISE MORE.
WHEN I COMPLAINED THAT I OFTEN WAKE UP WITH A NUMBNESS SPREADING ACROSS MY BODY, MY DOCTOR TOLD ME THAT MAYBE I SHOULD SEE A PSYCHIATRIST.
THAT IT WAS PROBABLY JUST MY TIRED MIND PLAYING TRICKS ON ME.
THE PAIN HAS KEPT ME FROM BEING ABLE TO DO EVEN SIMPLE TASKS FOR MYSELF AND MY FAMILY.

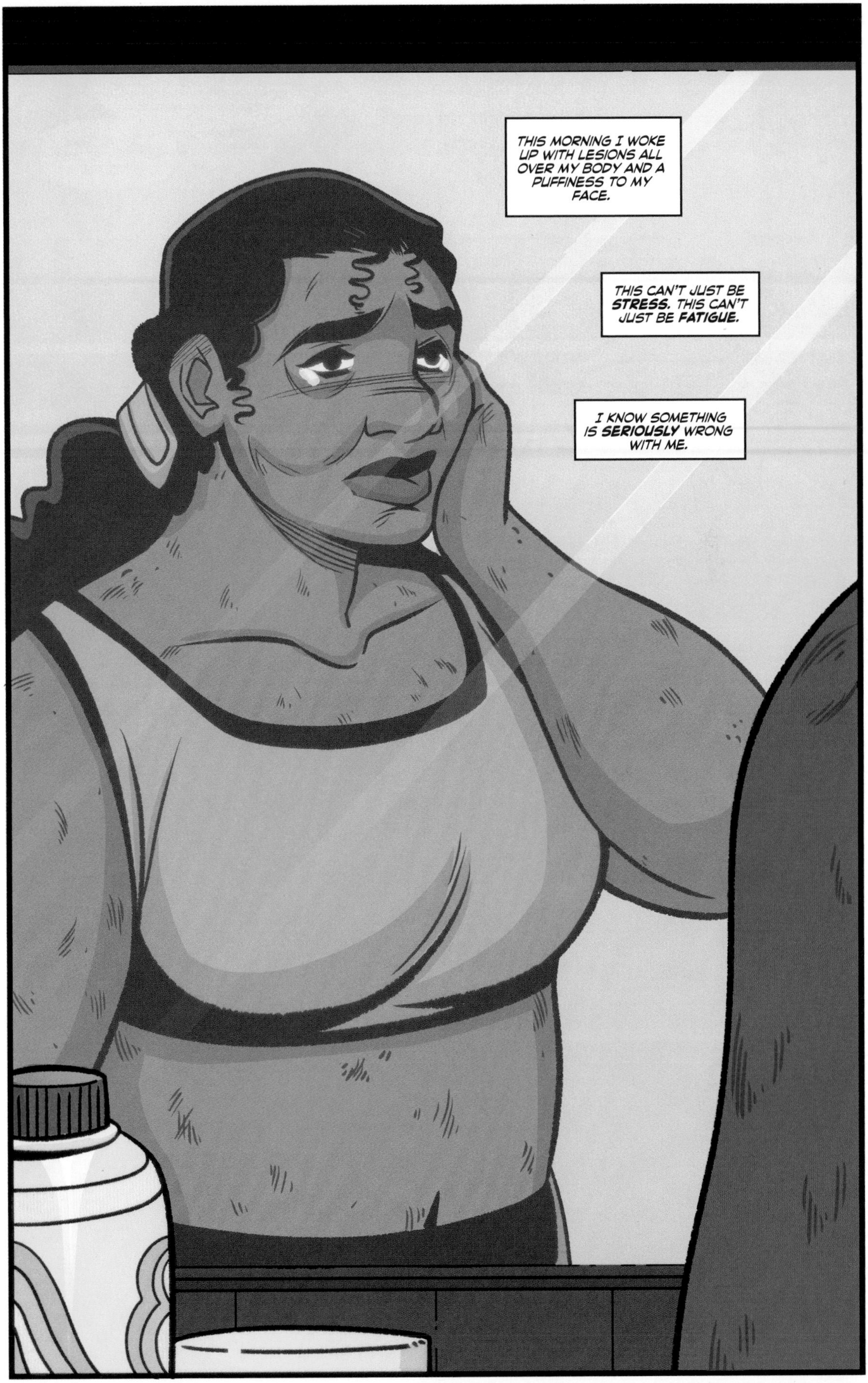
THIS MORNING I WOKE UP WITH LESIONS ALL OVER MY BODY AND A PUFFINESS TO MY FACE.
THIS CAN'T JUST BE **STRESS.** THIS CAN'T JUST BE **FATIGUE.**
I KNOW SOMETHING IS **SERIOUSLY** WRONG WITH ME.

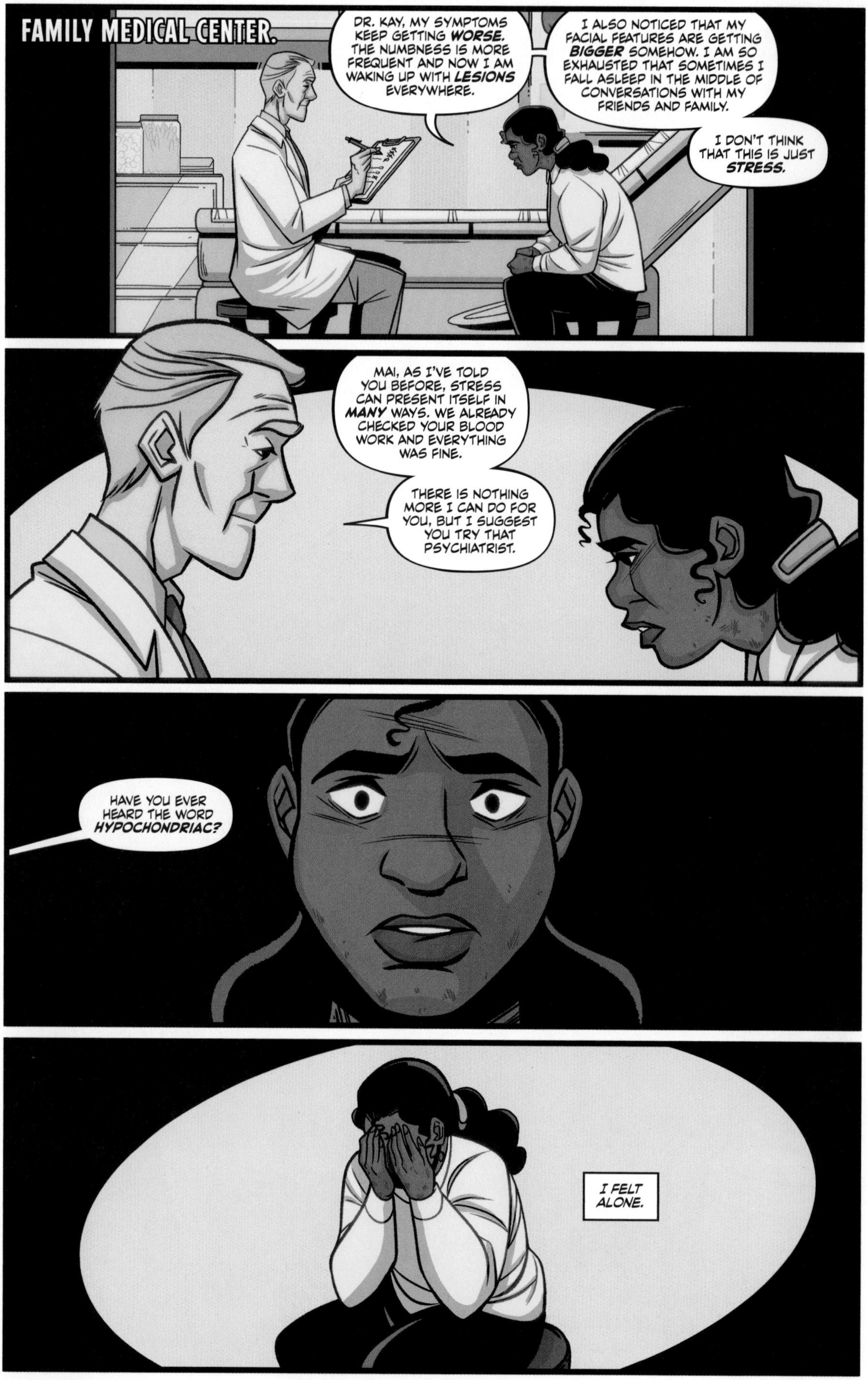
FAMILY MEDICAL CENTER.
DR. KAY, MY SYMPTOMS KEEP GETTING WORSE. THE NUMBNESS IS MORE FREQUENT AND NOW I AM WAKING UP WITH LESIONS EVERYWHERE.
I ALSO NOTICED THAT MY FACIAL FEATURES ARE GETTING BIGGER SOMEHOW. I AM SO EXHAUSTED THAT SOMETIMES I FALL ASLEEP IN THE MIDDLE OF CONVERSATIONS WITH MY FRIENDS AND FAMILY.
I DON'T THINK THAT THIS IS JUST STRESS.
MAI, AS I'VE TOLD YOU BEFORE, STRESS CAN PRESENT ITSELF IN MANY WAYS. WE ALREADY CHECKED YOUR BLOOD WORK AND EVERYTHING WAS FINE.
THERE IS NOTHING MORE I CAN DO FOR YOU, BUT I SUGGEST YOU TRY THAT PSYCHIATRIST.
HAVE YOU EVER HEARD THE WORD HYPOCHONDRIAC?
I FELT ALONE.

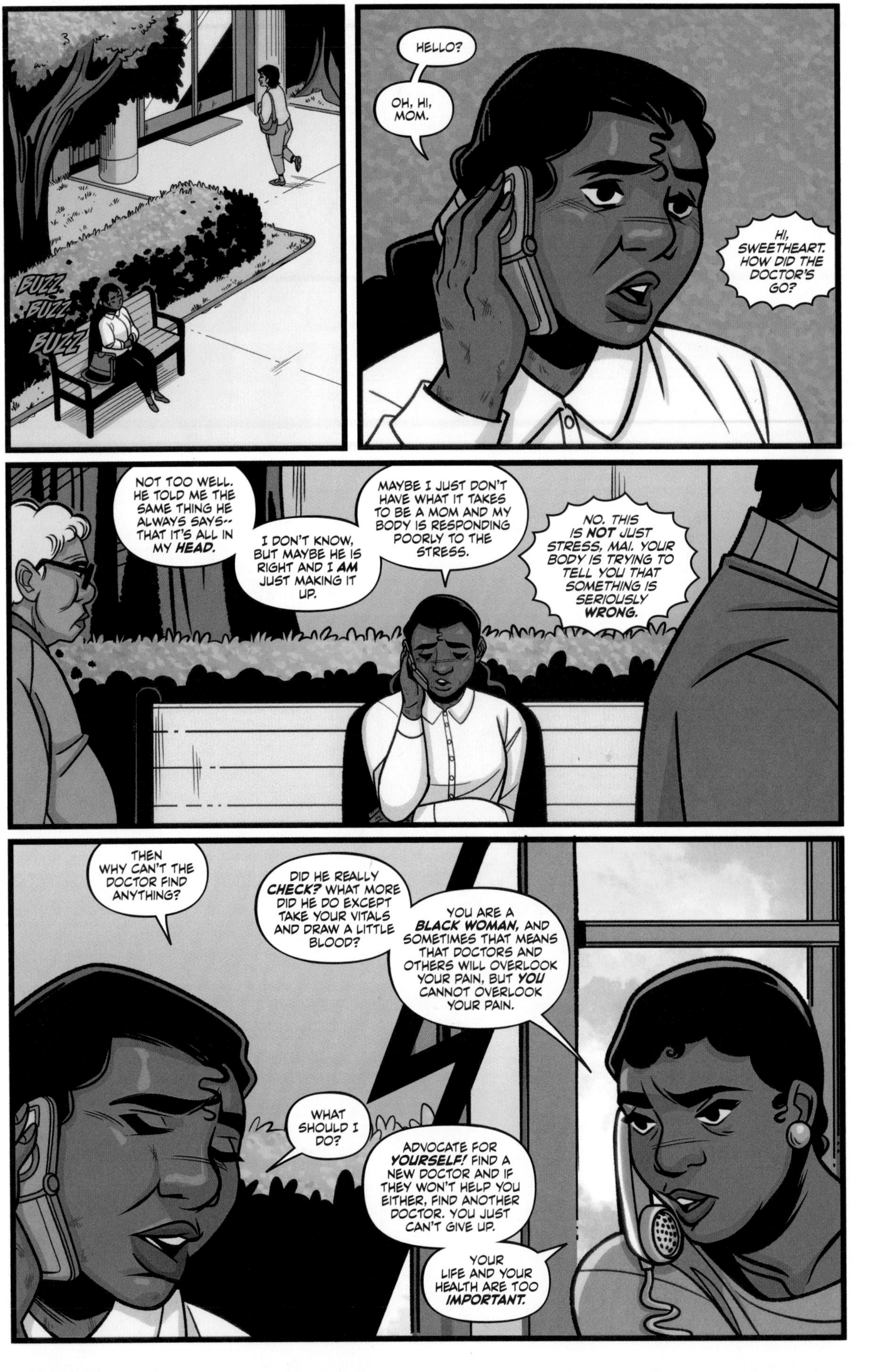
BUZZ
BUZZ
BUZZ
HELLO?
OH, HI, MOM.
HI, SWEETHEART. HOW DID THE DOCTOR'S GO?
NOT TOO WELL. HE TOLD ME THE SAME THING HE ALWAYS SAYS-- THAT IT'S ALL IN MY HEAD.
I DON'T KNOW, BUT MAYBE HE IS RIGHT AND I AM JUST MAKING IT UP.
MAYBE I JUST DON'T HAVE WHAT IT TAKES TO BE A MOM AND MY BODY IS RESPONDING POORLY TO THE STRESS.
NO. THIS IS NOT JUST STRESS, MAI. YOUR BODY IS TRYING TO TELL YOU THAT SOMETHING IS SERIOUSLY WRONG.
THEN WHY CAN'T THE DOCTOR FIND ANYTHING?
DID HE REALLY CHECK? WHAT MORE DID HE DO EXCEPT TAKE YOUR VITALS AND DRAW A LITTLE BLOOD?
YOU ARE A BLACK WOMAN, AND SOMETIMES THAT MEANS THAT DOCTORS AND OTHERS WILL OVERLOOK YOUR PAIN, BUT YOU CANNOT OVERLOOK YOUR PAIN.
WHAT SHOULD I DO?
ADVOCATE FOR YOURSELF! FIND A NEW DOCTOR AND IF THEY WON'T HELP YOU EITHER, FIND ANOTHER DOCTOR. YOU JUST CAN'T GIVE UP.
YOUR LIFE AND YOUR HEALTH ARE TOO IMPORTANT.

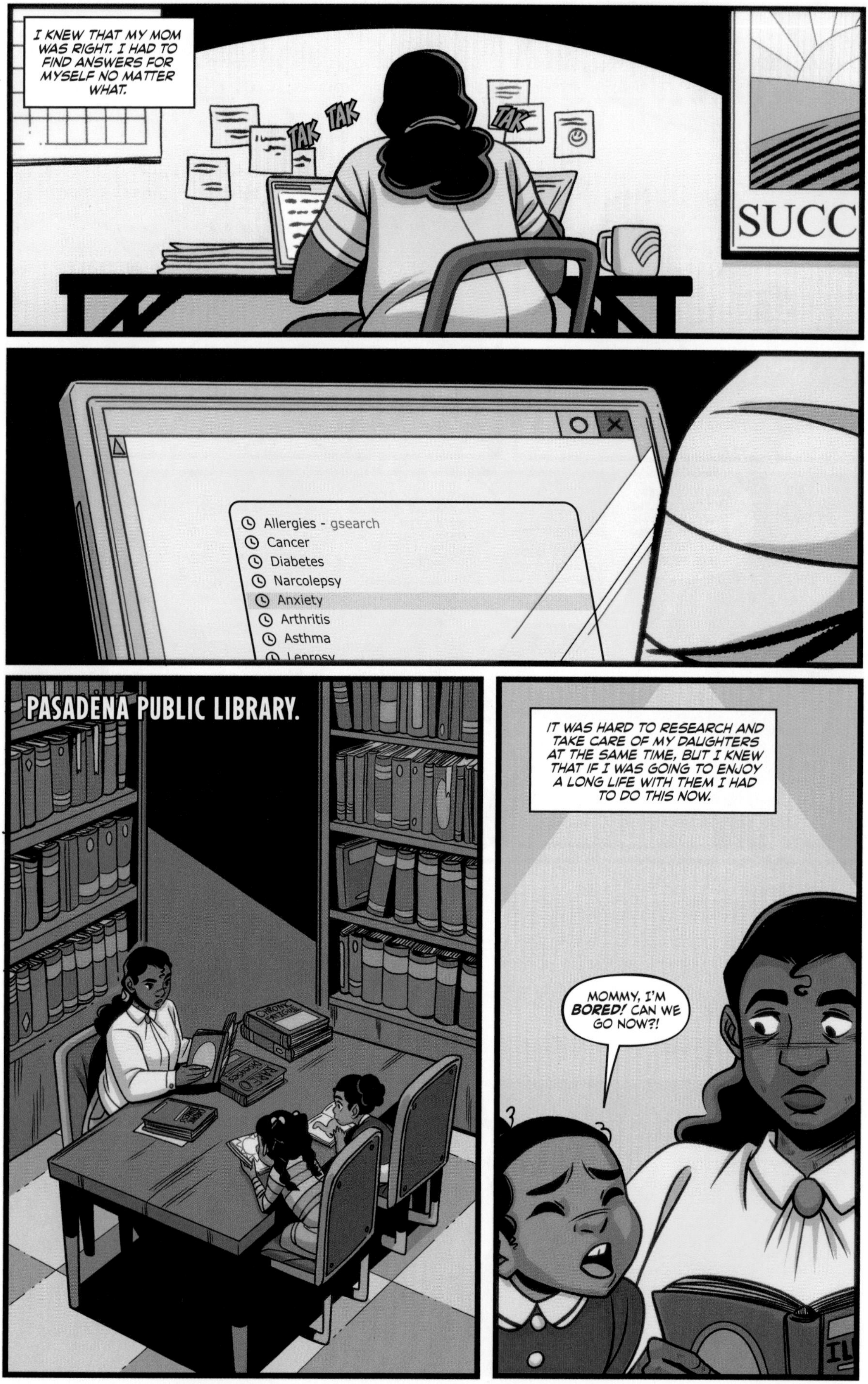
I KNEW THAT MY MOM WAS RIGHT. I HAD TO FIND ANSWERS FOR MYSELF NO MATTER WHAT.
TAK TAK
TAK
SUCC
Allergies - gsearch
Cancer
Diabetes
Narcolepsy
Anxiety
Arthritis
Asthma
Leprosy
PASADENA PUBLIC LIBRARY.
IT WAS HARD TO RESEARCH AND TAKE CARE OF MY DAUGHTERS AT THE SAME TIME, BUT I KNEW THAT IF I WAS GOING TO ENJOY A LONG LIFE WITH THEM I HAD TO DO THIS NOW.
MOMMY, I'M BORED! CAN WE GO NOW?!

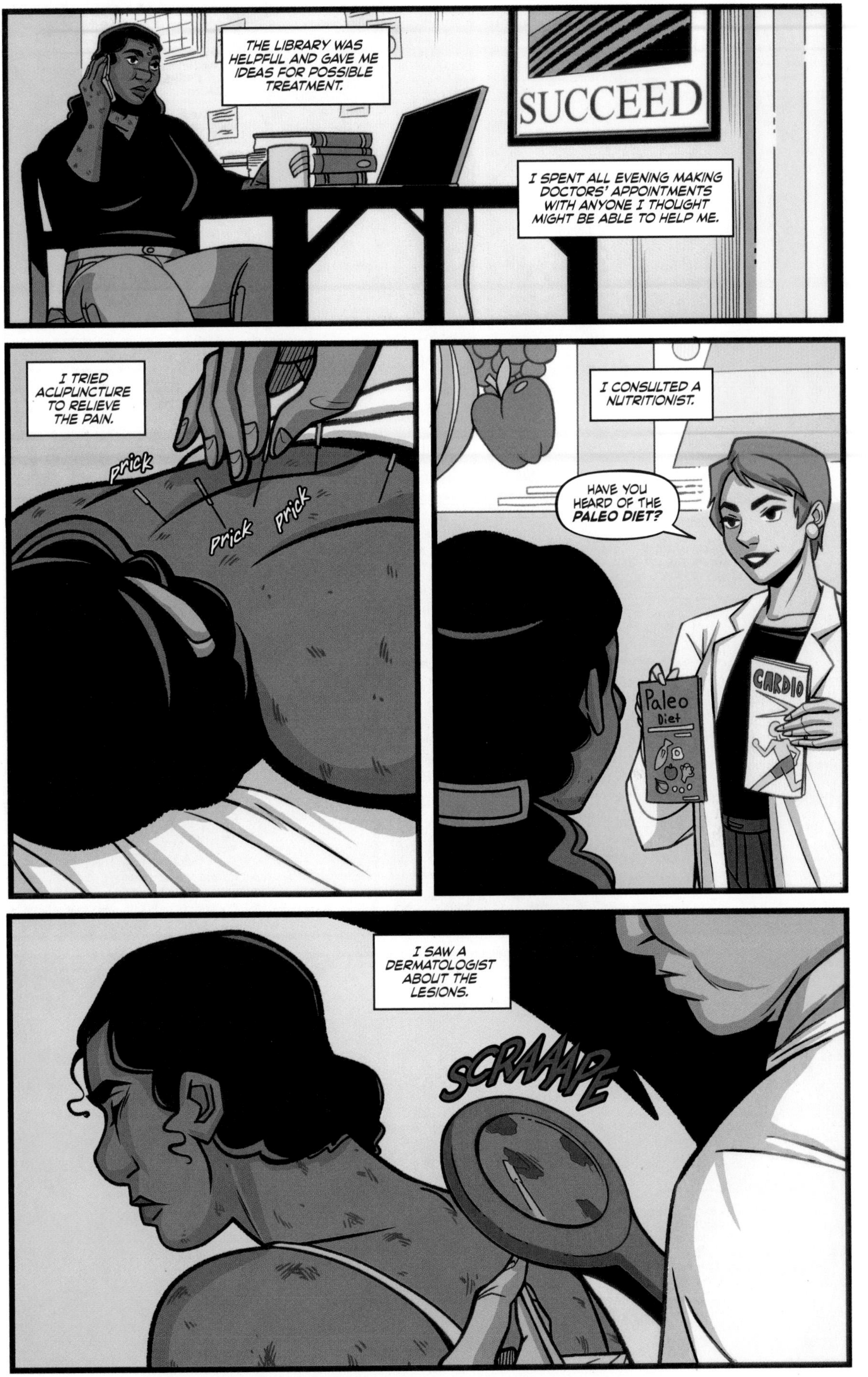
THE LIBRARY WAS HELPFUL AND GAVE ME IDEAS FOR POSSIBLE TREATMENT.
SUCCEED
I SPENT ALL EVENING MAKING DOCTORS' APPOINTMENTS WITH ANYONE I THOUGHT MIGHT BE ABLE TO HELP ME.
I TRIED ACUPUNCTURE TO RELIEVE THE PAIN.
prick
prick
prick
I CONSULTED A NUTRITIONIST.
HAVE YOU HEARD OF THE PALEO DIET?
Paleo Diet
CARDIO
I SAW A DERMATOLOGIST ABOUT THE LESIONS.
SCRAAAPE

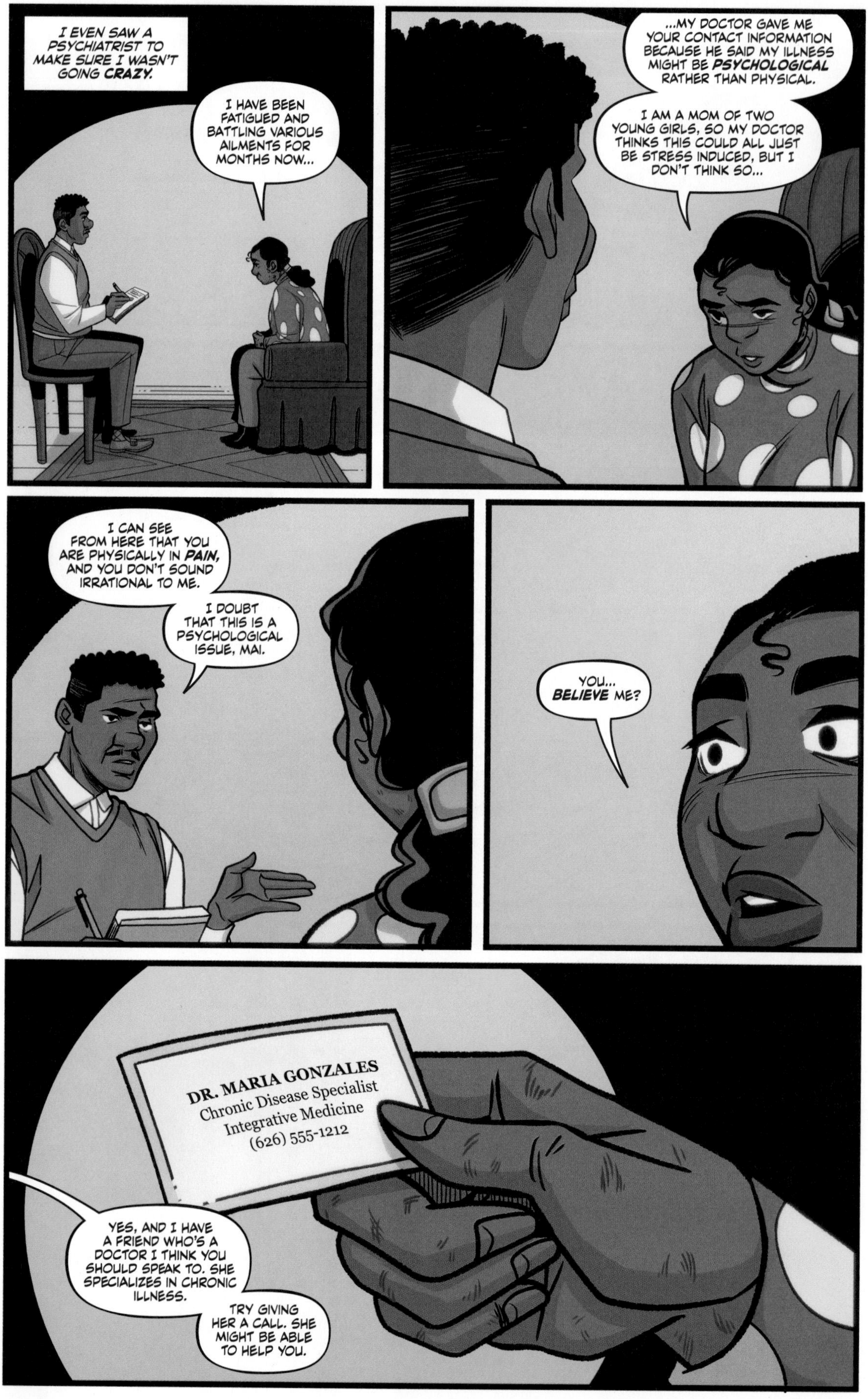

I EVEN SAW A PSYCHIATRIST TO MAKE SURE I WASN'T GOING **CRAZY.**
I HAVE BEEN FATIGUED AND BATTLING VARIOUS AILMENTS FOR MONTHS NOW...
...MY DOCTOR GAVE ME YOUR CONTACT INFORMATION BECAUSE HE SAID MY ILLNESS MIGHT BE **PSYCHOLOGICAL** RATHER THAN PHYSICAL.
I AM A MOM OF TWO YOUNG GIRLS, SO MY DOCTOR THINKS THIS COULD ALL JUST BE STRESS INDUCED, BUT I DON'T THINK SO...
I CAN SEE FROM HERE THAT YOU ARE PHYSICALLY IN **PAIN,** AND YOU DON'T SOUND IRRATIONAL TO ME.
I DOUBT THAT THIS IS A PSYCHOLOGICAL ISSUE, MAI.
YOU... **BELIEVE** ME?
DR. MARIA GONZALES
Chronic Disease Specialist
Integrative Medicine
(626) 555-1212
YES, AND I HAVE A FRIEND WHO'S A DOCTOR I THINK YOU SHOULD SPEAK TO. SHE SPECIALIZES IN CHRONIC ILLNESS.
TRY GIVING HER A CALL. SHE MIGHT BE ABLE TO HELP YOU.

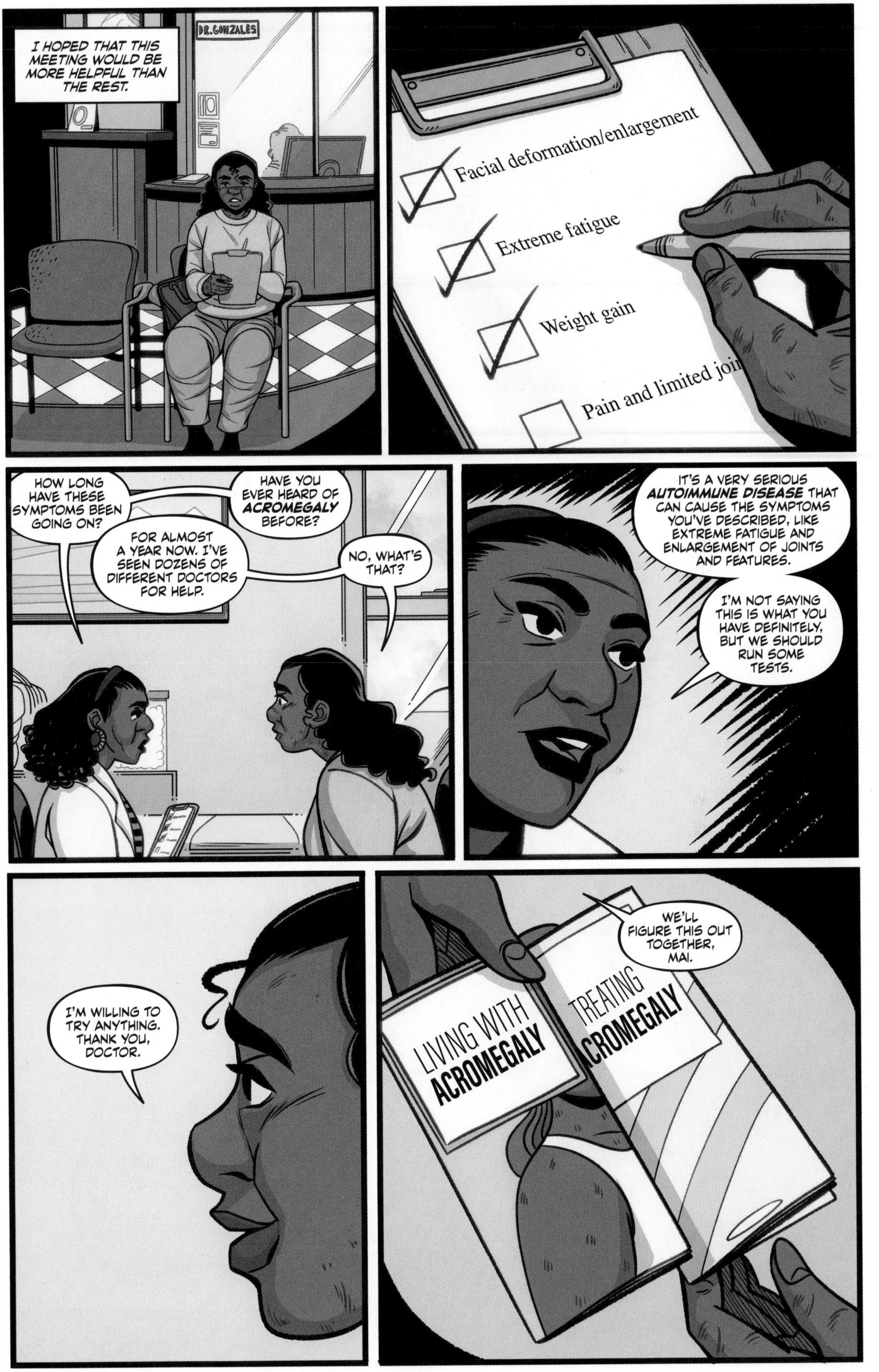
I HOPED THAT THIS MEETING WOULD BE MORE HELPFUL THAN THE REST.
DR. GONZALES
Facial deformation/enlargement
Extreme fatigue
Weight gain
Pain and limited joi
HOW LONG HAVE THESE SYMPTOMS BEEN GOING ON?
FOR ALMOST A YEAR NOW. I'VE SEEN DOZENS OF DIFFERENT DOCTORS FOR HELP.
HAVE YOU EVER HEARD OF ACROMEGALY BEFORE?
NO, WHAT'S THAT?
IT'S A VERY SERIOUS AUTOIMMUNE DISEASE THAT CAN CAUSE THE SYMPTOMS YOU'VE DESCRIBED, LIKE EXTREME FATIGUE AND ENLARGEMENT OF JOINTS AND FEATURES.
I'M NOT SAYING THIS IS WHAT YOU HAVE DEFINITELY, BUT WE SHOULD RUN SOME TESTS.
I'M WILLING TO TRY ANYTHING. THANK YOU, DOCTOR.
WE'LL FIGURE THIS OUT TOGETHER, MAI.
LIVING WITH ACROMEGALY
TREATING ACROMEGALY

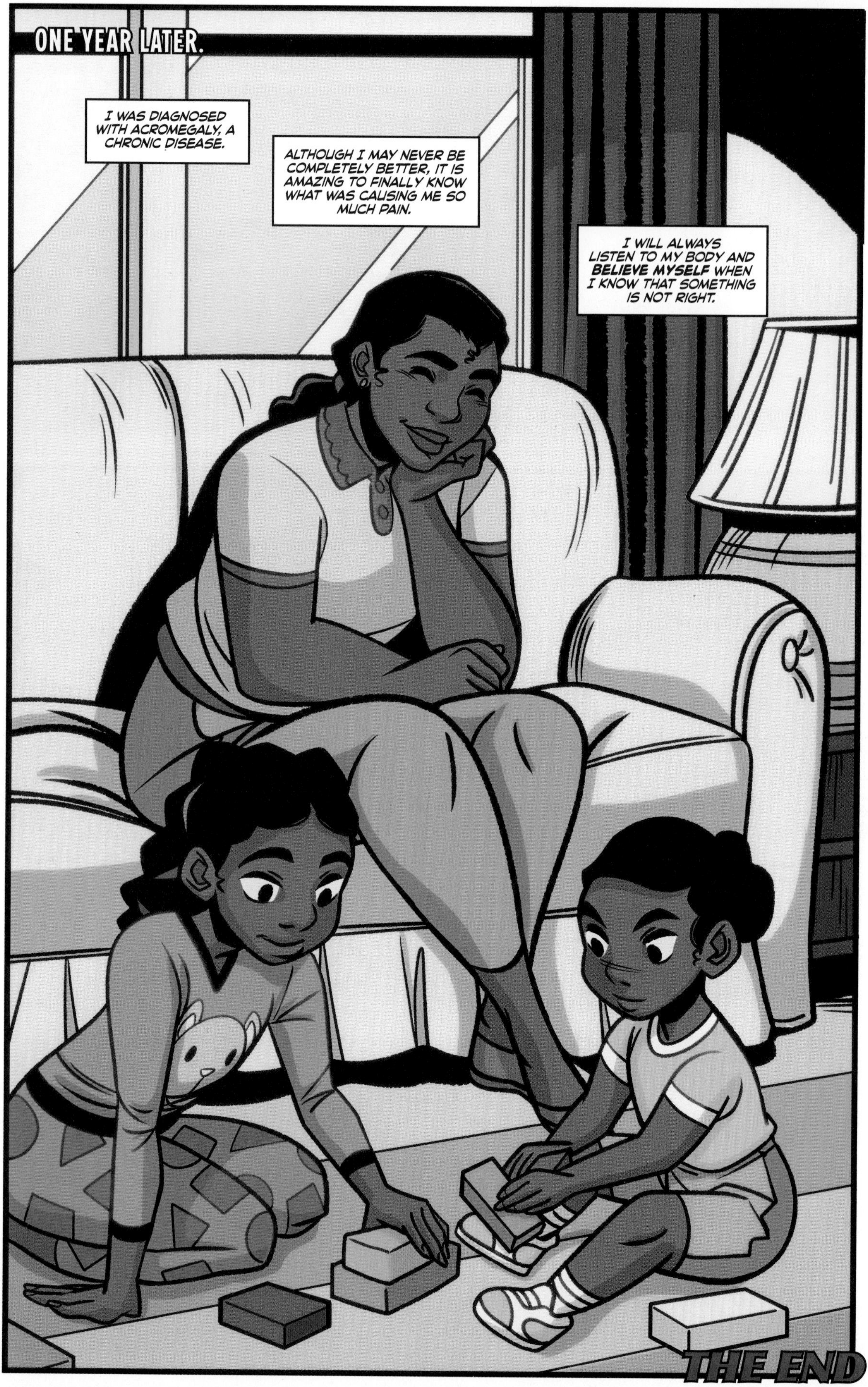
ONE YEAR LATER.
I WAS DIAGNOSED WITH ACROMEGALY, A CHRONIC DISEASE.
ALTHOUGH I MAY NEVER BE COMPLETELY BETTER, IT IS AMAZING TO FINALLY KNOW WHAT WAS CAUSING ME SO MUCH PAIN.
I WILL ALWAYS LISTEN TO MY BODY AND BELIEVE MYSELF WHEN I KNOW THAT SOMETHING IS NOT RIGHT.
THE END

DC REPRESENT!   "MY GRANNY WAS A HERO"

WRITER - TARA ROBERTS

Tara Roberts is a National Geographic Storytelling Fellow and a fellow at MIT's Open Documentary Lab. She spent 2019 following, diving with, and telling stories about Black scuba divers as they searched for and helped document the wrecks of slave ships around the world. Tara has also worked as an editor for *CosmoGirl*, *Essence*, AOL, *Ebony*, and *Heart & Soul* and has edited several books for girls. She founded her own magazine for women "too bold for boundaries." And she spent an amazing and fulfilling year backpacking around the world to find and tell stories about women social entrepreneurs, which led to the creation of a nonprofit that supported and funded their big ideas. Follow her on Instagram @storiesfromthedepths and @curvypath_tara.

ARTIST - YANCEY LABAT
COLORIST - MONICA KUBINA
LETTERER - DERON BENNETT

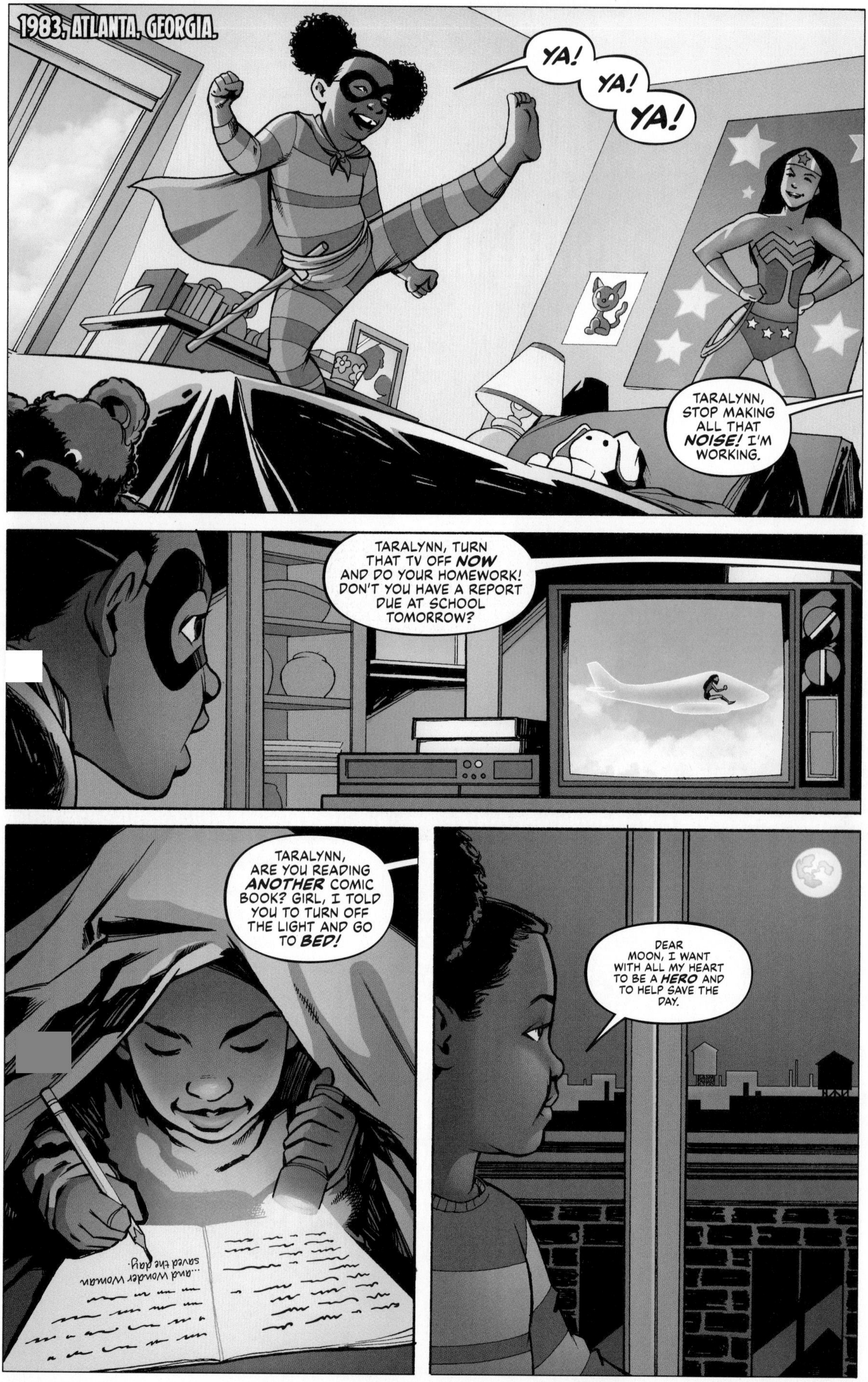
1983, ATLANTA, GEORGIA.
YA! YA! YA!
TARALYNN, STOP MAKING ALL THAT NOISE! I'M WORKING.
TARALYNN, TURN THAT TV OFF NOW AND DO YOUR HOMEWORK! DON'T YOU HAVE A REPORT DUE AT SCHOOL TOMORROW?
TARALYNN, ARE YOU READING ANOTHER COMIC BOOK? GIRL, I TOLD YOU TO TURN OFF THE LIGHT AND GO TO BED!
...and Wonder Woman saved the day.
DEAR MOON, I WANT WITH ALL MY HEART TO BE A HERO AND TO HELP SAVE THE DAY.

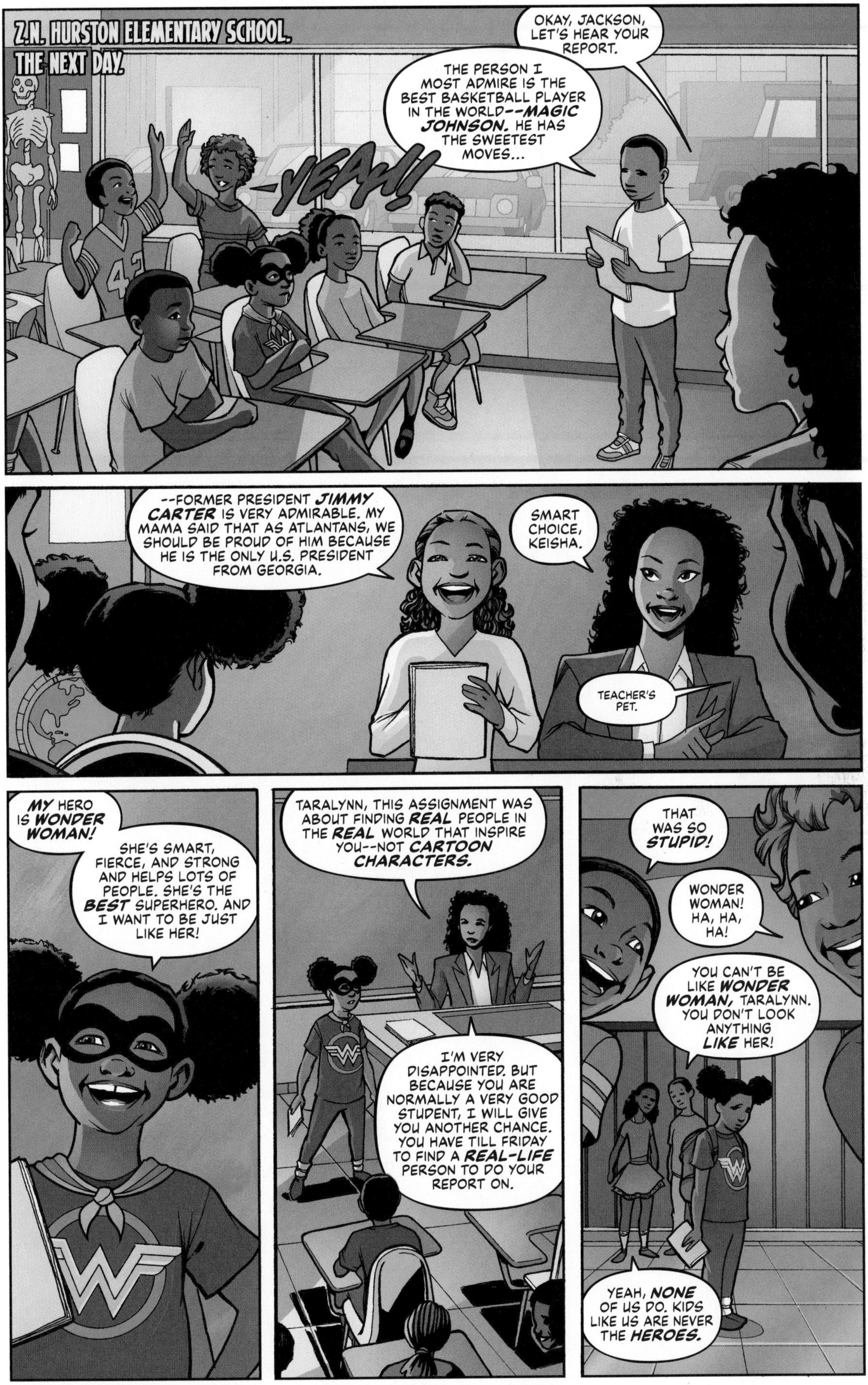
Z.N. HURSTON ELEMENTARY SCHOOL. THE NEXT DAY.
OKAY, JACKSON, LET'S HEAR YOUR REPORT.
THE PERSON I MOST ADMIRE IS THE BEST BASKETBALL PLAYER IN THE WORLD--MAGIC JOHNSON. HE HAS THE SWEETEST MOVES...
-YEAH!
--FORMER PRESIDENT JIMMY CARTER IS VERY ADMIRABLE. MY MAMA SAID THAT AS ATLANTANS, WE SHOULD BE PROUD OF HIM BECAUSE HE IS THE ONLY U.S. PRESIDENT FROM GEORGIA.
SMART CHOICE, KEISHA.
TEACHER'S PET.
MY HERO IS WONDER WOMAN!
SHE'S SMART, FIERCE, AND STRONG AND HELPS LOTS OF PEOPLE. SHE'S THE BEST SUPERHERO. AND I WANT TO BE JUST LIKE HER!
TARALYNN, THIS ASSIGNMENT WAS ABOUT FINDING REAL PEOPLE IN THE REAL WORLD THAT INSPIRE YOU--NOT CARTOON CHARACTERS.
I'M VERY DISAPPOINTED. BUT BECAUSE YOU ARE NORMALLY A VERY GOOD STUDENT, I WILL GIVE YOU ANOTHER CHANCE. YOU HAVE TILL FRIDAY TO FIND A REAL-LIFE PERSON TO DO YOUR REPORT ON.
THAT WAS SO STUPID!
WONDER WOMAN! HA, HA, HA!
YOU CAN'T BE LIKE WONDER WOMAN, TARALYNN. YOU DON'T LOOK ANYTHING LIKE HER!
YEAH, NONE OF US DO. KIDS LIKE US ARE NEVER THE HEROES.

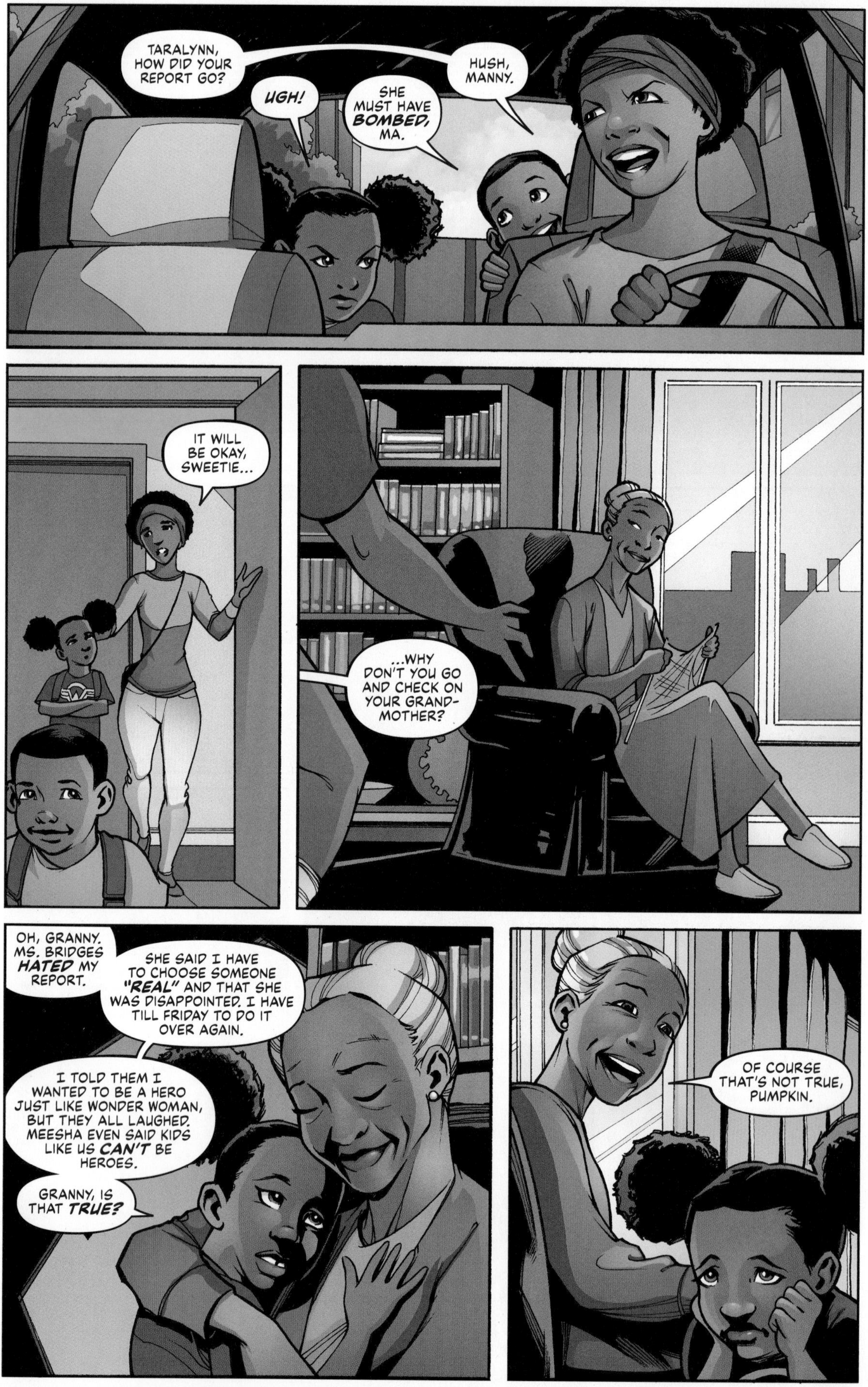
TARALYNN, HOW DID YOUR REPORT GO?
UGH!
SHE MUST HAVE BOMBED, MA.
HUSH, MANNY.
IT WILL BE OKAY, SWEETIE...
...WHY DON'T YOU GO AND CHECK ON YOUR GRAND-MOTHER?
OH, GRANNY. MS. BRIDGES HATED MY REPORT.
SHE SAID I HAVE TO CHOOSE SOMEONE "REAL" AND THAT SHE WAS DISAPPOINTED. I HAVE TILL FRIDAY TO DO IT OVER AGAIN.
I TOLD THEM I WANTED TO BE A HERO JUST LIKE WONDER WOMAN, BUT THEY ALL LAUGHED. MEESHA EVEN SAID KIDS LIKE US CAN'T BE HEROES.
GRANNY, IS THAT TRUE?
OF COURSE THAT'S NOT TRUE, PUMPKIN.

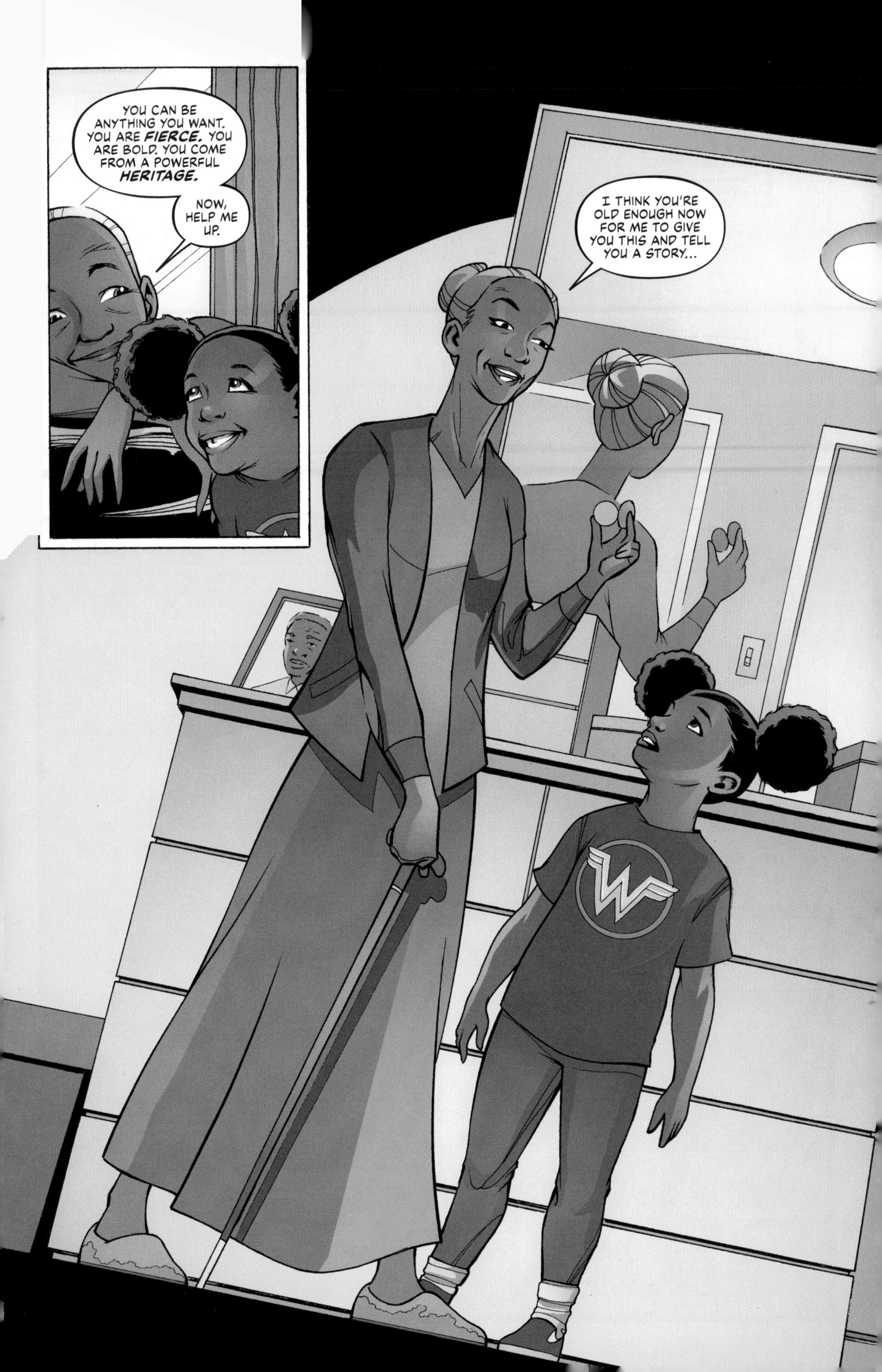
YOU CAN BE ANYTHING YOU WANT. YOU ARE **FIERCE.** YOU ARE BOLD. YOU COME FROM A POWERFUL **HERITAGE.**
NOW, HELP ME UP.
I THINK YOU'RE OLD ENOUGH NOW FOR ME TO GIVE YOU THIS AND TELL YOU A STORY...

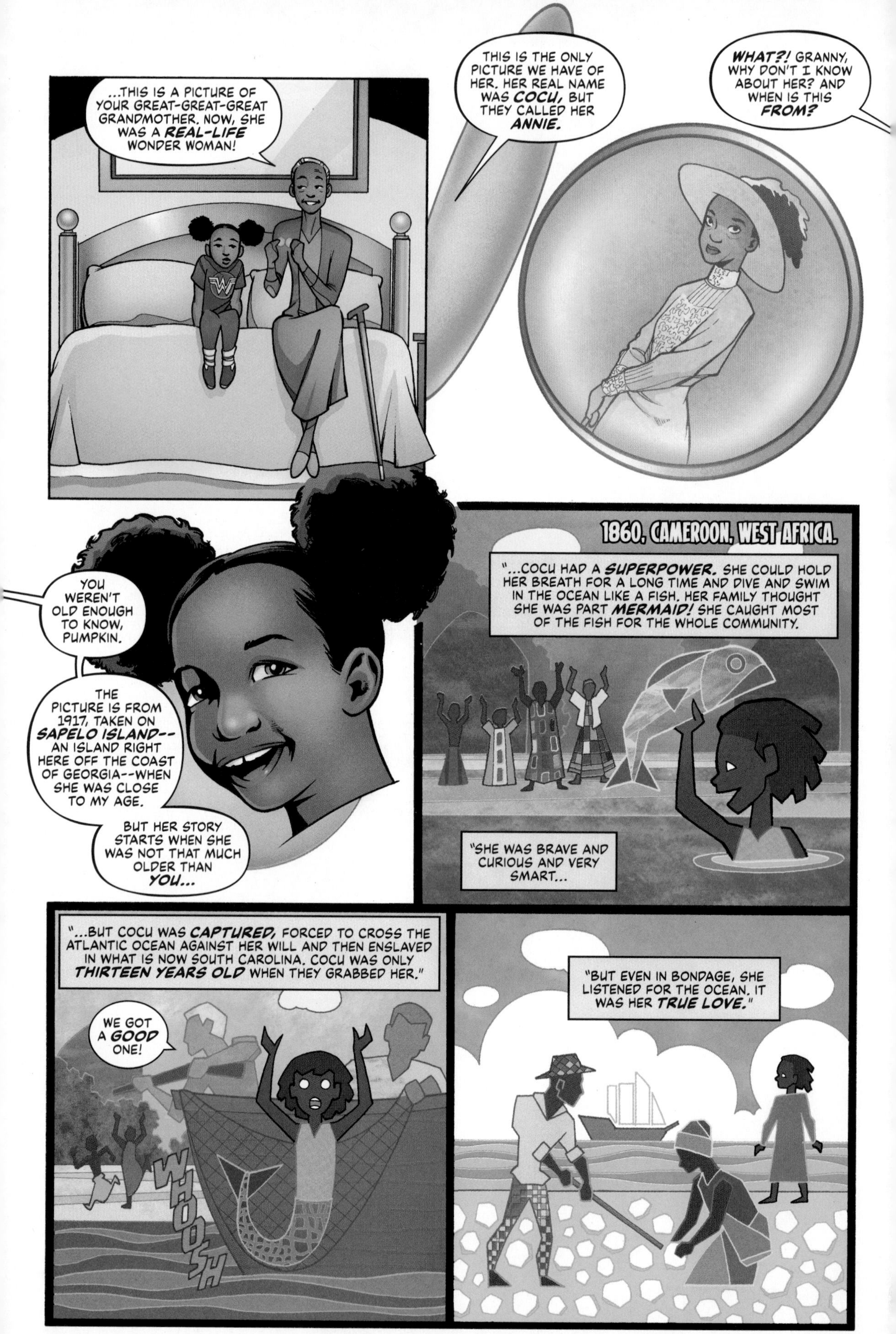
...THIS IS A PICTURE OF YOUR GREAT-GREAT-GREAT GRANDMOTHER. NOW, SHE WAS A REAL-LIFE WONDER WOMAN!
THIS IS THE ONLY PICTURE WE HAVE OF HER. HER REAL NAME WAS COCU, BUT THEY CALLED HER ANNIE.
WHAT?! GRANNY, WHY DON'T I KNOW ABOUT HER? AND WHEN IS THIS FROM?
YOU WEREN'T OLD ENOUGH TO KNOW, PUMPKIN.
THE PICTURE IS FROM 1917, TAKEN ON SAPELO ISLAND--AN ISLAND RIGHT HERE OFF THE COAST OF GEORGIA--WHEN SHE WAS CLOSE TO MY AGE.
BUT HER STORY STARTS WHEN SHE WAS NOT THAT MUCH OLDER THAN YOU...
1860, CAMEROON, WEST AFRICA.
"...COCU HAD A SUPERPOWER. SHE COULD HOLD HER BREATH FOR A LONG TIME AND DIVE AND SWIM IN THE OCEAN LIKE A FISH. HER FAMILY THOUGHT SHE WAS PART MERMAID! SHE CAUGHT MOST OF THE FISH FOR THE WHOLE COMMUNITY.
"SHE WAS BRAVE AND CURIOUS AND VERY SMART...
"...BUT COCU WAS CAPTURED, FORCED TO CROSS THE ATLANTIC OCEAN AGAINST HER WILL AND THEN ENSLAVED IN WHAT IS NOW SOUTH CAROLINA. COCU WAS ONLY THIRTEEN YEARS OLD WHEN THEY GRABBED HER."
WE GOT A GOOD ONE!
WHOOSH
"BUT EVEN IN BONDAGE, SHE LISTENED FOR THE OCEAN. IT WAS HER TRUE LOVE."

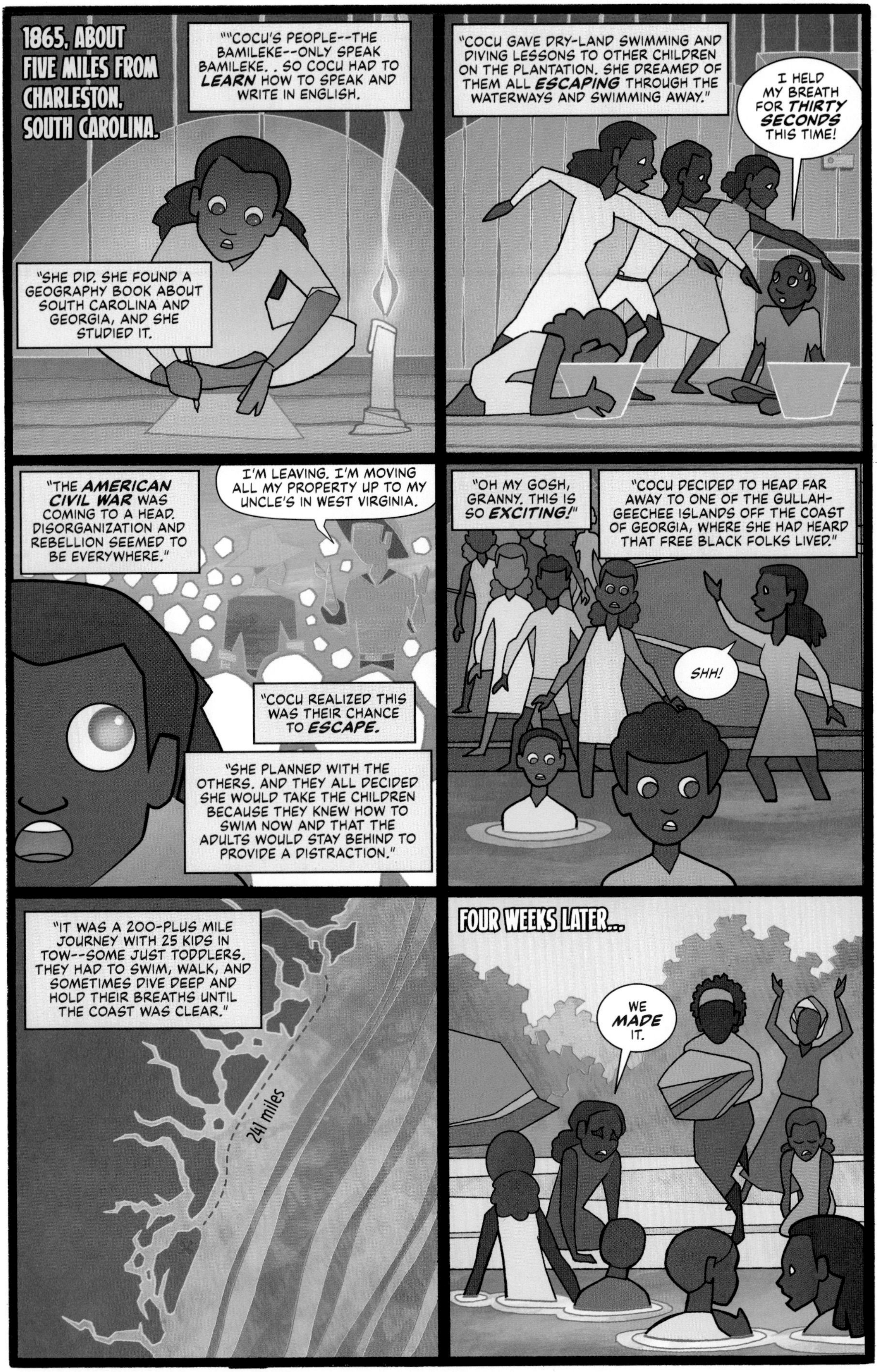
1865, ABOUT FIVE MILES FROM CHARLESTON, SOUTH CAROLINA.
""COCU'S PEOPLE--THE BAMILEKE--ONLY SPEAK BAMILEKE. . SO COCU HAD TO LEARN HOW TO SPEAK AND WRITE IN ENGLISH.
"SHE DID. SHE FOUND A GEOGRAPHY BOOK ABOUT SOUTH CAROLINA AND GEORGIA, AND SHE STUDIED IT.
"COCU GAVE DRY-LAND SWIMMING AND DIVING LESSONS TO OTHER CHILDREN ON THE PLANTATION. SHE DREAMED OF THEM ALL ESCAPING THROUGH THE WATERWAYS AND SWIMMING AWAY."
I HELD MY BREATH FOR THIRTY SECONDS THIS TIME!
"THE AMERICAN CIVIL WAR WAS COMING TO A HEAD. DISORGANIZATION AND REBELLION SEEMED TO BE EVERYWHERE."
I'M LEAVING. I'M MOVING ALL MY PROPERTY UP TO MY UNCLE'S IN WEST VIRGINIA.
"COCU REALIZED THIS WAS THEIR CHANCE TO ESCAPE.
"SHE PLANNED WITH THE OTHERS. AND THEY ALL DECIDED SHE WOULD TAKE THE CHILDREN BECAUSE THEY KNEW HOW TO SWIM NOW AND THAT THE ADULTS WOULD STAY BEHIND TO PROVIDE A DISTRACTION."
"OH MY GOSH, GRANNY. THIS IS SO EXCITING!"
"COCU DECIDED TO HEAD FAR AWAY TO ONE OF THE GULLAH-GEECHEE ISLANDS OFF THE COAST OF GEORGIA, WHERE SHE HAD HEARD THAT FREE BLACK FOLKS LIVED."
SHH!
"IT WAS A 200-PLUS MILE JOURNEY WITH 25 KIDS IN TOW--SOME JUST TODDLERS. THEY HAD TO SWIM, WALK, AND SOMETIMES DIVE DEEP AND HOLD THEIR BREATHS UNTIL THE COAST WAS CLEAR."
241 miles
FOUR WEEKS LATER...
WE MADE IT.

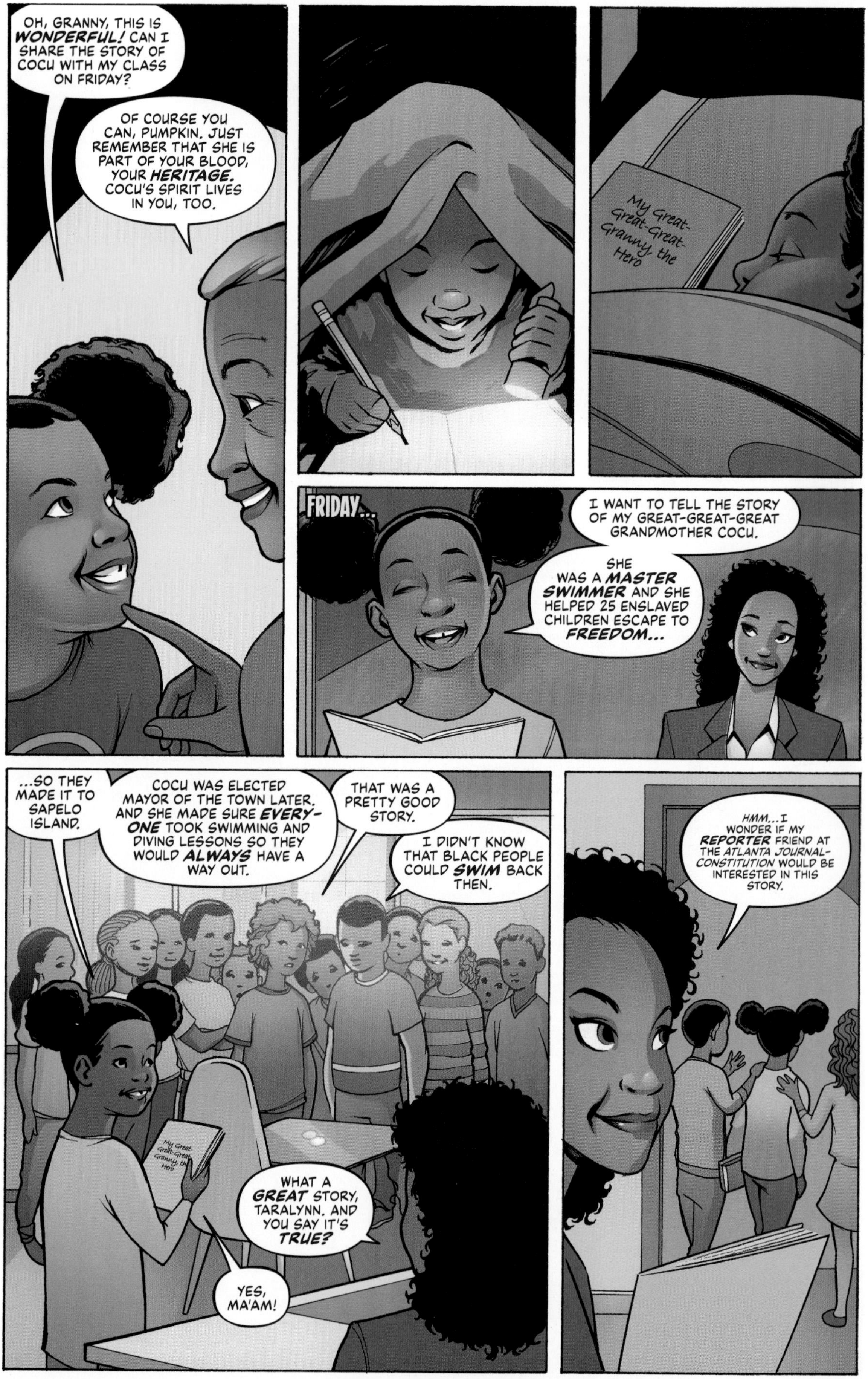
OH, GRANNY, THIS IS WONDERFUL! CAN I SHARE THE STORY OF COCU WITH MY CLASS ON FRIDAY?
OF COURSE YOU CAN, PUMPKIN. JUST REMEMBER THAT SHE IS PART OF YOUR BLOOD, YOUR HERITAGE. COCU'S SPIRIT LIVES IN YOU, TOO.
My Great-Great-Great-Granny, the Hero
FRIDAY...
I WANT TO TELL THE STORY OF MY GREAT-GREAT-GREAT GRANDMOTHER COCU.
SHE WAS A MASTER SWIMMER AND SHE HELPED 25 ENSLAVED CHILDREN ESCAPE TO FREEDOM...
...SO THEY MADE IT TO SAPELO ISLAND.
COCU WAS ELECTED MAYOR OF THE TOWN LATER. AND SHE MADE SURE EVERY-ONE TOOK SWIMMING AND DIVING LESSONS SO THEY WOULD ALWAYS HAVE A WAY OUT.
THAT WAS A PRETTY GOOD STORY.
I DIDN'T KNOW THAT BLACK PEOPLE COULD SWIM BACK THEN.
My Great-Great-Great-Granny, the Hero
WHAT A GREAT STORY, TARALYNN. AND YOU SAY IT'S TRUE?
YES, MA'AM!
HMM...I WONDER IF MY REPORTER FRIEND AT THE ATLANTA JOURNAL-CONSTITUTION WOULD BE INTERESTED IN THIS STORY.

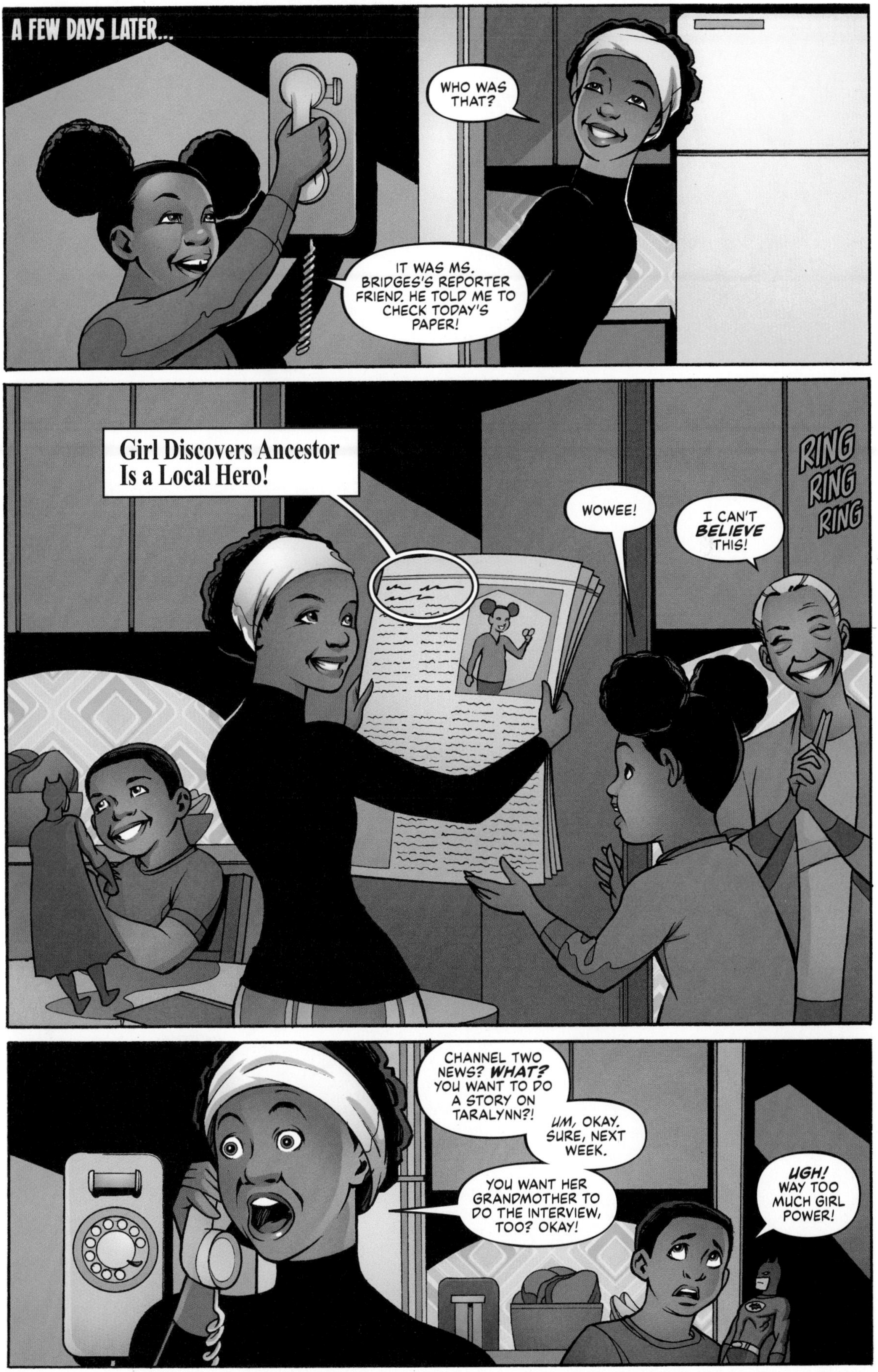
A FEW DAYS LATER...
WHO WAS THAT?
IT WAS MS. BRIDGES'S REPORTER FRIEND. HE TOLD ME TO CHECK TODAY'S PAPER!
Girl Discovers Ancestor Is a Local Hero!
WOWEE!
I CAN'T BELIEVE THIS!
RING RING RING
CHANNEL TWO NEWS? WHAT? YOU WANT TO DO A STORY ON TARALYNN?!
UM, OKAY. SURE, NEXT WEEK.
YOU WANT HER GRANDMOTHER TO DO THE INTERVIEW, TOO? OKAY!
UGH! WAY TOO MUCH GIRL POWER!

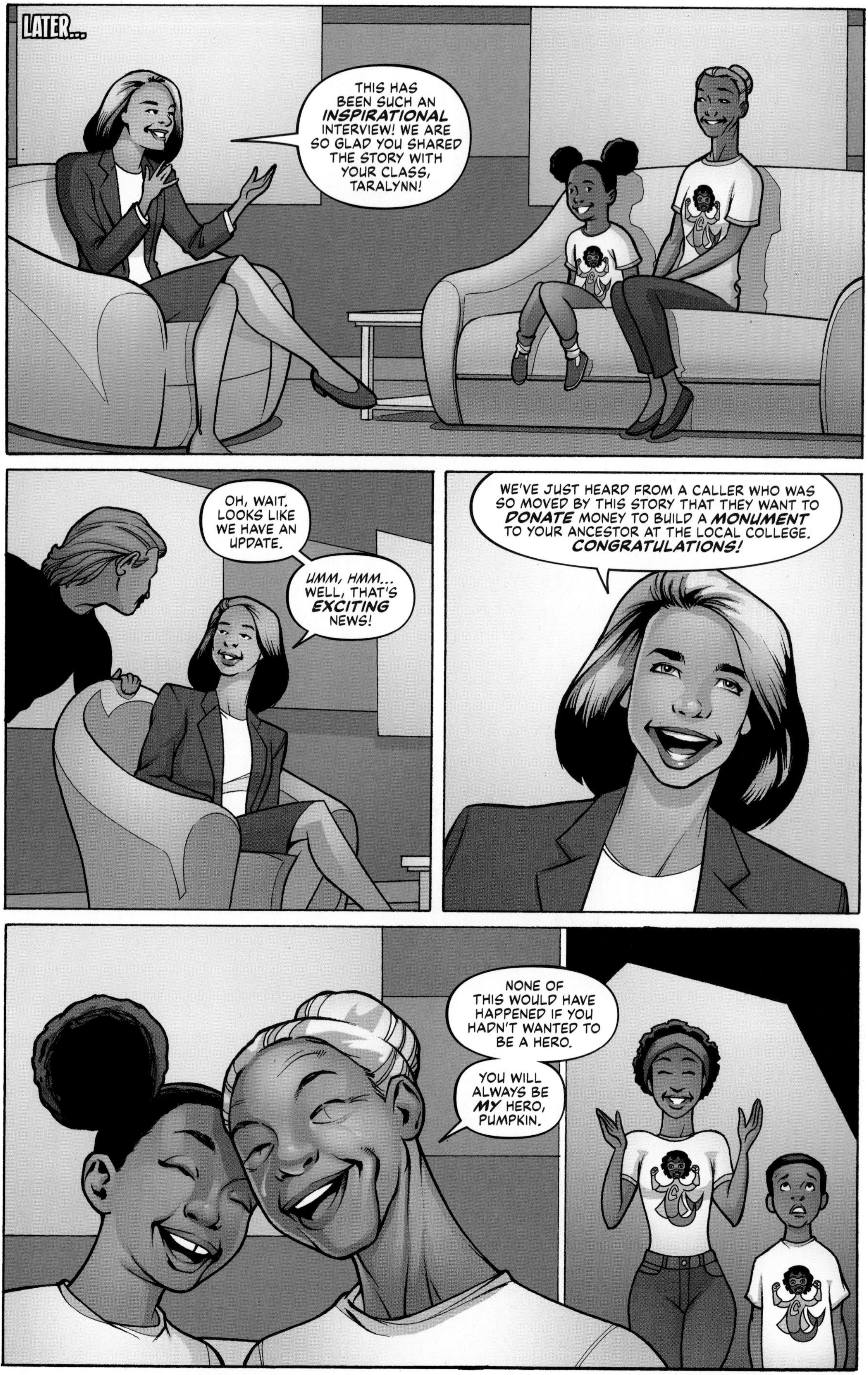
LATER...
THIS HAS BEEN SUCH AN INSPIRATIONAL INTERVIEW! WE ARE SO GLAD YOU SHARED THE STORY WITH YOUR CLASS, TARALYNN!
OH, WAIT. LOOKS LIKE WE HAVE AN UPDATE.
UMM, HMM... WELL, THAT'S EXCITING NEWS!
WE'VE JUST HEARD FROM A CALLER WHO WAS SO MOVED BY THIS STORY THAT THEY WANT TO DONATE MONEY TO BUILD A MONUMENT TO YOUR ANCESTOR AT THE LOCAL COLLEGE. CONGRATULATIONS!
NONE OF THIS WOULD HAVE HAPPENED IF YOU HADN'T WANTED TO BE A HERO.
YOU WILL ALWAYS BE MY HERO, PUMPKIN.

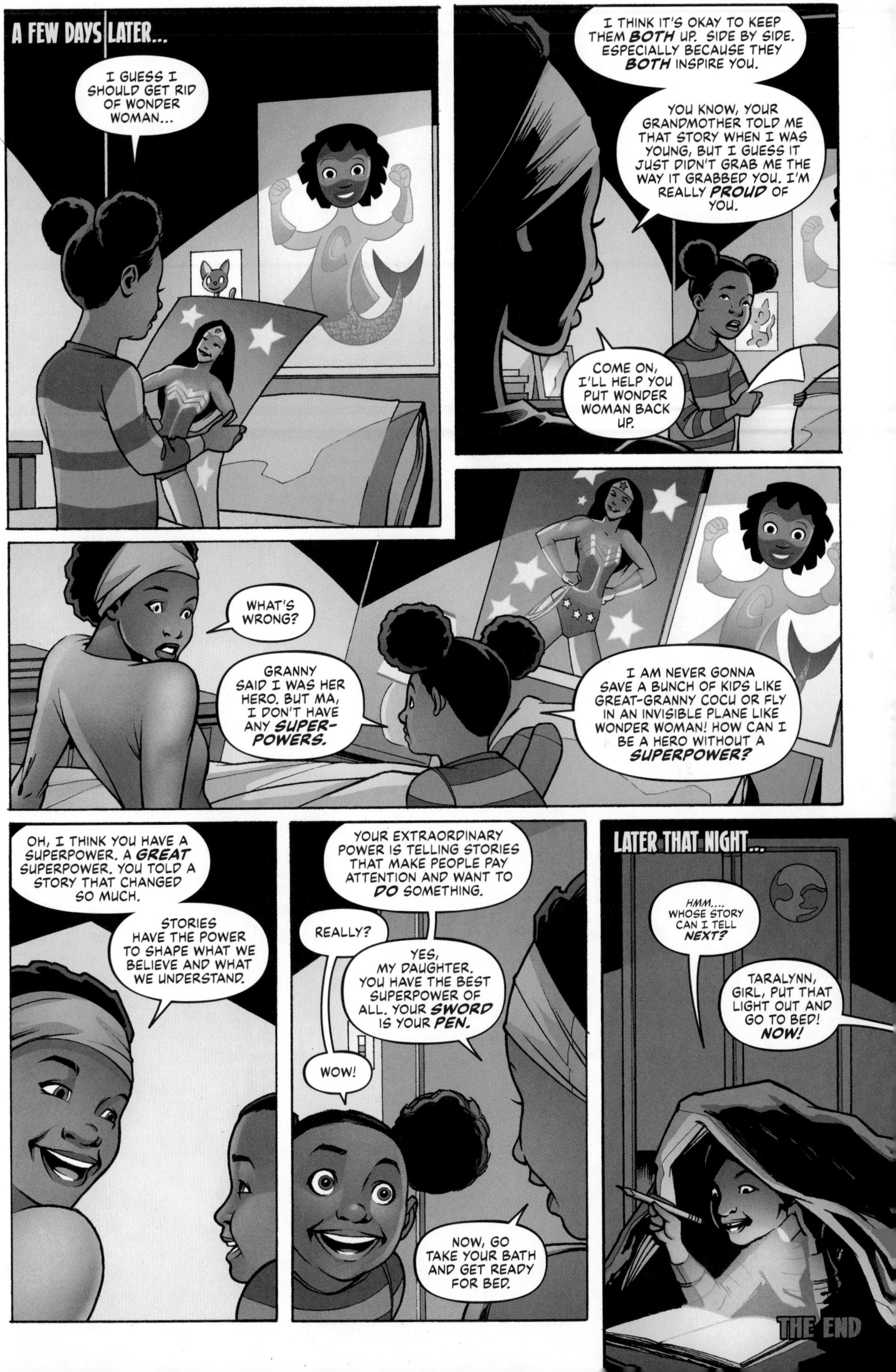
A FEW DAYS LATER...
I GUESS I SHOULD GET RID OF WONDER WOMAN...
I THINK IT'S OKAY TO KEEP THEM BOTH UP. SIDE BY SIDE. ESPECIALLY BECAUSE THEY BOTH INSPIRE YOU.
YOU KNOW, YOUR GRANDMOTHER TOLD ME THAT STORY WHEN I WAS YOUNG, BUT I GUESS IT JUST DIDN'T GRAB ME THE WAY IT GRABBED YOU. I'M REALLY PROUD OF YOU.
COME ON, I'LL HELP YOU PUT WONDER WOMAN BACK UP.
WHAT'S WRONG?
GRANNY SAID I WAS HER HERO. BUT MA, I DON'T HAVE ANY SUPER-POWERS.
I AM NEVER GONNA SAVE A BUNCH OF KIDS LIKE GREAT-GRANNY COCU OR FLY IN AN INVISIBLE PLANE LIKE WONDER WOMAN! HOW CAN I BE A HERO WITHOUT A SUPERPOWER?
OH, I THINK YOU HAVE A SUPERPOWER. A GREAT SUPERPOWER. YOU TOLD A STORY THAT CHANGED SO MUCH.
STORIES HAVE THE POWER TO SHAPE WHAT WE BELIEVE AND WHAT WE UNDERSTAND.
YOUR EXTRAORDINARY POWER IS TELLING STORIES THAT MAKE PEOPLE PAY ATTENTION AND WANT TO DO SOMETHING.
REALLY?
YES, MY DAUGHTER. YOU HAVE THE BEST SUPERPOWER OF ALL. YOUR SWORD IS YOUR PEN.
WOW!
NOW, GO TAKE YOUR BATH AND GET READY FOR BED.
LATER THAT NIGHT...
HMM.... WHOSE STORY CAN I TELL NEXT?
TARALYNN, GIRL, PUT THAT LIGHT OUT AND GO TO BED! NOW!
THE END

DC REPRESENT!

CHAPTER SIX
"THE LESSON"

WRITER & ARTIST - DOMINIKE "DOMO" STANTON

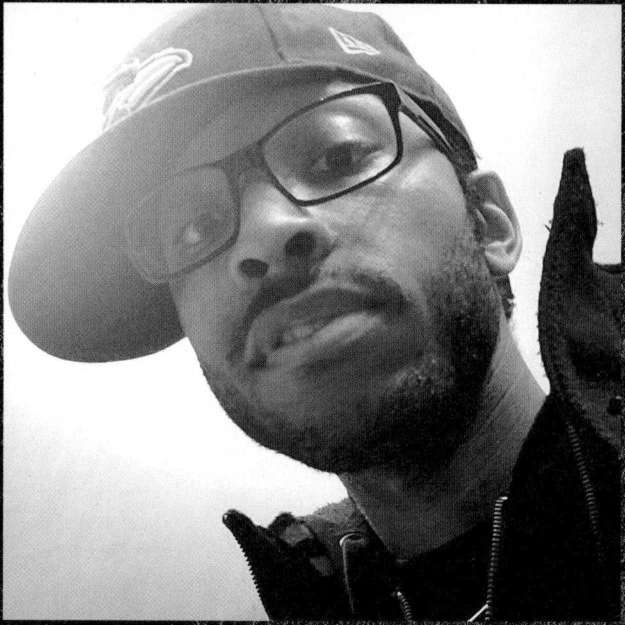

Dominike "DOMO" Stanton hails from Baltimore, Maryland. He studied illustration at Savannah College of Art and Design in Atlanta, Georgia, and has worked for 10 years building a career drawing various comics for Marvel, DC Comics, and Boom! Studios. He also worked as an animator on the FX cartoon *Archer*, and is one of his editors' favorite people. He will love you forever if you buy him shrimp and grits.

COLORIST - EMILIO LOPEZ
LETTERER - DERON BENNETT

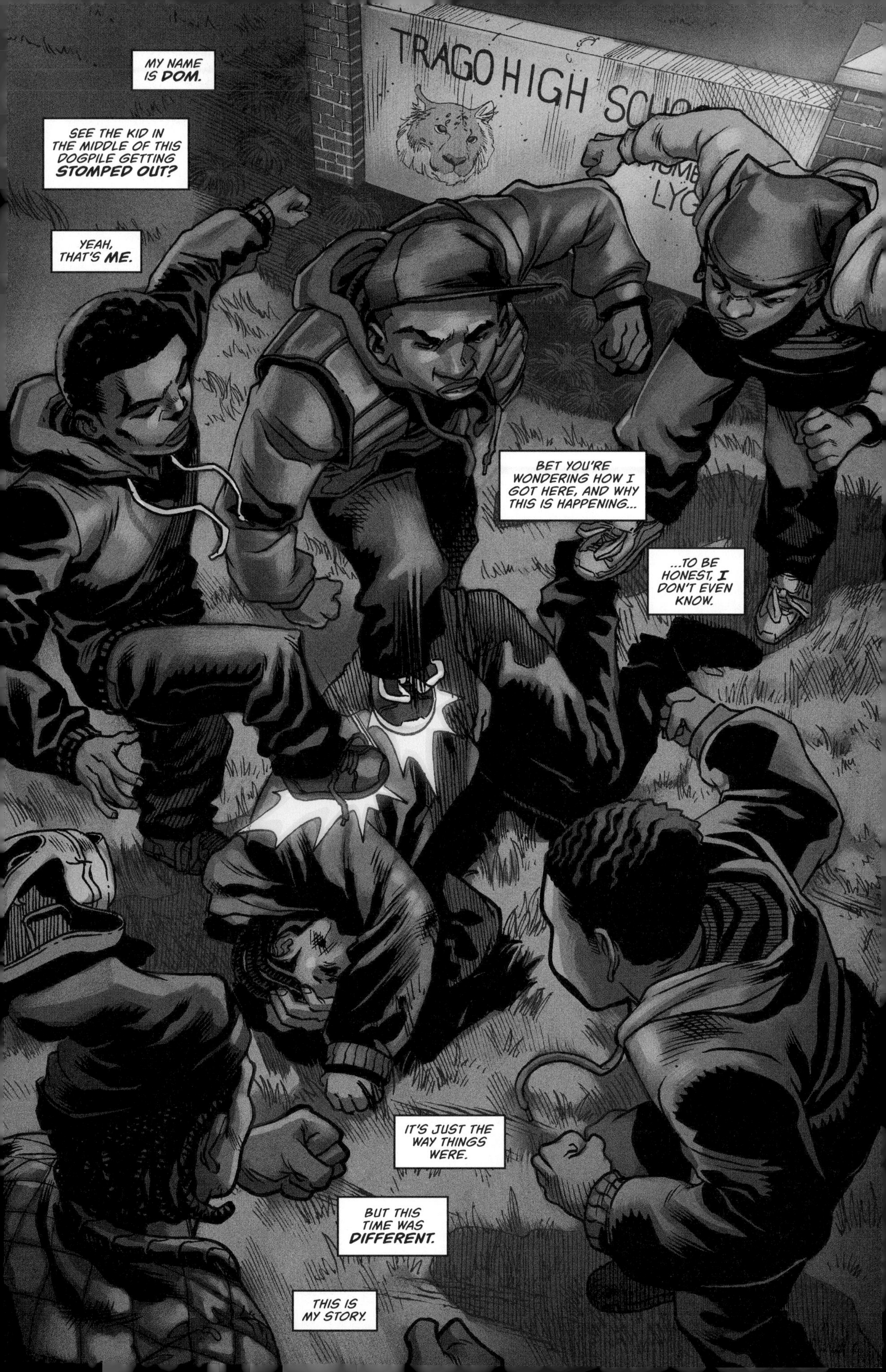
TRAGO HIGH SCHO
MY NAME IS DOM.
SEE THE KID IN THE MIDDLE OF THIS DOGPILE GETTING STOMPED OUT?
YEAH, THAT'S ME.
BET YOU'RE WONDERING HOW I GOT HERE, AND WHY THIS IS HAPPENING...
...TO BE HONEST, I DON'T EVEN KNOW.
IT'S JUST THE WAY THINGS WERE.
BUT THIS TIME WAS DIFFERENT.
THIS IS MY STORY.

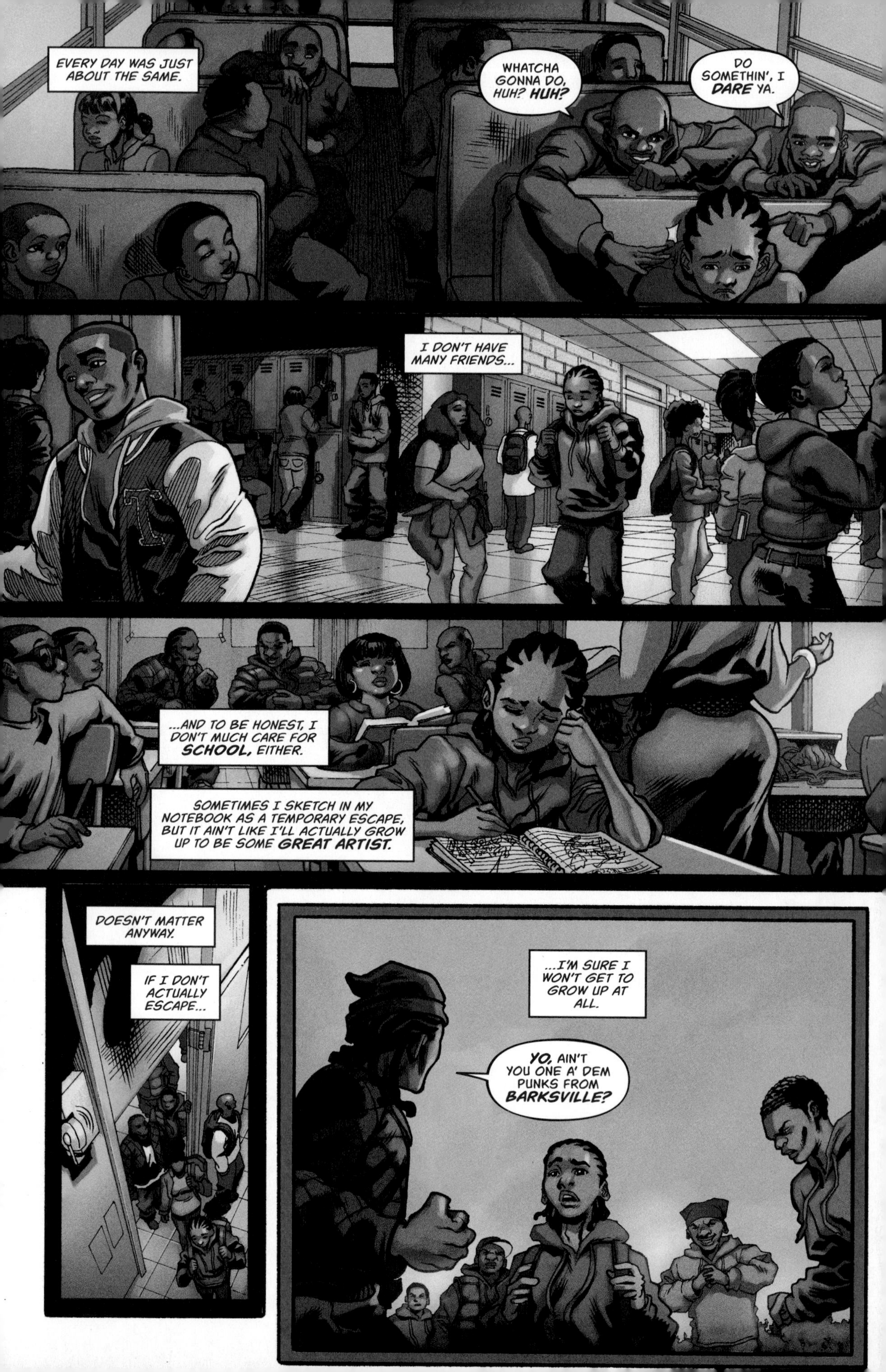
EVERY DAY WAS JUST ABOUT THE SAME.
WHATCHA GONNA DO, HUH? HUH?
DO SOMETHIN', I DARE YA.
I DON'T HAVE MANY FRIENDS...
...AND TO BE HONEST, I DON'T MUCH CARE FOR SCHOOL, EITHER.
SOMETIMES I SKETCH IN MY NOTEBOOK AS A TEMPORARY ESCAPE, BUT IT AIN'T LIKE I'LL ACTUALLY GROW UP TO BE SOME GREAT ARTIST.
DOESN'T MATTER ANYWAY.
IF I DON'T ACTUALLY ESCAPE...
...I'M SURE I WON'T GET TO GROW UP AT ALL.
YO, AIN'T YOU ONE A' DEM PUNKS FROM BARKSVILLE?

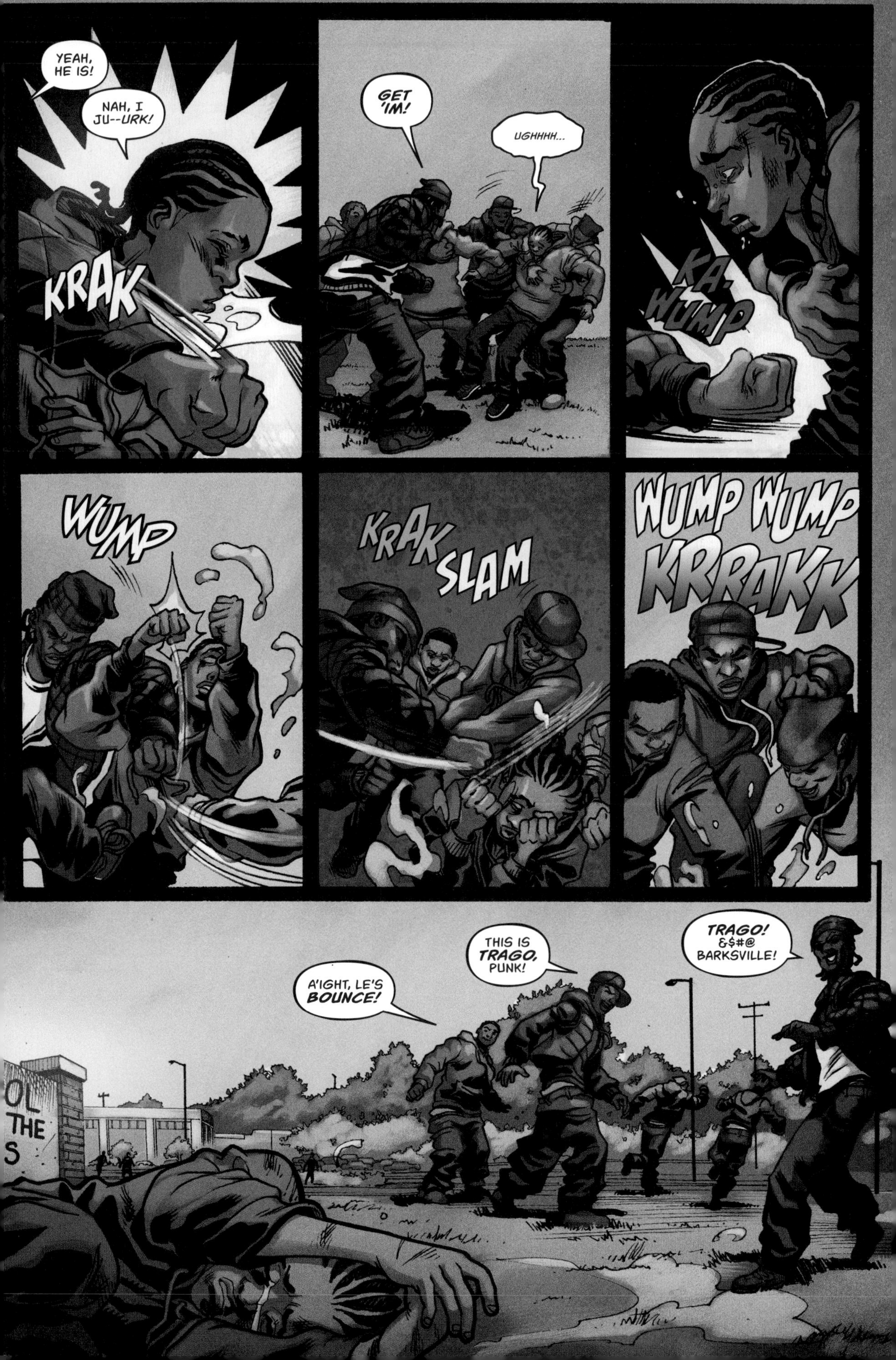
YEAH, HE IS!
NAH, I JU--URK!
KRAK
GET 'IM!
UGHHHH...
KA-WUMP
WUMP
KRAK SLAM
WUMP WUMP KRRAKK
A'IGHT, LE'S BOUNCE!
THIS IS TRAGO, PUNK!
TRAGO! &$#@ BARKSVILLE!
OL THE S

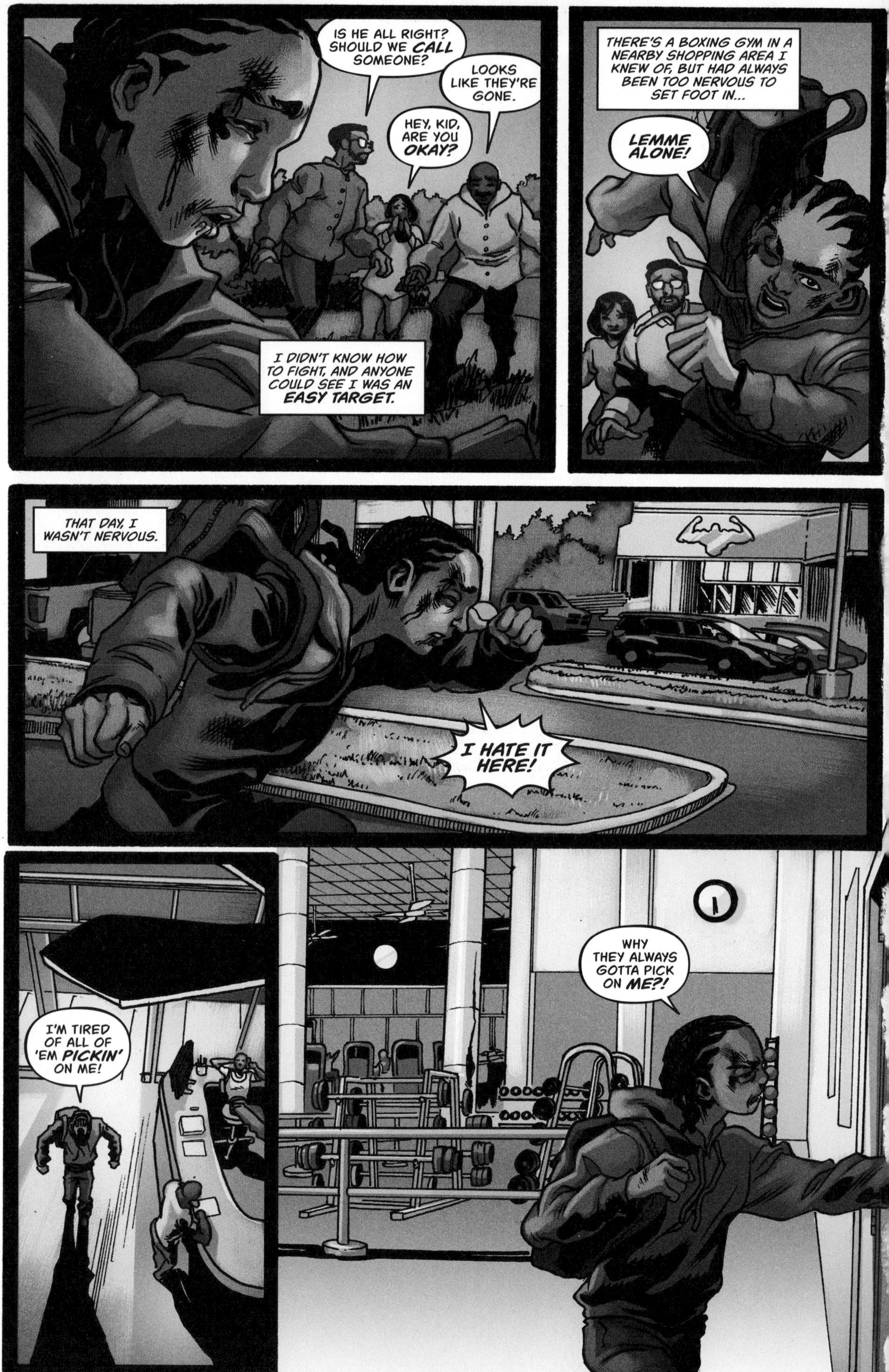
IS HE ALL RIGHT? SHOULD WE CALL SOMEONE?
LOOKS LIKE THEY'RE GONE.
HEY, KID, ARE YOU OKAY?
I DIDN'T KNOW HOW TO FIGHT, AND ANYONE COULD SEE I WAS AN EASY TARGET.
THERE'S A BOXING GYM IN A NEARBY SHOPPING AREA I KNEW OF, BUT HAD ALWAYS BEEN TOO NERVOUS TO SET FOOT IN...
LEMME ALONE!
THAT DAY, I WASN'T NERVOUS.
I HATE IT HERE!
I'M TIRED OF ALL OF 'EM PICKIN' ON ME!
WHY THEY ALWAYS GOTTA PICK ON ME?!

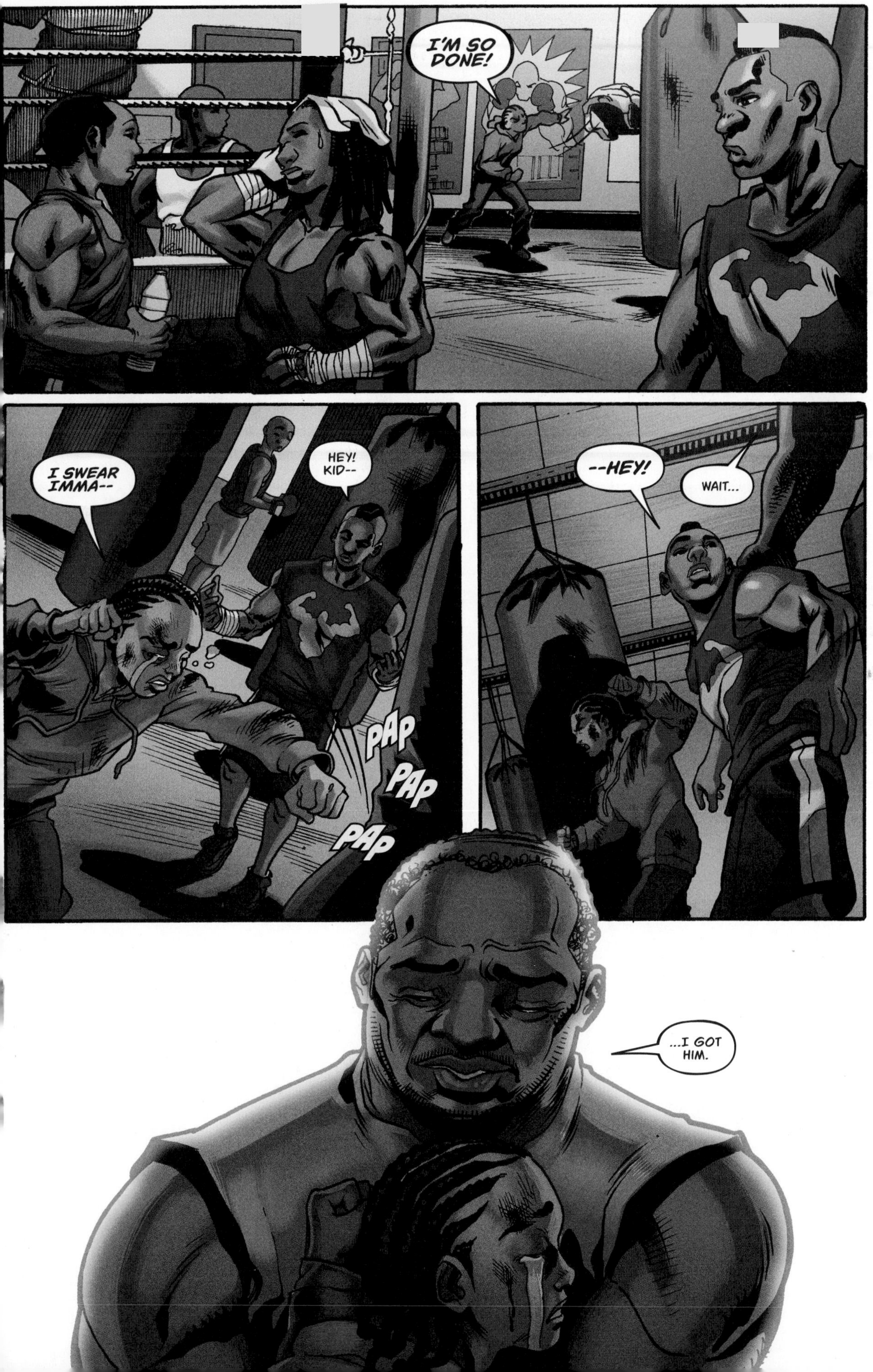
I'M SO DONE!
I SWEAR IMMA--
HEY! KID--
PAP
PAP
PAP
--HEY!
WAIT...
...I GOT HIM.

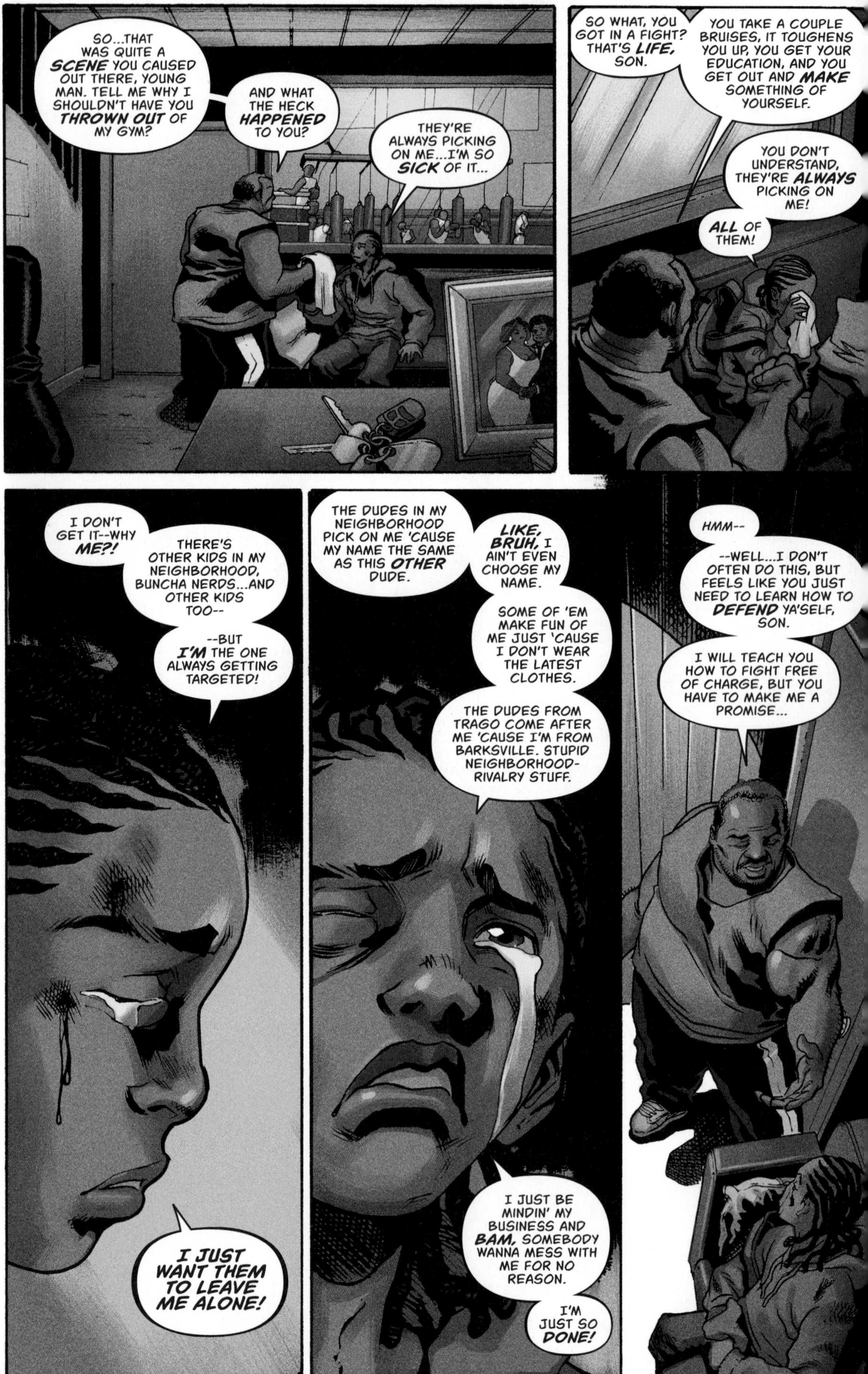

SO...THAT WAS QUITE A SCENE YOU CAUSED OUT THERE, YOUNG MAN. TELL ME WHY I SHOULDN'T HAVE YOU THROWN OUT OF MY GYM?
AND WHAT THE HECK HAPPENED TO YOU?
THEY'RE ALWAYS PICKING ON ME...I'M SO SICK OF IT...
SO WHAT, YOU GOT IN A FIGHT? THAT'S LIFE, SON.
YOU TAKE A COUPLE BRUISES, IT TOUGHENS YOU UP, YOU GET YOUR EDUCATION, AND YOU GET OUT AND MAKE SOMETHING OF YOURSELF.
YOU DON'T UNDERSTAND, THEY'RE ALWAYS PICKING ON ME!
ALL OF THEM!
I DON'T GET IT--WHY ME?!
THERE'S OTHER KIDS IN MY NEIGHBORHOOD, BUNCHA NERDS...AND OTHER KIDS TOO--
--BUT I'M THE ONE ALWAYS GETTING TARGETED!
I JUST WANT THEM TO LEAVE ME ALONE!
THE DUDES IN MY NEIGHBORHOOD PICK ON ME 'CAUSE MY NAME THE SAME AS THIS OTHER DUDE.
LIKE, BRUH, I AIN'T EVEN CHOOSE MY NAME.
SOME OF 'EM MAKE FUN OF ME JUST 'CAUSE I DON'T WEAR THE LATEST CLOTHES.
THE DUDES FROM TRAGO COME AFTER ME 'CAUSE I'M FROM BARKSVILLE. STUPID NEIGHBORHOOD-RIVALRY STUFF.
I JUST BE MINDIN' MY BUSINESS AND BAM, SOMEBODY WANNA MESS WITH ME FOR NO REASON.
I'M JUST SO DONE!
HMM--
--WELL...I DON'T OFTEN DO THIS, BUT FEELS LIKE YOU JUST NEED TO LEARN HOW TO DEFEND YA'SELF, SON.
I WILL TEACH YOU HOW TO FIGHT FREE OF CHARGE, BUT YOU HAVE TO MAKE ME A PROMISE...

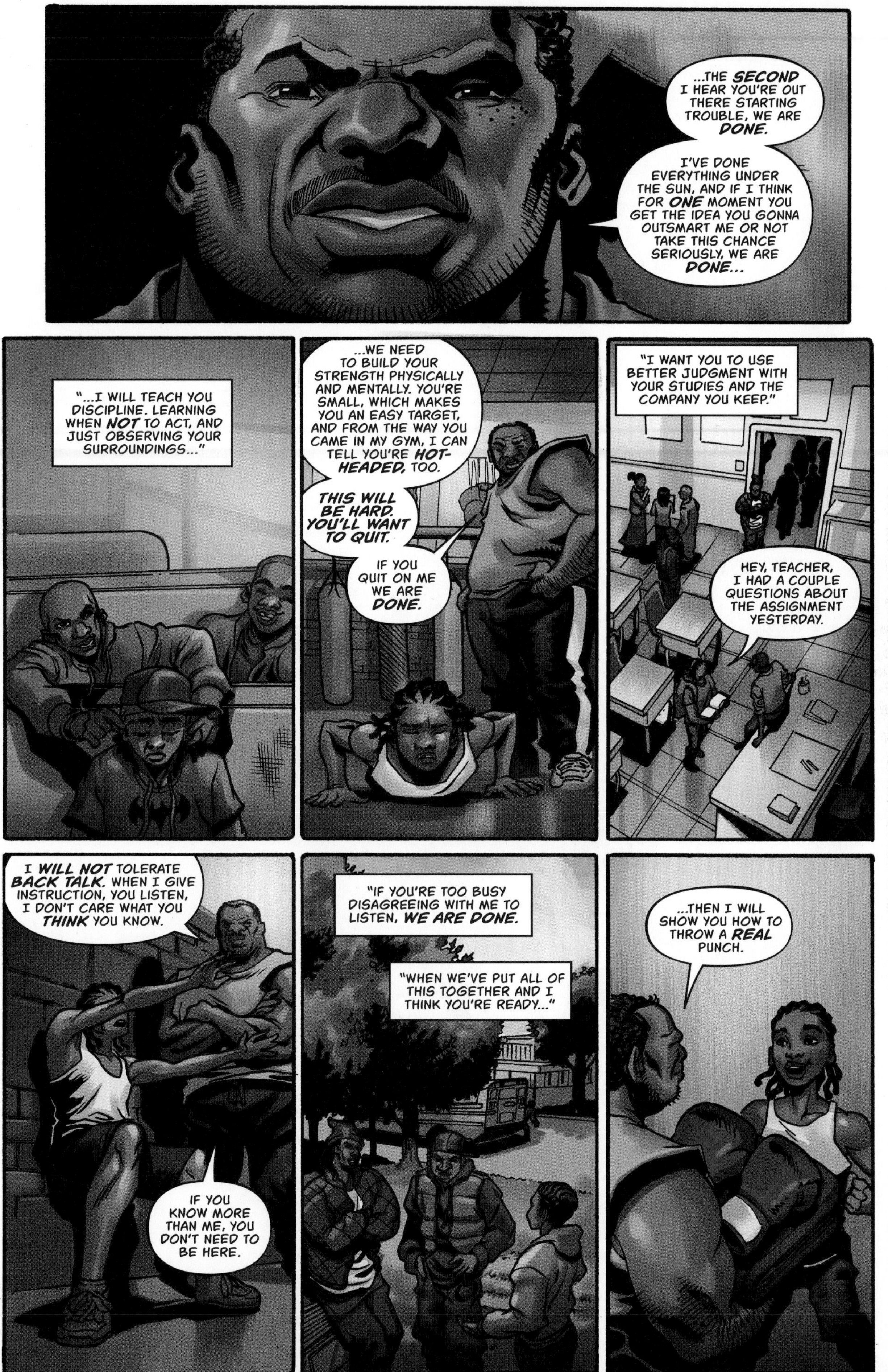
...THE SECOND I HEAR YOU'RE OUT THERE STARTING TROUBLE, WE ARE DONE.
I'VE DONE EVERYTHING UNDER THE SUN, AND IF I THINK FOR ONE MOMENT YOU GET THE IDEA YOU GONNA OUTSMART ME OR NOT TAKE THIS CHANCE SERIOUSLY, WE ARE DONE...
"...I WILL TEACH YOU DISCIPLINE. LEARNING WHEN NOT TO ACT, AND JUST OBSERVING YOUR SURROUNDINGS..."
...WE NEED TO BUILD YOUR STRENGTH PHYSICALLY AND MENTALLY. YOU'RE SMALL, WHICH MAKES YOU AN EASY TARGET, AND FROM THE WAY YOU CAME IN MY GYM, I CAN TELL YOU'RE HOT-HEADED, TOO.
THIS WILL BE HARD. YOU'LL WANT TO QUIT.
IF YOU QUIT ON ME WE ARE DONE.
"I WANT YOU TO USE BETTER JUDGMENT WITH YOUR STUDIES AND THE COMPANY YOU KEEP."
HEY, TEACHER, I HAD A COUPLE QUESTIONS ABOUT THE ASSIGNMENT YESTERDAY.
I WILL NOT TOLERATE BACK TALK. WHEN I GIVE INSTRUCTION, YOU LISTEN, I DON'T CARE WHAT YOU THINK YOU KNOW.
IF YOU KNOW MORE THAN ME, YOU DON'T NEED TO BE HERE.
"IF YOU'RE TOO BUSY DISAGREEING WITH ME TO LISTEN, WE ARE DONE."
"WHEN WE'VE PUT ALL OF THIS TOGETHER AND I THINK YOU'RE READY..."
...THEN I WILL SHOW YOU HOW TO THROW A REAL PUNCH.

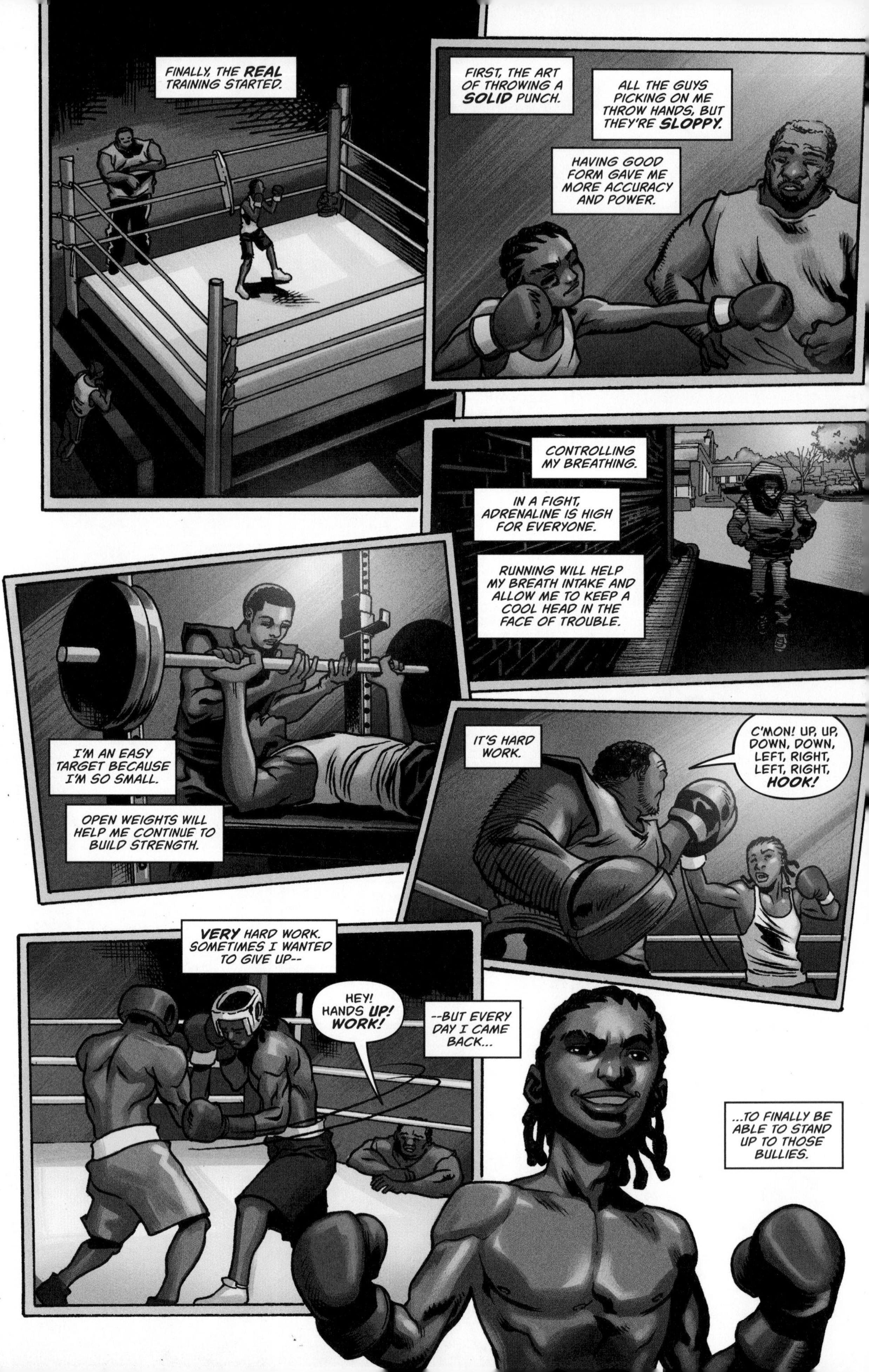
FINALLY, THE REAL TRAINING STARTED.
FIRST, THE ART OF THROWING A SOLID PUNCH.
ALL THE GUYS PICKING ON ME THROW HANDS, BUT THEY'RE SLOPPY.
HAVING GOOD FORM GAVE ME MORE ACCURACY AND POWER.
CONTROLLING MY BREATHING.
IN A FIGHT, ADRENALINE IS HIGH FOR EVERYONE.
RUNNING WILL HELP MY BREATH INTAKE AND ALLOW ME TO KEEP A COOL HEAD IN THE FACE OF TROUBLE.
I'M AN EASY TARGET BECAUSE I'M SO SMALL.
OPEN WEIGHTS WILL HELP ME CONTINUE TO BUILD STRENGTH.
IT'S HARD WORK.
C'MON! UP, UP, DOWN, DOWN, LEFT, RIGHT, LEFT, RIGHT, HOOK!
VERY HARD WORK. SOMETIMES I WANTED TO GIVE UP--
HEY! HANDS UP! WORK!
--BUT EVERY DAY I CAME BACK...
...TO FINALLY BE ABLE TO STAND UP TO THOSE BULLIES.

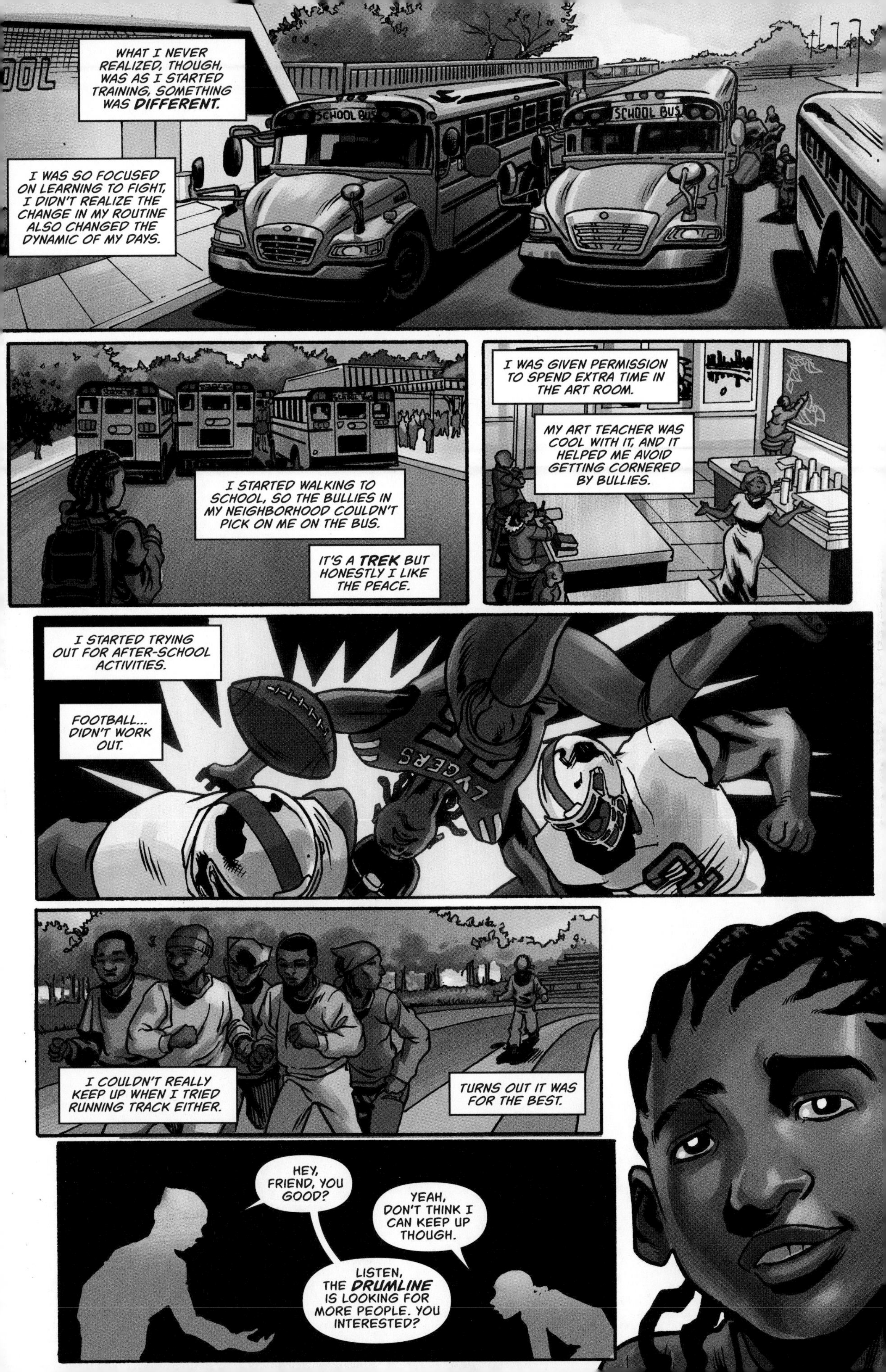

OOL
WHAT I NEVER REALIZED, THOUGH, WAS AS I STARTED TRAINING, SOMETHING WAS **DIFFERENT.**
SCHOOL BUS
SCHOOL BUS
I WAS SO FOCUSED ON LEARNING TO FIGHT, I DIDN'T REALIZE THE CHANGE IN MY ROUTINE ALSO CHANGED THE DYNAMIC OF MY DAYS.
I STARTED WALKING TO SCHOOL, SO THE BULLIES IN MY NEIGHBORHOOD COULDN'T PICK ON ME ON THE BUS.
IT'S A **TREK** BUT HONESTLY I LIKE THE PEACE.
I WAS GIVEN PERMISSION TO SPEND EXTRA TIME IN THE ART ROOM.
MY ART TEACHER WAS COOL WITH IT, AND IT HELPED ME AVOID GETTING CORNERED BY BULLIES.
I STARTED TRYING OUT FOR AFTER-SCHOOL ACTIVITIES.
FOOTBALL... DIDN'T WORK OUT.
LYGERS
I COULDN'T REALLY KEEP UP WHEN I TRIED RUNNING TRACK EITHER.
TURNS OUT IT WAS FOR THE BEST.
HEY, FRIEND, YOU GOOD?
YEAH, DON'T THINK I CAN KEEP UP THOUGH.
LISTEN, THE **DRUMLINE** IS LOOKING FOR MORE PEOPLE. YOU INTERESTED?

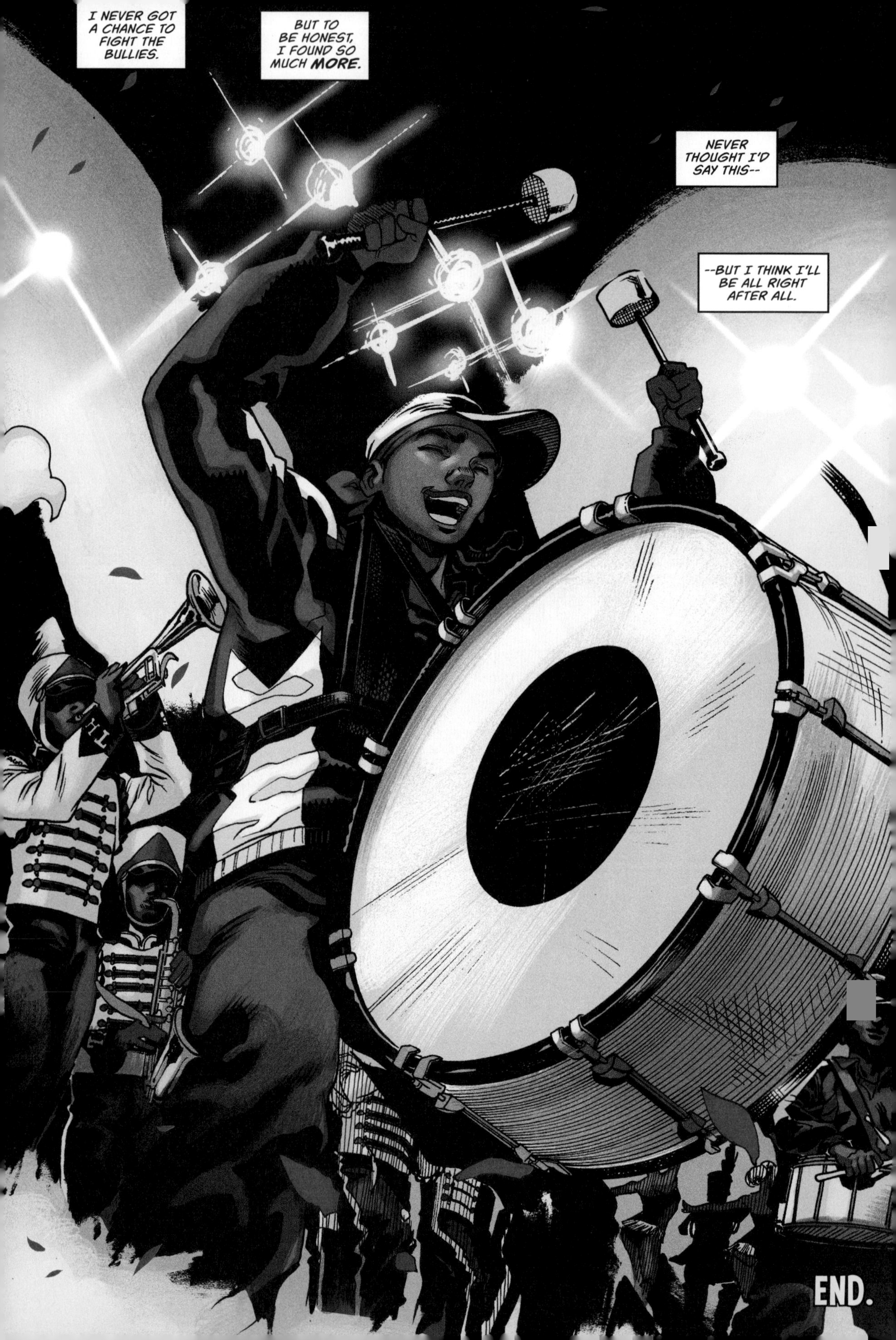
I NEVER GOT A CHANCE TO FIGHT THE BULLIES.
BUT TO BE HONEST, I FOUND SO MUCH MORE.
NEVER THOUGHT I'D SAY THIS--
--BUT I THINK I'LL BE ALL RIGHT AFTER ALL.
END.

CHAPTER SEVEN

ESENT! "FIGHT FIRE WITH SPRAY CANS"

WRITER - ONYEKACHI AKALONU

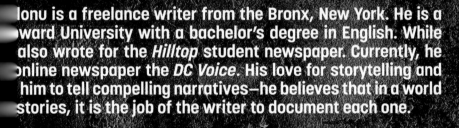

lonu is a freelance writer from the Bronx, New York. He is a
ward University with a bachelor's degree in English. While
also wrote for the *Hilltop* student newspaper. Currently, he
online newspaper the *DC Voice*. His love for storytelling and
him to tell compelling narratives—he believes that in a world
stories, it is the job of the writer to document each one.

ARTIST - VALENTINE DE LANDRO
COLORIST - MARISSA LOUISE
LETTERER - DERON BENNETT

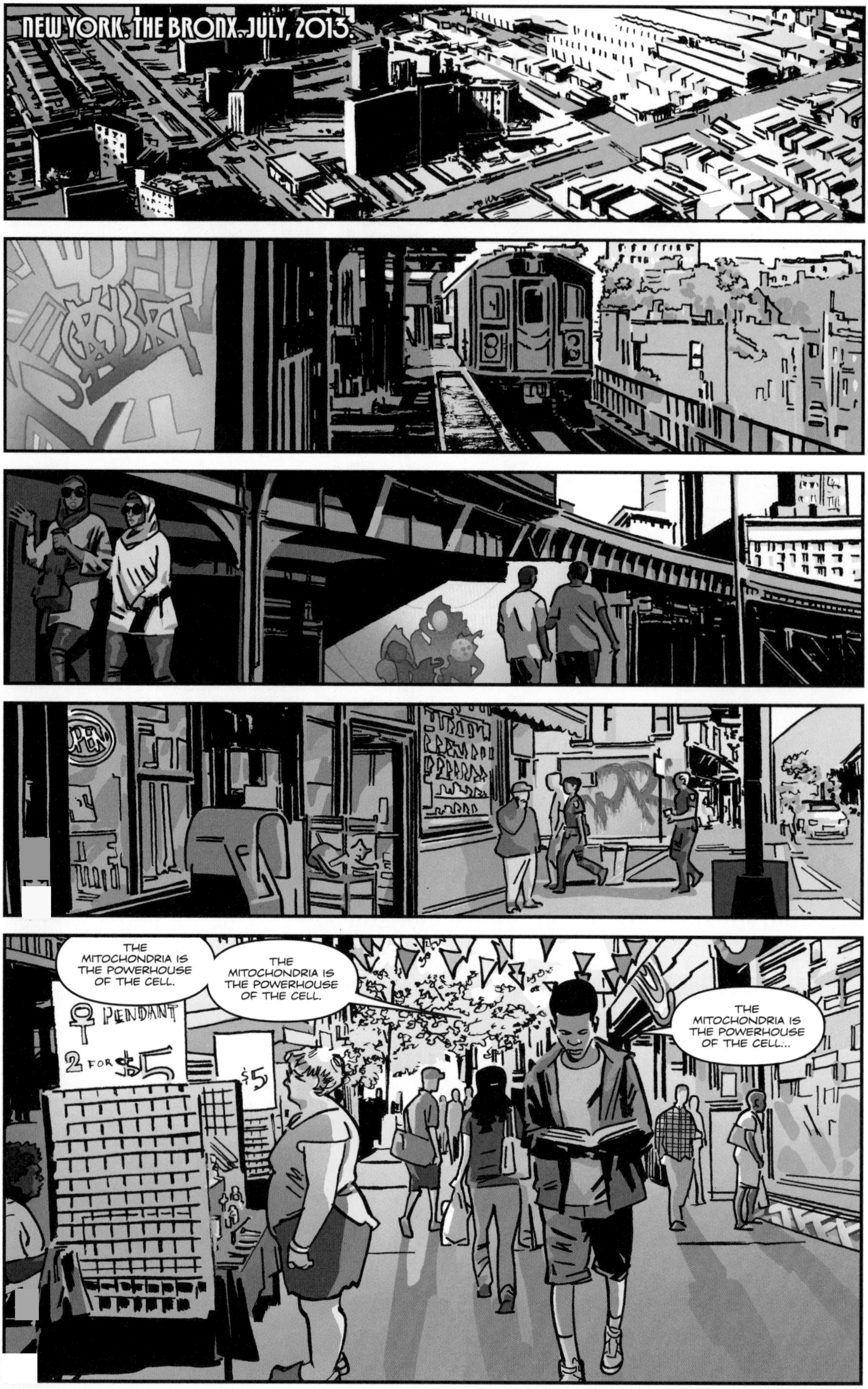
NEW YORK. THE BRONX. JULY, 2013.
OPEN
THE MITOCHONDRIA IS THE POWERHOUSE OF THE CELL.
THE MITOCHONDRIA IS THE POWERHOUSE OF THE CELL.
PENDANT 2 FOR $5
$5
THE MITOCHONDRIA IS THE POWERHOUSE OF THE CELL...

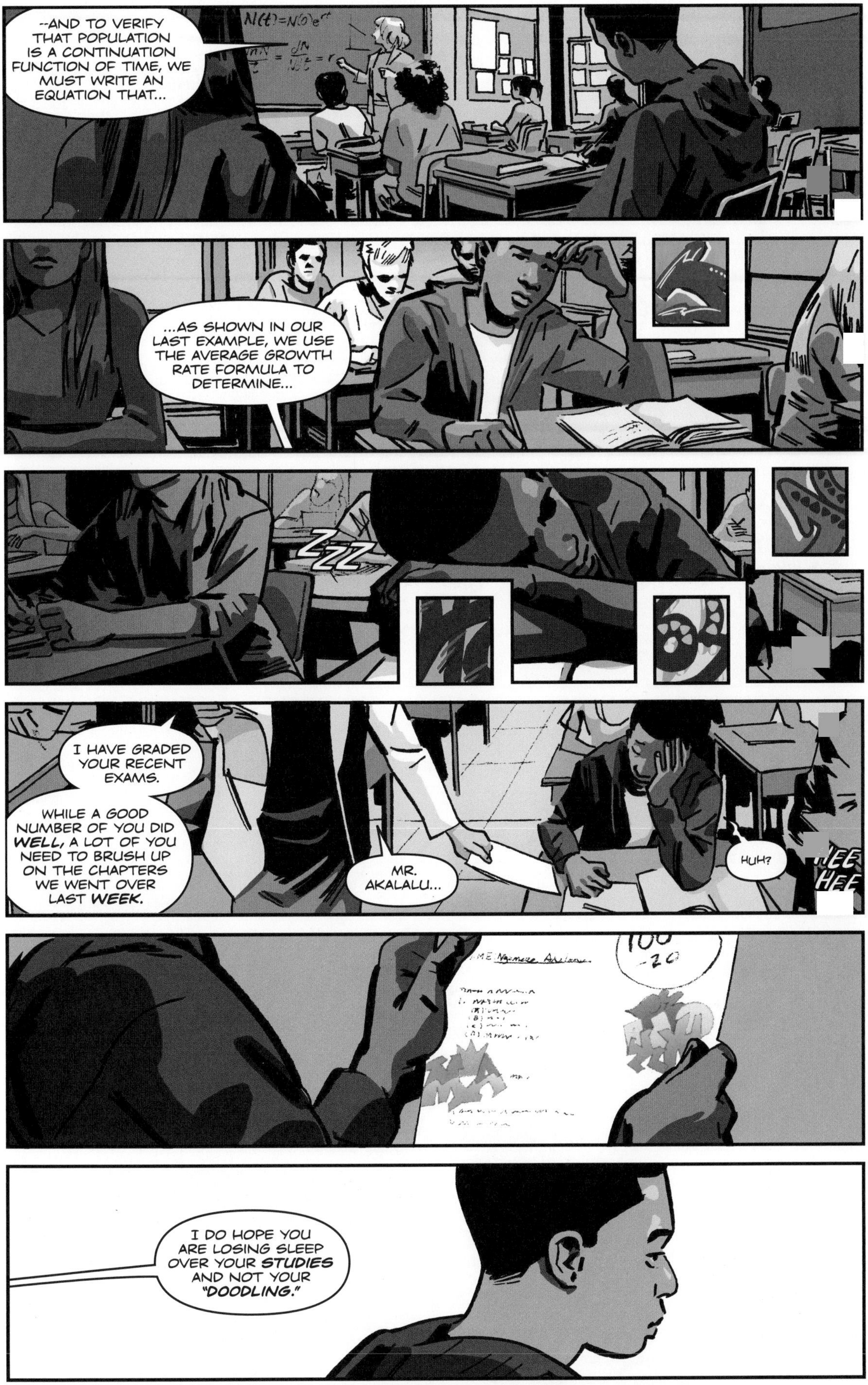
--AND TO VERIFY THAT POPULATION IS A CONTINUATION FUNCTION OF TIME, WE MUST WRITE AN EQUATION THAT...
...AS SHOWN IN OUR LAST EXAMPLE, WE USE THE AVERAGE GROWTH RATE FORMULA TO DETERMINE...
ZZZ
I HAVE GRADED YOUR RECENT EXAMS.
WHILE A GOOD NUMBER OF YOU DID WELL, A LOT OF YOU NEED TO BRUSH UP ON THE CHAPTERS WE WENT OVER LAST WEEK.
MR. AKALALU...
HUH?
HEE HEE
I DO HOPE YOU ARE LOSING SLEEP OVER YOUR STUDIES AND NOT YOUR "DOODLING."

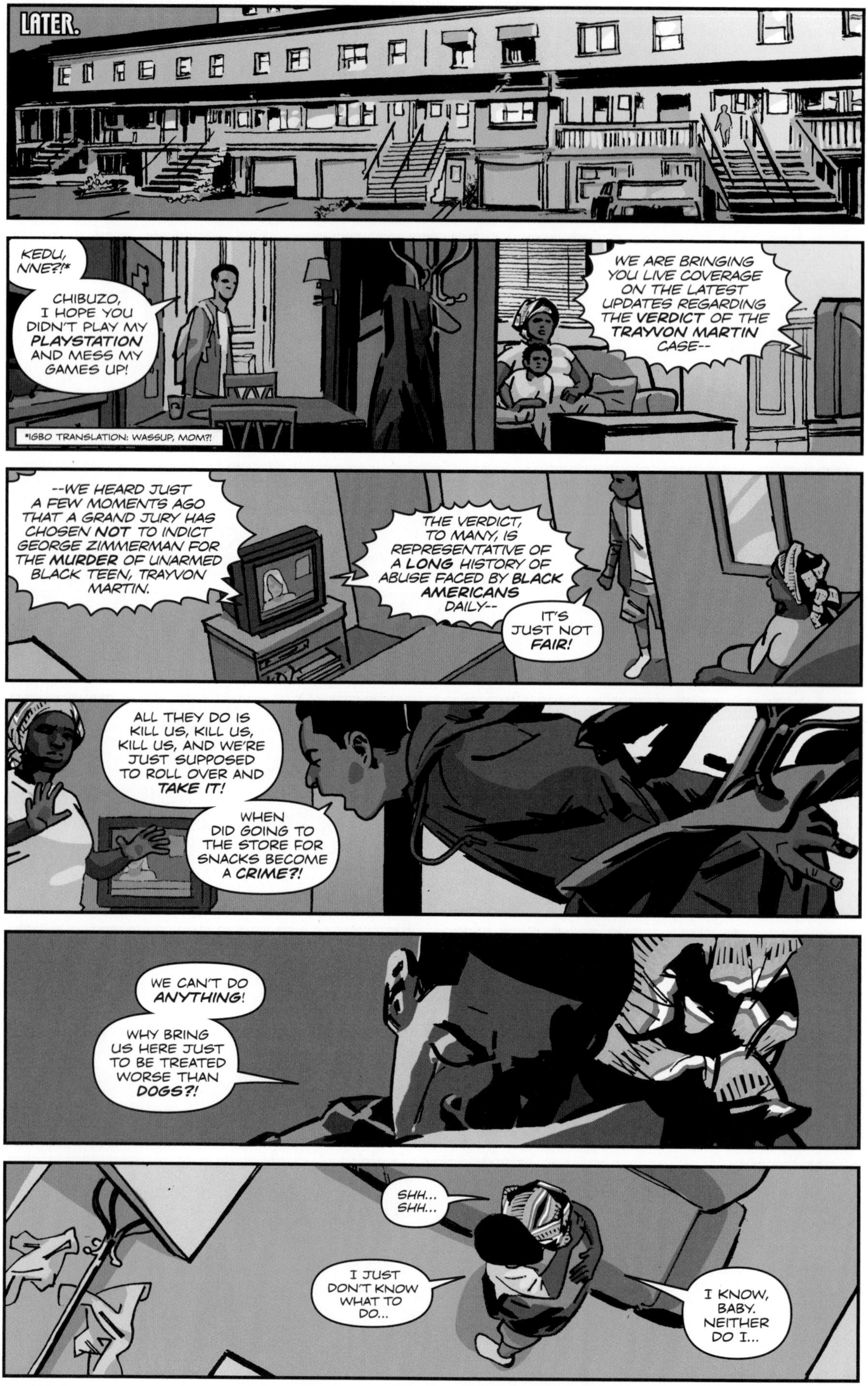
LATER.
KEDU, NNE?!*
CHIBUZO, I HOPE YOU DIDN'T PLAY MY PLAYSTATION AND MESS MY GAMES UP!
WE ARE BRINGING YOU LIVE COVERAGE ON THE LATEST UPDATES REGARDING THE VERDICT OF THE TRAYVON MARTIN CASE--
*IGBO TRANSLATION: WASSUP, MOM?!
--WE HEARD JUST A FEW MOMENTS AGO THAT A GRAND JURY HAS CHOSEN NOT TO INDICT GEORGE ZIMMERMAN FOR THE MURDER OF UNARMED BLACK TEEN, TRAYVON MARTIN.
THE VERDICT, TO MANY, IS REPRESENTATIVE OF A LONG HISTORY OF ABUSE FACED BY BLACK AMERICANS DAILY--
IT'S JUST NOT FAIR!
ALL THEY DO IS KILL US, KILL US, KILL US, AND WE'RE JUST SUPPOSED TO ROLL OVER AND TAKE IT!
WHEN DID GOING TO THE STORE FOR SNACKS BECOME A CRIME?!
WE CAN'T DO ANYTHING!
WHY BRING US HERE JUST TO BE TREATED WORSE THAN DOGS?!
SHH... SHH...
I JUST DON'T KNOW WHAT TO DO...
I KNOW, BABY. NEITHER DO I...

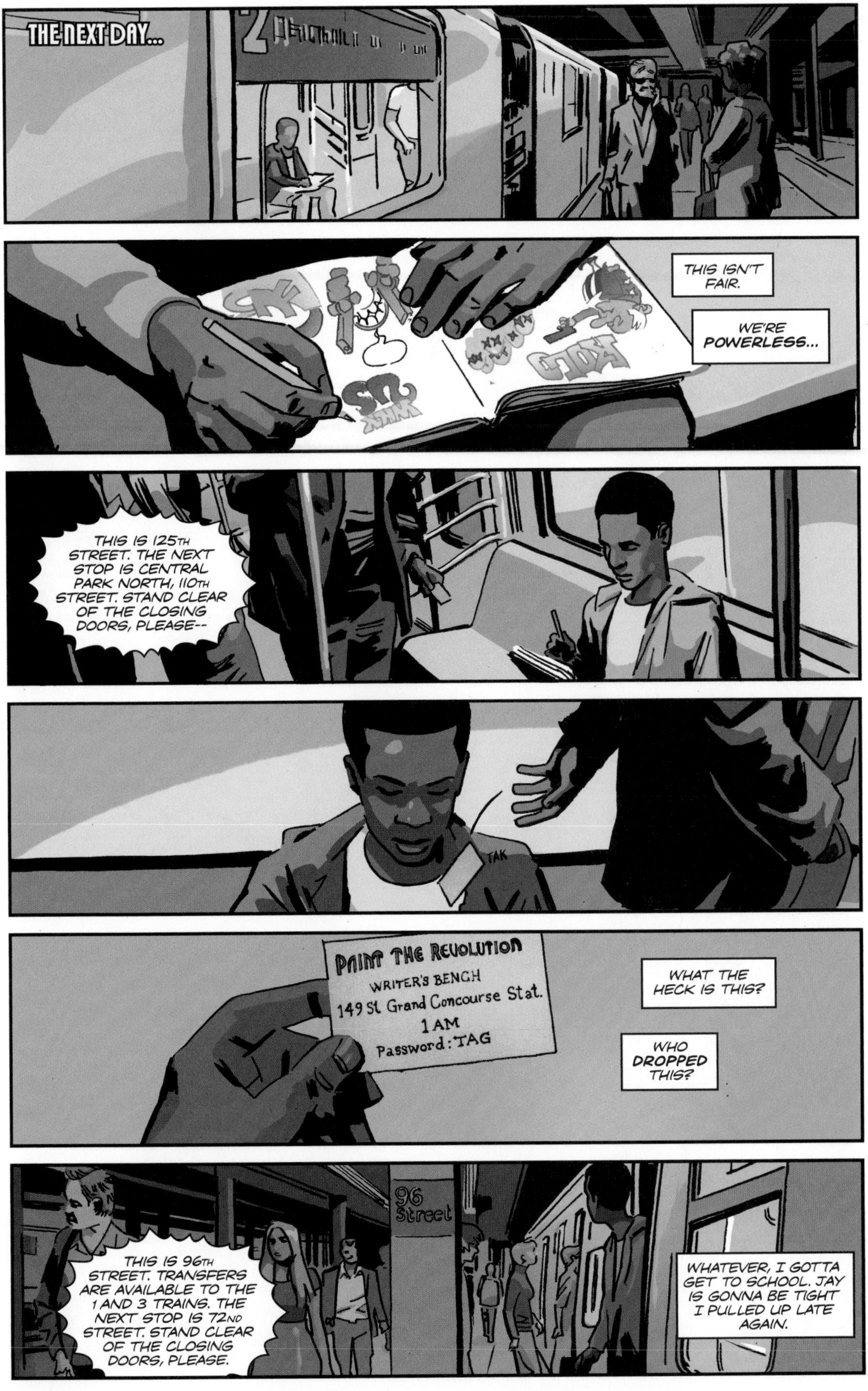
THE NEXT DAY...
THIS ISN'T FAIR.
WE'RE POWERLESS...
THIS IS 125TH STREET. THE NEXT STOP IS CENTRAL PARK NORTH, 110TH STREET. STAND CLEAR OF THE CLOSING DOORS, PLEASE--
TAK
PAINT THE REVOLUTION
WRITER'S BENCH
149 St Grand Concourse Stat.
1 AM
Password: TAG
WHAT THE HECK IS THIS?
WHO DROPPED THIS?
96 Street
THIS IS 96TH STREET. TRANSFERS ARE AVAILABLE TO THE 1 AND 3 TRAINS. THE NEXT STOP IS 72ND STREET. STAND CLEAR OF THE CLOSING DOORS, PLEASE.
WHATEVER, I GOTTA GET TO SCHOOL. JAY IS GONNA BE TIGHT I PULLED UP LATE AGAIN.

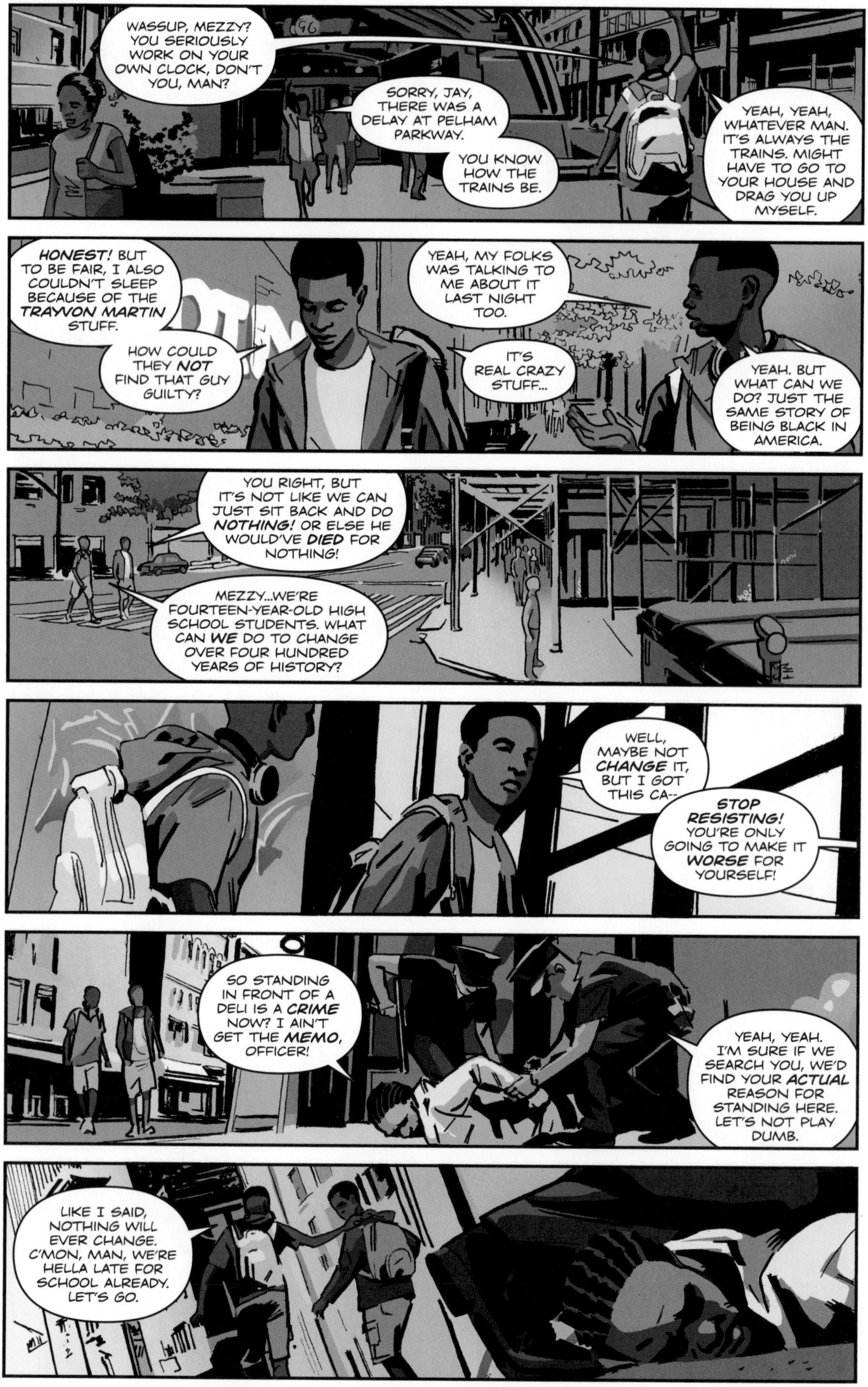
WASSUP, MEZZY? YOU SERIOUSLY WORK ON YOUR OWN CLOCK, DON'T YOU, MAN?
SORRY, JAY, THERE WAS A DELAY AT PELHAM PARKWAY.
YOU KNOW HOW THE TRAINS BE.
YEAH, YEAH, WHATEVER MAN. IT'S ALWAYS THE TRAINS. MIGHT HAVE TO GO TO YOUR HOUSE AND DRAG YOU UP MYSELF.
HONEST! BUT TO BE FAIR, I ALSO COULDN'T SLEEP BECAUSE OF THE TRAYVON MARTIN STUFF.
HOW COULD THEY NOT FIND THAT GUY GUILTY?
YEAH, MY FOLKS WAS TALKING TO ME ABOUT IT LAST NIGHT TOO.
IT'S REAL CRAZY STUFF...
YEAH. BUT WHAT CAN WE DO? JUST THE SAME STORY OF BEING BLACK IN AMERICA.
YOU RIGHT, BUT IT'S NOT LIKE WE CAN JUST SIT BACK AND DO NOTHING! OR ELSE HE WOULD'VE DIED FOR NOTHING!
MEZZY...WE'RE FOURTEEN-YEAR-OLD HIGH SCHOOL STUDENTS. WHAT CAN WE DO TO CHANGE OVER FOUR HUNDRED YEARS OF HISTORY?
WELL, MAYBE NOT CHANGE IT, BUT I GOT THIS CA--
STOP RESISTING! YOU'RE ONLY GOING TO MAKE IT WORSE FOR YOURSELF!
SO STANDING IN FRONT OF A DELI IS A CRIME NOW? I AIN'T GET THE MEMO, OFFICER!
YEAH, YEAH. I'M SURE IF WE SEARCH YOU, WE'D FIND YOUR ACTUAL REASON FOR STANDING HERE. LET'S NOT PLAY DUMB.
LIKE I SAID, NOTHING WILL EVER CHANGE. C'MON, MAN, WE'RE HELLA LATE FOR SCHOOL ALREADY. LET'S GO.

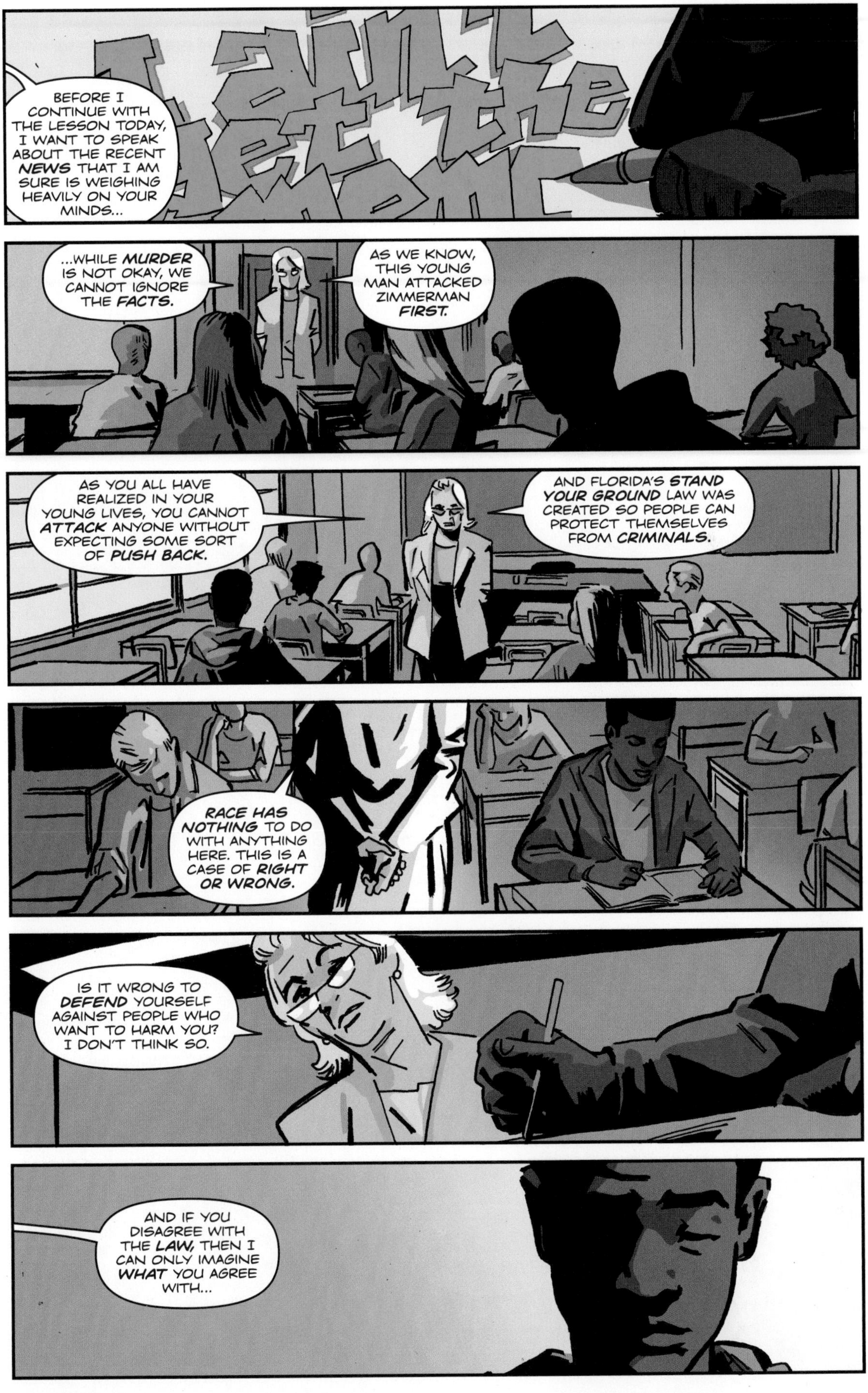
BEFORE I CONTINUE WITH THE LESSON TODAY, I WANT TO SPEAK ABOUT THE RECENT NEWS THAT I AM SURE IS WEIGHING HEAVILY ON YOUR MINDS...
...WHILE MURDER IS NOT OKAY, WE CANNOT IGNORE THE FACTS.
AS WE KNOW, THIS YOUNG MAN ATTACKED ZIMMERMAN FIRST.
AS YOU ALL HAVE REALIZED IN YOUR YOUNG LIVES, YOU CANNOT ATTACK ANYONE WITHOUT EXPECTING SOME SORT OF PUSH BACK.
AND FLORIDA'S STAND YOUR GROUND LAW WAS CREATED SO PEOPLE CAN PROTECT THEMSELVES FROM CRIMINALS.
RACE HAS NOTHING TO DO WITH ANYTHING HERE. THIS IS A CASE OF RIGHT OR WRONG.
IS IT WRONG TO DEFEND YOURSELF AGAINST PEOPLE WHO WANT TO HARM YOU? I DON'T THINK SO.
AND IF YOU DISAGREE WITH THE LAW, THEN I CAN ONLY IMAGINE WHAT YOU AGREE WITH...

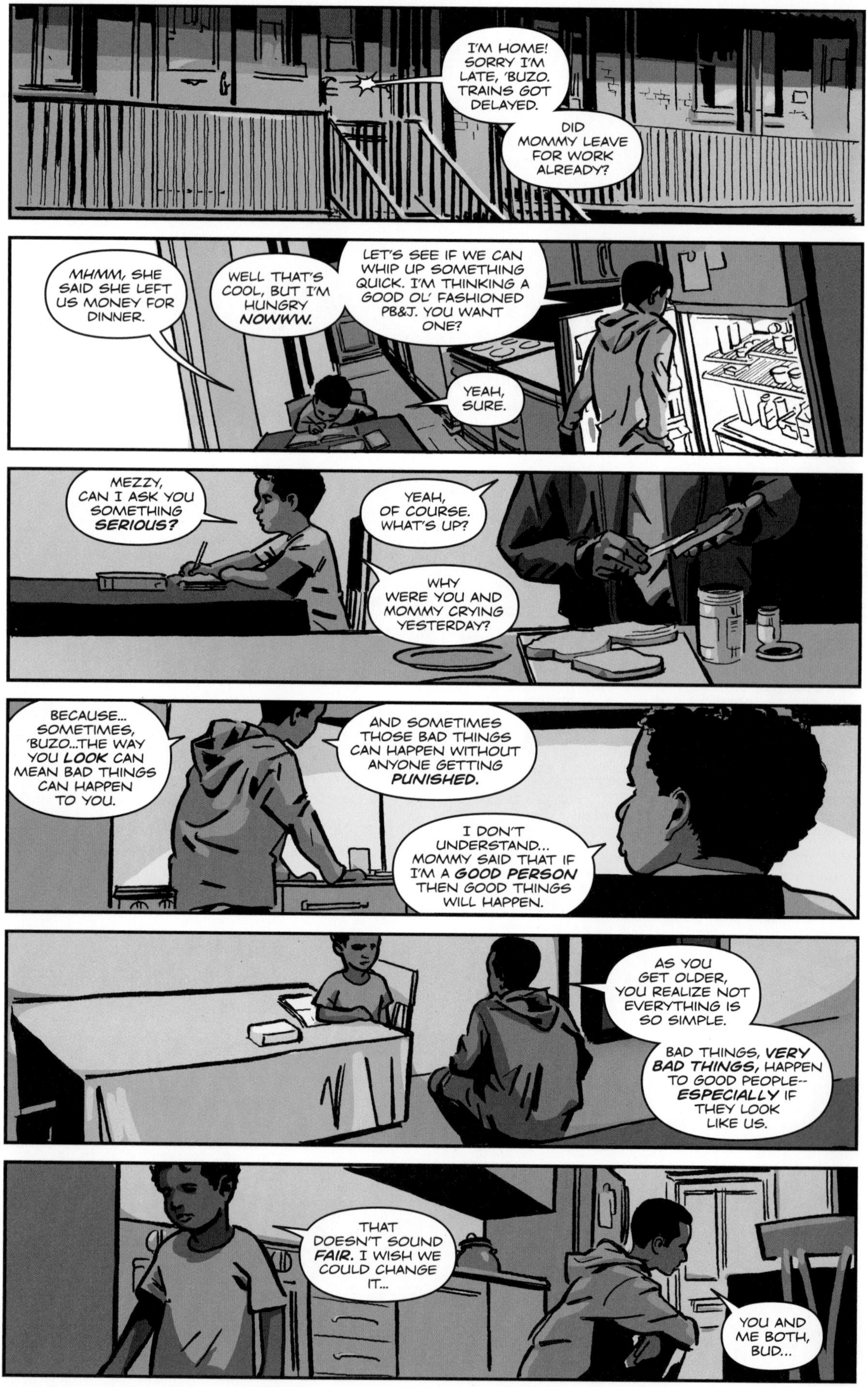
I'M HOME! SORRY I'M LATE, 'BUZO. TRAINS GOT DELAYED.
DID MOMMY LEAVE FOR WORK ALREADY?
MHMM, SHE SAID SHE LEFT US MONEY FOR DINNER.
WELL THAT'S COOL, BUT I'M HUNGRY NOWWW.
LET'S SEE IF WE CAN WHIP UP SOMETHING QUICK. I'M THINKING A GOOD OL' FASHIONED PB&J. YOU WANT ONE?
YEAH, SURE.
MEZZY, CAN I ASK YOU SOMETHING SERIOUS?
YEAH, OF COURSE. WHAT'S UP?
WHY WERE YOU AND MOMMY CRYING YESTERDAY?
BECAUSE... SOMETIMES, 'BUZO...THE WAY YOU LOOK CAN MEAN BAD THINGS CAN HAPPEN TO YOU.
AND SOMETIMES THOSE BAD THINGS CAN HAPPEN WITHOUT ANYONE GETTING PUNISHED.
I DON'T UNDERSTAND... MOMMY SAID THAT IF I'M A GOOD PERSON THEN GOOD THINGS WILL HAPPEN.
AS YOU GET OLDER, YOU REALIZE NOT EVERYTHING IS SO SIMPLE.
BAD THINGS, VERY BAD THINGS, HAPPEN TO GOOD PEOPLE-- ESPECIALLY IF THEY LOOK LIKE US.
THAT DOESN'T SOUND FAIR. I WISH WE COULD CHANGE IT...
YOU AND ME BOTH, BUD...

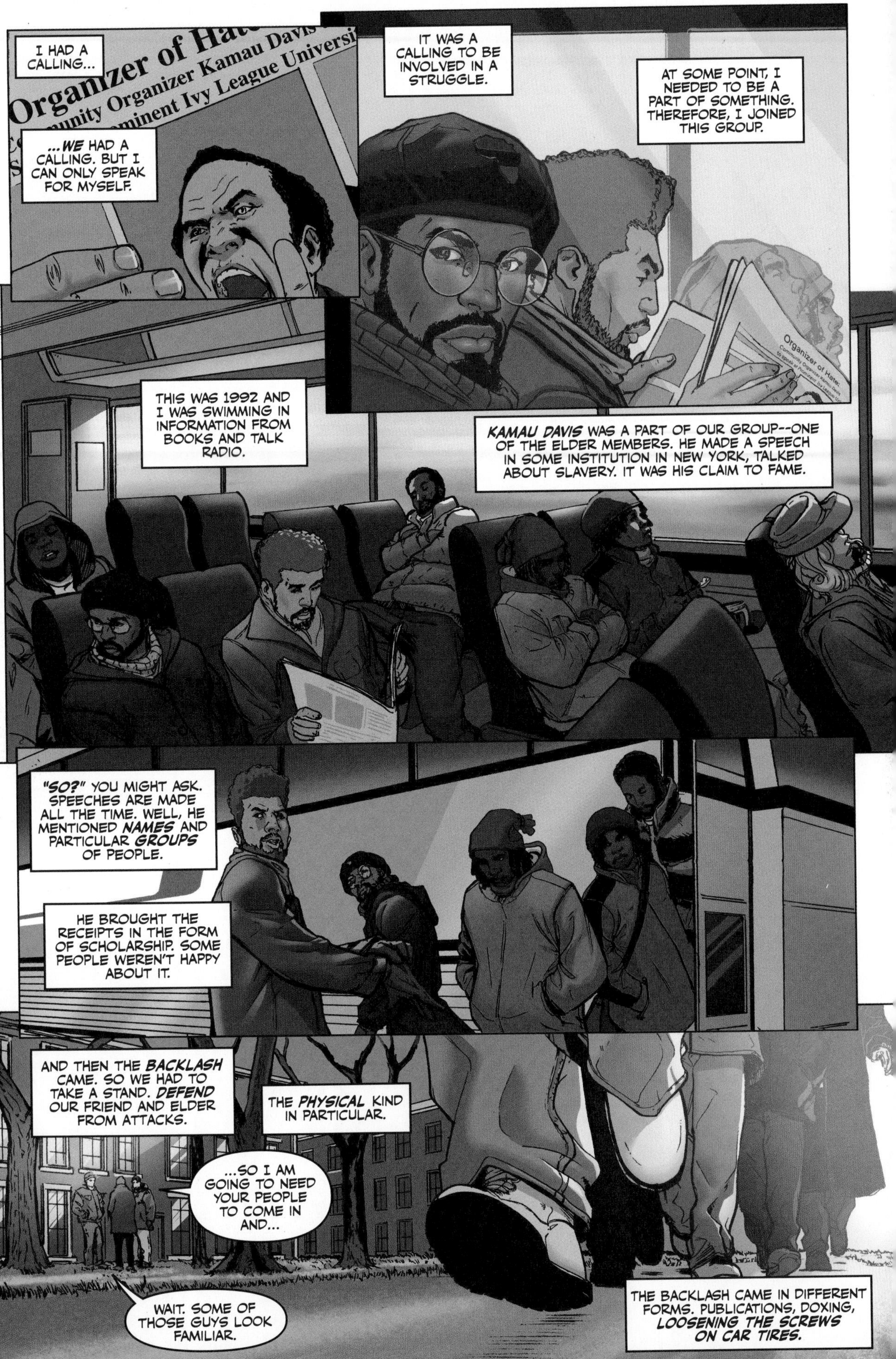

I HAD A CALLING...
Organizer of Hate
Community Organizer Kamau Davis
Prominent Ivy League Universi
...WE HAD A CALLING. BUT I CAN ONLY SPEAK FOR MYSELF.
IT WAS A CALLING TO BE INVOLVED IN A STRUGGLE.
AT SOME POINT, I NEEDED TO BE A PART OF SOMETHING. THEREFORE, I JOINED THIS GROUP.
THIS WAS 1992 AND I WAS SWIMMING IN INFORMATION FROM BOOKS AND TALK RADIO.
KAMAU DAVIS WAS A PART OF OUR GROUP--ONE OF THE ELDER MEMBERS. HE MADE A SPEECH IN SOME INSTITUTION IN NEW YORK, TALKED ABOUT SLAVERY. IT WAS HIS CLAIM TO FAME.
"SO?" YOU MIGHT ASK. SPEECHES ARE MADE ALL THE TIME. WELL, HE MENTIONED NAMES AND PARTICULAR GROUPS OF PEOPLE.
HE BROUGHT THE RECEIPTS IN THE FORM OF SCHOLARSHIP. SOME PEOPLE WEREN'T HAPPY ABOUT IT.
AND THEN THE BACKLASH CAME. SO WE HAD TO TAKE A STAND. DEFEND OUR FRIEND AND ELDER FROM ATTACKS.
THE PHYSICAL KIND IN PARTICULAR.
...SO I AM GOING TO NEED YOUR PEOPLE TO COME IN AND...
WAIT. SOME OF THOSE GUYS LOOK FAMILIAR.
THE BACKLASH CAME IN DIFFERENT FORMS. PUBLICATIONS, DOXING, LOOSENING THE SCREWS ON CAR TIRES.

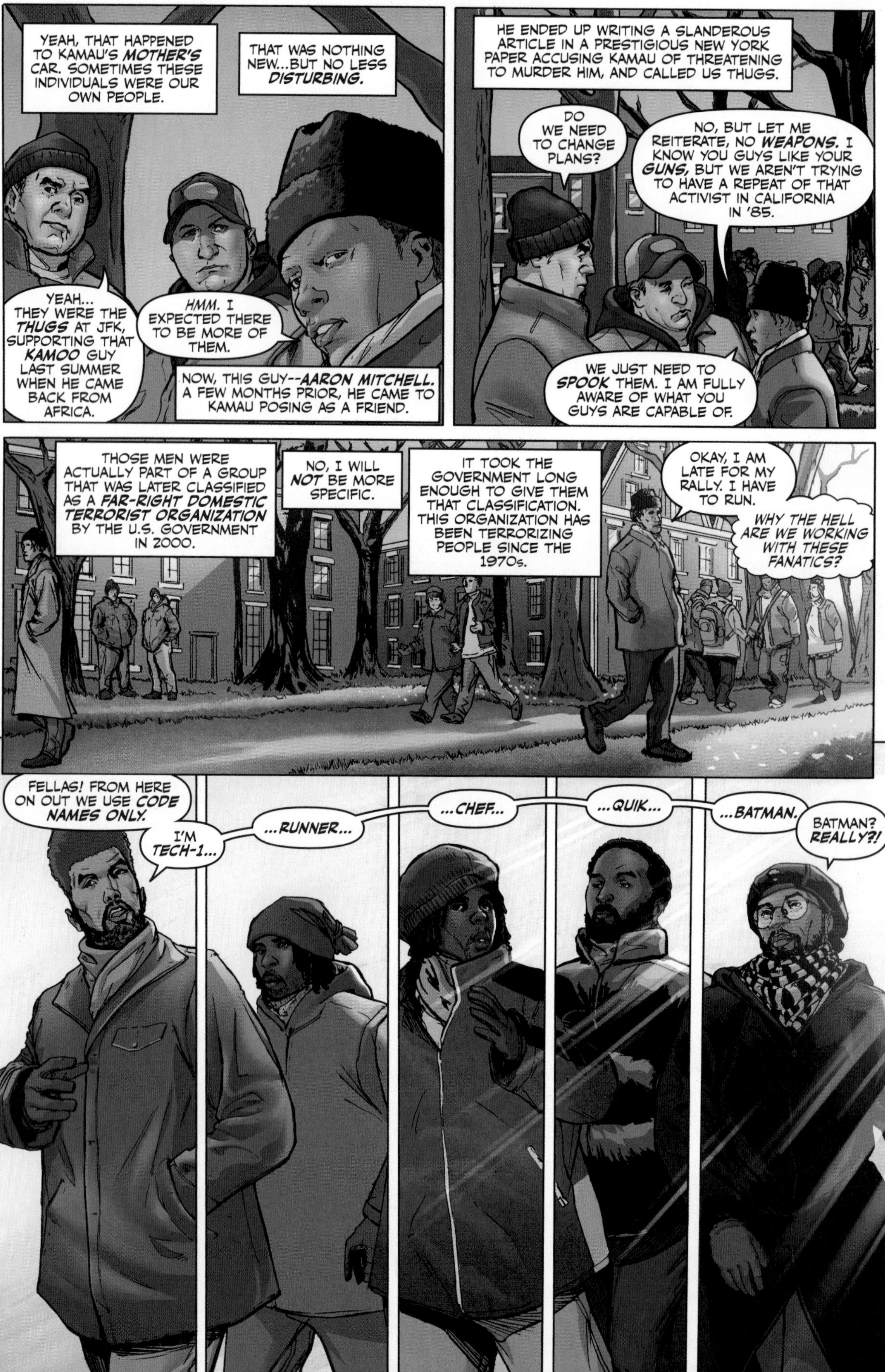
YEAH, THAT HAPPENED TO KAMAU'S MOTHER'S CAR. SOMETIMES THESE INDIVIDUALS WERE OUR OWN PEOPLE.
THAT WAS NOTHING NEW...BUT NO LESS DISTURBING.
YEAH... THEY WERE THE THUGS AT JFK, SUPPORTING THAT KAMOO GUY LAST SUMMER WHEN HE CAME BACK FROM AFRICA.
HMM. I EXPECTED THERE TO BE MORE OF THEM.
NOW, THIS GUY--AARON MITCHELL. A FEW MONTHS PRIOR, HE CAME TO KAMAU POSING AS A FRIEND.
HE ENDED UP WRITING A SLANDEROUS ARTICLE IN A PRESTIGIOUS NEW YORK PAPER ACCUSING KAMAU OF THREATENING TO MURDER HIM, AND CALLED US THUGS.
DO WE NEED TO CHANGE PLANS?
NO, BUT LET ME REITERATE, NO WEAPONS. I KNOW YOU GUYS LIKE YOUR GUNS, BUT WE AREN'T TRYING TO HAVE A REPEAT OF THAT ACTIVIST IN CALIFORNIA IN '85.
WE JUST NEED TO SPOOK THEM. I AM FULLY AWARE OF WHAT YOU GUYS ARE CAPABLE OF.
THOSE MEN WERE ACTUALLY PART OF A GROUP THAT WAS LATER CLASSIFIED AS A FAR-RIGHT DOMESTIC TERRORIST ORGANIZATION BY THE U.S. GOVERNMENT IN 2000.
NO, I WILL NOT BE MORE SPECIFIC.
IT TOOK THE GOVERNMENT LONG ENOUGH TO GIVE THEM THAT CLASSIFICATION. THIS ORGANIZATION HAS BEEN TERRORIZING PEOPLE SINCE THE 1970s.
OKAY, I AM LATE FOR MY RALLY. I HAVE TO RUN.
WHY THE HELL ARE WE WORKING WITH THESE FANATICS?
FELLAS! FROM HERE ON OUT WE USE CODE NAMES ONLY.
I'M TECH-1...
...RUNNER...
...CHEF...
...QUIK...
...BATMAN.
BATMAN? REALLY?!

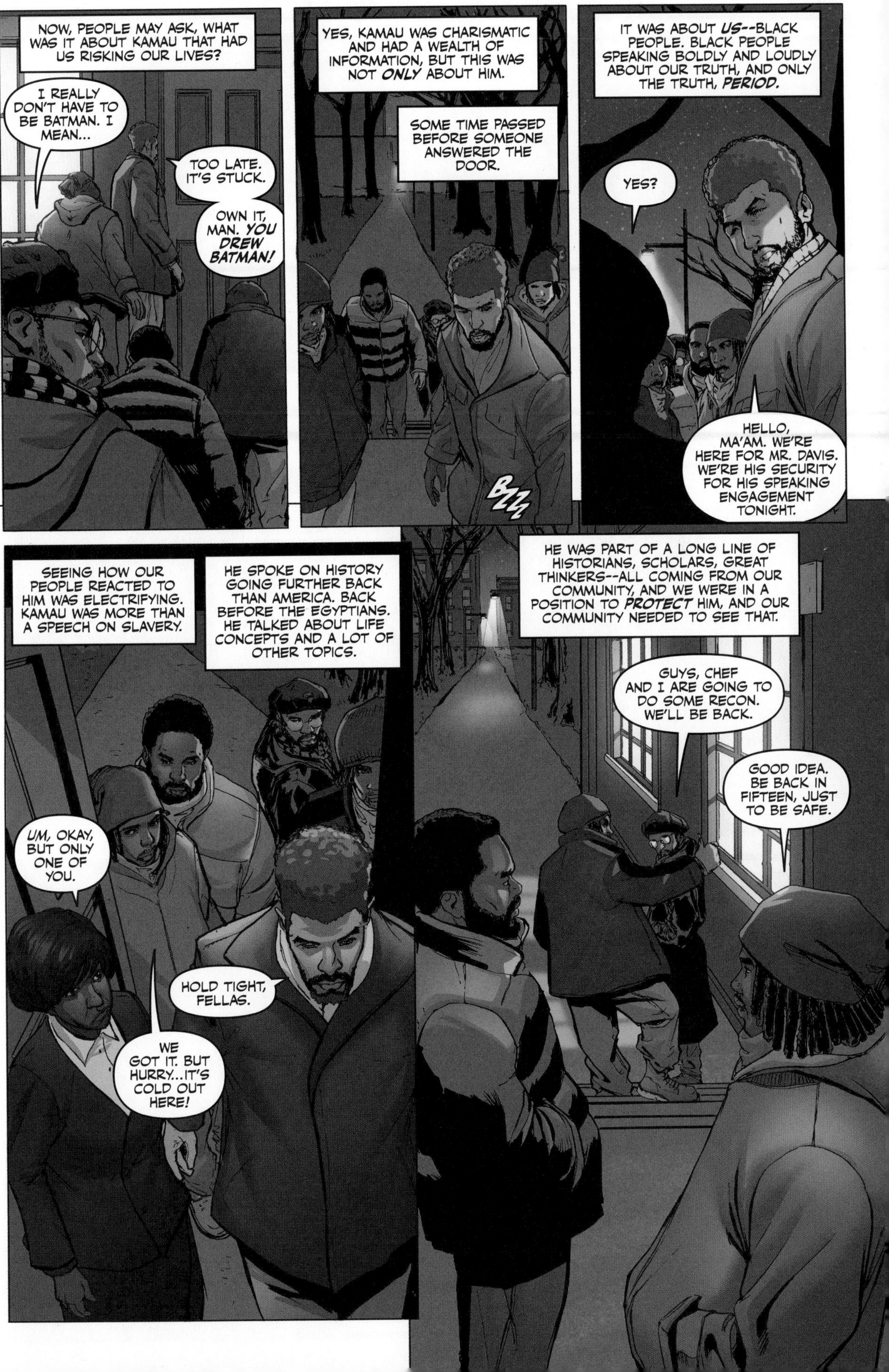
NOW, PEOPLE MAY ASK, WHAT WAS IT ABOUT KAMAU THAT HAD US RISKING OUR LIVES?
I REALLY DON'T HAVE TO BE BATMAN. I MEAN...
TOO LATE. IT'S STUCK.
OWN IT, MAN. YOU DREW BATMAN!
YES, KAMAU WAS CHARISMATIC AND HAD A WEALTH OF INFORMATION, BUT THIS WAS NOT ONLY ABOUT HIM.
SOME TIME PASSED BEFORE SOMEONE ANSWERED THE DOOR.
BZZ
IT WAS ABOUT US--BLACK PEOPLE. BLACK PEOPLE SPEAKING BOLDLY AND LOUDLY ABOUT OUR TRUTH, AND ONLY THE TRUTH, PERIOD.
YES?
HELLO, MA'AM. WE'RE HERE FOR MR. DAVIS. WE'RE HIS SECURITY FOR HIS SPEAKING ENGAGEMENT TONIGHT.
SEEING HOW OUR PEOPLE REACTED TO HIM WAS ELECTRIFYING. KAMAU WAS MORE THAN A SPEECH ON SLAVERY.
HE SPOKE ON HISTORY GOING FURTHER BACK THAN AMERICA. BACK BEFORE THE EGYPTIANS. HE TALKED ABOUT LIFE CONCEPTS AND A LOT OF OTHER TOPICS.
UM, OKAY, BUT ONLY ONE OF YOU.
HOLD TIGHT, FELLAS.
WE GOT IT. BUT HURRY...IT'S COLD OUT HERE!
HE WAS PART OF A LONG LINE OF HISTORIANS, SCHOLARS, GREAT THINKERS--ALL COMING FROM OUR COMMUNITY, AND WE WERE IN A POSITION TO PROTECT HIM, AND OUR COMMUNITY NEEDED TO SEE THAT.
GUYS, CHEF AND I ARE GOING TO DO SOME RECON. WE'LL BE BACK.
GOOD IDEA. BE BACK IN FIFTEEN, JUST TO BE SAFE.

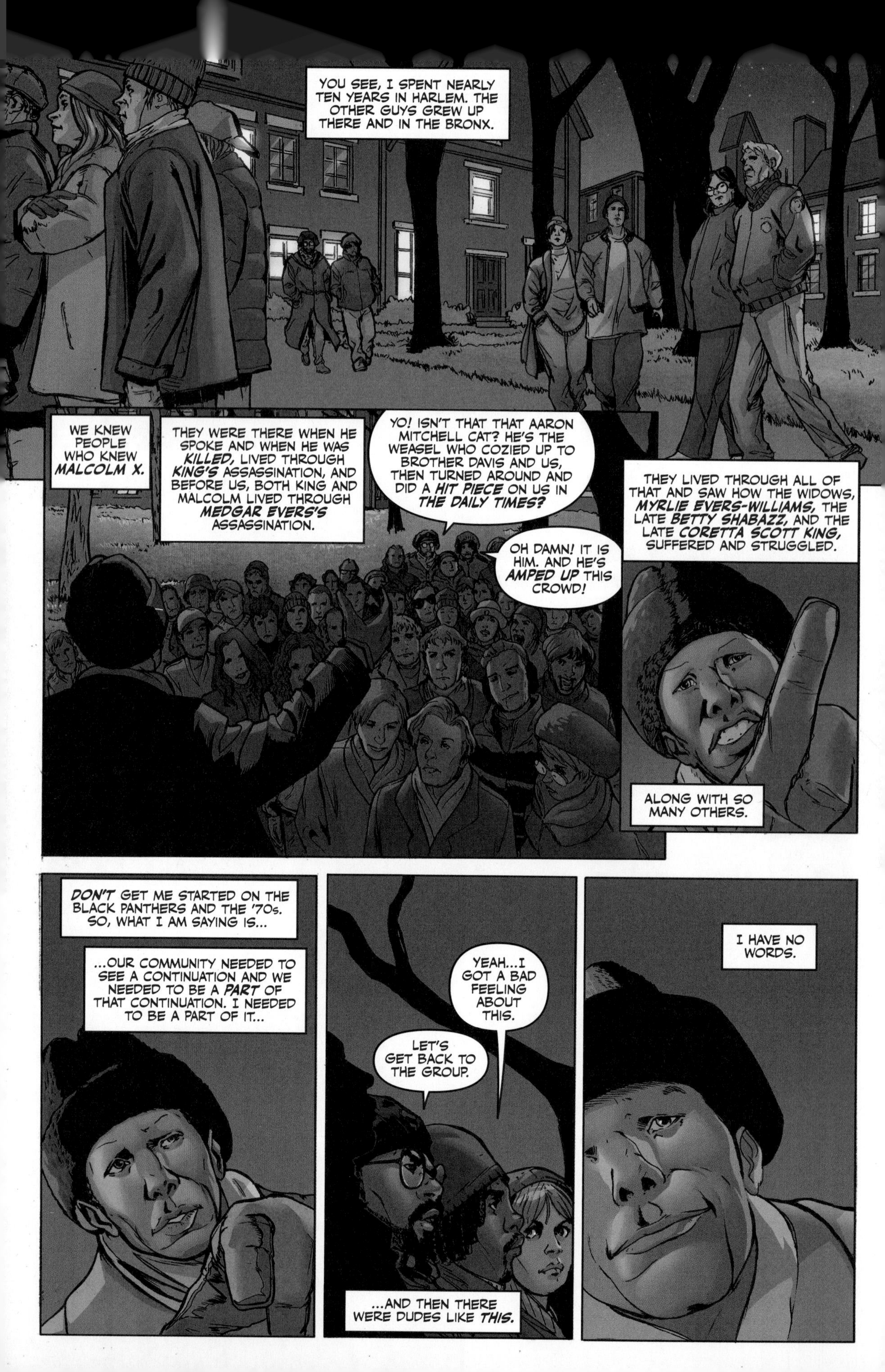
YOU SEE, I SPENT NEARLY TEN YEARS IN HARLEM. THE OTHER GUYS GREW UP THERE AND IN THE BRONX.
WE KNEW PEOPLE WHO KNEW MALCOLM X.
THEY WERE THERE WHEN HE SPOKE AND WHEN HE WAS KILLED, LIVED THROUGH KING'S ASSASSINATION, AND BEFORE US, BOTH KING AND MALCOLM LIVED THROUGH MEDGAR EVERS'S ASSASSINATION.
YO! ISN'T THAT THAT AARON MITCHELL CAT? HE'S THE WEASEL WHO COZIED UP TO BROTHER DAVIS AND US, THEN TURNED AROUND AND DID A HIT PIECE ON US IN THE DAILY TIMES?
OH DAMN! IT IS HIM. AND HE'S AMPED UP THIS CROWD!
THEY LIVED THROUGH ALL OF THAT AND SAW HOW THE WIDOWS, MYRLIE EVERS-WILLIAMS, THE LATE BETTY SHABAZZ, AND THE LATE CORETTA SCOTT KING, SUFFERED AND STRUGGLED.
ALONG WITH SO MANY OTHERS.
DON'T GET ME STARTED ON THE BLACK PANTHERS AND THE '70s. SO, WHAT I AM SAYING IS...
...OUR COMMUNITY NEEDED TO SEE A CONTINUATION AND WE NEEDED TO BE A PART OF THAT CONTINUATION. I NEEDED TO BE A PART OF IT...
YEAH...I GOT A BAD FEELING ABOUT THIS.
LET'S GET BACK TO THE GROUP.
...AND THEN THERE WERE DUDES LIKE THIS.
I HAVE NO WORDS.

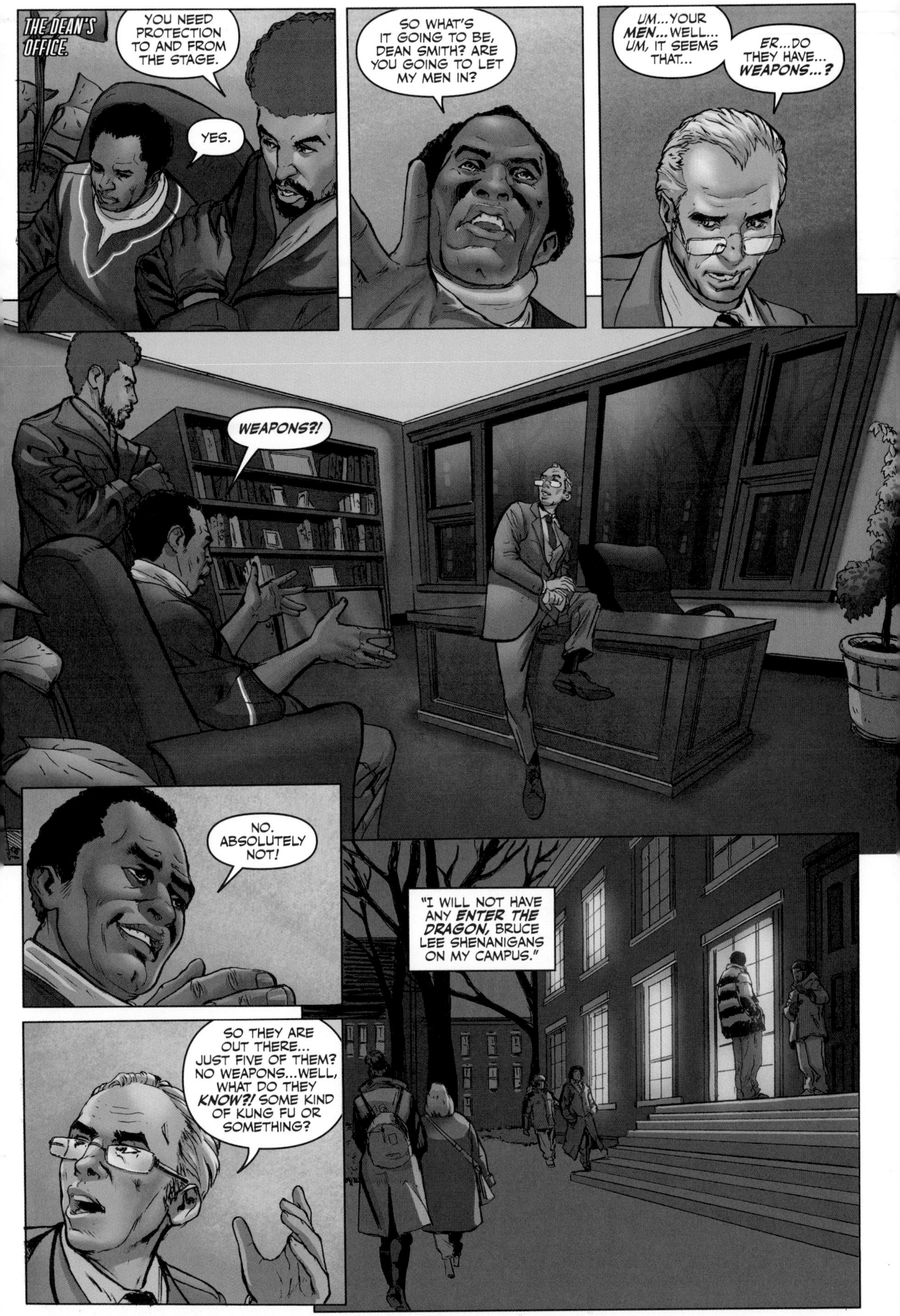
THE DEAN'S OFFICE.
YOU NEED PROTECTION TO AND FROM THE STAGE.
YES.
SO WHAT'S IT GOING TO BE, DEAN SMITH? ARE YOU GOING TO LET MY MEN IN?
UM... YOUR MEN... WELL... UM, IT SEEMS THAT...
ER... DO THEY HAVE... WEAPONS...?
WEAPONS?!
NO. ABSOLUTELY NOT!
"I WILL NOT HAVE ANY ENTER THE DRAGON, BRUCE LEE SHENANIGANS ON MY CAMPUS."
SO THEY ARE OUT THERE... JUST FIVE OF THEM? NO WEAPONS... WELL, WHAT DO THEY KNOW?! SOME KIND OF KUNG FU OR SOMETHING?

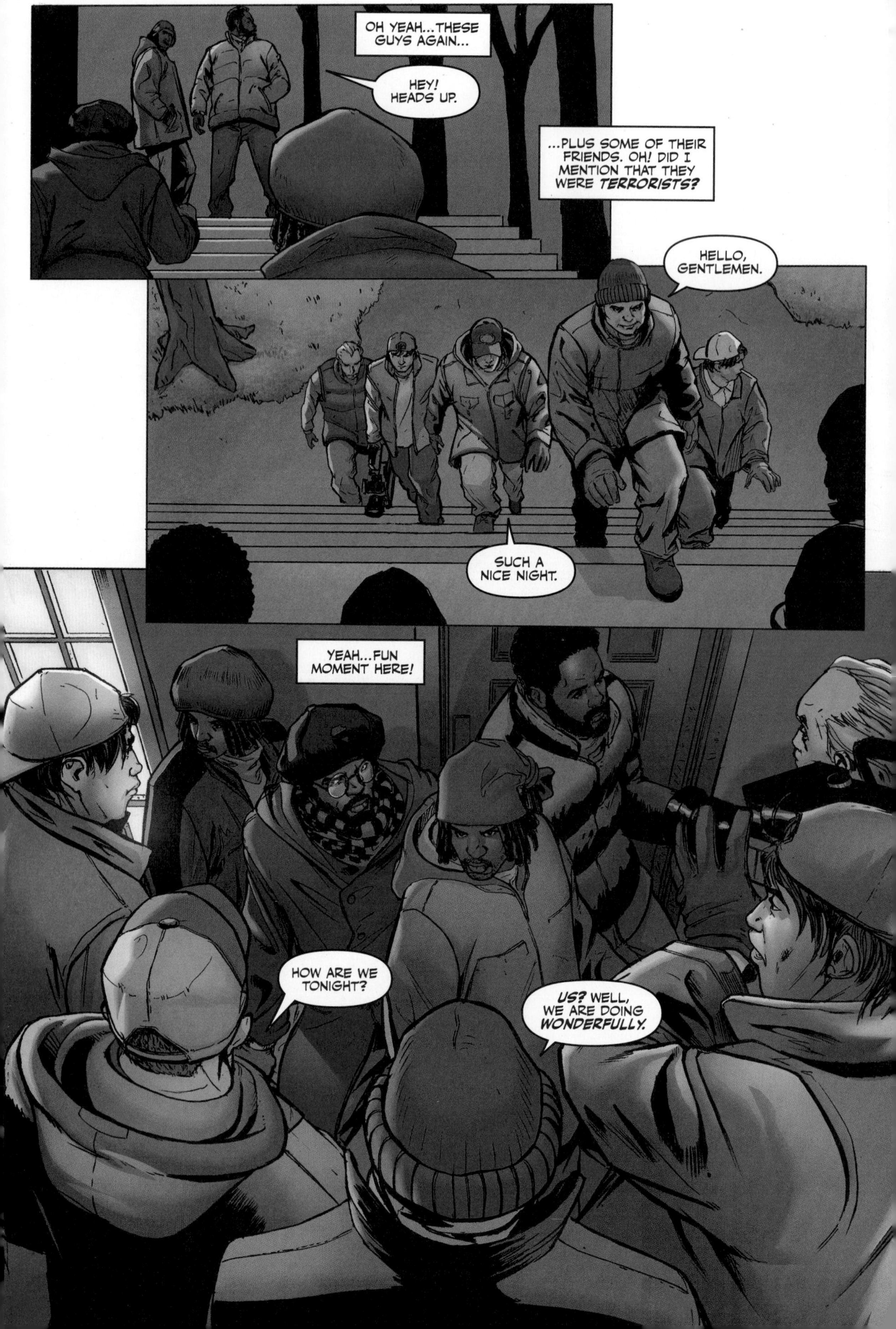
OH YEAH...THESE GUYS AGAIN...
HEY! HEADS UP.
...PLUS SOME OF THEIR FRIENDS. OH! DID I MENTION THAT THEY WERE TERRORISTS?
HELLO, GENTLEMEN.
SUCH A NICE NIGHT.
YEAH...FUN MOMENT HERE!
HOW ARE WE TONIGHT?
US? WELL, WE ARE DOING WONDERFULLY.

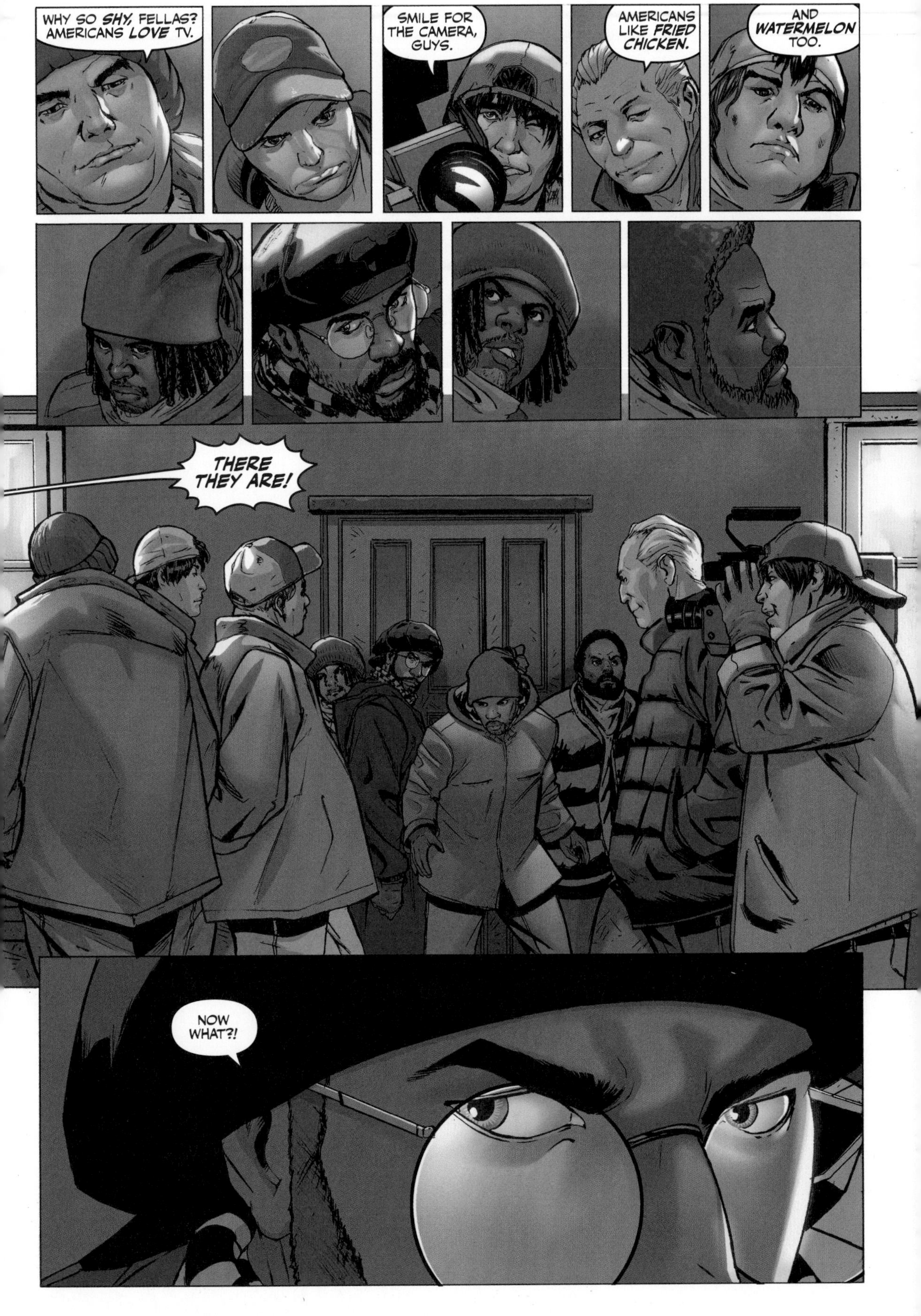
WHY SO SHY, FELLAS? AMERICANS LOVE TV.
SMILE FOR THE CAMERA, GUYS.
AMERICANS LIKE FRIED CHICKEN.
AND WATERMELON TOO.
THERE THEY ARE!
NOW WHAT?!

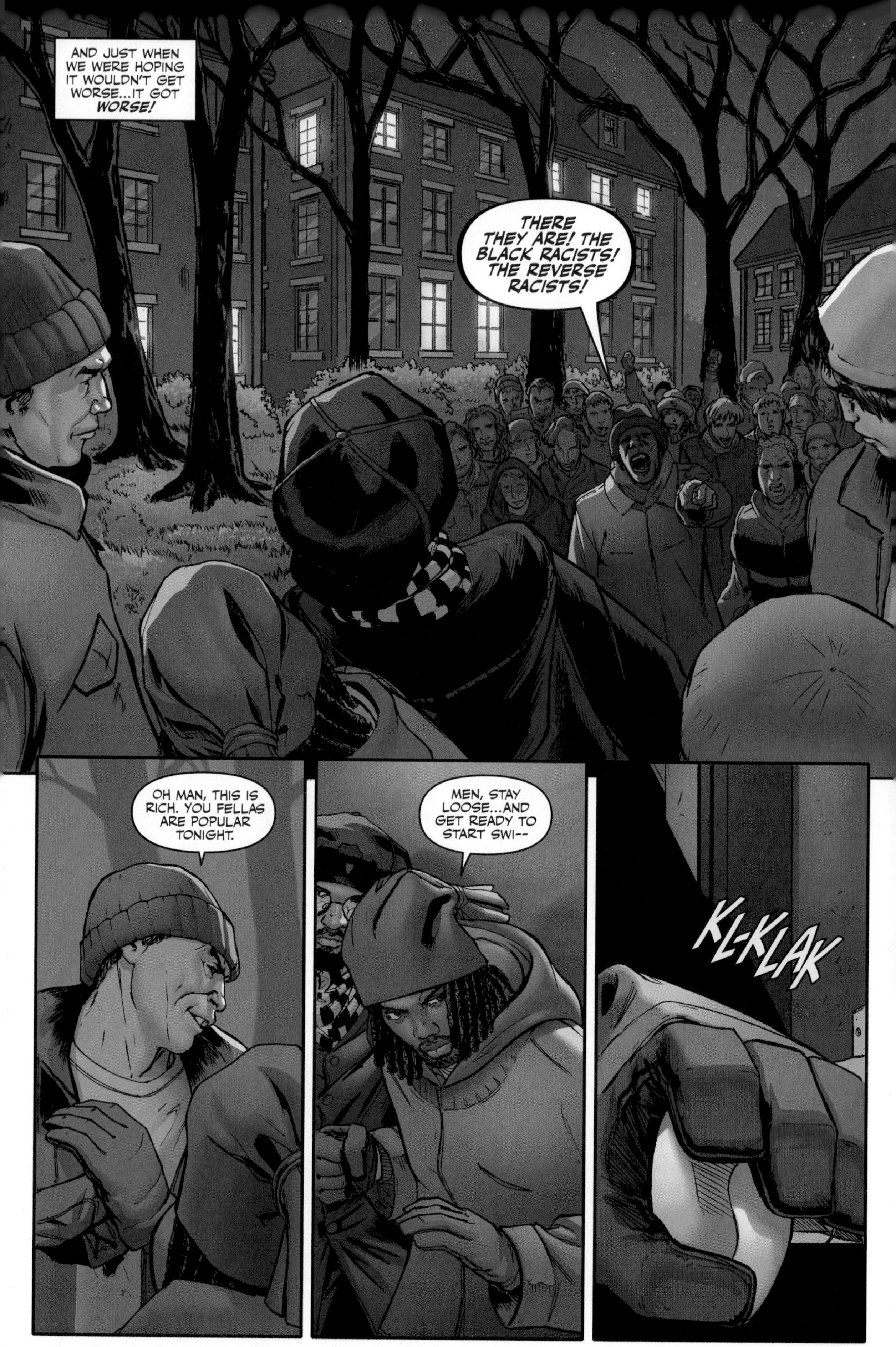
AND JUST WHEN WE WERE HOPING IT WOULDN'T GET WORSE...IT GOT WORSE!
THERE THEY ARE! THE BLACK RACISTS! THE REVERSE RACISTS!
OH MAN, THIS IS RICH. YOU FELLAS ARE POPULAR TONIGHT.
MEN, STAY LOOSE...AND GET READY TO START SWI--
KL-KLAK

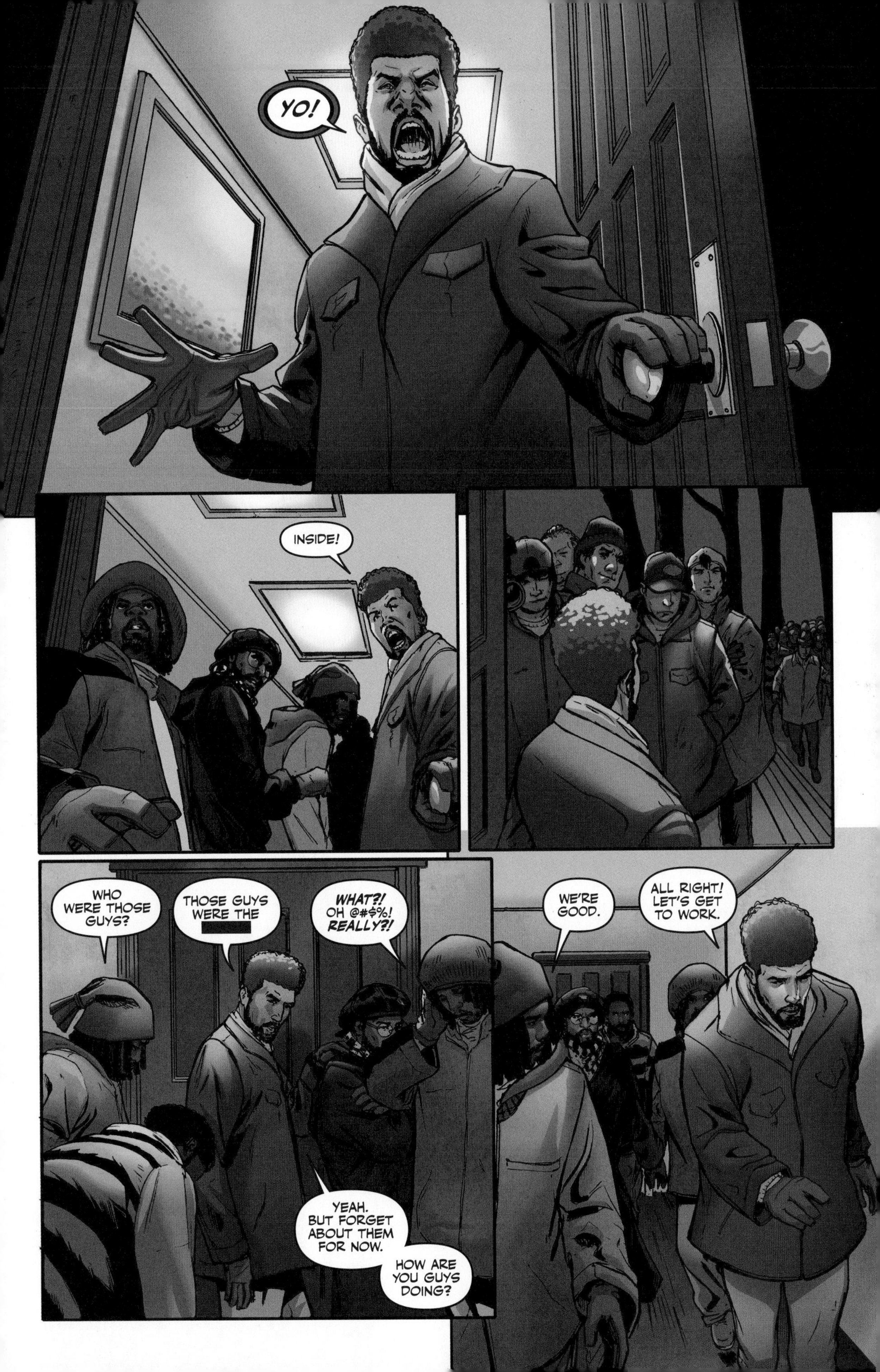
YO!
INSIDE!
WHO WERE THOSE GUYS?
THOSE GUYS WERE THE [redacted]
WHAT?! OH @#$%! REALLY?!
YEAH. BUT FORGET ABOUT THEM FOR NOW.
HOW ARE YOU GUYS DOING?
WE'RE GOOD.
ALL RIGHT! LET'S GET TO WORK.

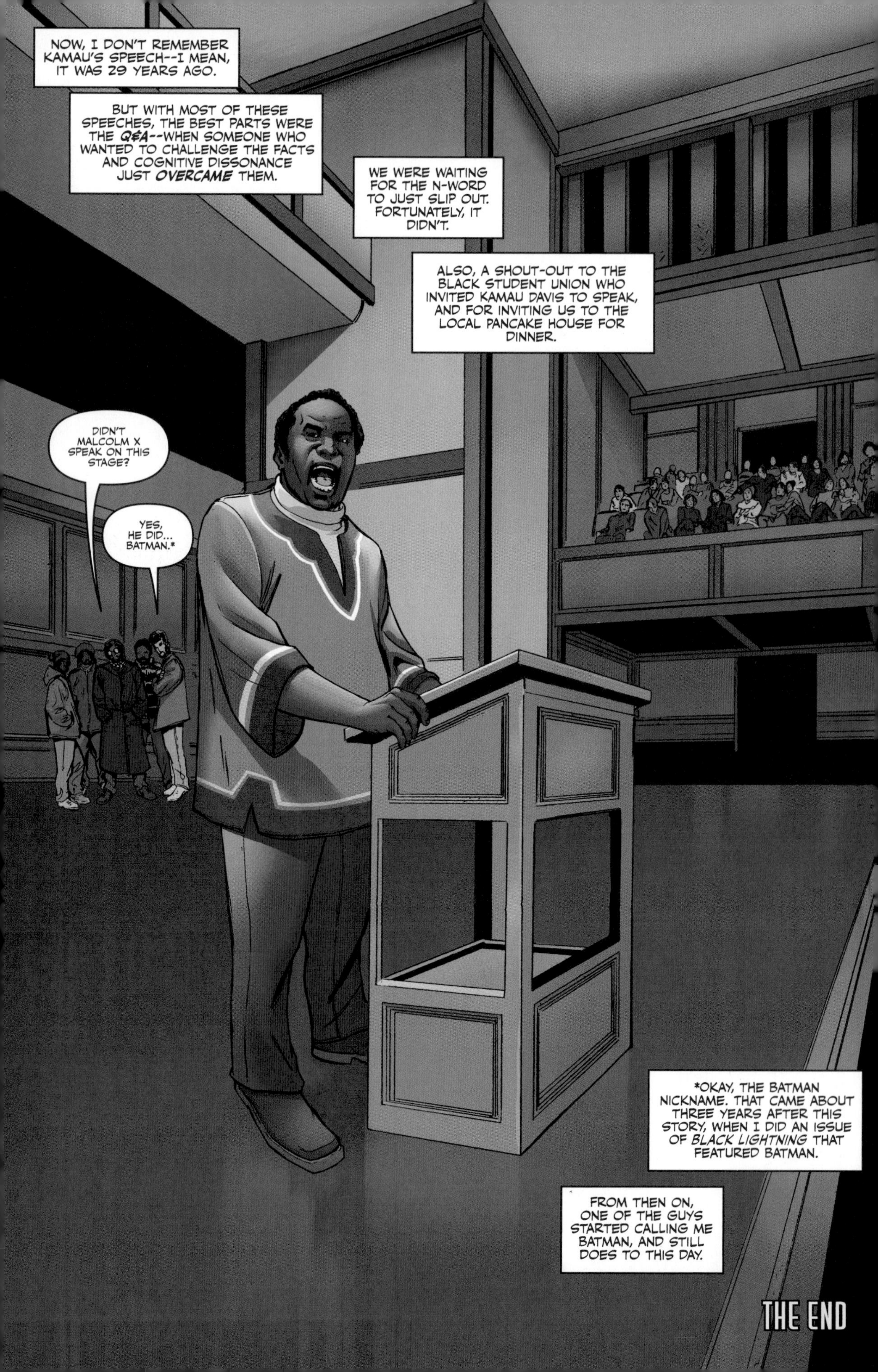
NOW, I DON'T REMEMBER KAMAU'S SPEECH--I MEAN, IT WAS 29 YEARS AGO.
BUT WITH MOST OF THESE SPEECHES, THE BEST PARTS WERE THE *Q&A*--WHEN SOMEONE WHO WANTED TO CHALLENGE THE FACTS AND COGNITIVE DISSONANCE JUST *OVERCAME* THEM.
WE WERE WAITING FOR THE N-WORD TO JUST SLIP OUT. FORTUNATELY, IT DIDN'T.
ALSO, A SHOUT-OUT TO THE BLACK STUDENT UNION WHO INVITED KAMAU DAVIS TO SPEAK, AND FOR INVITING US TO THE LOCAL PANCAKE HOUSE FOR DINNER.
DIDN'T MALCOLM X SPEAK ON THIS STAGE?
YES, HE DID... BATMAN.*
*OKAY, THE BATMAN NICKNAME. THAT CAME ABOUT THREE YEARS AFTER THIS STORY, WHEN I DID AN ISSUE OF *BLACK LIGHTNING* THAT FEATURED BATMAN.
FROM THEN ON, ONE OF THE GUYS STARTED CALLING ME BATMAN, AND STILL DOES TO THIS DAY.
THE END

DC REPRESENT!

CHAPTER NINE
"WEIGHT OF THE WORLD"

WRITER - JUSTIN ELLIS

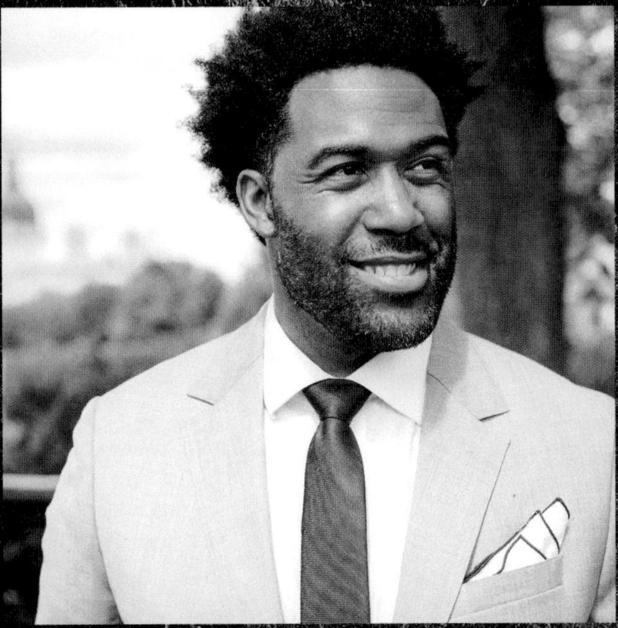

Justin Ellis is a writer, editor, and producer whose work has appeared in *ESPN The Magazine*, the *Atlantic*, the *New York Times*, and *GQ*. He is the projects editor for Defector, a worker-owned media company founded in 2020. His TV credits include *Wyatt Cenac's Problem Areas* on HBO and Jigsaw Productions' *How to Fix a Drug Scandal* on Netflix. He is currently at work on his first book, *The Cruelty of Nice Folks*, an examination of the history of Black families in Minnesota and the subtle racism that arises in seemingly progressive parts of America, for Harper.

ARTIST - TRAVEL FOREMAN
COLORIST - REX LOKUS
LETTERER - DERON BENNETT

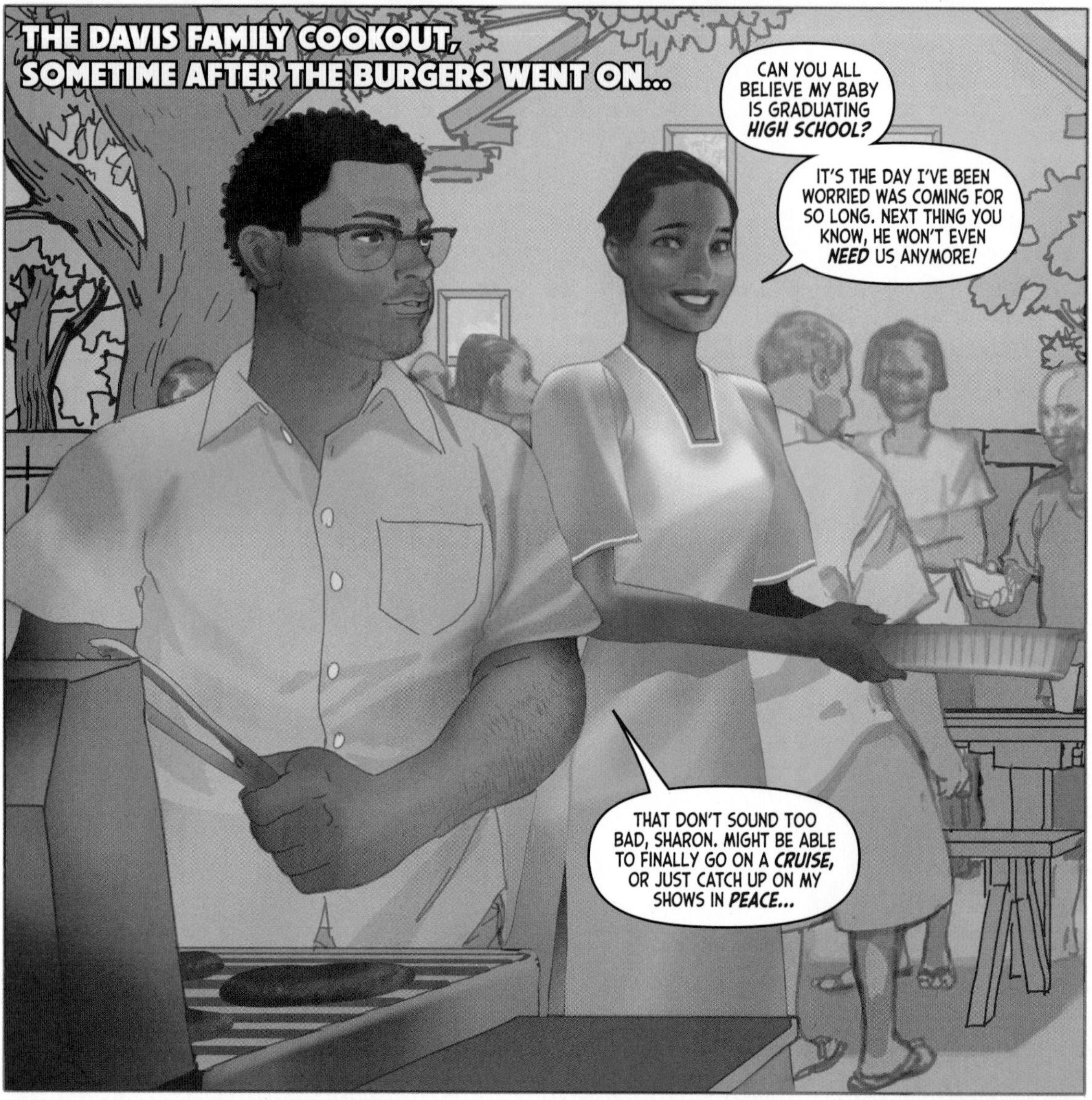
THE DAVIS FAMILY COOKOUT, SOMETIME AFTER THE BURGERS WENT ON...
CAN YOU ALL BELIEVE MY BABY IS GRADUATING HIGH SCHOOL?
IT'S THE DAY I'VE BEEN WORRIED WAS COMING FOR SO LONG. NEXT THING YOU KNOW, HE WON'T EVEN NEED US ANYMORE!
THAT DON'T SOUND TOO BAD, SHARON. MIGHT BE ABLE TO FINALLY GO ON A CRUISE, OR JUST CATCH UP ON MY SHOWS IN PEACE...

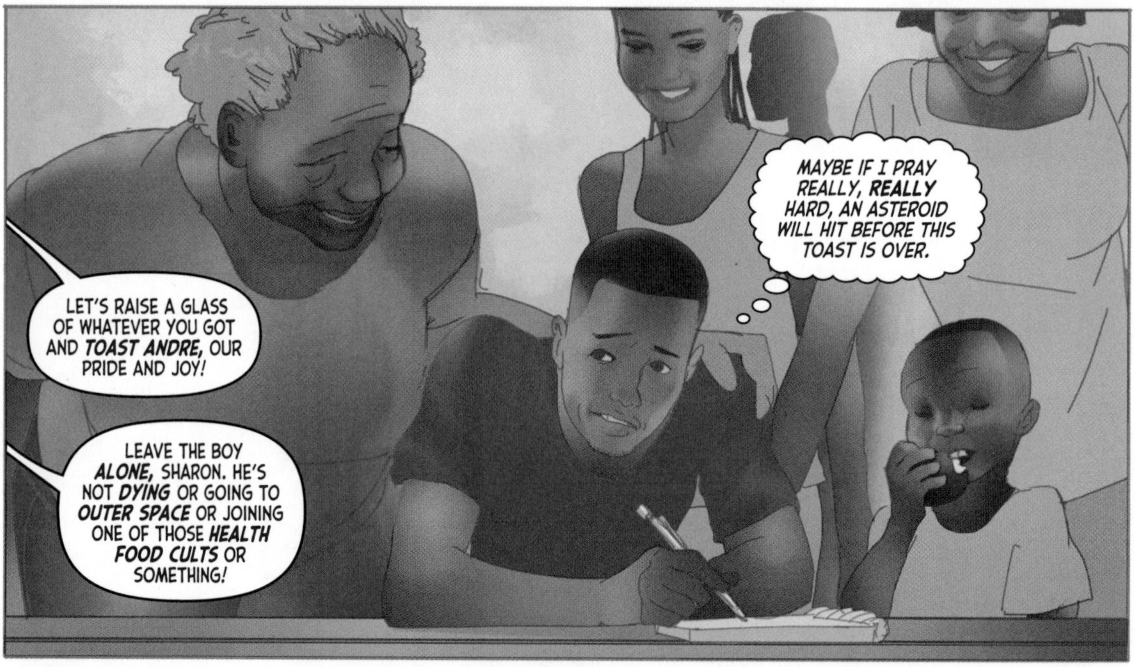
LET'S RAISE A GLASS OF WHATEVER YOU GOT AND TOAST ANDRE, OUR PRIDE AND JOY!
MAYBE IF I PRAY REALLY, REALLY HARD, AN ASTEROID WILL HIT BEFORE THIS TOAST IS OVER.
LEAVE THE BOY ALONE, SHARON. HE'S NOT DYING OR GOING TO OUTER SPACE OR JOINING ONE OF THOSE HEALTH FOOD CULTS OR SOMETHING!

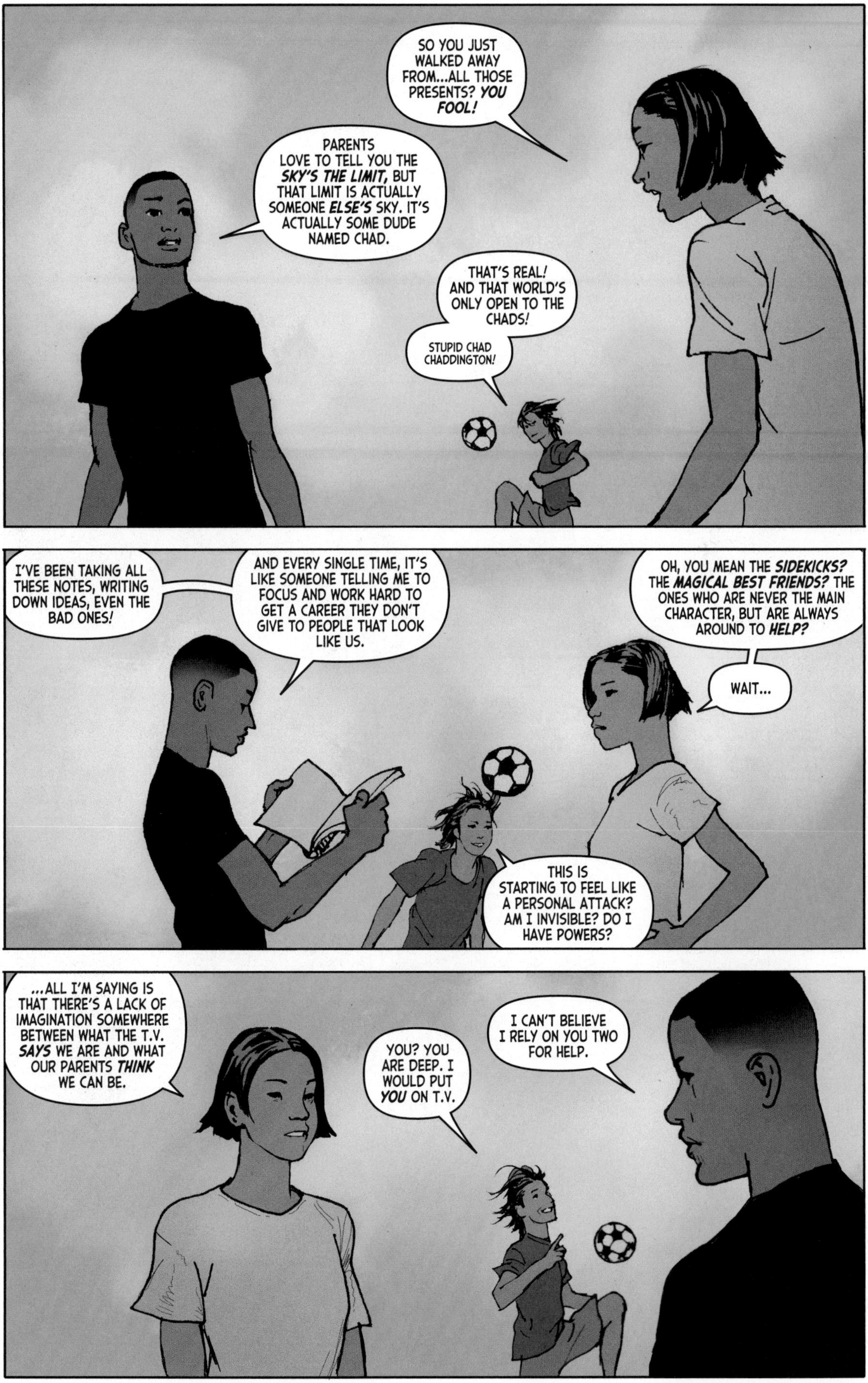
PARENTS LOVE TO TELL YOU THE ***SKY'S THE LIMIT,*** BUT THAT LIMIT IS ACTUALLY SOMEONE ***ELSE'S*** SKY. IT'S ACTUALLY SOME DUDE NAMED CHAD.
SO YOU JUST WALKED AWAY FROM...ALL THOSE PRESENTS? ***YOU FOOL!***
THAT'S REAL! AND THAT WORLD'S ONLY OPEN TO THE CHADS!
STUPID CHAD CHADDINGTON!
I'VE BEEN TAKING ALL THESE NOTES, WRITING DOWN IDEAS, EVEN THE BAD ONES!
AND EVERY SINGLE TIME, IT'S LIKE SOMEONE TELLING ME TO FOCUS AND WORK HARD TO GET A CAREER THEY DON'T GIVE TO PEOPLE THAT LOOK LIKE US.
OH, YOU MEAN THE ***SIDEKICKS?*** THE ***MAGICAL BEST FRIENDS?*** THE ONES WHO ARE NEVER THE MAIN CHARACTER, BUT ARE ALWAYS AROUND TO ***HELP?***
WAIT...
THIS IS STARTING TO FEEL LIKE A PERSONAL ATTACK? AM I INVISIBLE? DO I HAVE POWERS?
...ALL I'M SAYING IS THAT THERE'S A LACK OF IMAGINATION SOMEWHERE BETWEEN WHAT THE T.V. ***SAYS*** WE ARE AND WHAT OUR PARENTS ***THINK*** WE CAN BE.
YOU? YOU ARE DEEP. I WOULD PUT ***YOU*** ON T.V.
I CAN'T BELIEVE I RELY ON YOU TWO FOR HELP.

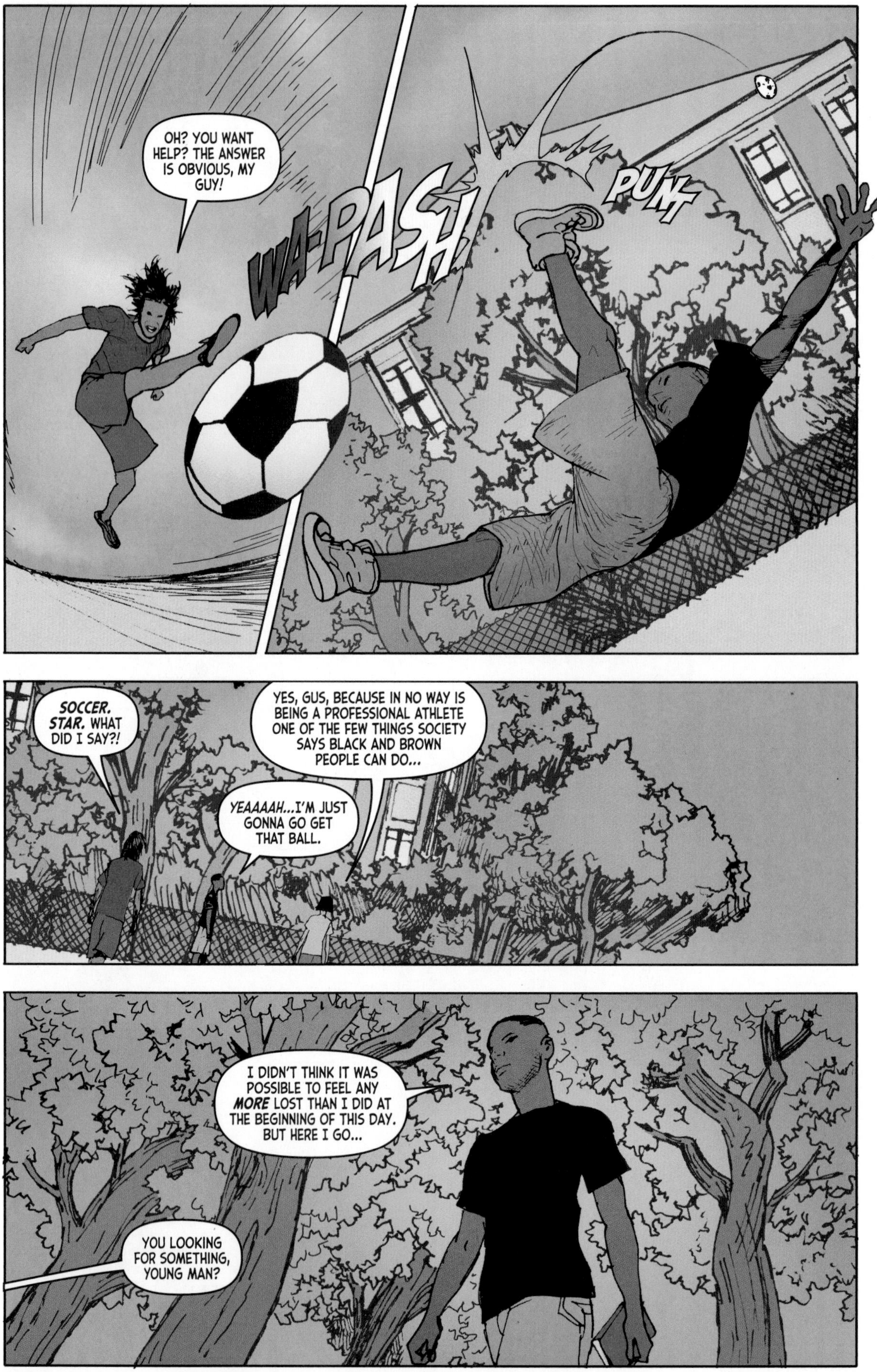
OH? YOU WANT HELP? THE ANSWER IS OBVIOUS, MY GUY!
WA-PASH
PUNT
SOCCER. STAR. WHAT DID I SAY?!
YES, GUS, BECAUSE IN NO WAY IS BEING A PROFESSIONAL ATHLETE ONE OF THE FEW THINGS SOCIETY SAYS BLACK AND BROWN PEOPLE CAN DO...
YEAAAAH...I'M JUST GONNA GO GET THAT BALL.
I DIDN'T THINK IT WAS POSSIBLE TO FEEL ANY MORE LOST THAN I DID AT THE BEGINNING OF THIS DAY. BUT HERE I GO...
YOU LOOKING FOR SOMETHING, YOUNG MAN?

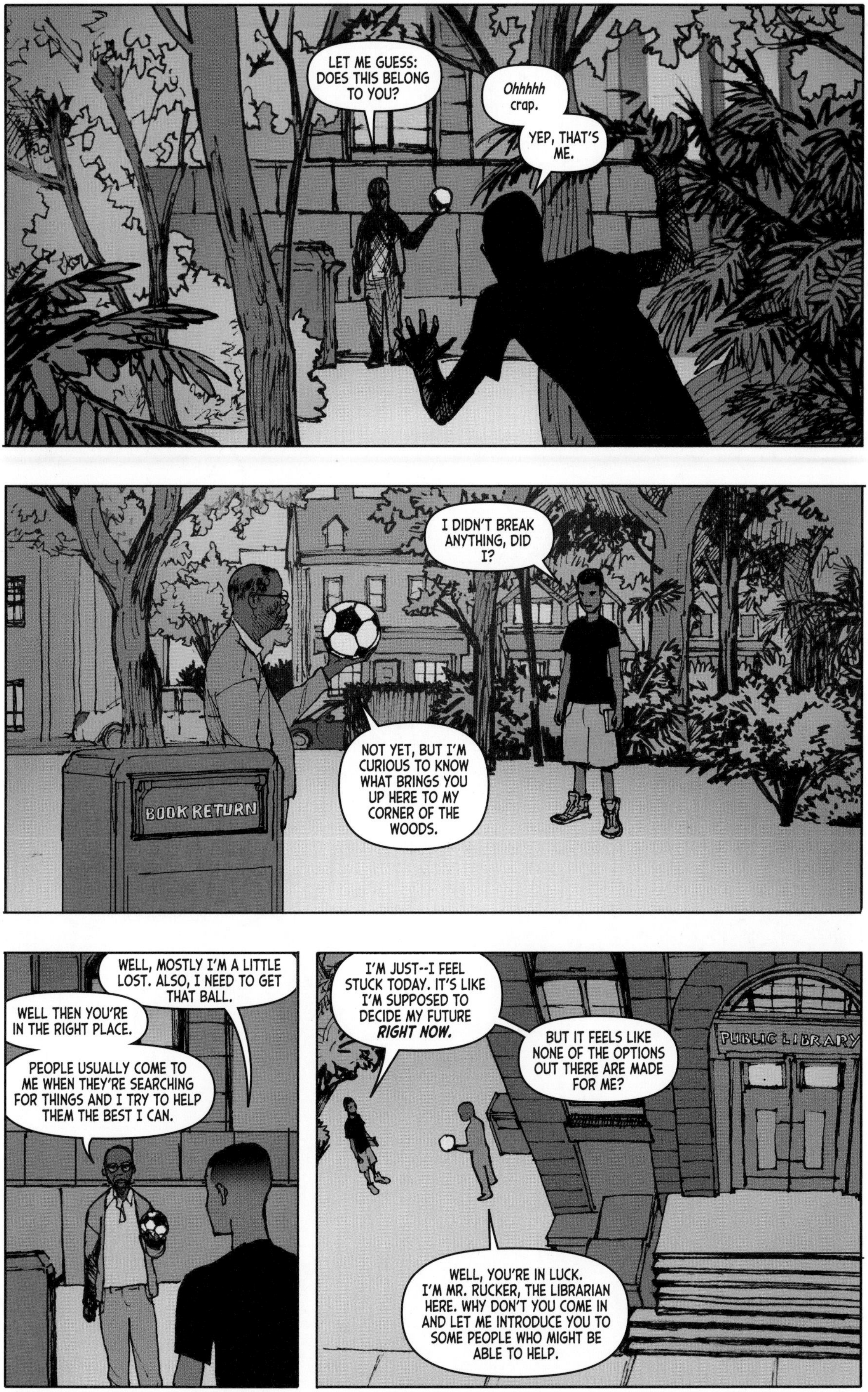
LET ME GUESS: DOES THIS BELONG TO YOU?
Ohhhhh crap.
YEP, THAT'S ME.
I DIDN'T BREAK ANYTHING, DID I?
NOT YET, BUT I'M CURIOUS TO KNOW WHAT BRINGS YOU UP HERE TO MY CORNER OF THE WOODS.
BOOK RETURN
WELL, MOSTLY I'M A LITTLE LOST. ALSO, I NEED TO GET THAT BALL.
WELL THEN YOU'RE IN THE RIGHT PLACE.
PEOPLE USUALLY COME TO ME WHEN THEY'RE SEARCHING FOR THINGS AND I TRY TO HELP THEM THE BEST I CAN.
I'M JUST--I FEEL STUCK TODAY. IT'S LIKE I'M SUPPOSED TO DECIDE MY FUTURE ***RIGHT NOW.***
BUT IT FEELS LIKE NONE OF THE OPTIONS OUT THERE ARE MADE FOR ME?
PUBLIC LIBRARY
WELL, YOU'RE IN LUCK. I'M MR. RUCKER, THE LIBRARIAN HERE. WHY DON'T YOU COME IN AND LET ME INTRODUCE YOU TO SOME PEOPLE WHO MIGHT BE ABLE TO HELP.

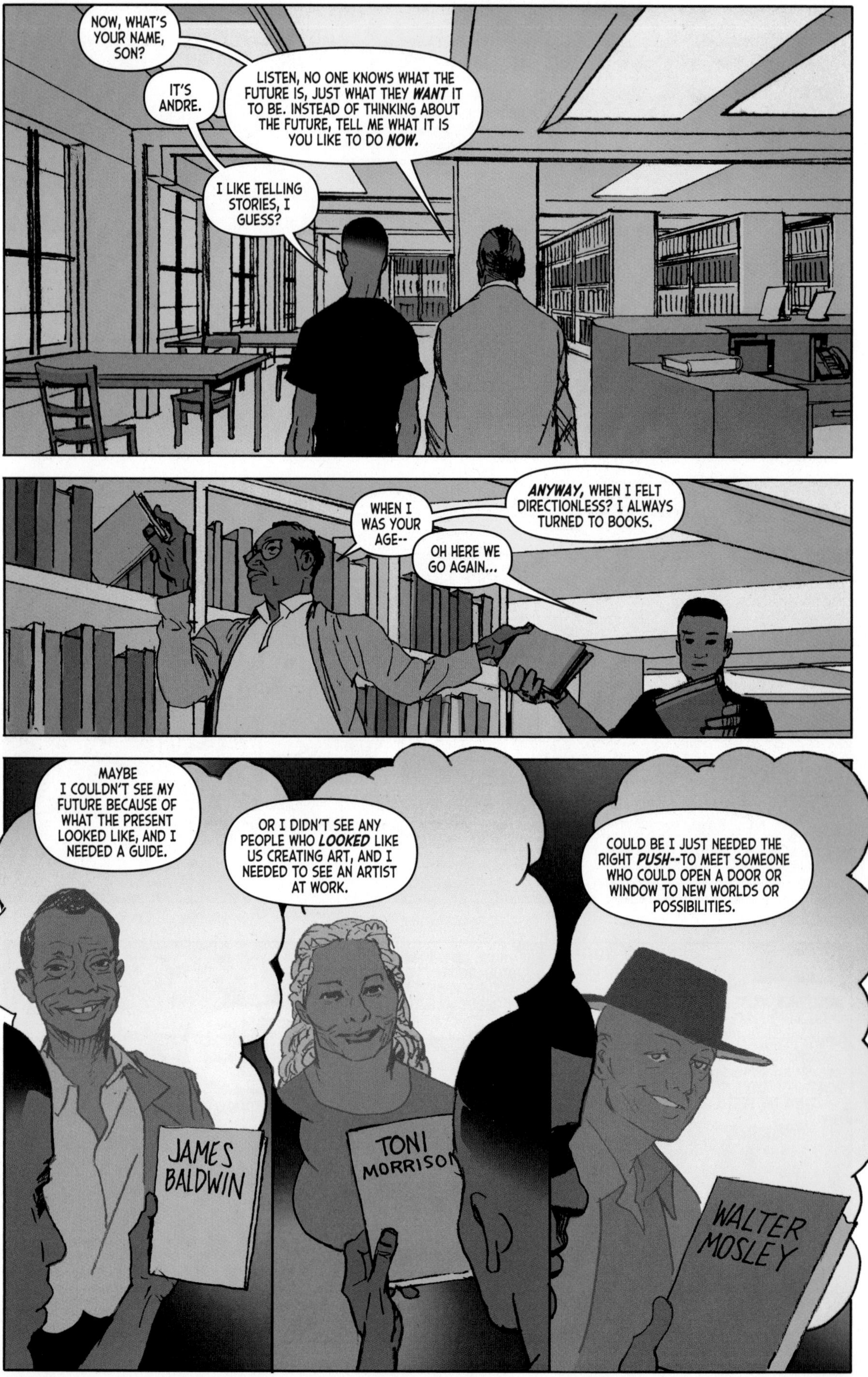
NOW, WHAT'S YOUR NAME, SON?
IT'S ANDRE.
LISTEN, NO ONE KNOWS WHAT THE FUTURE IS, JUST WHAT THEY *WANT* IT TO BE. INSTEAD OF THINKING ABOUT THE FUTURE, TELL ME WHAT IT IS YOU LIKE TO DO *NOW.*
I LIKE TELLING STORIES, I GUESS?
WHEN I WAS YOUR AGE--
OH HERE WE GO AGAIN...
ANYWAY, WHEN I FELT DIRECTIONLESS? I ALWAYS TURNED TO BOOKS.
MAYBE I COULDN'T SEE MY FUTURE BECAUSE OF WHAT THE PRESENT LOOKED LIKE, AND I NEEDED A GUIDE.
OR I DIDN'T SEE ANY PEOPLE WHO *LOOKED* LIKE US CREATING ART, AND I NEEDED TO SEE AN ARTIST AT WORK.
COULD BE I JUST NEEDED THE RIGHT *PUSH*--TO MEET SOMEONE WHO COULD OPEN A DOOR OR WINDOW TO NEW WORLDS OR POSSIBILITIES.
JAMES BALDWIN
TONI MORRISON
WALTER MOSLEY

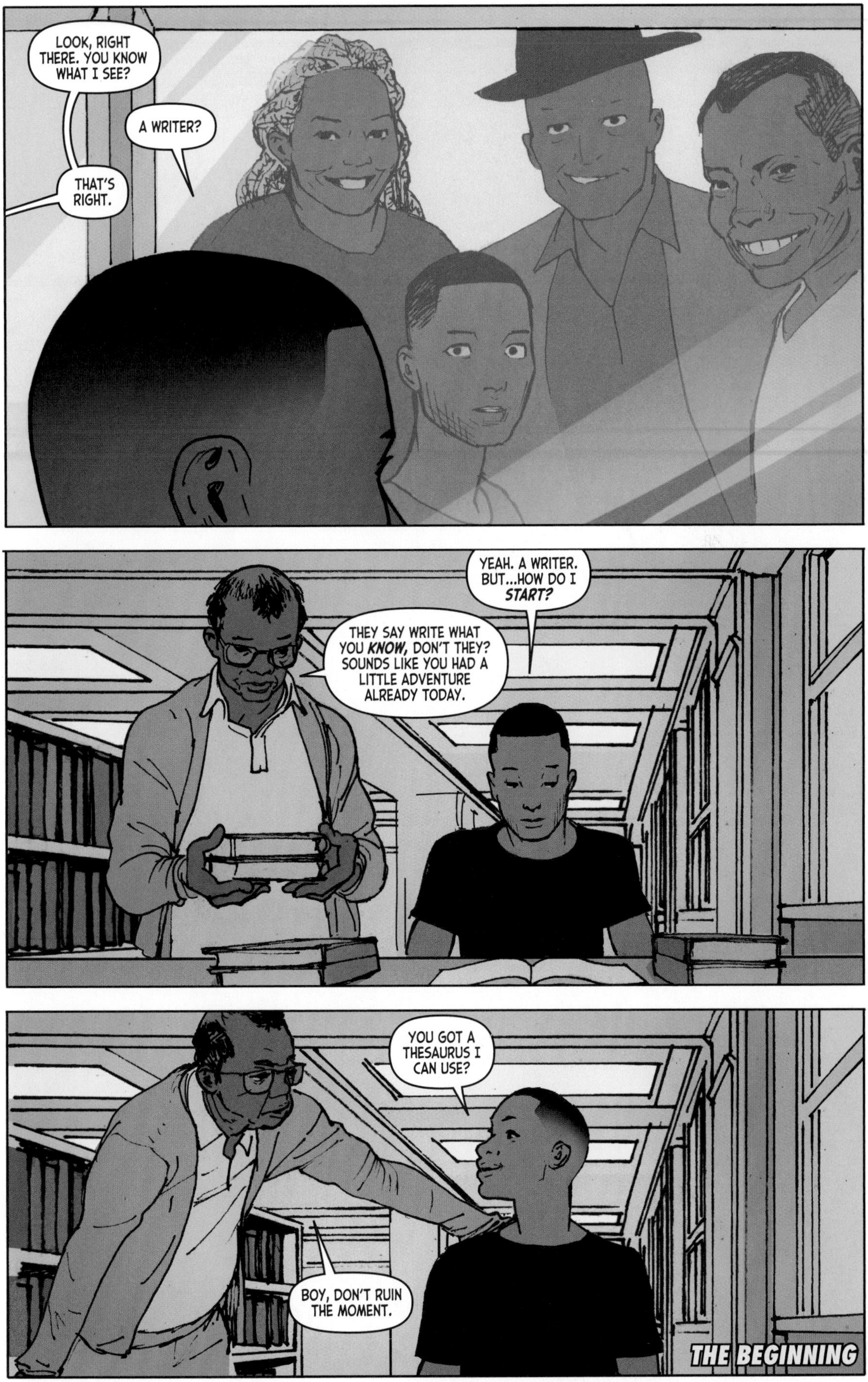
LOOK, RIGHT THERE. YOU KNOW WHAT I SEE?
A WRITER?
THAT'S RIGHT.
YEAH. A WRITER. BUT...HOW DO I *START?*
THEY SAY WRITE WHAT YOU *KNOW,* DON'T THEY? SOUNDS LIKE YOU HAD A LITTLE ADVENTURE ALREADY TODAY.
YOU GOT A THESAURUS I CAN USE?
BOY, DON'T RUIN THE MOMENT.
THE BEGINNING

DC REPRESENT!

CHAPTER TEN
"THE FLIGHTLESS BIRD"

WRITER - FREDERICK JOSEPH

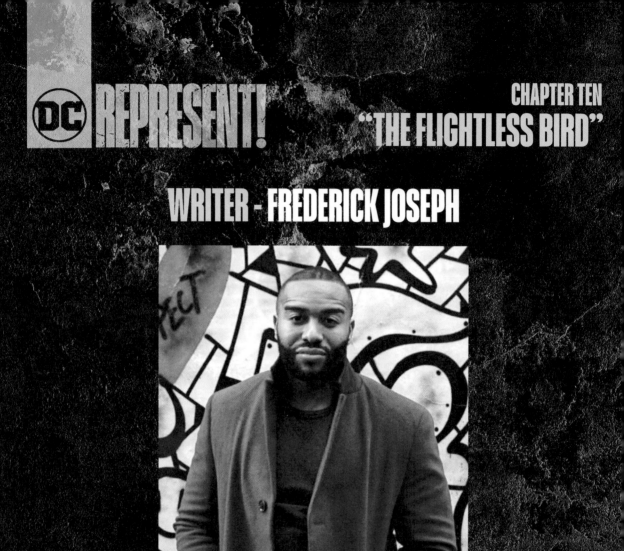

Frederick Joseph is a *New York Times* bestselling author, a *Forbes* 30 Under 30 listee for marketing and advertising, an activist, and a philanthropist, with more than 10 years of marketing experience.

He is also the sole creator of the largest GoFundMe campaign in history, the #BlackPantherChallenge, and of the largest individual COVID-19 support effort, the #RentRelief campaign, which has raised over three million dollars.

Frederick has been honored with the 2018 Comic-Con Bob Clampett Humanitarian Award and is a member of the Root's 2018 list of the 100 most influential African Americans.

ARTIST - KERON GRANT
LETTERER - DERON BENNETT

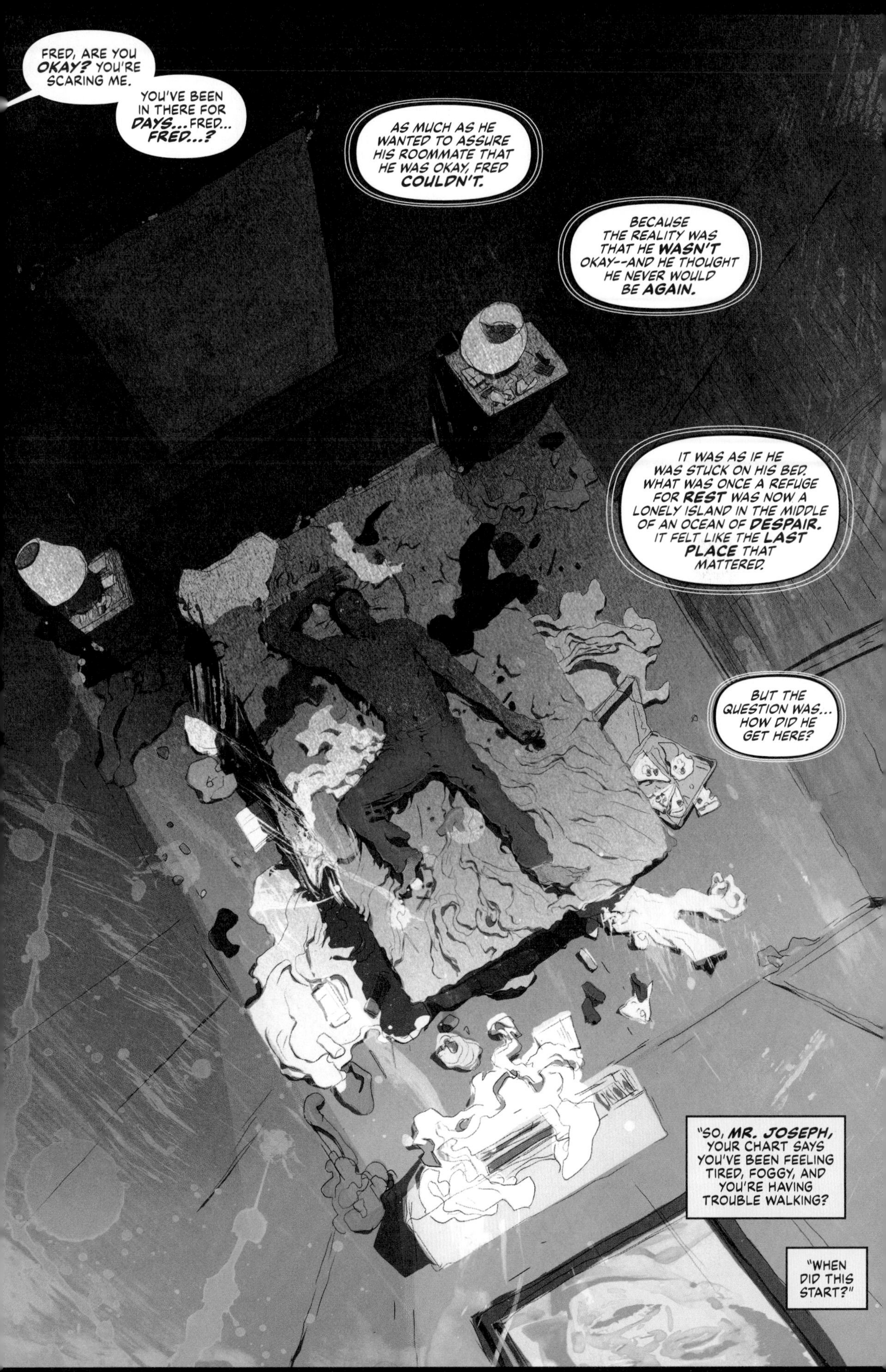
FRED, ARE YOU OKAY? YOU'RE SCARING ME.
YOU'VE BEEN IN THERE FOR DAYS... FRED... FRED...?
AS MUCH AS HE WANTED TO ASSURE HIS ROOMMATE THAT HE WAS OKAY, FRED COULDN'T.
BECAUSE THE REALITY WAS THAT HE WASN'T OKAY--AND HE THOUGHT HE NEVER WOULD BE AGAIN.
IT WAS AS IF HE WAS STUCK ON HIS BED. WHAT WAS ONCE A REFUGE FOR REST WAS NOW A LONELY ISLAND IN THE MIDDLE OF AN OCEAN OF DESPAIR. IT FELT LIKE THE LAST PLACE THAT MATTERED.
BUT THE QUESTION WAS... HOW DID HE GET HERE?
"SO, MR. JOSEPH, YOUR CHART SAYS YOU'VE BEEN FEELING TIRED, FOGGY, AND YOU'RE HAVING TROUBLE WALKING?
"WHEN DID THIS START?"

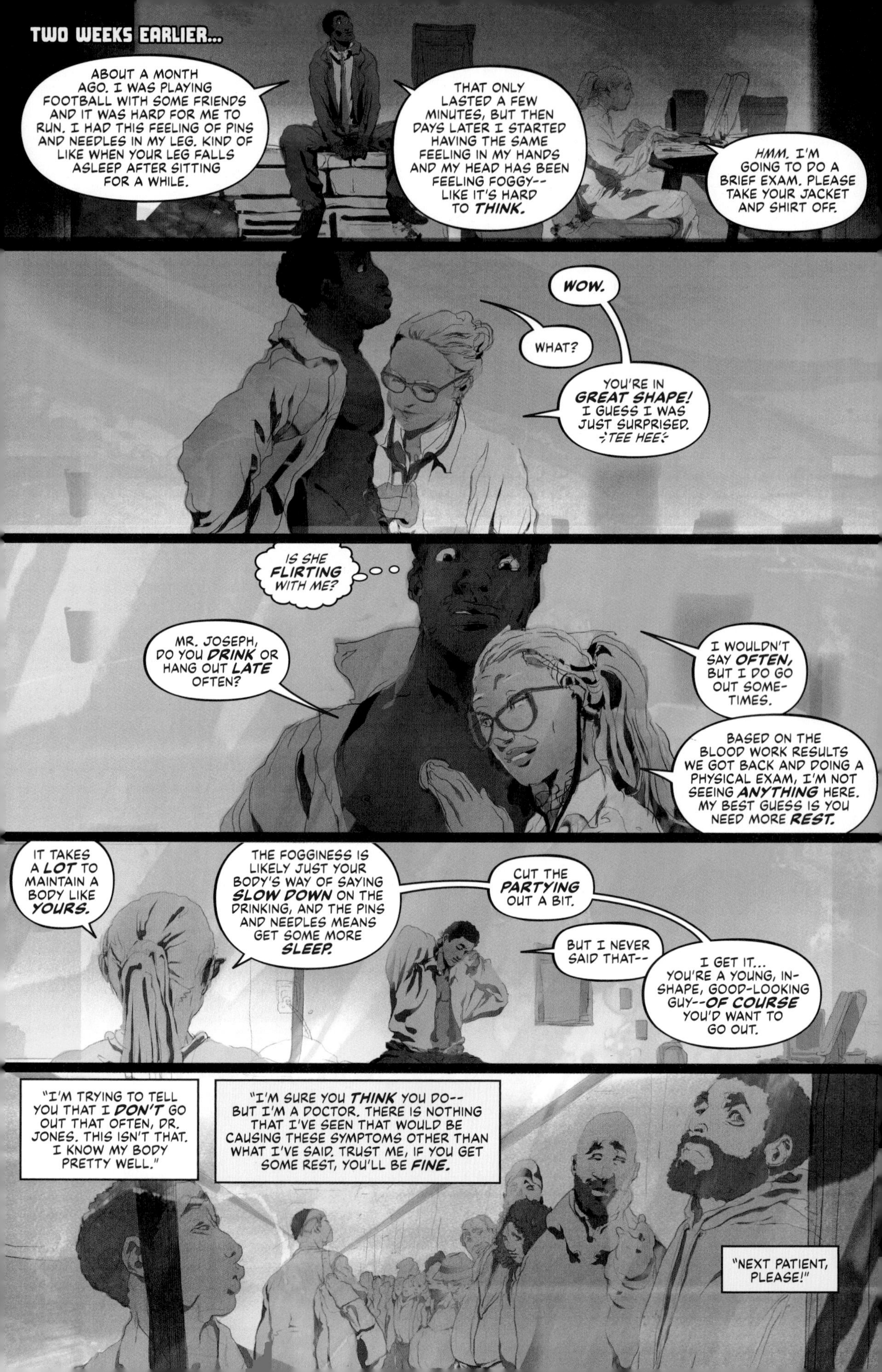
TWO WEEKS EARLIER...
ABOUT A MONTH AGO. I WAS PLAYING FOOTBALL WITH SOME FRIENDS AND IT WAS HARD FOR ME TO RUN. I HAD THIS FEELING OF PINS AND NEEDLES IN MY LEG. KIND OF LIKE WHEN YOUR LEG FALLS ASLEEP AFTER SITTING FOR A WHILE.
THAT ONLY LASTED A FEW MINUTES, BUT THEN DAYS LATER I STARTED HAVING THE SAME FEELING IN MY HANDS AND MY HEAD HAS BEEN FEELING FOGGY-- LIKE IT'S HARD TO THINK.
HMM. I'M GOING TO DO A BRIEF EXAM. PLEASE TAKE YOUR JACKET AND SHIRT OFF.
WOW.
WHAT?
YOU'RE IN GREAT SHAPE! I GUESS I WAS JUST SURPRISED. TEE HEE
IS SHE FLIRTING WITH ME?
MR. JOSEPH, DO YOU DRINK OR HANG OUT LATE OFTEN?
I WOULDN'T SAY OFTEN, BUT I DO GO OUT SOME-TIMES.
BASED ON THE BLOOD WORK RESULTS WE GOT BACK AND DOING A PHYSICAL EXAM, I'M NOT SEEING ANYTHING HERE. MY BEST GUESS IS YOU NEED MORE REST.
IT TAKES A LOT TO MAINTAIN A BODY LIKE YOURS.
THE FOGGINESS IS LIKELY JUST YOUR BODY'S WAY OF SAYING SLOW DOWN ON THE DRINKING, AND THE PINS AND NEEDLES MEANS GET SOME MORE SLEEP.
CUT THE PARTYING OUT A BIT.
BUT I NEVER SAID THAT--
I GET IT... YOU'RE A YOUNG, IN-SHAPE, GOOD-LOOKING GUY--OF COURSE YOU'D WANT TO GO OUT.
"I'M TRYING TO TELL YOU THAT I DON'T GO OUT THAT OFTEN, DR. JONES. THIS ISN'T THAT. I KNOW MY BODY PRETTY WELL."
"I'M SURE YOU THINK YOU DO-- BUT I'M A DOCTOR. THERE IS NOTHING THAT I'VE SEEN THAT WOULD BE CAUSING THESE SYMPTOMS OTHER THAN WHAT I'VE SAID. TRUST ME, IF YOU GET SOME REST, YOU'LL BE FINE.
"NEXT PATIENT, PLEASE!"

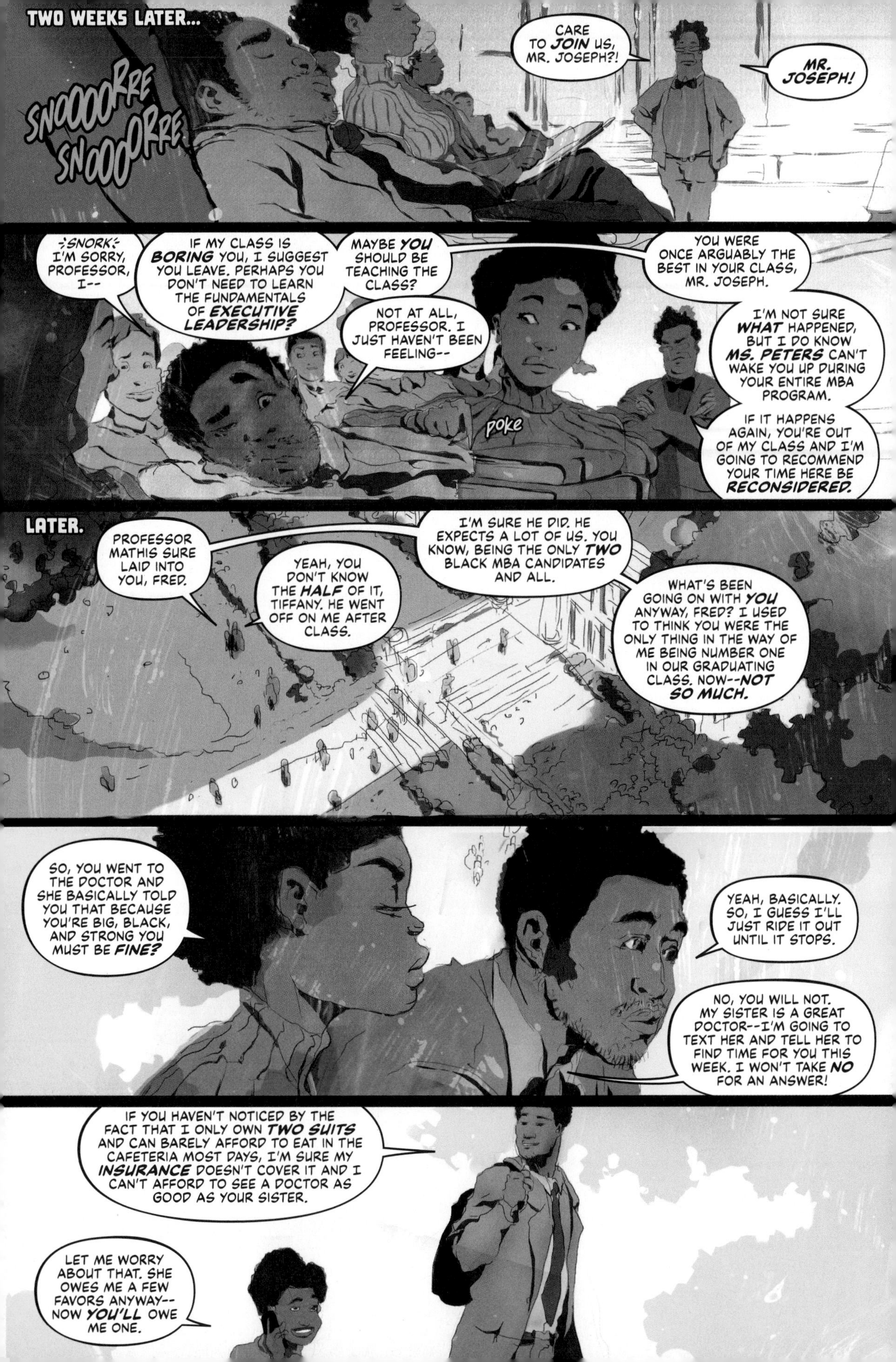

TWO WEEKS LATER...
SNOOOORRE SNOOOORRE
CARE TO JOIN US, MR. JOSEPH?!
MR. JOSEPH!
-SNORK- I'M SORRY, PROFESSOR, I--
IF MY CLASS IS BORING YOU, I SUGGEST YOU LEAVE. PERHAPS YOU DON'T NEED TO LEARN THE FUNDAMENTALS OF EXECUTIVE LEADERSHIP?
MAYBE YOU SHOULD BE TEACHING THE CLASS?
NOT AT ALL, PROFESSOR. I JUST HAVEN'T BEEN FEELING--
YOU WERE ONCE ARGUABLY THE BEST IN YOUR CLASS, MR. JOSEPH.
I'M NOT SURE WHAT HAPPENED, BUT I DO KNOW MS. PETERS CAN'T WAKE YOU UP DURING YOUR ENTIRE MBA PROGRAM.
IF IT HAPPENS AGAIN, YOU'RE OUT OF MY CLASS AND I'M GOING TO RECOMMEND YOUR TIME HERE BE RECONSIDERED.
POKE
LATER.
PROFESSOR MATHIS SURE LAID INTO YOU, FRED.
YEAH, YOU DON'T KNOW THE HALF OF IT, TIFFANY. HE WENT OFF ON ME AFTER CLASS.
I'M SURE HE DID. HE EXPECTS A LOT OF US. YOU KNOW, BEING THE ONLY TWO BLACK MBA CANDIDATES AND ALL.
WHAT'S BEEN GOING ON WITH YOU ANYWAY, FRED? I USED TO THINK YOU WERE THE ONLY THING IN THE WAY OF ME BEING NUMBER ONE IN OUR GRADUATING CLASS. NOW--NOT SO MUCH.
SO, YOU WENT TO THE DOCTOR AND SHE BASICALLY TOLD YOU THAT BECAUSE YOU'RE BIG, BLACK, AND STRONG YOU MUST BE FINE?
YEAH, BASICALLY. SO, I GUESS I'LL JUST RIDE IT OUT UNTIL IT STOPS.
NO, YOU WILL NOT. MY SISTER IS A GREAT DOCTOR--I'M GOING TO TEXT HER AND TELL HER TO FIND TIME FOR YOU THIS WEEK. I WON'T TAKE NO FOR AN ANSWER!
IF YOU HAVEN'T NOTICED BY THE FACT THAT I ONLY OWN TWO SUITS AND CAN BARELY AFFORD TO EAT IN THE CAFETERIA MOST DAYS, I'M SURE MY INSURANCE DOESN'T COVER IT AND I CAN'T AFFORD TO SEE A DOCTOR AS GOOD AS YOUR SISTER.
LET ME WORRY ABOUT THAT. SHE OWES ME A FEW FAVORS ANYWAY--NOW YOU'LL OWE ME ONE.

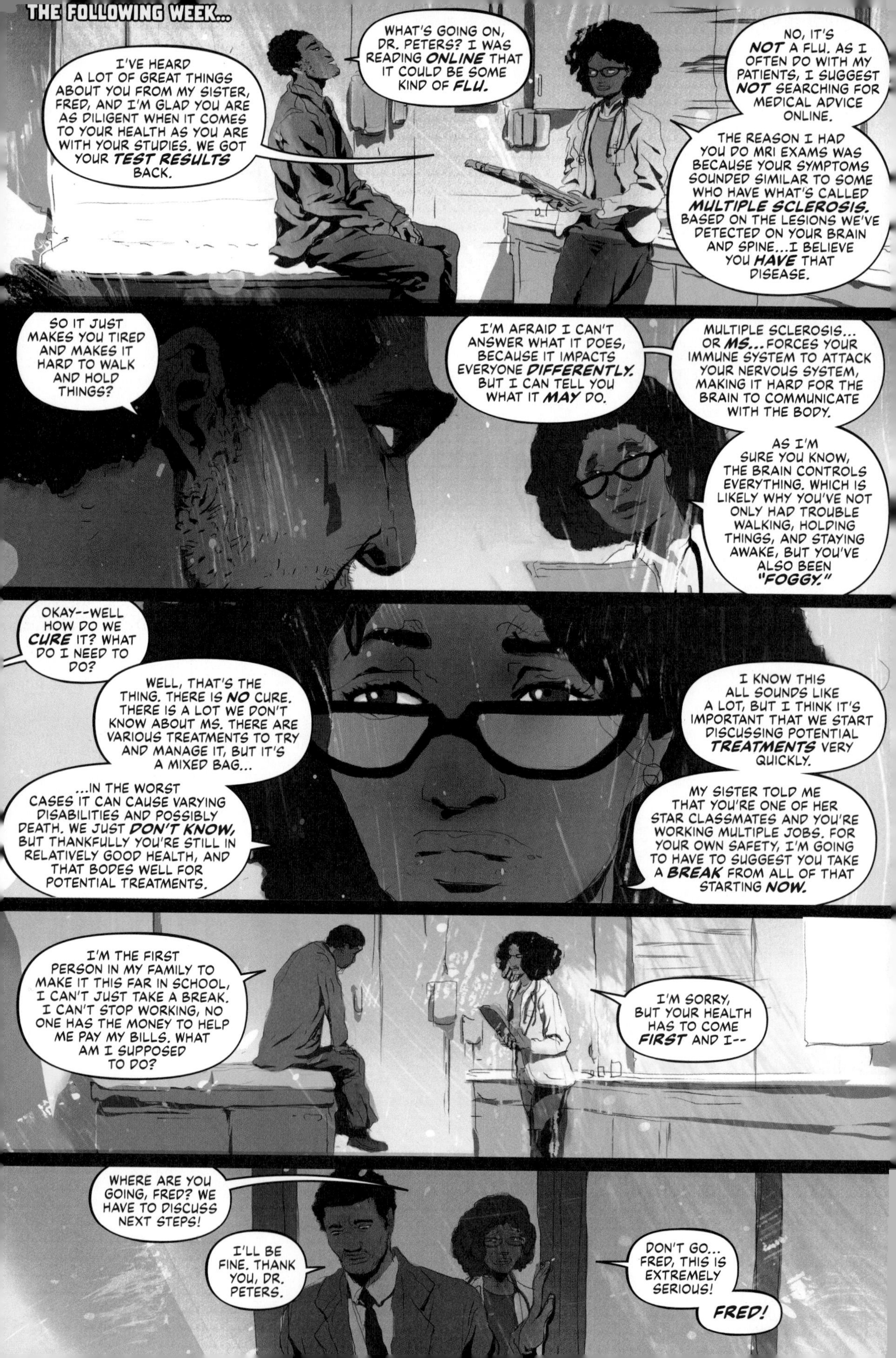
THE FOLLOWING WEEK...
WHAT'S GOING ON, DR. PETERS? I WAS READING ONLINE THAT IT COULD BE SOME KIND OF FLU.
I'VE HEARD A LOT OF GREAT THINGS ABOUT YOU FROM MY SISTER, FRED, AND I'M GLAD YOU ARE AS DILIGENT WHEN IT COMES TO YOUR HEALTH AS YOU ARE WITH YOUR STUDIES. WE GOT YOUR TEST RESULTS BACK.
NO, IT'S NOT A FLU. AS I OFTEN DO WITH MY PATIENTS, I SUGGEST NOT SEARCHING FOR MEDICAL ADVICE ONLINE.
THE REASON I HAD YOU DO MRI EXAMS WAS BECAUSE YOUR SYMPTOMS SOUNDED SIMILAR TO SOME WHO HAVE WHAT'S CALLED MULTIPLE SCLEROSIS. BASED ON THE LESIONS WE'VE DETECTED ON YOUR BRAIN AND SPINE...I BELIEVE YOU HAVE THAT DISEASE.
MULTIPLE SCLEROSIS... OR MS...FORCES YOUR IMMUNE SYSTEM TO ATTACK YOUR NERVOUS SYSTEM, MAKING IT HARD FOR THE BRAIN TO COMMUNICATE WITH THE BODY.
SO IT JUST MAKES YOU TIRED AND MAKES IT HARD TO WALK AND HOLD THINGS?
I'M AFRAID I CAN'T ANSWER WHAT IT DOES, BECAUSE IT IMPACTS EVERYONE DIFFERENTLY. BUT I CAN TELL YOU WHAT IT MAY DO.
AS I'M SURE YOU KNOW, THE BRAIN CONTROLS EVERYTHING. WHICH IS LIKELY WHY YOU'VE NOT ONLY HAD TROUBLE WALKING, HOLDING THINGS, AND STAYING AWAKE, BUT YOU'VE ALSO BEEN "FOGGY."
OKAY--WELL HOW DO WE CURE IT? WHAT DO I NEED TO DO?
WELL, THAT'S THE THING. THERE IS NO CURE. THERE IS A LOT WE DON'T KNOW ABOUT MS. THERE ARE VARIOUS TREATMENTS TO TRY AND MANAGE IT, BUT IT'S A MIXED BAG...
...IN THE WORST CASES IT CAN CAUSE VARYING DISABILITIES AND POSSIBLY DEATH. WE JUST DON'T KNOW, BUT THANKFULLY YOU'RE STILL IN RELATIVELY GOOD HEALTH, AND THAT BODES WELL FOR POTENTIAL TREATMENTS.
I KNOW THIS ALL SOUNDS LIKE A LOT, BUT I THINK IT'S IMPORTANT THAT WE START DISCUSSING POTENTIAL TREATMENTS VERY QUICKLY.
MY SISTER TOLD ME THAT YOU'RE ONE OF HER STAR CLASSMATES AND YOU'RE WORKING MULTIPLE JOBS. FOR YOUR OWN SAFETY, I'M GOING TO HAVE TO SUGGEST YOU TAKE A BREAK FROM ALL OF THAT STARTING NOW.
I'M THE FIRST PERSON IN MY FAMILY TO MAKE IT THIS FAR IN SCHOOL, I CAN'T JUST TAKE A BREAK. I CAN'T STOP WORKING, NO ONE HAS THE MONEY TO HELP ME PAY MY BILLS. WHAT AM I SUPPOSED TO DO?
I'M SORRY, BUT YOUR HEALTH HAS TO COME FIRST AND I--
WHERE ARE YOU GOING, FRED? WE HAVE TO DISCUSS NEXT STEPS!
I'LL BE FINE. THANK YOU, DR. PETERS.
DON'T GO... FRED, THIS IS EXTREMELY SERIOUS!
FRED!

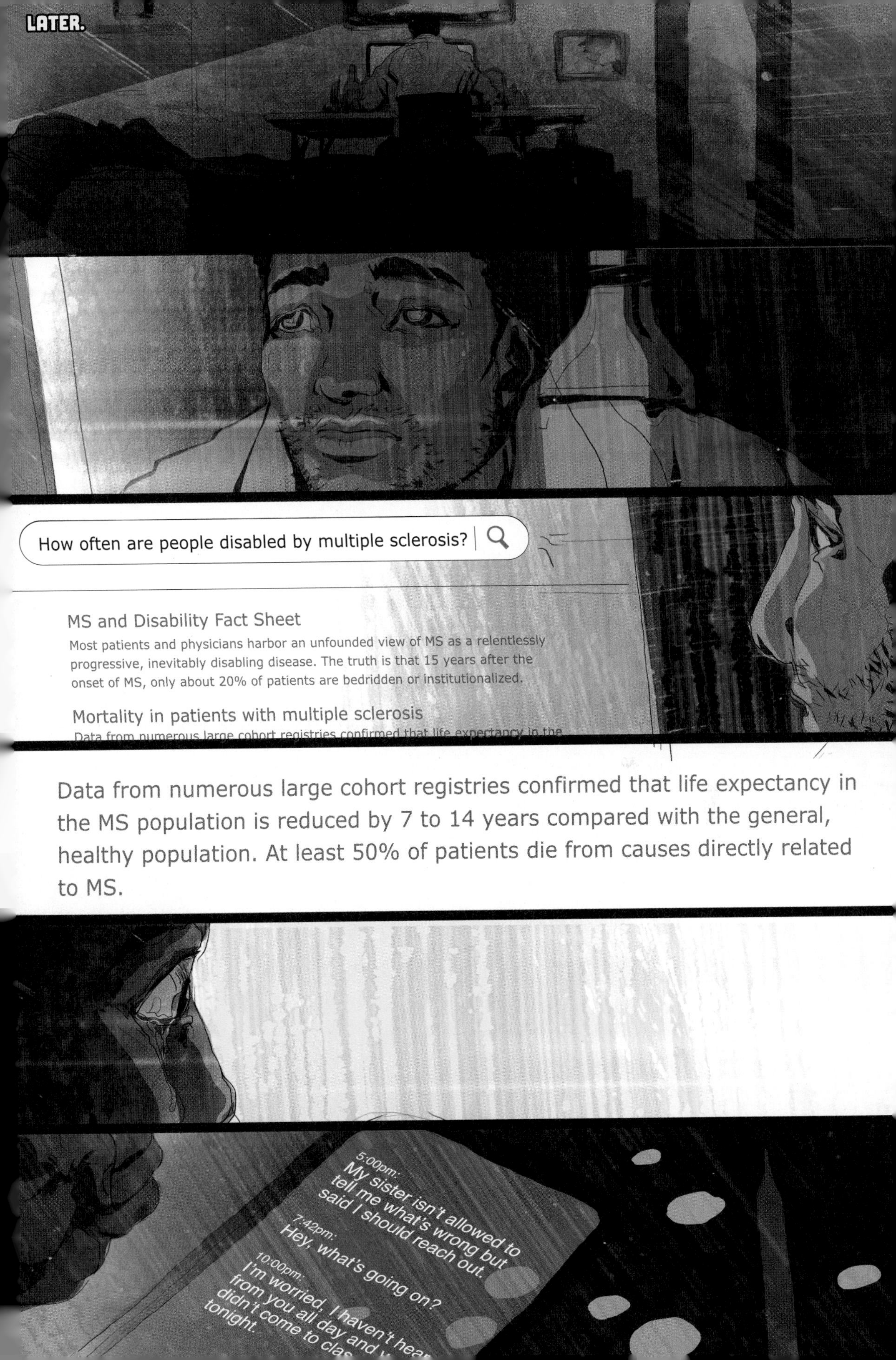
LATER.
How often are people disabled by multiple sclerosis?
MS and Disability Fact Sheet
Most patients and physicians harbor an unfounded view of MS as a relentlessly progressive, inevitably disabling disease. The truth is that 15 years after the onset of MS, only about 20% of patients are bedridden or institutionalized.
Mortality in patients with multiple sclerosis
Data from numerous large cohort registries confirmed that life expectancy in the
Data from numerous large cohort registries confirmed that life expectancy in the MS population is reduced by 7 to 14 years compared with the general, healthy population. At least 50% of patients die from causes directly related to MS.
5:00pm:
My sister isn't allowed to tell me what's wrong but said I should reach out.
7:42pm:
Hey, what's going on?
10:00pm:
I'm worried, I haven't hea
from you all day and
didn't come to clas
tonight.

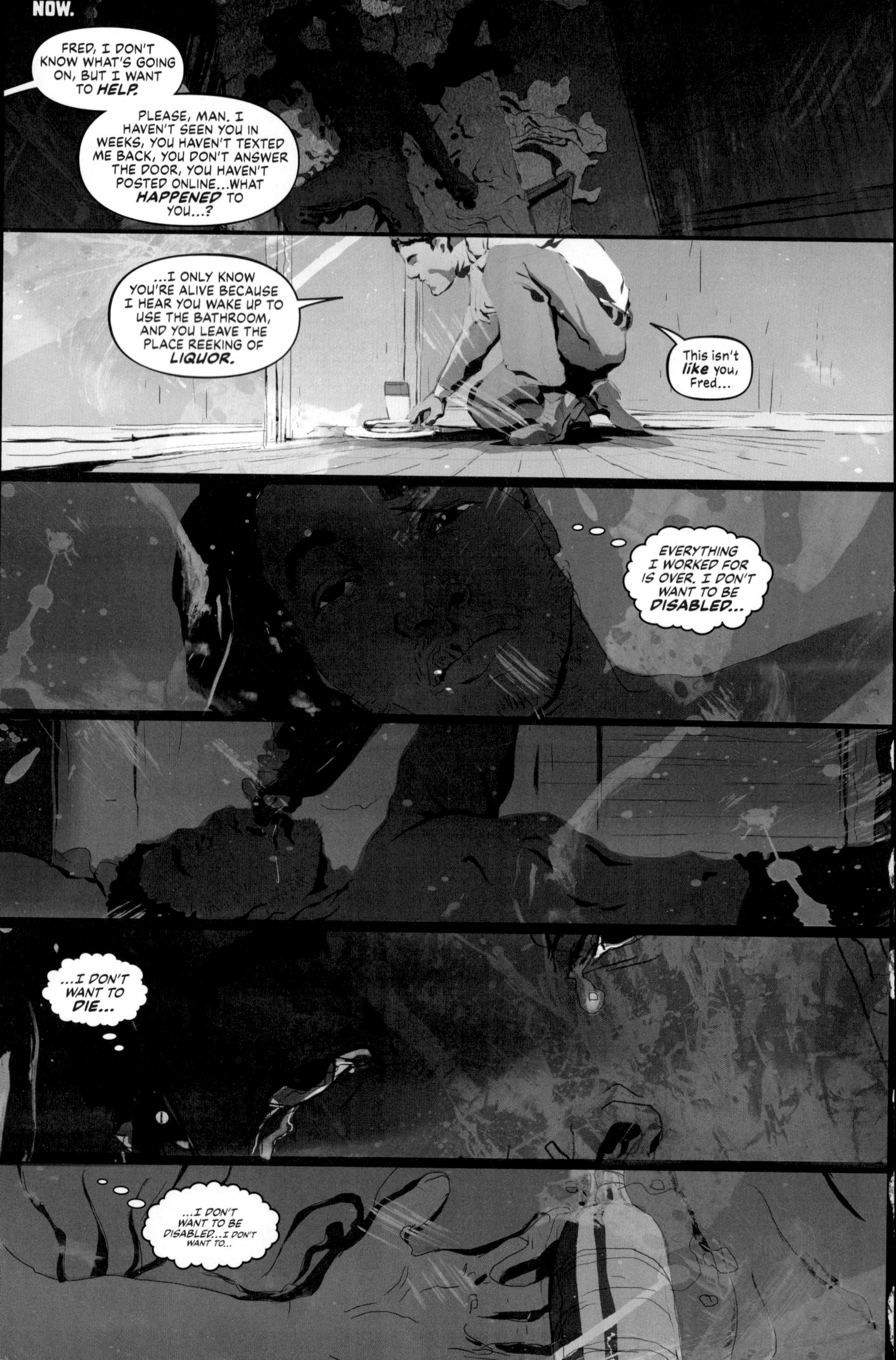
NOW.
FRED, I DON'T KNOW WHAT'S GOING ON, BUT I WANT TO HELP.
PLEASE, MAN. I HAVEN'T SEEN YOU IN WEEKS, YOU HAVEN'T TEXTED ME BACK, YOU DON'T ANSWER THE DOOR, YOU HAVEN'T POSTED ONLINE...WHAT HAPPENED TO YOU...?
...I ONLY KNOW YOU'RE ALIVE BECAUSE I HEAR YOU WAKE UP TO USE THE BATHROOM, AND YOU LEAVE THE PLACE REEKING OF LIQUOR.
This isn't like you, Fred...
EVERYTHING I WORKED FOR IS OVER. I DON'T WANT TO BE DISABLED...
...I DON'T WANT TO DIE...
...I DON'T WANT TO BE DISABLED...I DON'T WANT TO...

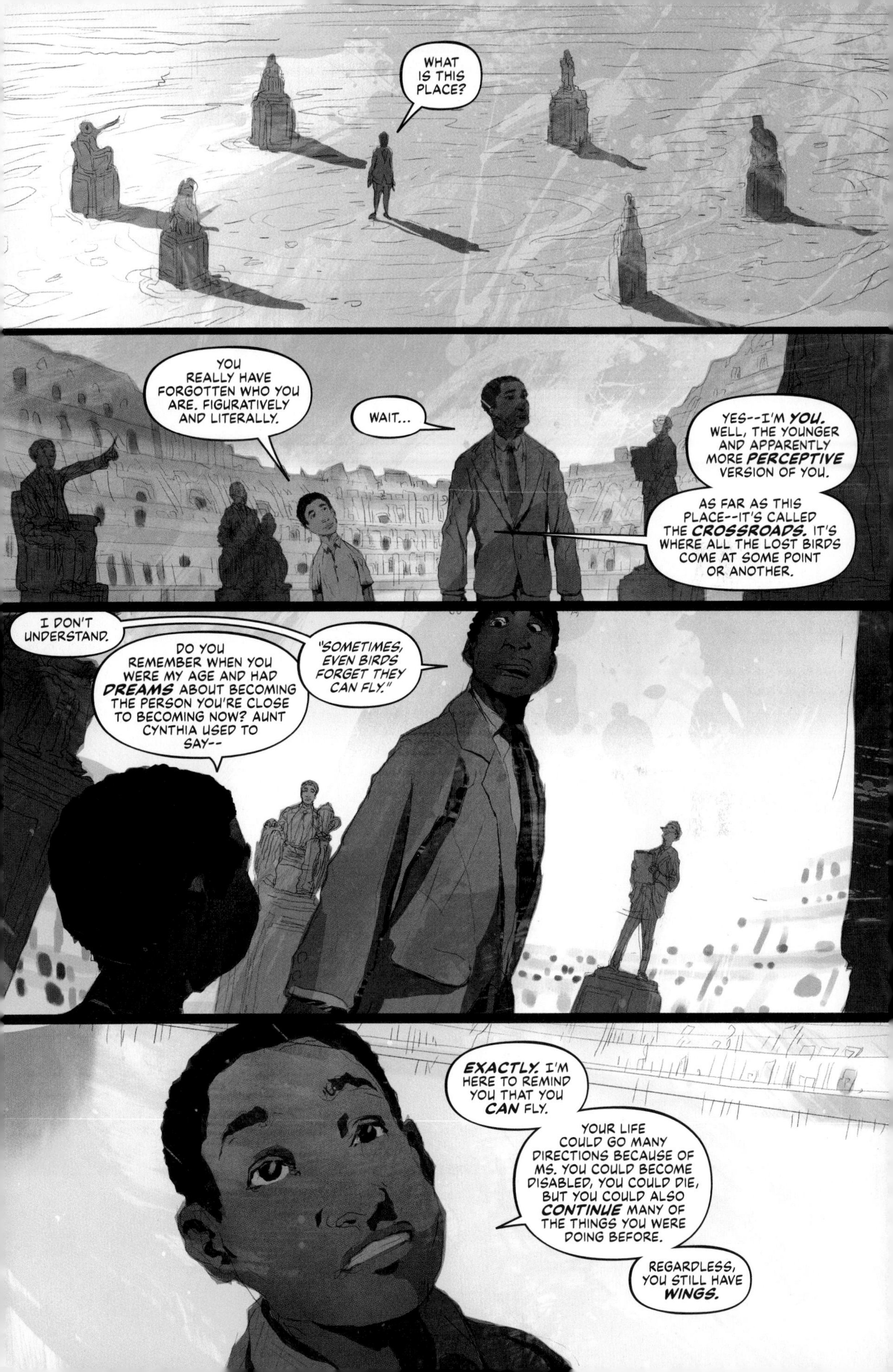
WHAT IS THIS PLACE?
YOU REALLY HAVE FORGOTTEN WHO YOU ARE. FIGURATIVELY AND LITERALLY.
WAIT...
YES--I'M YOU. WELL, THE YOUNGER AND APPARENTLY MORE PERCEPTIVE VERSION OF YOU.
AS FAR AS THIS PLACE--IT'S CALLED THE CROSSROADS. IT'S WHERE ALL THE LOST BIRDS COME AT SOME POINT OR ANOTHER.
I DON'T UNDERSTAND.
DO YOU REMEMBER WHEN YOU WERE MY AGE AND HAD DREAMS ABOUT BECOMING THE PERSON YOU'RE CLOSE TO BECOMING NOW? AUNT CYNTHIA USED TO SAY--
"SOMETIMES, EVEN BIRDS FORGET THEY CAN FLY."
EXACTLY. I'M HERE TO REMIND YOU THAT YOU CAN FLY.
YOUR LIFE COULD GO MANY DIRECTIONS BECAUSE OF MS. YOU COULD BECOME DISABLED, YOU COULD DIE, BUT YOU COULD ALSO CONTINUE MANY OF THE THINGS YOU WERE DOING BEFORE.
REGARDLESS, YOU STILL HAVE WINGS.

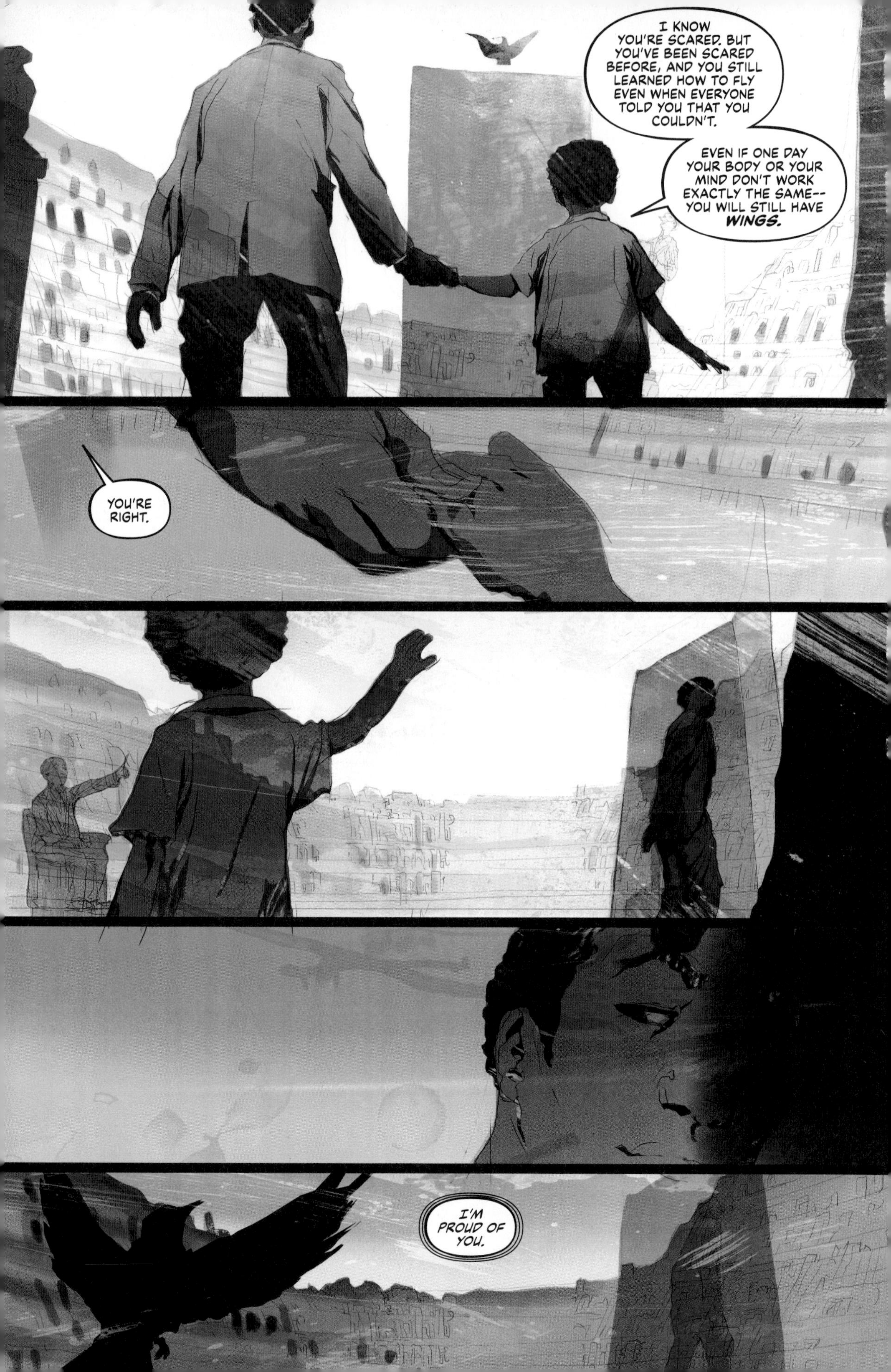
I KNOW YOU'RE SCARED. BUT YOU'VE BEEN SCARED BEFORE, AND YOU STILL LEARNED HOW TO FLY EVEN WHEN EVERYONE TOLD YOU THAT YOU COULDN'T.
EVEN IF ONE DAY YOUR BODY OR YOUR MIND DON'T WORK EXACTLY THE SAME-- YOU WILL STILL HAVE *WINGS.*
YOU'RE RIGHT.
I'M PROUD OF YOU.

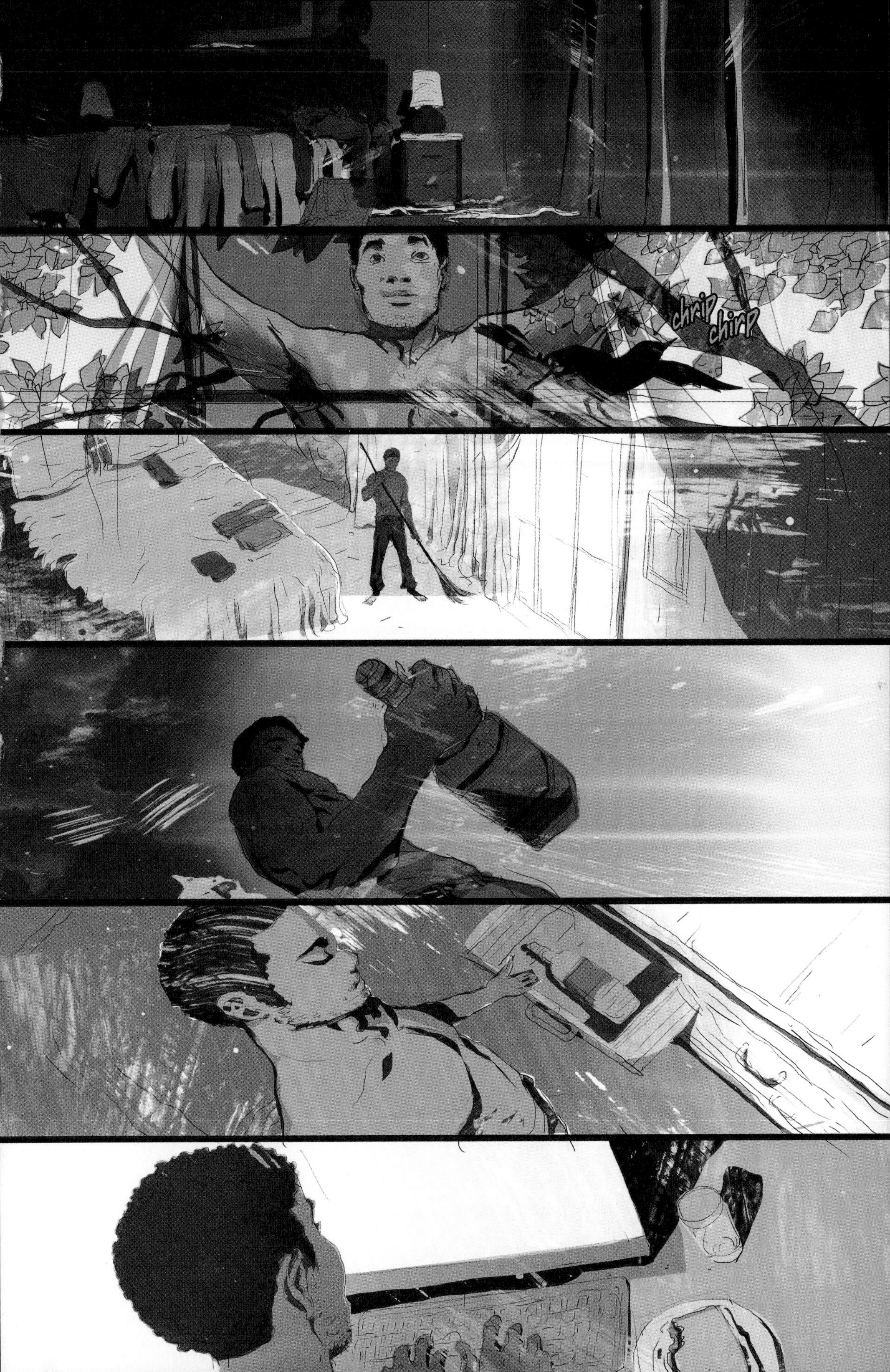
chrip chirp

HERE GOES NOTHING...

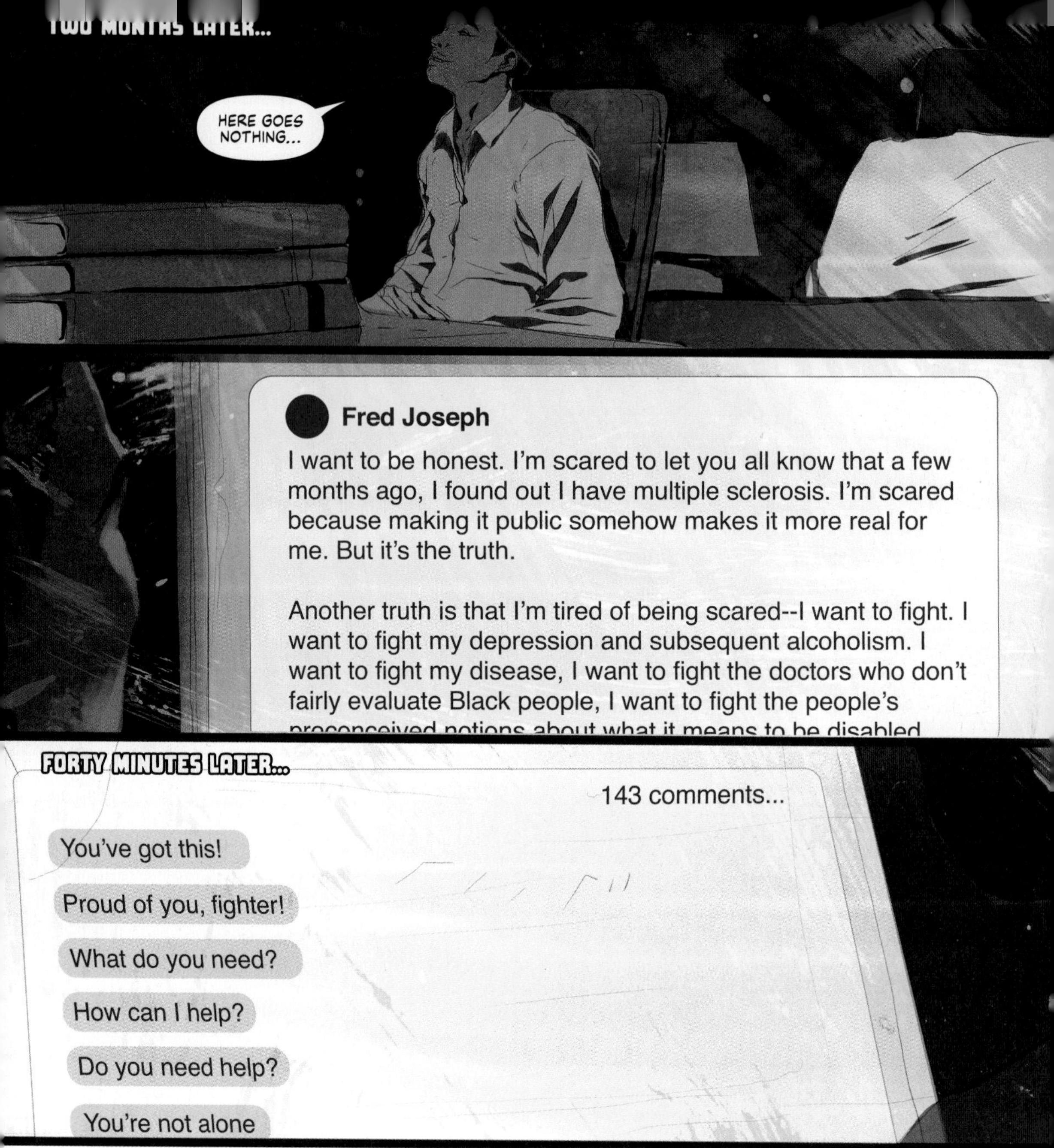

Fred Joseph

I want to be honest. I'm scared to let you all know that a few months ago, I found out I have multiple sclerosis. I'm scared because making it public somehow makes it more real for me. But it's the truth.

Another truth is that I'm tired of being scared--I want to fight. I want to fight my depression and subsequent alcoholism. I want to fight my disease, I want to fight the doctors who don't fairly evaluate Black people, I want to fight the people's preconceived notions about what it means to be disabled

FORTY MINUTES LATER...

143 comments...

You've got this!

Proud of you, fighter!

What do you need?

How can I help?

Do you need help?

You're not alone

Hey Fred,

I know it's been a while since freshman year of college, but I wanted to reach out about your post telling people you have multiple sclerosis. My father and I also have MS, and I wanted to let you know I'm here if you ever need me.

I know it can feel like it sometimes--but you're not alone. Let's fight.

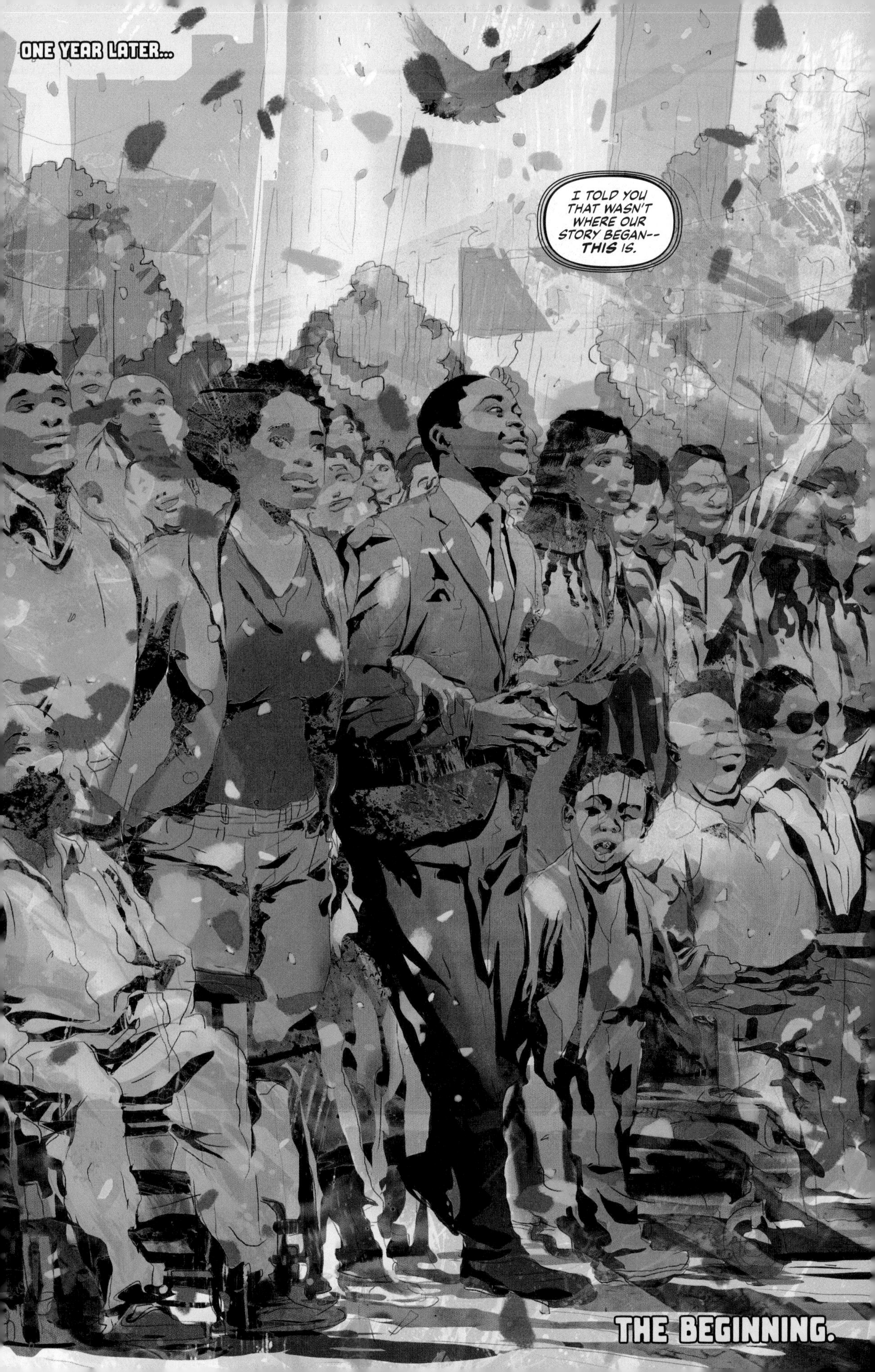
ONE YEAR LATER...
I TOLD YOU THAT WASN'T WHERE OUR STORY BEGAN-- THIS IS.
THE BEGINNING.

CHAPTER ELEVEN
"AMERICAN MONGREL"

WRITER & ARTIST - GABE ELTAEB

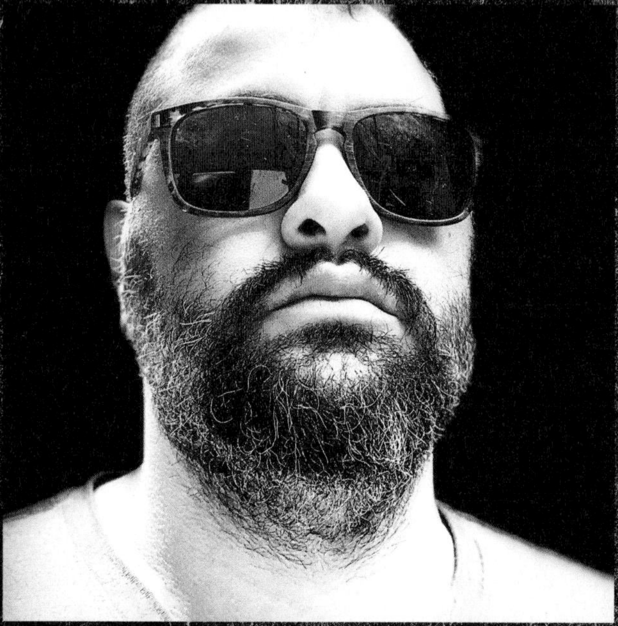

Gabriel Abdulati Eltaeb was born in Greeley, Colorado, in 1978. He has been drawing ever since he can remember. At 13 years old, he fell in love with comics when he saw *X-Men* #1 by Jim Lee, Scott Williams, and Chris Claremont. He decided then and there that when he grew up, he would be a comic book artist working alongside Lee, his artistic hero. A wedding, three children, a college degree, multiple small art jobs, and a few dozen rejection letters later, Gabe was hired to work at WildStorm in the fall of 2007. Gabe has been a freelance comic book color artist since 2011. He lives in San Diego with his lovely wife, Adrienne, and his two older children, Minnie and Peter.

LETTERER - DERON BENNETT

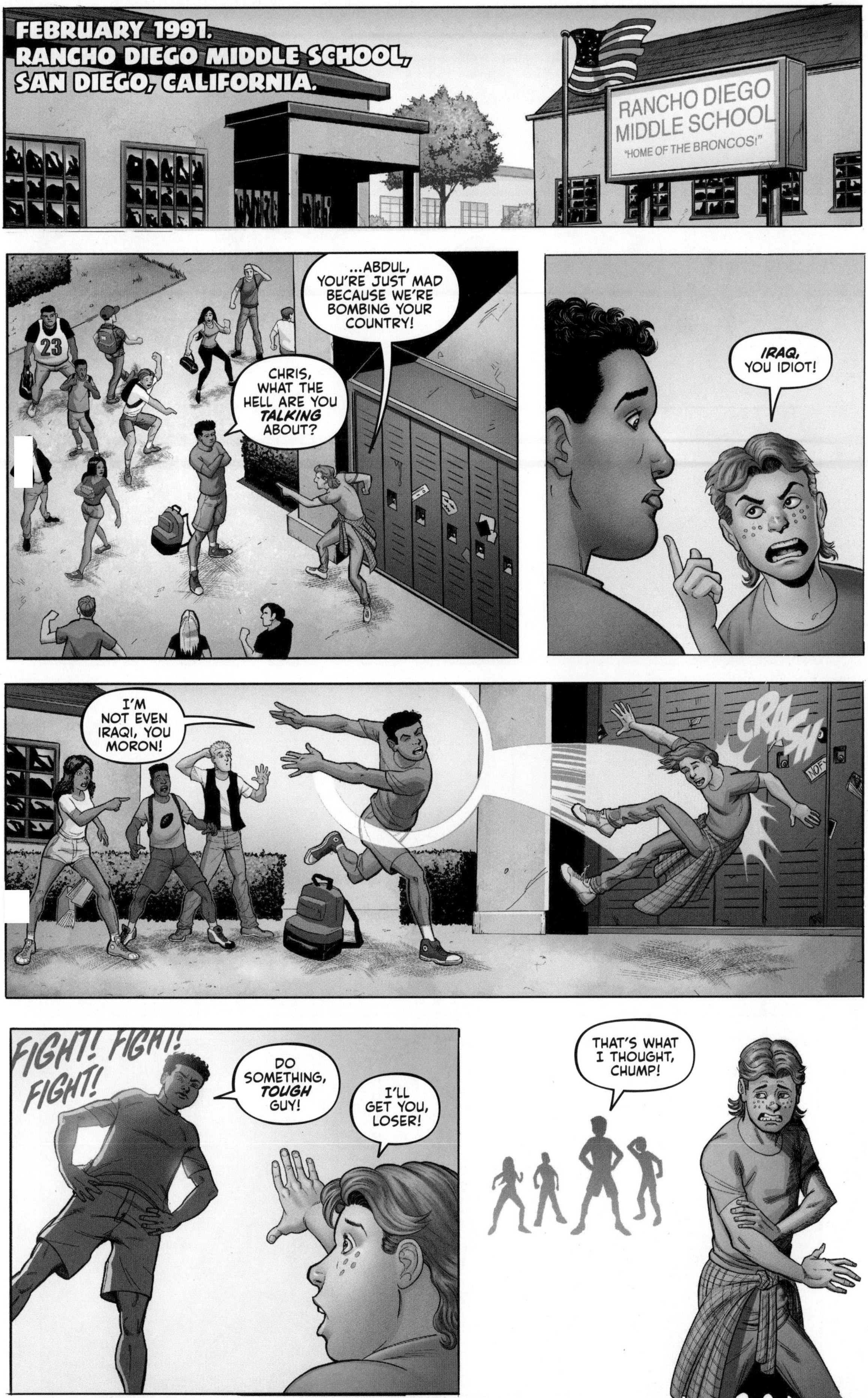

FEBRUARY 1991. RANCHO DIEGO MIDDLE SCHOOL, SAN DIEGO, CALIFORNIA.
RANCHO DIEGO MIDDLE SCHOOL
"HOME OF THE BRONCOS!"
...ABDUL, YOU'RE JUST MAD BECAUSE WE'RE BOMBING YOUR COUNTRY!
CHRIS, WHAT THE HELL ARE YOU *TALKING* ABOUT?
IRAQ, YOU IDIOT!
I'M NOT EVEN IRAQI, YOU MORON!
CRASH
FIGHT! FIGHT! FIGHT!
DO SOMETHING, *TOUGH* GUY!
I'LL GET YOU, LOSER!
THAT'S WHAT I THOUGHT, CHUMP!

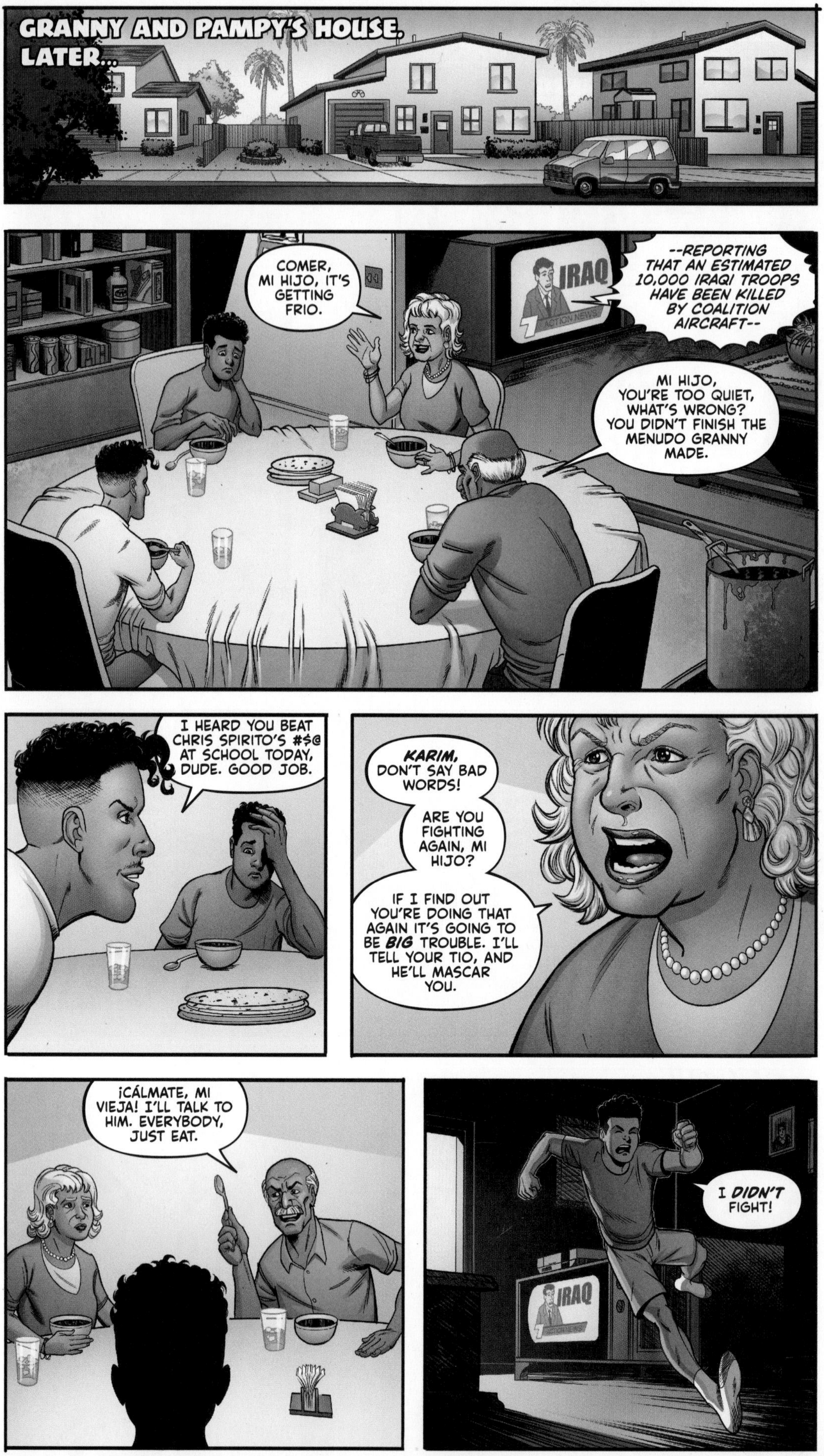
GRANNY AND PAMPY'S HOUSE. LATER...
COMER, MI HIJO, IT'S GETTING FRIO.
--REPORTING THAT AN ESTIMATED 10,000 IRAQI TROOPS HAVE BEEN KILLED BY COALITION AIRCRAFT--
IRAQ
7 ACTION NEWS
MI HIJO, YOU'RE TOO QUIET, WHAT'S WRONG? YOU DIDN'T FINISH THE MENUDO GRANNY MADE.
I HEARD YOU BEAT CHRIS SPIRITO'S #$@ AT SCHOOL TODAY, DUDE. GOOD JOB.
KARIM, DON'T SAY BAD WORDS!
ARE YOU FIGHTING AGAIN, MI HIJO?
IF I FIND OUT YOU'RE DOING THAT AGAIN IT'S GOING TO BE BIG TROUBLE. I'LL TELL YOUR TIO, AND HE'LL MASCAR YOU.
¡CÁLMATE, MI VIEJA! I'LL TALK TO HIM. EVERYBODY, JUST EAT.
IRAQ
I DIDN'T FIGHT!

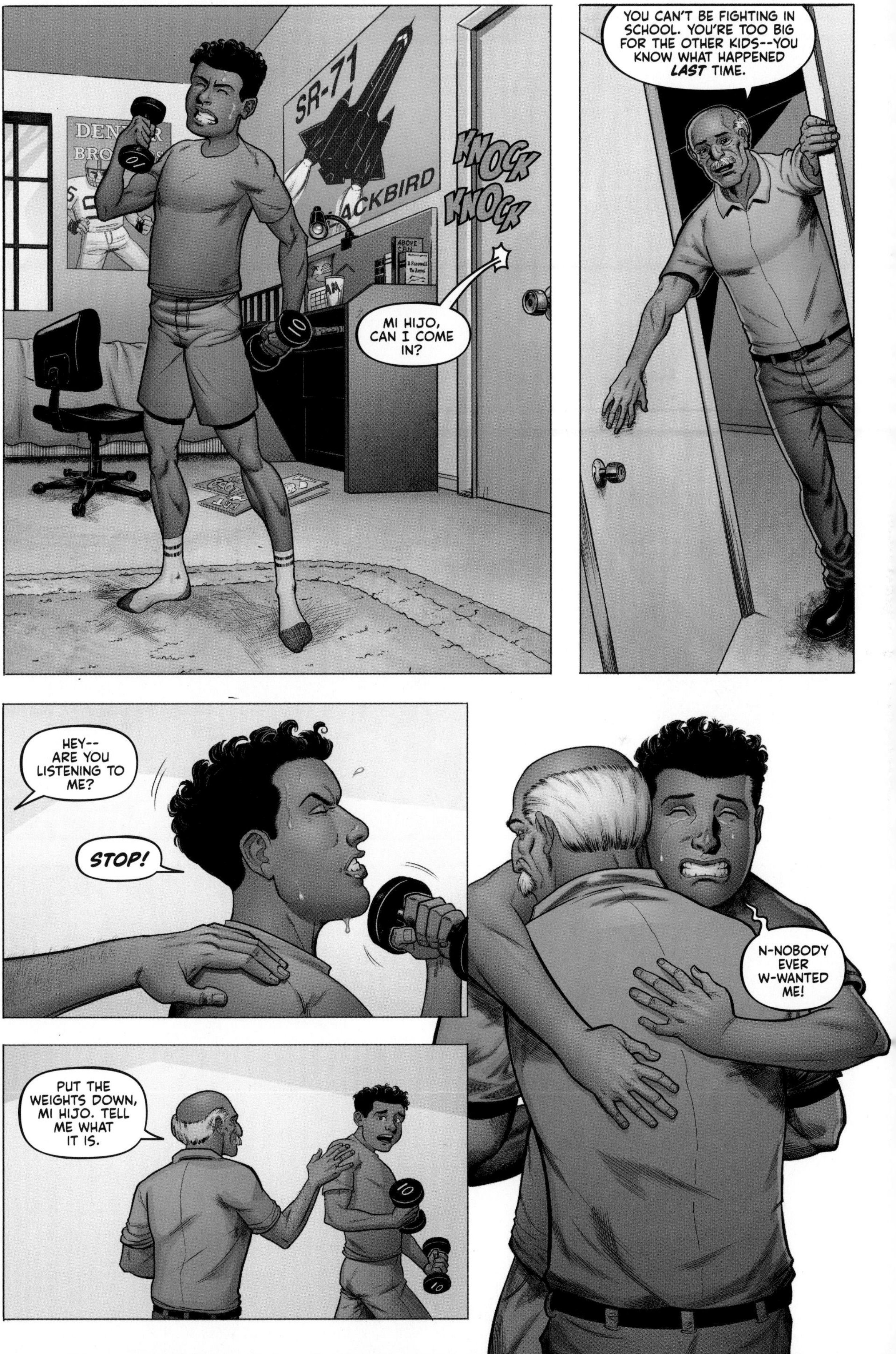
SR-71
BLACKBIRD
KNOCK KNOCK
MI HIJO, CAN I COME IN?
YOU CAN'T BE FIGHTING IN SCHOOL. YOU'RE TOO BIG FOR THE OTHER KIDS--YOU KNOW WHAT HAPPENED LAST TIME.
HEY-- ARE YOU LISTENING TO ME?
STOP!
PUT THE WEIGHTS DOWN, MI HIJO. TELL ME WHAT IT IS.
N-NOBODY EVER W-WANTED ME!

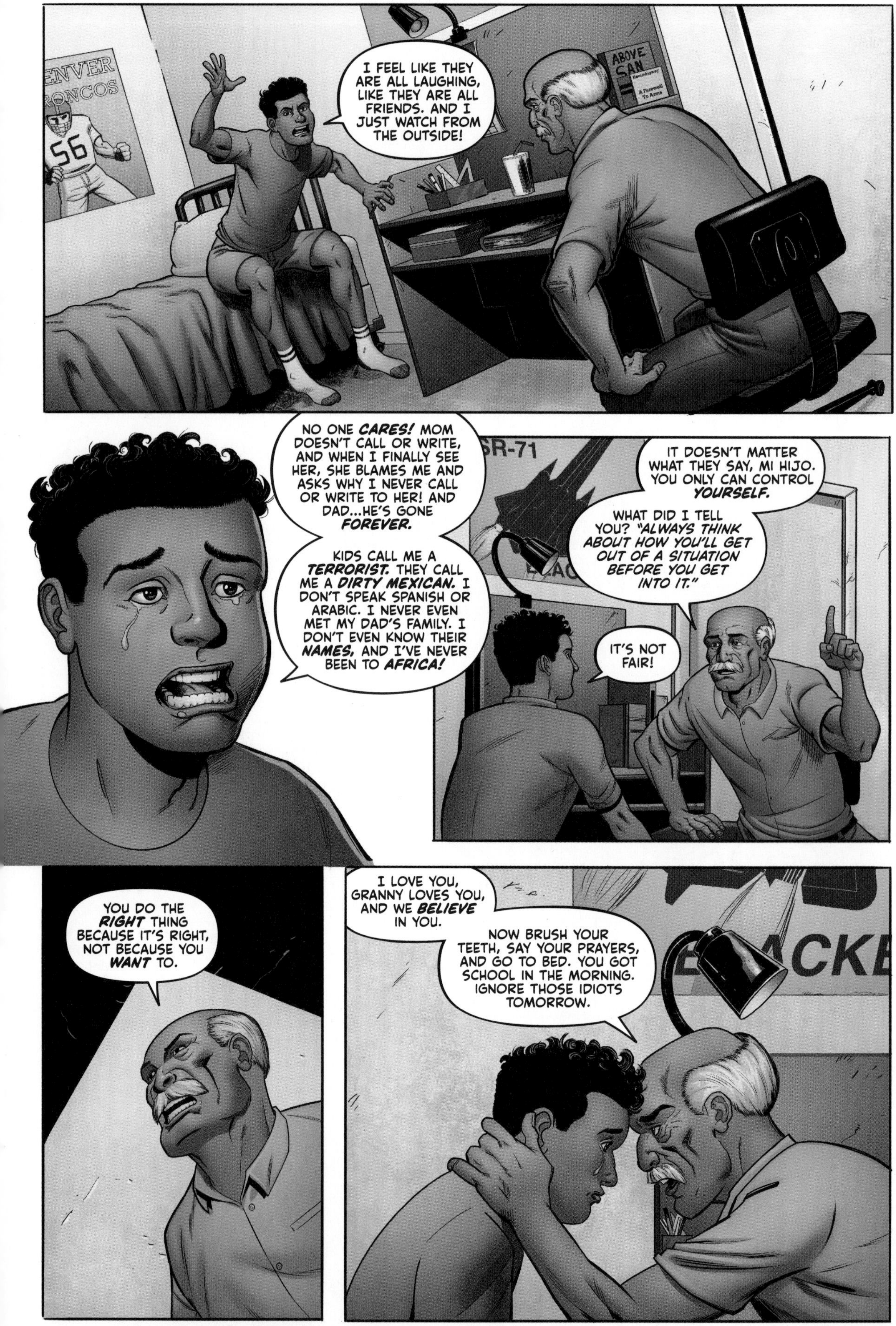

DENVER BRONCOS
56
I FEEL LIKE THEY ARE ALL LAUGHING, LIKE THEY ARE ALL FRIENDS. AND I JUST WATCH FROM THE OUTSIDE!
ABOVE SAN
A Farewell To Arms
NO ONE CARES! MOM DOESN'T CALL OR WRITE, AND WHEN I FINALLY SEE HER, SHE BLAMES ME AND ASKS WHY I NEVER CALL OR WRITE TO HER! AND DAD...HE'S GONE FOREVER.
KIDS CALL ME A TERRORIST. THEY CALL ME A DIRTY MEXICAN. I DON'T SPEAK SPANISH OR ARABIC. I NEVER EVEN MET MY DAD'S FAMILY. I DON'T EVEN KNOW THEIR NAMES, AND I'VE NEVER BEEN TO AFRICA!
SR-71
IT DOESN'T MATTER WHAT THEY SAY, MI HIJO. YOU ONLY CAN CONTROL YOURSELF.
WHAT DID I TELL YOU? "ALWAYS THINK ABOUT HOW YOU'LL GET OUT OF A SITUATION BEFORE YOU GET INTO IT."
IT'S NOT FAIR!
YOU DO THE RIGHT THING BECAUSE IT'S RIGHT, NOT BECAUSE YOU WANT TO.
I LOVE YOU, GRANNY LOVES YOU, AND WE BELIEVE IN YOU.
NOW BRUSH YOUR TEETH, SAY YOUR PRAYERS, AND GO TO BED. YOU GOT SCHOOL IN THE MORNING. IGNORE THOSE IDIOTS TOMORROW.

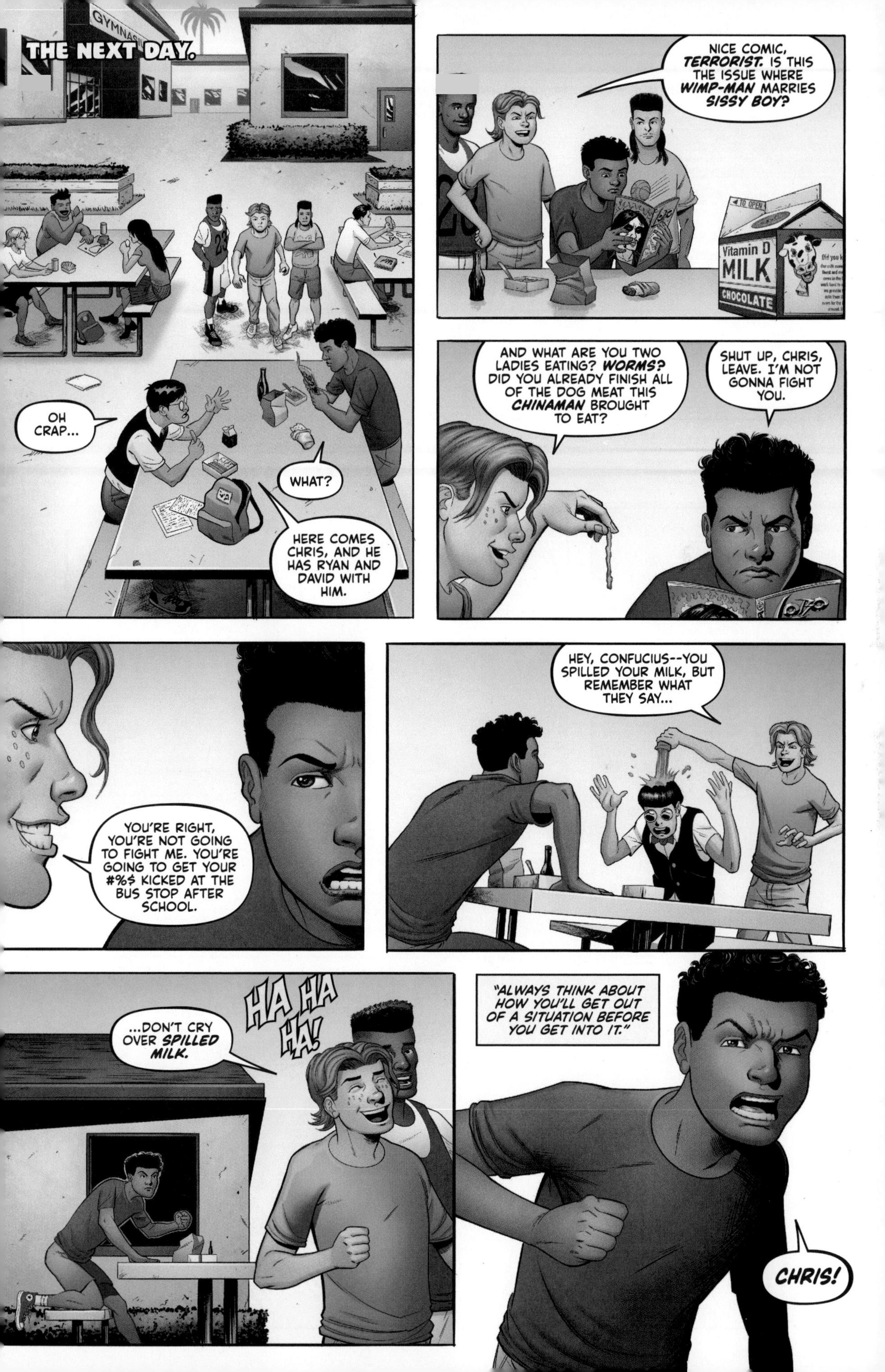
THE NEXT DAY.
GYMNASIU
OH CRAP...
WHAT?
HERE COMES CHRIS, AND HE HAS RYAN AND DAVID WITH HIM.
NICE COMIC, TERRORIST. IS THIS THE ISSUE WHERE WIMP-MAN MARRIES SISSY BOY?
TO OPEN
Vitamin D MILK
CHOCOLATE
AND WHAT ARE YOU TWO LADIES EATING? WORMS? DID YOU ALREADY FINISH ALL OF THE DOG MEAT THIS CHINAMAN BROUGHT TO EAT?
SHUT UP, CHRIS, LEAVE. I'M NOT GONNA FIGHT YOU.
YOU'RE RIGHT, YOU'RE NOT GOING TO FIGHT ME. YOU'RE GOING TO GET YOUR #%$ KICKED AT THE BUS STOP AFTER SCHOOL.
HEY, CONFUCIUS--YOU SPILLED YOUR MILK, BUT REMEMBER WHAT THEY SAY...
...DON'T CRY OVER SPILLED MILK.
HA HA HA!
"ALWAYS THINK ABOUT HOW YOU'LL GET OUT OF A SITUATION BEFORE YOU GET INTO IT."
CHRIS!

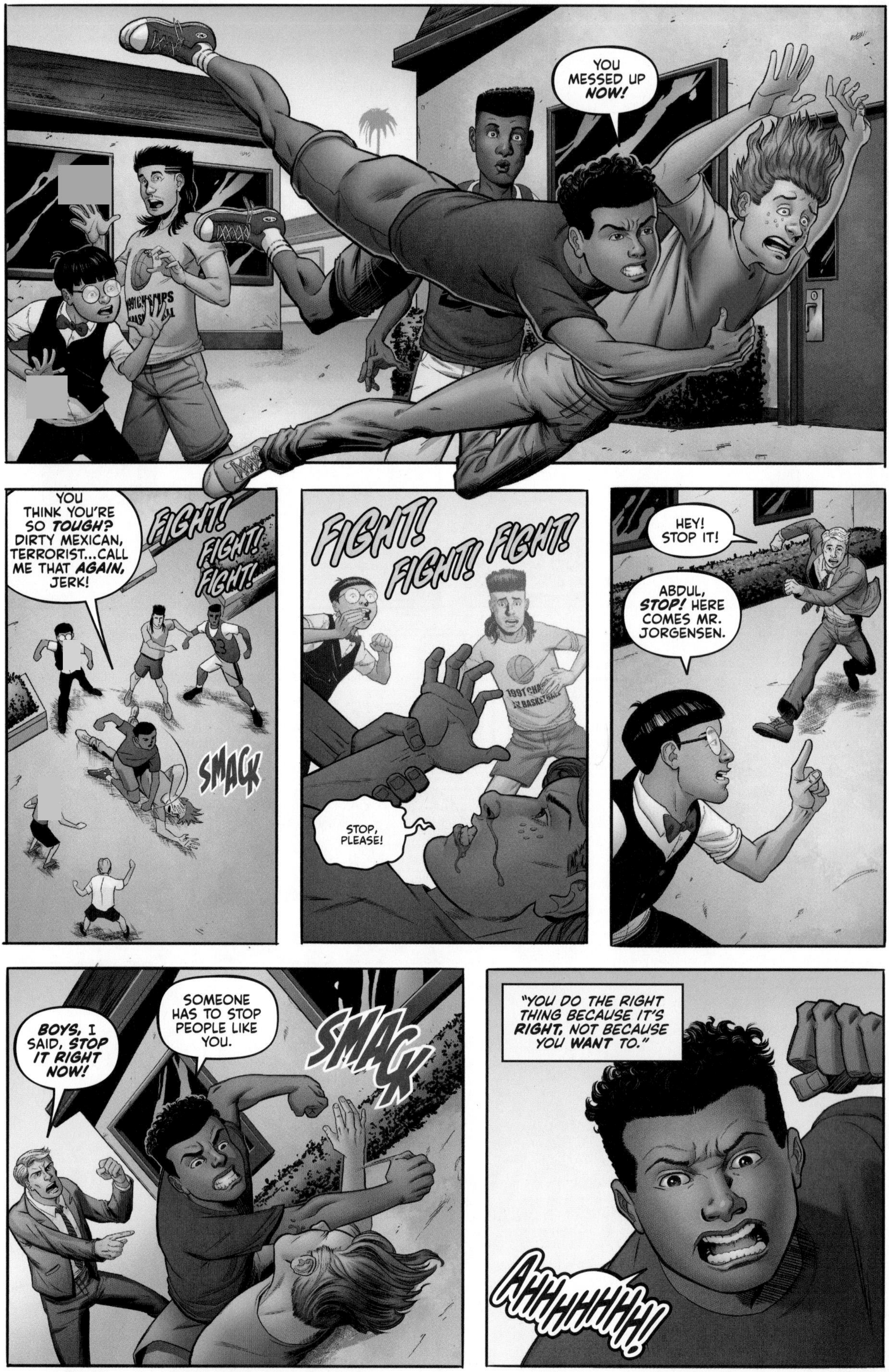
YOU MESSED UP NOW!
YOU THINK YOU'RE SO TOUGH? DIRTY MEXICAN, TERRORIST...CALL ME THAT AGAIN, JERK!
FIGHT! FIGHT! FIGHT!
SMACK
FIGHT! FIGHT! FIGHT!
STOP, PLEASE!
HEY! STOP IT!
ABDUL, STOP! HERE COMES MR. JORGENSEN.
BOYS, I SAID, STOP IT RIGHT NOW!
SOMEONE HAS TO STOP PEOPLE LIKE YOU.
SMACK
"YOU DO THE RIGHT THING BECAUSE IT'S RIGHT, NOT BECAUSE YOU WANT TO."
AHHHHHHH!

LATER...

FIVE DAYS...

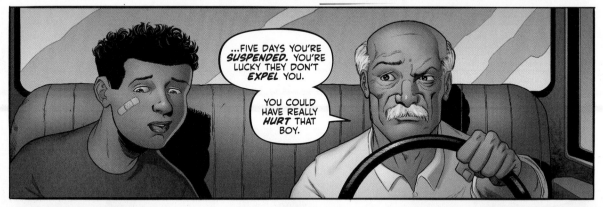

...FIVE DAYS YOU'RE *SUSPENDED.* YOU'RE LUCKY THEY DON'T *EXPEL* YOU.

YOU COULD HAVE REALLY *HURT* THAT BOY.

HE *DESERVED* IT. HE CALLED ME A TERRORIST AND SAID SEAN EATS *DOGS!*

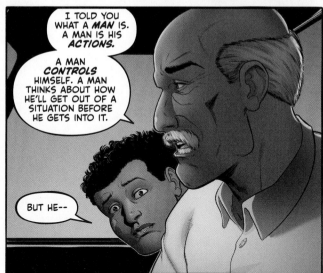

I TOLD YOU WHAT A *MAN* IS. A MAN IS HIS *ACTIONS.*

A MAN *CONTROLS* HIMSELF. A MAN THINKS ABOUT HOW HE'LL GET OUT OF A SITUATION BEFORE HE GETS INTO IT.

BUT HE--

¡YA PÁRALE! SILENCIO!

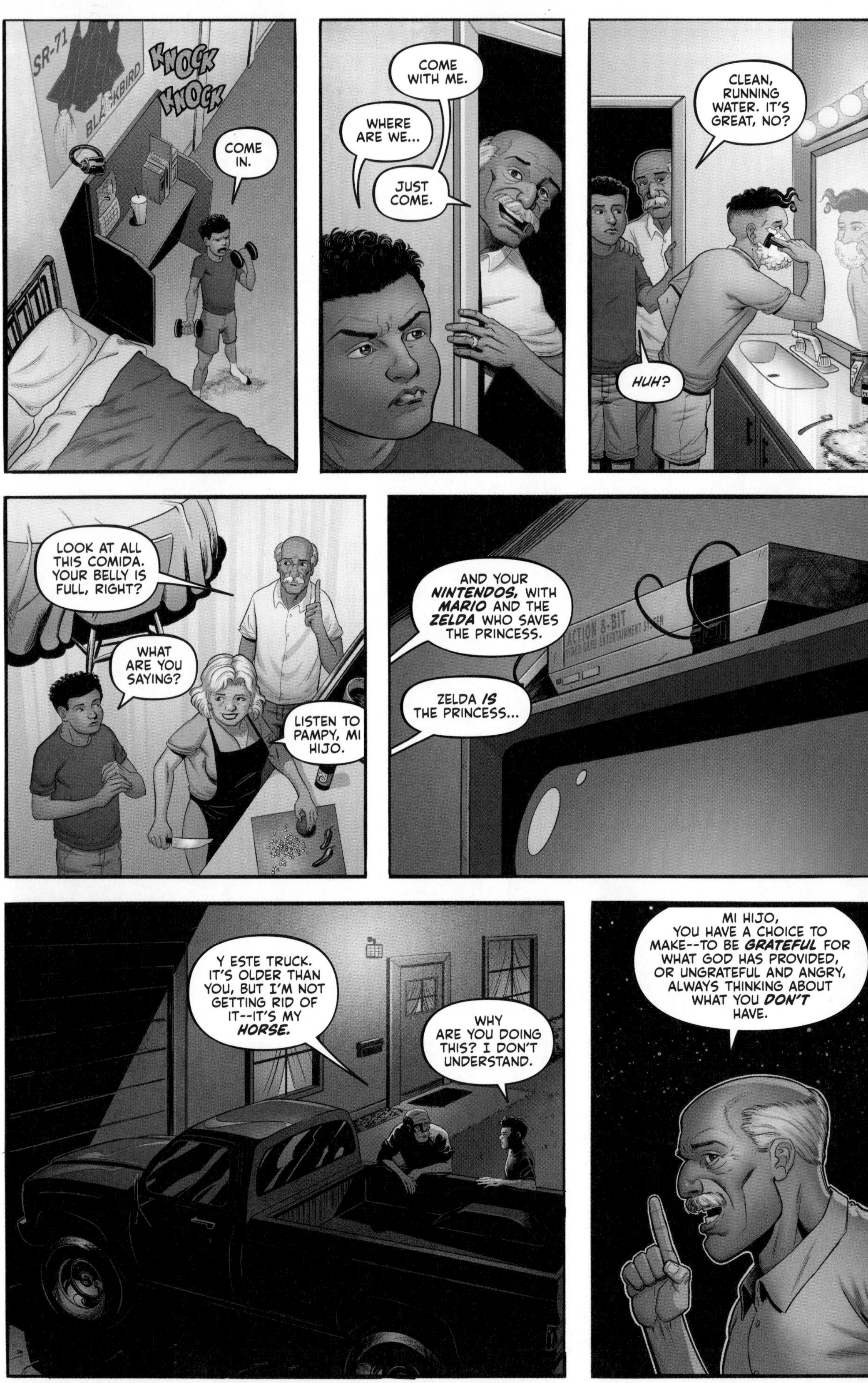
SR-71
BLACKBIRD
KNOCK KNOCK
COME IN.
COME WITH ME.
WHERE ARE WE...
JUST COME.
CLEAN, RUNNING WATER. IT'S GREAT, NO?
HUH?
LOOK AT ALL THIS COMIDA. YOUR BELLY IS FULL, RIGHT?
WHAT ARE YOU SAYING?
LISTEN TO PAMPY, MI HIJO.
AND YOUR NINTENDOS, WITH MARIO AND THE ZELDA WHO SAVES THE PRINCESS.
ZELDA IS THE PRINCESS...
ACTION 8-BIT
Y ESTE TRUCK. IT'S OLDER THAN YOU, BUT I'M NOT GETTING RID OF IT--IT'S MY HORSE.
WHY ARE YOU DOING THIS? I DON'T UNDERSTAND.
MI HIJO, YOU HAVE A CHOICE TO MAKE--TO BE GRATEFUL FOR WHAT GOD HAS PROVIDED, OR UNGRATEFUL AND ANGRY, ALWAYS THINKING ABOUT WHAT YOU DON'T HAVE.

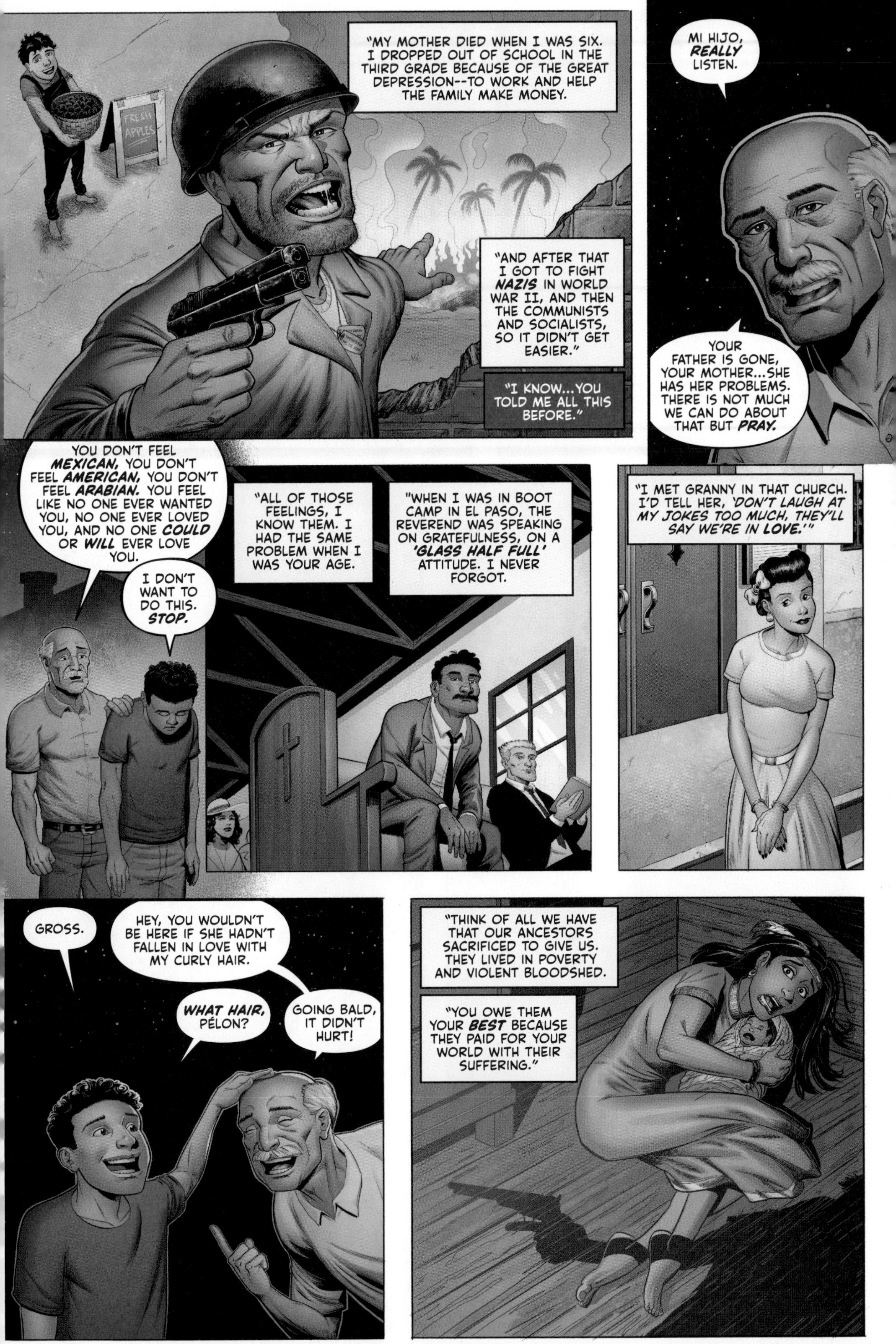

FRESH APPLES
"MY MOTHER DIED WHEN I WAS SIX. I DROPPED OUT OF SCHOOL IN THE THIRD GRADE BECAUSE OF THE GREAT DEPRESSION--TO WORK AND HELP THE FAMILY MAKE MONEY.
"AND AFTER THAT I GOT TO FIGHT NAZIS IN WORLD WAR II, AND THEN THE COMMUNISTS AND SOCIALISTS, SO IT DIDN'T GET EASIER."
"I KNOW...YOU TOLD ME ALL THIS BEFORE."
MI HIJO, REALLY LISTEN.
YOUR FATHER IS GONE, YOUR MOTHER...SHE HAS HER PROBLEMS. THERE IS NOT MUCH WE CAN DO ABOUT THAT BUT PRAY.
YOU DON'T FEEL MEXICAN, YOU DON'T FEEL AMERICAN, YOU DON'T FEEL ARABIAN. YOU FEEL LIKE NO ONE EVER WANTED YOU, NO ONE EVER LOVED YOU, AND NO ONE COULD OR WILL EVER LOVE YOU.
I DON'T WANT TO DO THIS. STOP.
"ALL OF THOSE FEELINGS, I KNOW THEM. I HAD THE SAME PROBLEM WHEN I WAS YOUR AGE.
"WHEN I WAS IN BOOT CAMP IN EL PASO, THE REVEREND WAS SPEAKING ON GRATEFULNESS, ON A 'GLASS HALF FULL' ATTITUDE. I NEVER FORGOT.
"I MET GRANNY IN THAT CHURCH. I'D TELL HER, 'DON'T LAUGH AT MY JOKES TOO MUCH, THEY'LL SAY WE'RE IN LOVE.'"
GROSS.
HEY, YOU WOULDN'T BE HERE IF SHE HADN'T FALLEN IN LOVE WITH MY CURLY HAIR.
WHAT HAIR, PÉLON?
GOING BALD, IT DIDN'T HURT!
"THINK OF ALL WE HAVE THAT OUR ANCESTORS SACRIFICED TO GIVE US. THEY LIVED IN POVERTY AND VIOLENT BLOODSHED.
"YOU OWE THEM YOUR BEST BECAUSE THEY PAID FOR YOUR WORLD WITH THEIR SUFFERING."

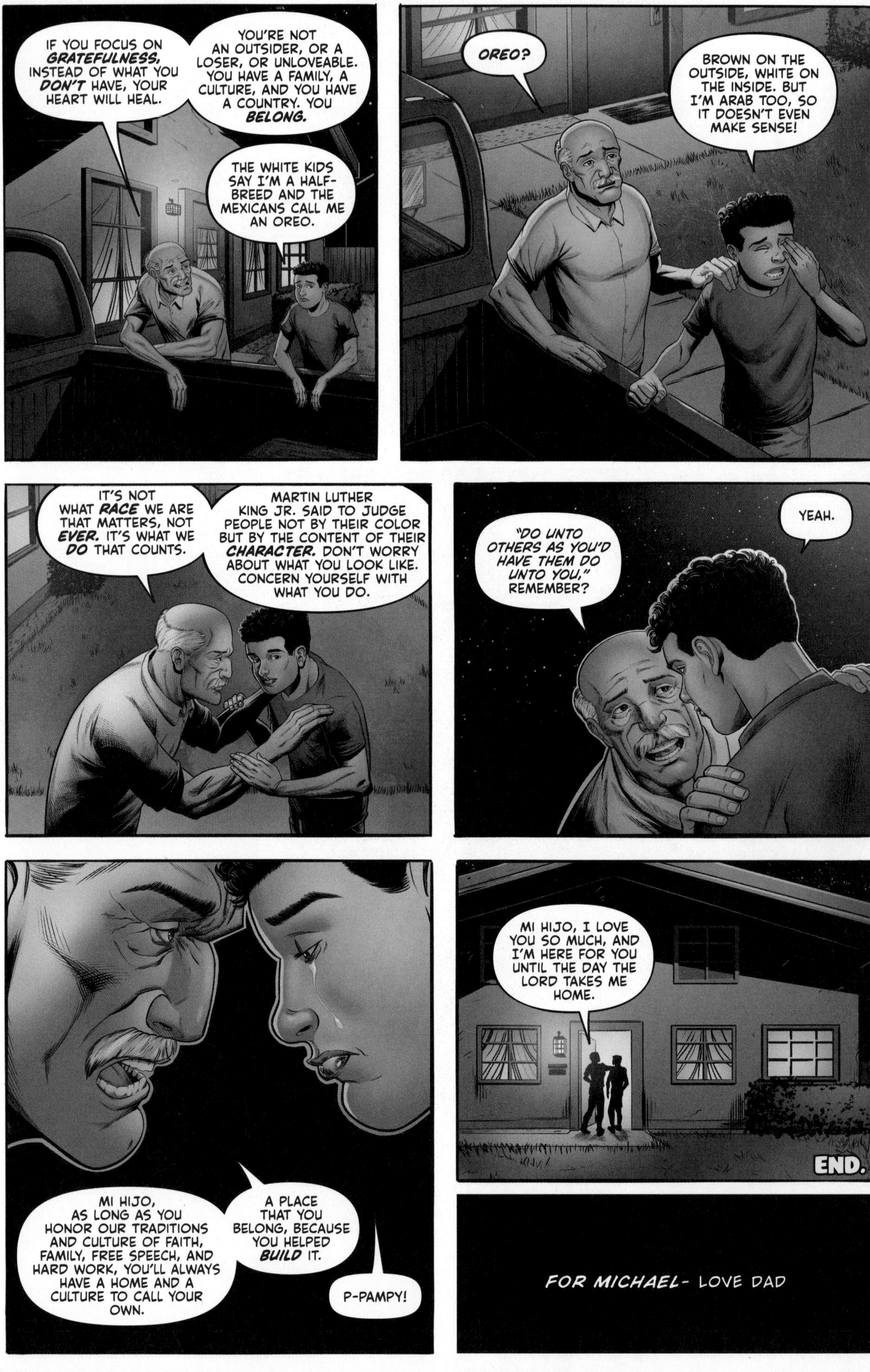
IF YOU FOCUS ON GRATEFULNESS, INSTEAD OF WHAT YOU DON'T HAVE, YOUR HEART WILL HEAL.
YOU'RE NOT AN OUTSIDER, OR A LOSER, OR UNLOVEABLE. YOU HAVE A FAMILY, A CULTURE, AND YOU HAVE A COUNTRY. YOU BELONG.
THE WHITE KIDS SAY I'M A HALF-BREED AND THE MEXICANS CALL ME AN OREO.
OREO?
BROWN ON THE OUTSIDE, WHITE ON THE INSIDE. BUT I'M ARAB TOO, SO IT DOESN'T EVEN MAKE SENSE!
IT'S NOT WHAT RACE WE ARE THAT MATTERS, NOT EVER. IT'S WHAT WE DO THAT COUNTS.
MARTIN LUTHER KING JR. SAID TO JUDGE PEOPLE NOT BY THEIR COLOR BUT BY THE CONTENT OF THEIR CHARACTER. DON'T WORRY ABOUT WHAT YOU LOOK LIKE. CONCERN YOURSELF WITH WHAT YOU DO.
"DO UNTO OTHERS AS YOU'D HAVE THEM DO UNTO YOU," REMEMBER?
YEAH.
MI HIJO, AS LONG AS YOU HONOR OUR TRADITIONS AND CULTURE OF FAITH, FAMILY, FREE SPEECH, AND HARD WORK, YOU'LL ALWAYS HAVE A HOME AND A CULTURE TO CALL YOUR OWN.
A PLACE THAT YOU BELONG, BECAUSE YOU HELPED BUILD IT.
P-PAMPY!
MI HIJO, I LOVE YOU SO MUCH, AND I'M HERE FOR YOU UNTIL THE DAY THE LORD TAKES ME HOME.
END.
FOR MICHAEL- LOVE DAD

DC REPRESENT!

CHAPTER TWELVE

"THE WATER'S EDGE WITHIN REACH"

WRITER - DAN LIBURD

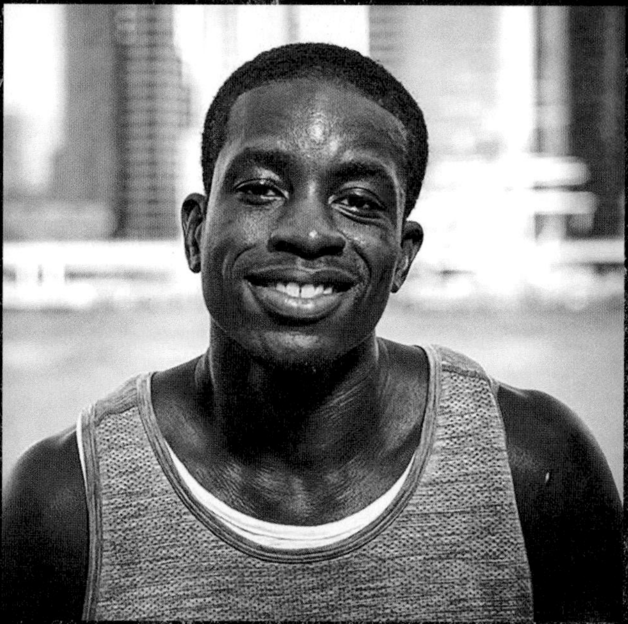

Dan Liburd has over a decade of experience working with professional athletes and as an NFL and NBA strength and conditioning coach. Liburd earned his bachelor's degree in exercise science from Boston University. He received his master of science degree in health and human performance from Canisius College and is currently working toward his PhD in health and human performance at Concordia University Chicago. Liburd holds a variety of certifications in strength and conditioning, health and sport nutrition, Olympic weight lifting, manual therapy techniques, and movement assessment. His professional experience includes stints with several pro teams including the Buffalo Bills and the Pittsburgh Steelers, and he currently works as a head strength and conditioning coach in the NBA. Liburd has also worked as a strength coach for several collegiate strength and conditioning programs including the Boston University Terriers, Springfield College Pride, and American International College Yellow Jackets, and as a performance specialist at private training facilities such as Mike Boyle Strength & Conditioning as well as Peak Performance Physical Therapy.

ARTIST - KOI TURNBULL
COLORIST - TONY AVIÑA
LETTERER - DERON BENNETT

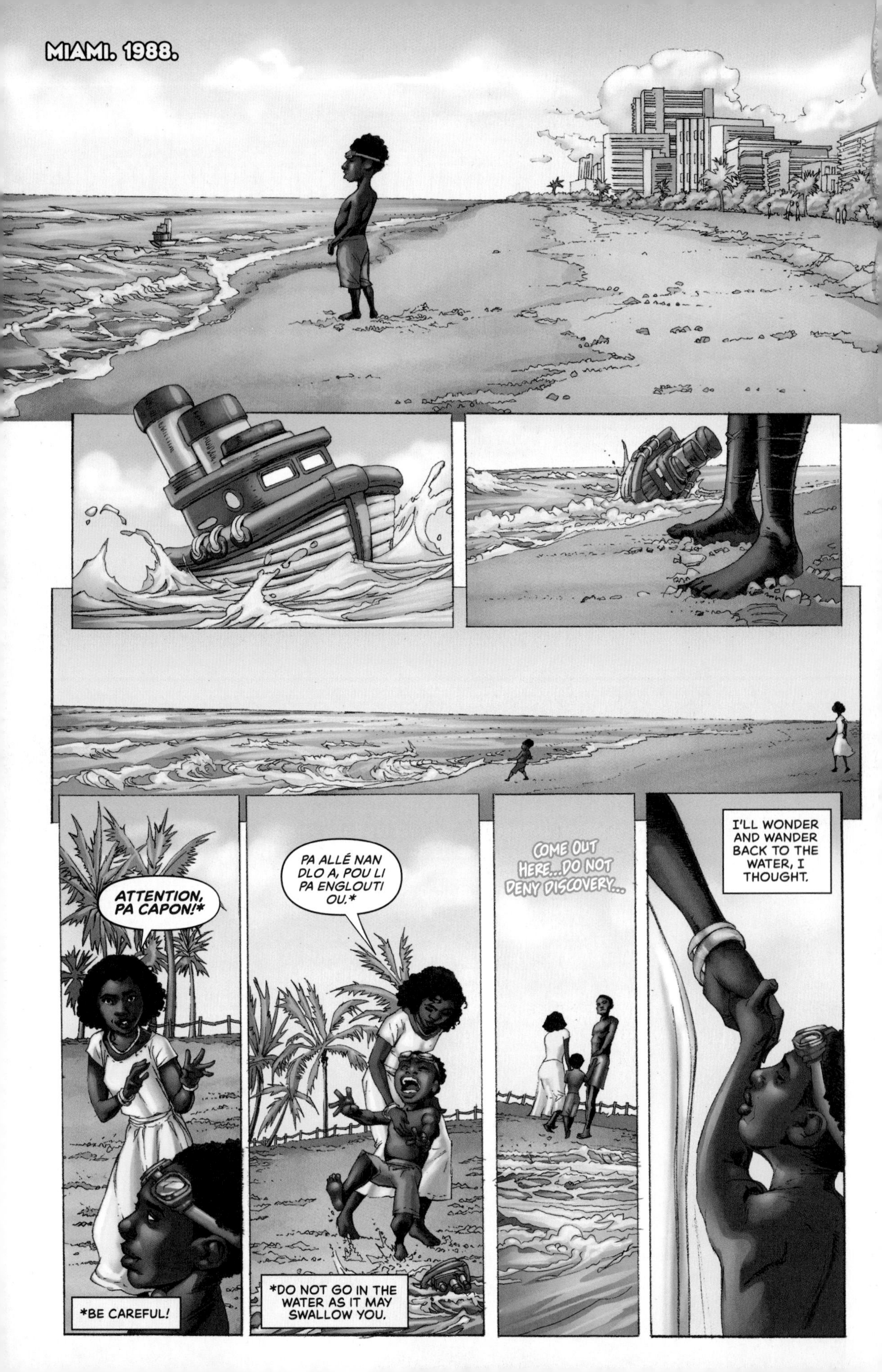

MIAMI. 1988.
ATTENTION, PA CAPON!*
*BE CAREFUL!
PA ALLÉ NAN DLO A, POU LI PA ENGLOUTI OU.*
*DO NOT GO IN THE WATER AS IT MAY SWALLOW YOU.
COME OUT HERE...DO NOT DENY DISCOVERY...
I'LL WONDER AND WANDER BACK TO THE WATER, I THOUGHT.

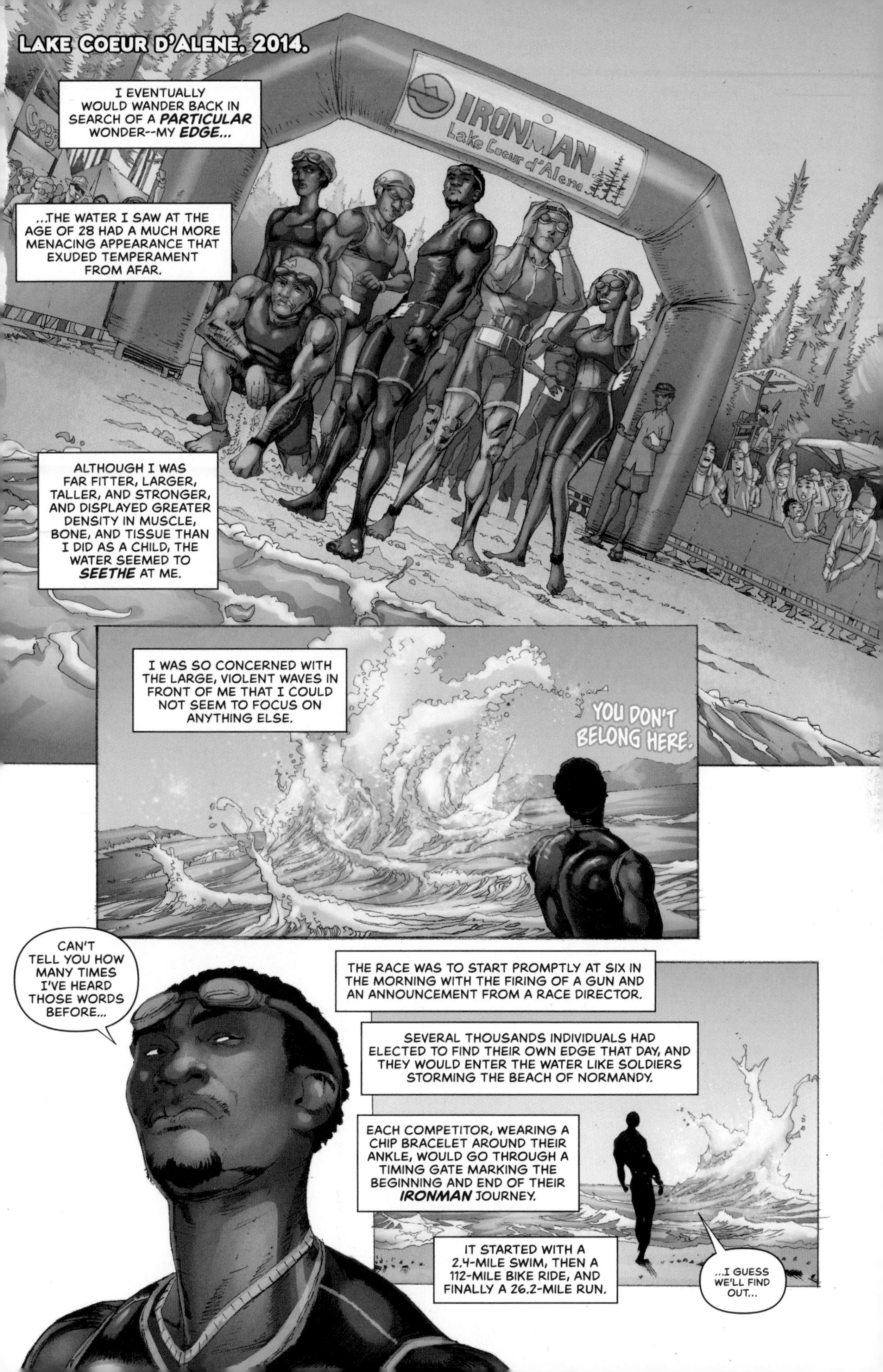
LAKE COEUR D'ALENE. 2014.
I EVENTUALLY WOULD WANDER BACK IN SEARCH OF A PARTICULAR WONDER--MY EDGE...
IRONMAN Lake Coeur d'Alene
...THE WATER I SAW AT THE AGE OF 28 HAD A MUCH MORE MENACING APPEARANCE THAT EXUDED TEMPERAMENT FROM AFAR.
ALTHOUGH I WAS FAR FITTER, LARGER, TALLER, AND STRONGER, AND DISPLAYED GREATER DENSITY IN MUSCLE, BONE, AND TISSUE THAN I DID AS A CHILD, THE WATER SEEMED TO SEETHE AT ME.
I WAS SO CONCERNED WITH THE LARGE, VIOLENT WAVES IN FRONT OF ME THAT I COULD NOT SEEM TO FOCUS ON ANYTHING ELSE.
YOU DON'T BELONG HERE.
CAN'T TELL YOU HOW MANY TIMES I'VE HEARD THOSE WORDS BEFORE...
THE RACE WAS TO START PROMPTLY AT SIX IN THE MORNING WITH THE FIRING OF A GUN AND AN ANNOUNCEMENT FROM A RACE DIRECTOR.
SEVERAL THOUSANDS INDIVIDUALS HAD ELECTED TO FIND THEIR OWN EDGE THAT DAY, AND THEY WOULD ENTER THE WATER LIKE SOLDIERS STORMING THE BEACH OF NORMANDY.
EACH COMPETITOR, WEARING A CHIP BRACELET AROUND THEIR ANKLE, WOULD GO THROUGH A TIMING GATE MARKING THE BEGINNING AND END OF THEIR IRONMAN JOURNEY.
IT STARTED WITH A 2.4-MILE SWIM, THEN A 112-MILE BIKE RIDE, AND FINALLY A 26.2-MILE RUN.
...I GUESS WE'LL FIND OUT...

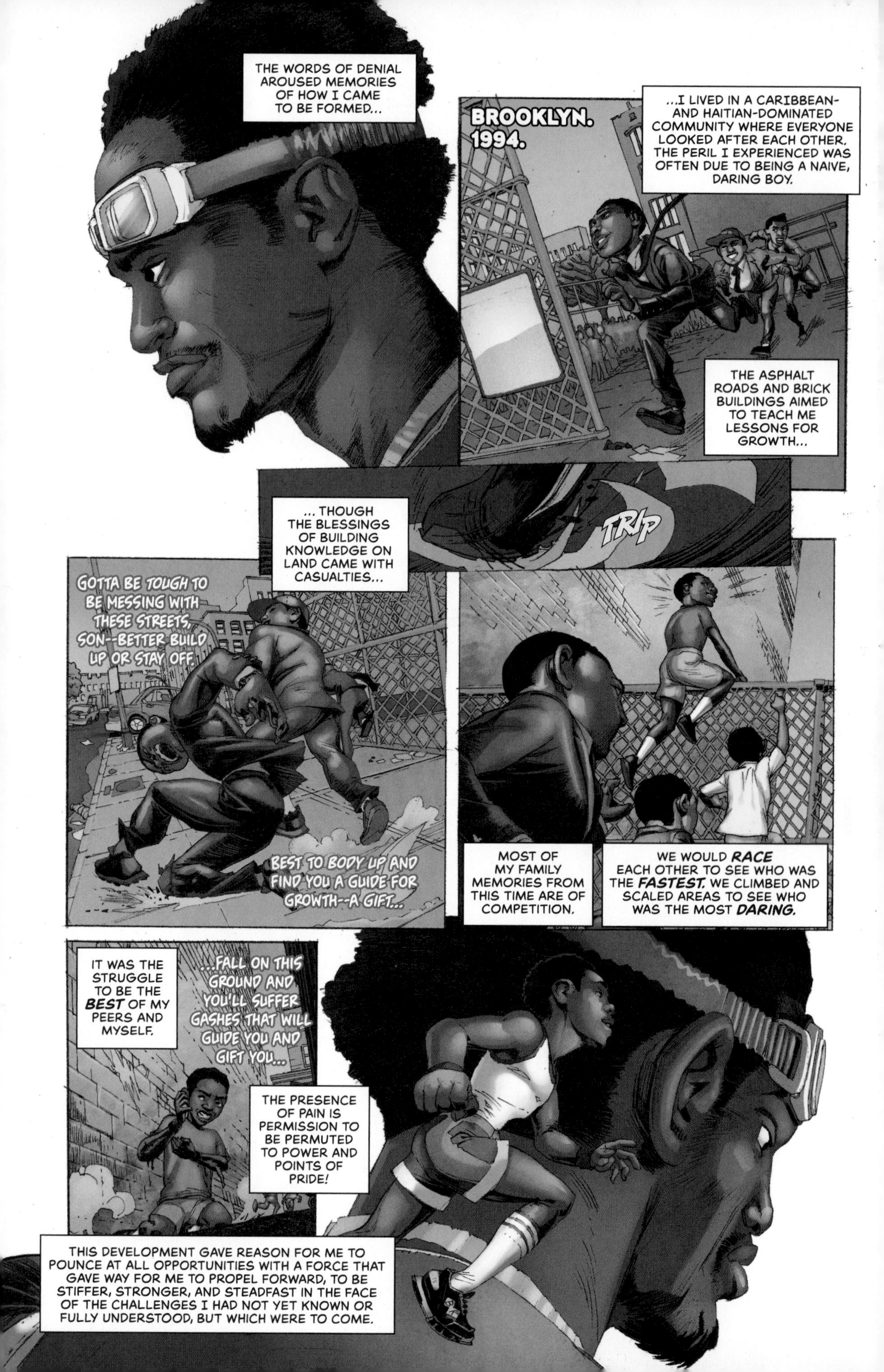
THE WORDS OF DENIAL AROUSED MEMORIES OF HOW I CAME TO BE FORMED...
BROOKLYN. 1994.
...I LIVED IN A CARIBBEAN- AND HAITIAN-DOMINATED COMMUNITY WHERE EVERYONE LOOKED AFTER EACH OTHER. THE PERIL I EXPERIENCED WAS OFTEN DUE TO BEING A NAIVE, DARING BOY.
THE ASPHALT ROADS AND BRICK BUILDINGS AIMED TO TEACH ME LESSONS FOR GROWTH...
... THOUGH THE BLESSINGS OF BUILDING KNOWLEDGE ON LAND CAME WITH CASUALTIES...
TRIP
GOTTA BE TOUGH TO BE MESSING WITH THESE STREETS, SON--BETTER BUILD UP OR STAY OFF.
BEST TO BODY UP AND FIND YOU A GUIDE FOR GROWTH--A GIFT...
MOST OF MY FAMILY MEMORIES FROM THIS TIME ARE OF COMPETITION.
WE WOULD RACE EACH OTHER TO SEE WHO WAS THE FASTEST. WE CLIMBED AND SCALED AREAS TO SEE WHO WAS THE MOST DARING.
IT WAS THE STRUGGLE TO BE THE BEST OF MY PEERS AND MYSELF.
...FALL ON THIS GROUND AND YOU'LL SUFFER GASHES THAT WILL GUIDE YOU AND GIFT YOU...
THE PRESENCE OF PAIN IS PERMISSION TO BE PERMUTED TO POWER AND POINTS OF PRIDE!
THIS DEVELOPMENT GAVE REASON FOR ME TO POUNCE AT ALL OPPORTUNITIES WITH A FORCE THAT GAVE WAY FOR ME TO PROPEL FORWARD, TO BE STIFFER, STRONGER, AND STEADFAST IN THE FACE OF THE CHALLENGES I HAD NOT YET KNOWN OR FULLY UNDERSTOOD, BUT WHICH WERE TO COME.

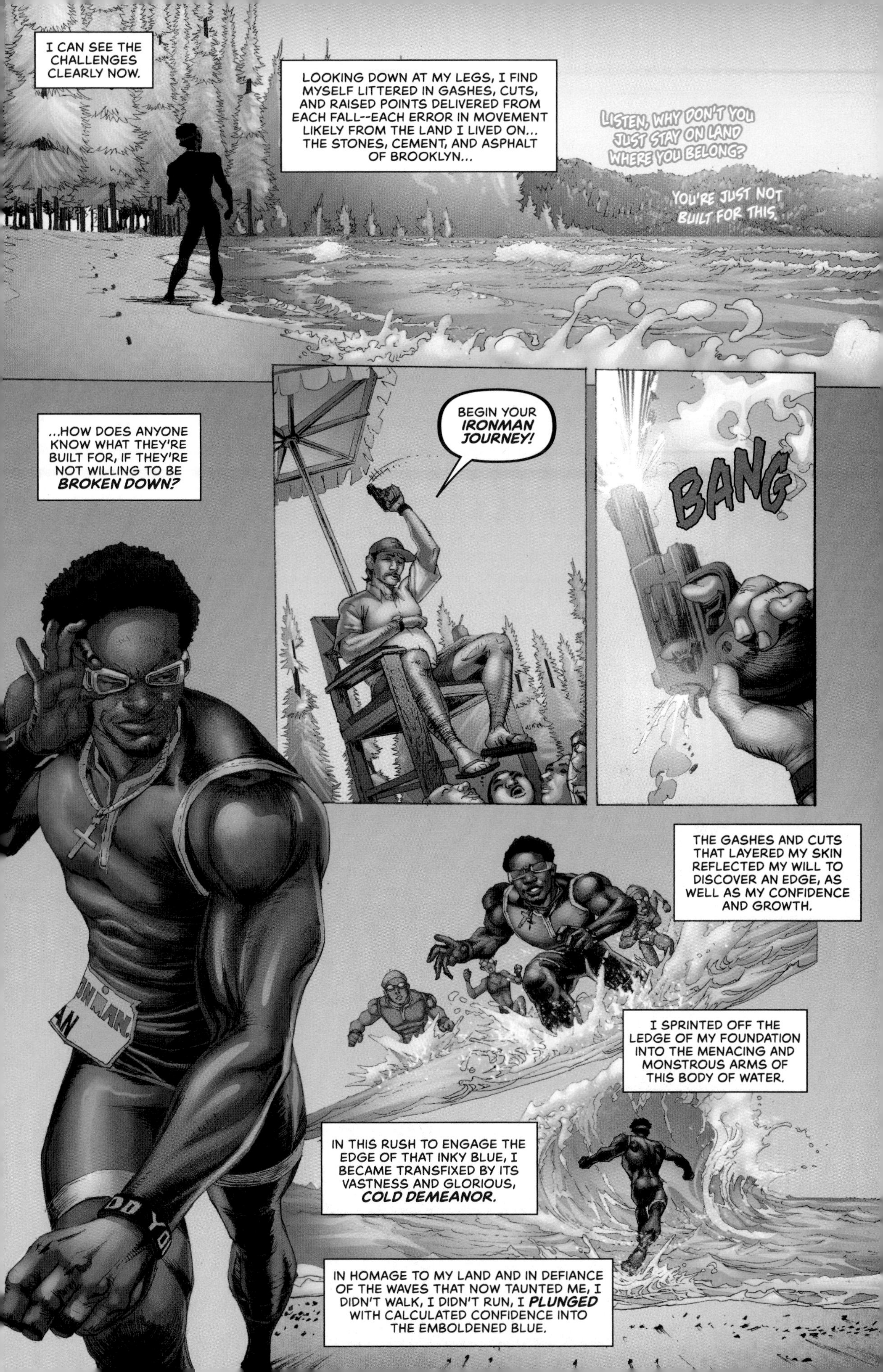
I CAN SEE THE CHALLENGES CLEARLY NOW.
LOOKING DOWN AT MY LEGS, I FIND MYSELF LITTERED IN GASHES, CUTS, AND RAISED POINTS DELIVERED FROM EACH FALL--EACH ERROR IN MOVEMENT LIKELY FROM THE LAND I LIVED ON... THE STONES, CEMENT, AND ASPHALT OF BROOKLYN...
LISTEN, WHY DON'T YOU JUST STAY ON LAND WHERE YOU BELONG?
YOU'RE JUST NOT BUILT FOR THIS.
...HOW DOES ANYONE KNOW WHAT THEY'RE BUILT FOR, IF THEY'RE NOT WILLING TO BE ***BROKEN DOWN?***
BEGIN YOUR ***IRONMAN JOURNEY!***
BANG
THE GASHES AND CUTS THAT LAYERED MY SKIN REFLECTED MY WILL TO DISCOVER AN EDGE, AS WELL AS MY CONFIDENCE AND GROWTH.
I SPRINTED OFF THE LEDGE OF MY FOUNDATION INTO THE MENACING AND MONSTROUS ARMS OF THIS BODY OF WATER.
IN THIS RUSH TO ENGAGE THE EDGE OF THAT INKY BLUE, I BECAME TRANSFIXED BY ITS VASTNESS AND GLORIOUS, ***COLD DEMEANOR.***
IN HOMAGE TO MY LAND AND IN DEFIANCE OF THE WAVES THAT NOW TAUNTED ME, I DIDN'T WALK, I DIDN'T RUN, I ***PLUNGED*** WITH CALCULATED CONFIDENCE INTO THE EMBOLDENED BLUE.

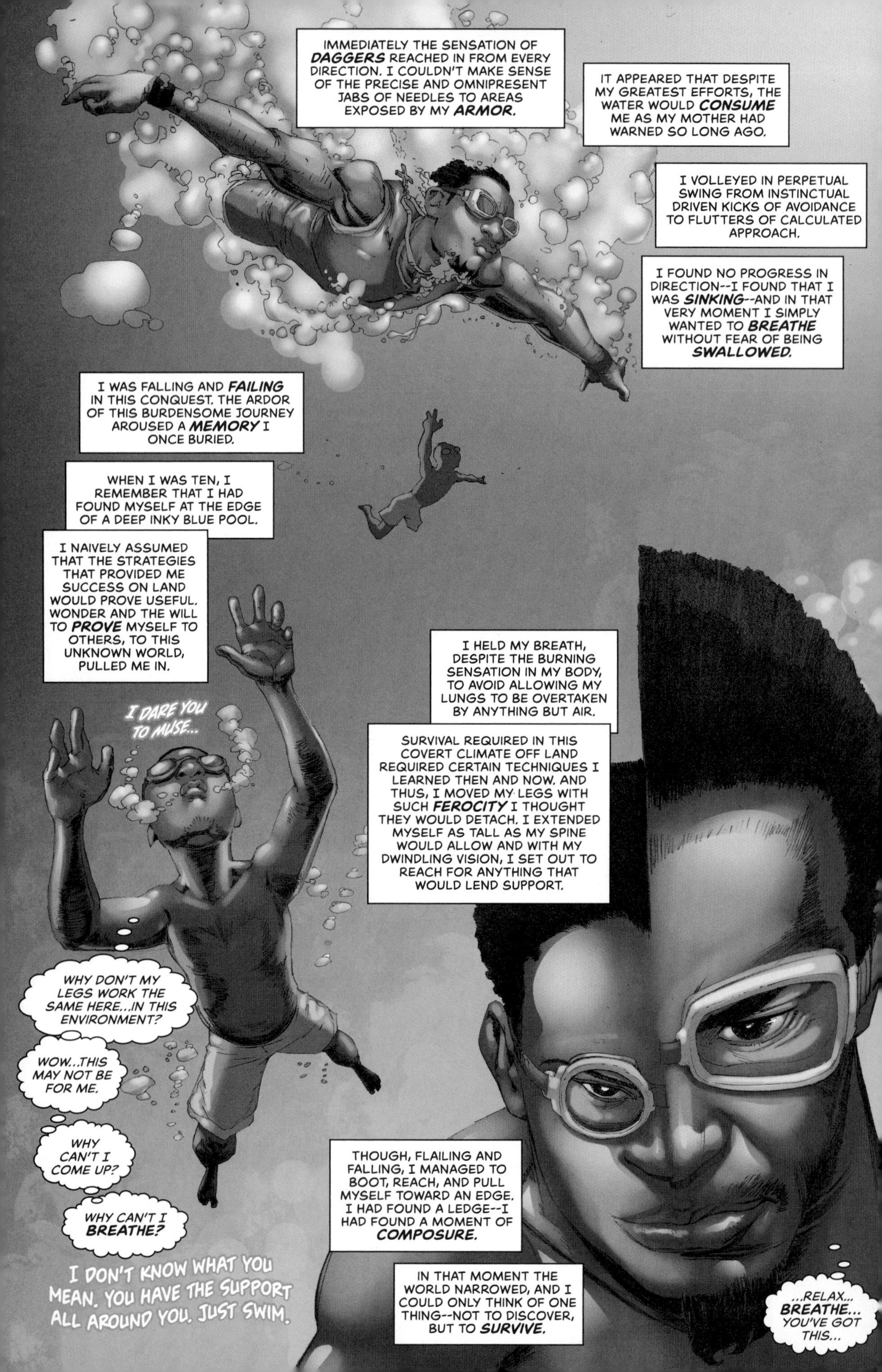
IMMEDIATELY THE SENSATION OF DAGGERS REACHED IN FROM EVERY DIRECTION. I COULDN'T MAKE SENSE OF THE PRECISE AND OMNIPRESENT JABS OF NEEDLES TO AREAS EXPOSED BY MY ARMOR.
IT APPEARED THAT DESPITE MY GREATEST EFFORTS, THE WATER WOULD CONSUME ME AS MY MOTHER HAD WARNED SO LONG AGO.
I VOLLEYED IN PERPETUAL SWING FROM INSTINCTUAL DRIVEN KICKS OF AVOIDANCE TO FLUTTERS OF CALCULATED APPROACH.
I FOUND NO PROGRESS IN DIRECTION--I FOUND THAT I WAS SINKING--AND IN THAT VERY MOMENT I SIMPLY WANTED TO BREATHE WITHOUT FEAR OF BEING SWALLOWED.
I WAS FALLING AND FAILING IN THIS CONQUEST. THE ARDOR OF THIS BURDENSOME JOURNEY AROUSED A MEMORY I ONCE BURIED.
WHEN I WAS TEN, I REMEMBER THAT I HAD FOUND MYSELF AT THE EDGE OF A DEEP INKY BLUE POOL.
I NAIVELY ASSUMED THAT THE STRATEGIES THAT PROVIDED ME SUCCESS ON LAND WOULD PROVE USEFUL. WONDER AND THE WILL TO PROVE MYSELF TO OTHERS, TO THIS UNKNOWN WORLD, PULLED ME IN.
I DARE YOU TO MUSE...
WHY DON'T MY LEGS WORK THE SAME HERE...IN THIS ENVIRONMENT?
WOW...THIS MAY NOT BE FOR ME.
WHY CAN'T I COME UP?
WHY CAN'T I BREATHE?
I DON'T KNOW WHAT YOU MEAN. YOU HAVE THE SUPPORT ALL AROUND YOU. JUST SWIM.
I HELD MY BREATH, DESPITE THE BURNING SENSATION IN MY BODY, TO AVOID ALLOWING MY LUNGS TO BE OVERTAKEN BY ANYTHING BUT AIR.
SURVIVAL REQUIRED IN THIS COVERT CLIMATE OFF LAND REQUIRED CERTAIN TECHNIQUES I LEARNED THEN AND NOW. AND THUS, I MOVED MY LEGS WITH SUCH FEROCITY I THOUGHT THEY WOULD DETACH. I EXTENDED MYSELF AS TALL AS MY SPINE WOULD ALLOW AND WITH MY DWINDLING VISION, I SET OUT TO REACH FOR ANYTHING THAT WOULD LEND SUPPORT.
THOUGH, FLAILING AND FALLING, I MANAGED TO BOOT, REACH, AND PULL MYSELF TOWARD AN EDGE. I HAD FOUND A LEDGE--I HAD FOUND A MOMENT OF COMPOSURE.
IN THAT MOMENT THE WORLD NARROWED, AND I COULD ONLY THINK OF ONE THING--NOT TO DISCOVER, BUT TO SURVIVE.
...RELAX... BREATHE... YOU'VE GOT THIS...

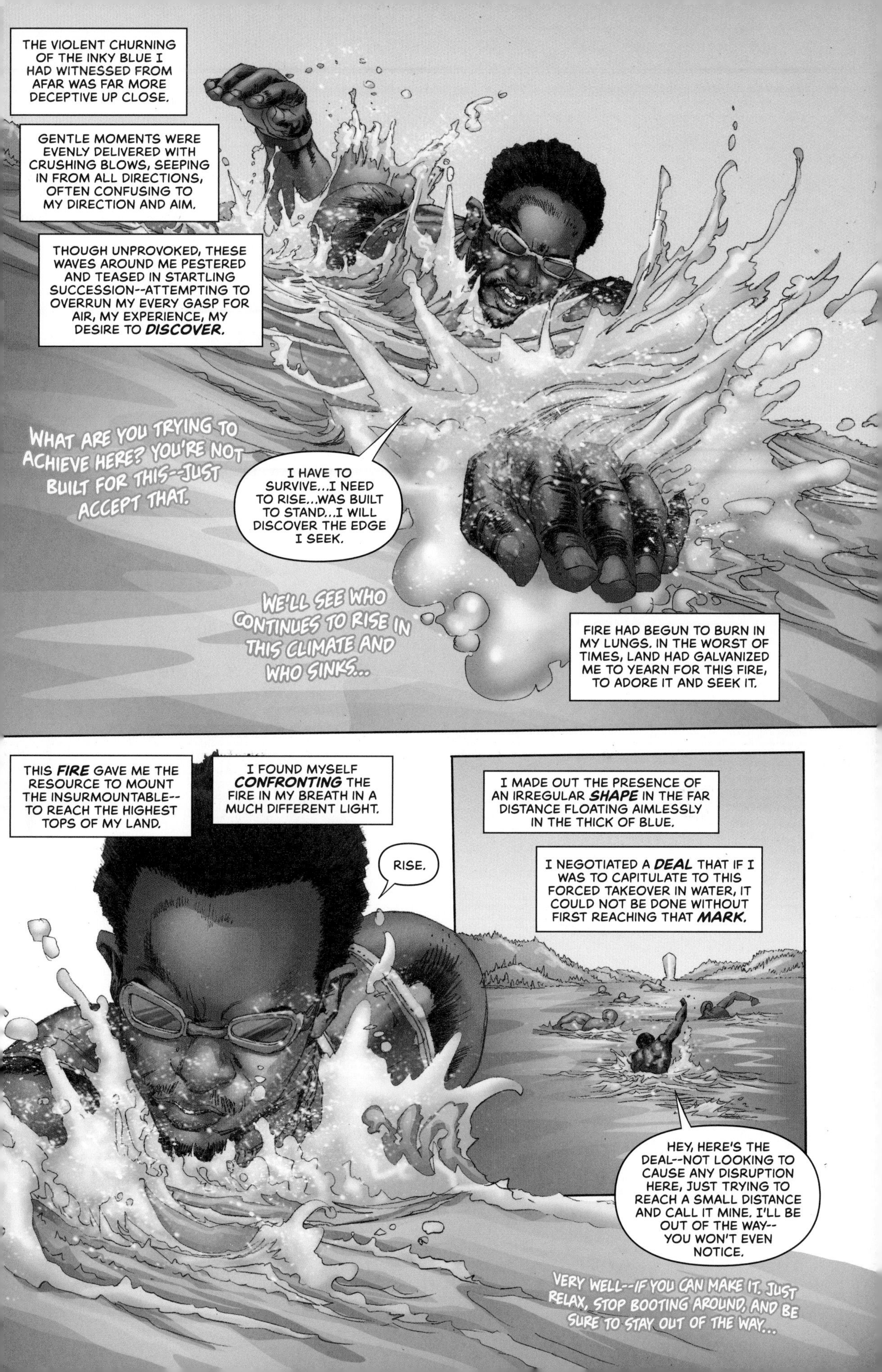
THE VIOLENT CHURNING OF THE INKY BLUE I HAD WITNESSED FROM AFAR WAS FAR MORE DECEPTIVE UP CLOSE.
GENTLE MOMENTS WERE EVENLY DELIVERED WITH CRUSHING BLOWS, SEEPING IN FROM ALL DIRECTIONS, OFTEN CONFUSING TO MY DIRECTION AND AIM.
THOUGH UNPROVOKED, THESE WAVES AROUND ME PESTERED AND TEASED IN STARTLING SUCCESSION--ATTEMPTING TO OVERRUN MY EVERY GASP FOR AIR, MY EXPERIENCE, MY DESIRE TO DISCOVER.
WHAT ARE YOU TRYING TO ACHIEVE HERE? YOU'RE NOT BUILT FOR THIS--JUST ACCEPT THAT.
I HAVE TO SURVIVE...I NEED TO RISE...WAS BUILT TO STAND...I WILL DISCOVER THE EDGE I SEEK.
WE'LL SEE WHO CONTINUES TO RISE IN THIS CLIMATE AND WHO SINKS...
FIRE HAD BEGUN TO BURN IN MY LUNGS. IN THE WORST OF TIMES, LAND HAD GALVANIZED ME TO YEARN FOR THIS FIRE, TO ADORE IT AND SEEK IT.
THIS FIRE GAVE ME THE RESOURCE TO MOUNT THE INSURMOUNTABLE--TO REACH THE HIGHEST TOPS OF MY LAND.
I FOUND MYSELF CONFRONTING THE FIRE IN MY BREATH IN A MUCH DIFFERENT LIGHT.
RISE.
I MADE OUT THE PRESENCE OF AN IRREGULAR SHAPE IN THE FAR DISTANCE FLOATING AIMLESSLY IN THE THICK OF BLUE.
I NEGOTIATED A DEAL THAT IF I WAS TO CAPITULATE TO THIS FORCED TAKEOVER IN WATER, IT COULD NOT BE DONE WITHOUT FIRST REACHING THAT MARK.
HEY, HERE'S THE DEAL--NOT LOOKING TO CAUSE ANY DISRUPTION HERE, JUST TRYING TO REACH A SMALL DISTANCE AND CALL IT MINE. I'LL BE OUT OF THE WAY--YOU WON'T EVEN NOTICE.
VERY WELL--IF YOU CAN MAKE IT. JUST RELAX, STOP BOOTING AROUND, AND BE SURE TO STAY OUT OF THE WAY...

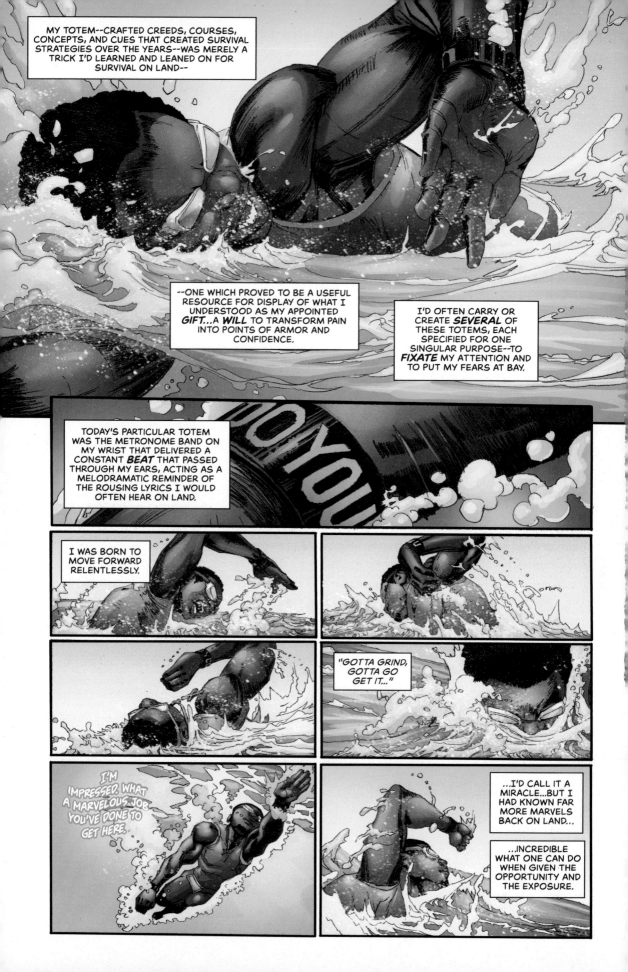

MY TOTEM--CRAFTED CREEDS, COURSES, CONCEPTS, AND CUES THAT CREATED SURVIVAL STRATEGIES OVER THE YEARS--WAS MERELY A TRICK I'D LEARNED AND LEANED ON FOR SURVIVAL ON LAND--

--ONE WHICH PROVED TO BE A USEFUL RESOURCE FOR DISPLAY OF WHAT I UNDERSTOOD AS MY APPOINTED *GIFT*...A *WILL* TO TRANSFORM PAIN INTO POINTS OF ARMOR AND CONFIDENCE.

I'D OFTEN CARRY OR CREATE *SEVERAL* OF THESE TOTEMS, EACH SPECIFIED FOR ONE SINGULAR PURPOSE--TO *FIXATE* MY ATTENTION AND TO PUT MY FEARS AT BAY.

TODAY'S PARTICULAR TOTEM WAS THE METRONOME BAND ON MY WRIST THAT DELIVERED A CONSTANT *BEAT* THAT PASSED THROUGH MY EARS, ACTING AS A MELODRAMATIC REMINDER OF THE ROUSING LYRICS I WOULD OFTEN HEAR ON LAND.

I WAS BORN TO MOVE FORWARD RELENTLESSLY.

"GOTTA GRIND, GOTTA GO GET IT..."

I'M IMPRESSED. WHAT A MARVELOUS JOB YOU'VE DONE TO GET HERE.

...I'D CALL IT A MIRACLE...BUT I HAD KNOWN FAR MORE MARVELS BACK ON LAND...

...INCREDIBLE WHAT ONE CAN DO WHEN GIVEN THE OPPORTUNITY AND THE EXPOSURE.

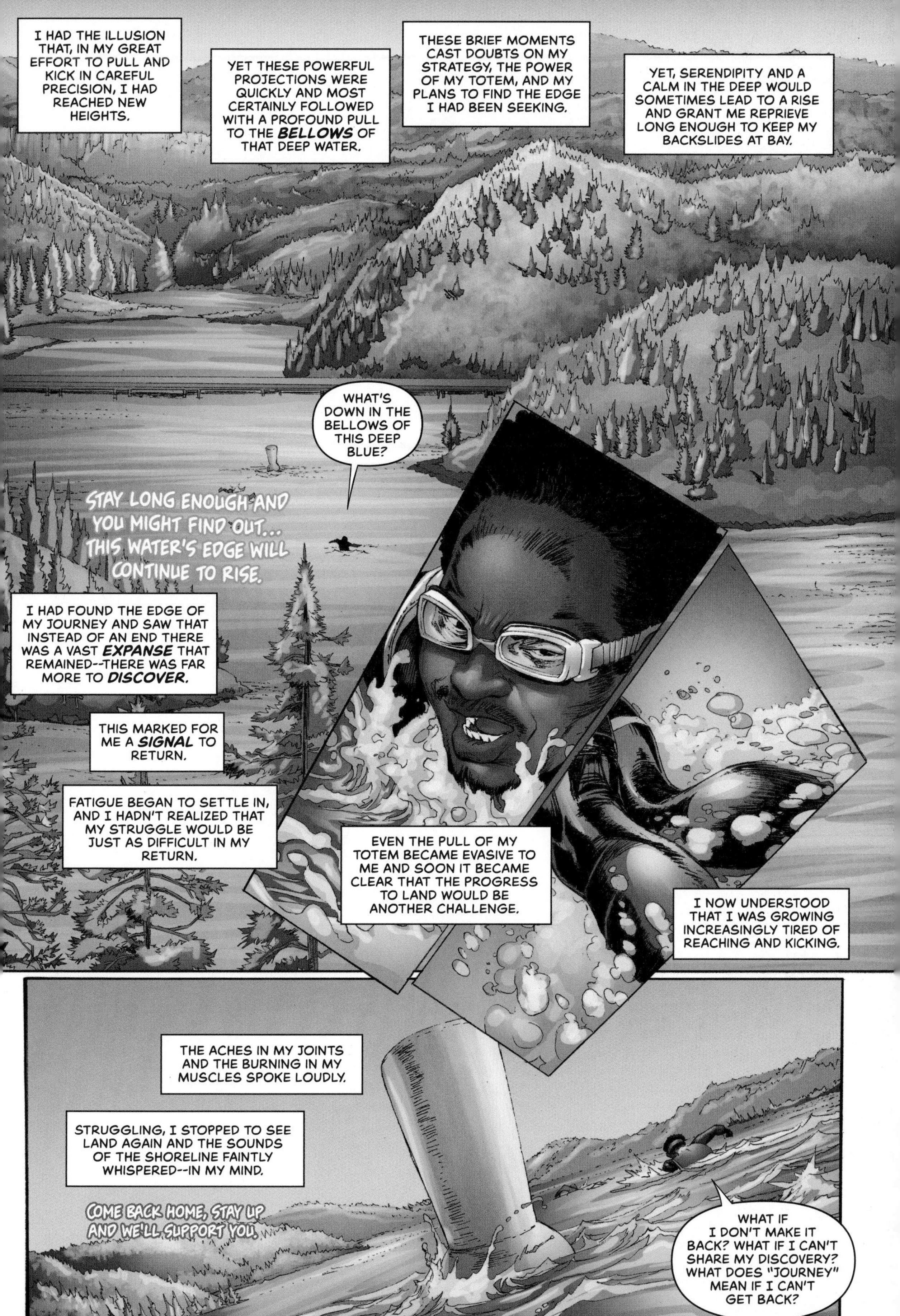
I HAD THE ILLUSION THAT, IN MY GREAT EFFORT TO PULL AND KICK IN CAREFUL PRECISION, I HAD REACHED NEW HEIGHTS.
YET THESE POWERFUL PROJECTIONS WERE QUICKLY AND MOST CERTAINLY FOLLOWED WITH A PROFOUND PULL TO THE BELLOWS OF THAT DEEP WATER.
THESE BRIEF MOMENTS CAST DOUBTS ON MY STRATEGY, THE POWER OF MY TOTEM, AND MY PLANS TO FIND THE EDGE I HAD BEEN SEEKING.
YET, SERENDIPITY AND A CALM IN THE DEEP WOULD SOMETIMES LEAD TO A RISE AND GRANT ME REPRIEVE LONG ENOUGH TO KEEP MY BACKSLIDES AT BAY.
WHAT'S DOWN IN THE BELLOWS OF THIS DEEP BLUE?
STAY LONG ENOUGH AND YOU MIGHT FIND OUT... THIS WATER'S EDGE WILL CONTINUE TO RISE.
I HAD FOUND THE EDGE OF MY JOURNEY AND SAW THAT INSTEAD OF AN END THERE WAS A VAST EXPANSE THAT REMAINED--THERE WAS FAR MORE TO DISCOVER.
THIS MARKED FOR ME A SIGNAL TO RETURN.
FATIGUE BEGAN TO SETTLE IN, AND I HADN'T REALIZED THAT MY STRUGGLE WOULD BE JUST AS DIFFICULT IN MY RETURN.
EVEN THE PULL OF MY TOTEM BECAME EVASIVE TO ME AND SOON IT BECAME CLEAR THAT THE PROGRESS TO LAND WOULD BE ANOTHER CHALLENGE.
I NOW UNDERSTOOD THAT I WAS GROWING INCREASINGLY TIRED OF REACHING AND KICKING.
THE ACHES IN MY JOINTS AND THE BURNING IN MY MUSCLES SPOKE LOUDLY.
STRUGGLING, I STOPPED TO SEE LAND AGAIN AND THE SOUNDS OF THE SHORELINE FAINTLY WHISPERED--IN MY MIND.
COME BACK HOME, STAY UP AND WE'LL SUPPORT YOU.
WHAT IF I DON'T MAKE IT BACK? WHAT IF I CAN'T SHARE MY DISCOVERY? WHAT DOES "JOURNEY" MEAN IF I CAN'T GET BACK?

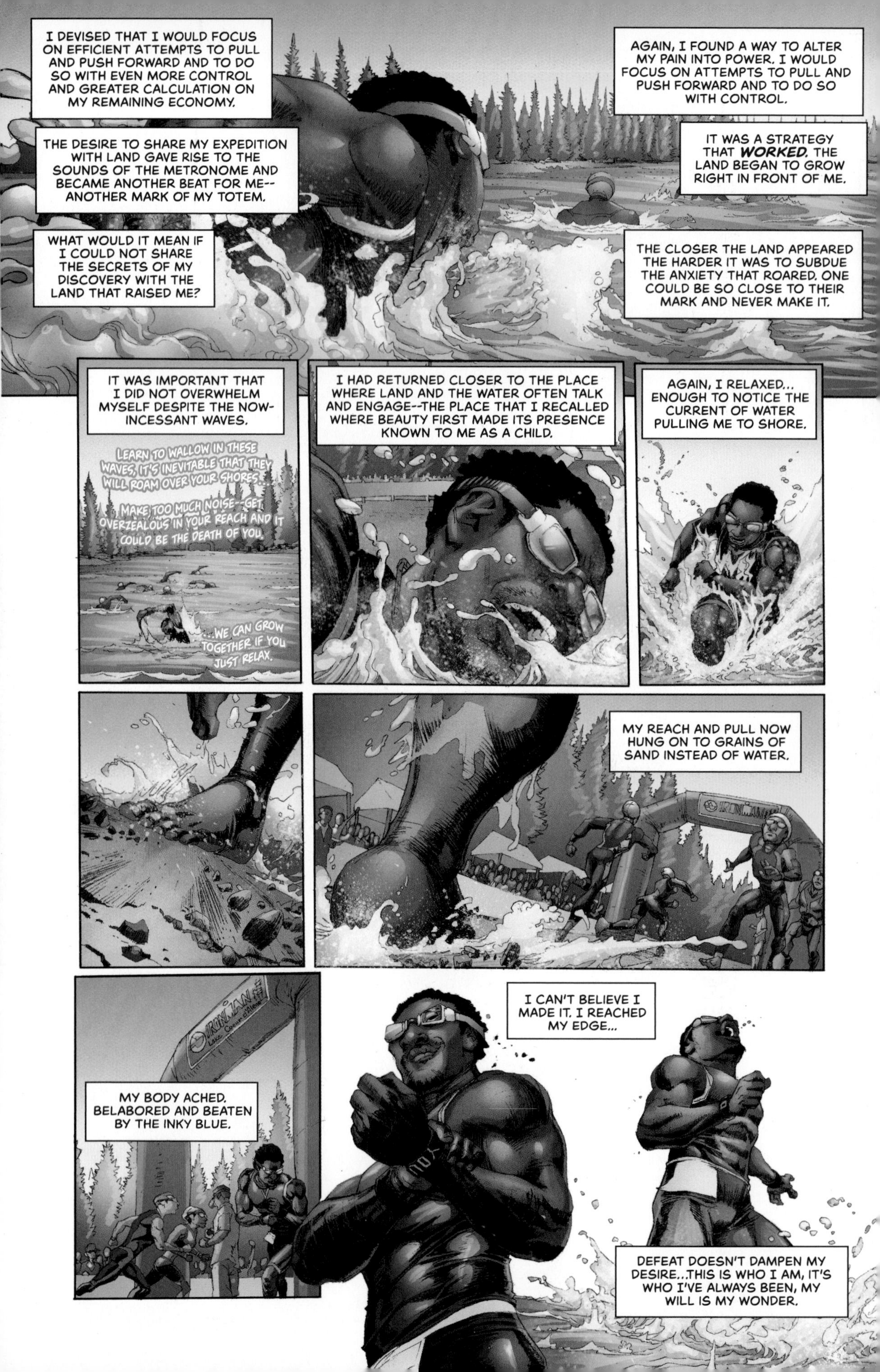
I DEVISED THAT I WOULD FOCUS ON EFFICIENT ATTEMPTS TO PULL AND PUSH FORWARD AND TO DO SO WITH EVEN MORE CONTROL AND GREATER CALCULATION ON MY REMAINING ECONOMY.
THE DESIRE TO SHARE MY EXPEDITION WITH LAND GAVE RISE TO THE SOUNDS OF THE METRONOME AND BECAME ANOTHER BEAT FOR ME--ANOTHER MARK OF MY TOTEM.
WHAT WOULD IT MEAN IF I COULD NOT SHARE THE SECRETS OF MY DISCOVERY WITH THE LAND THAT RAISED ME?
AGAIN, I FOUND A WAY TO ALTER MY PAIN INTO POWER. I WOULD FOCUS ON ATTEMPTS TO PULL AND PUSH FORWARD AND TO DO SO WITH CONTROL.
IT WAS A STRATEGY THAT ***WORKED.*** THE LAND BEGAN TO GROW RIGHT IN FRONT OF ME.
THE CLOSER THE LAND APPEARED THE HARDER IT WAS TO SUBDUE THE ANXIETY THAT ROARED. ONE COULD BE SO CLOSE TO THEIR MARK AND NEVER MAKE IT.
IT WAS IMPORTANT THAT I DID NOT OVERWHELM MYSELF DESPITE THE NOW-INCESSANT WAVES.
LEARN TO WALLOW IN THESE WAVES, IT'S INEVITABLE THAT THEY WILL ROAM OVER YOUR SHORES...
MAKE TOO MUCH NOISE--GET OVERZEALOUS IN YOUR REACH AND IT COULD BE THE DEATH OF YOU.
...WE CAN GROW TOGETHER IF YOU JUST RELAX.
I HAD RETURNED CLOSER TO THE PLACE WHERE LAND AND THE WATER OFTEN TALK AND ENGAGE--THE PLACE THAT I RECALLED WHERE BEAUTY FIRST MADE ITS PRESENCE KNOWN TO ME AS A CHILD.
AGAIN, I RELAXED... ENOUGH TO NOTICE THE CURRENT OF WATER PULLING ME TO SHORE.
MY REACH AND PULL NOW HUNG ON TO GRAINS OF SAND INSTEAD OF WATER.
IRONMAN
MY BODY ACHED. BELABORED AND BEATEN BY THE INKY BLUE.
I CAN'T BELIEVE I MADE IT. I REACHED MY EDGE...
DEFEAT DOESN'T DAMPEN MY DESIRE...THIS IS WHO I AM, IT'S WHO I'VE ALWAYS BEEN, MY WILL IS MY WONDER.

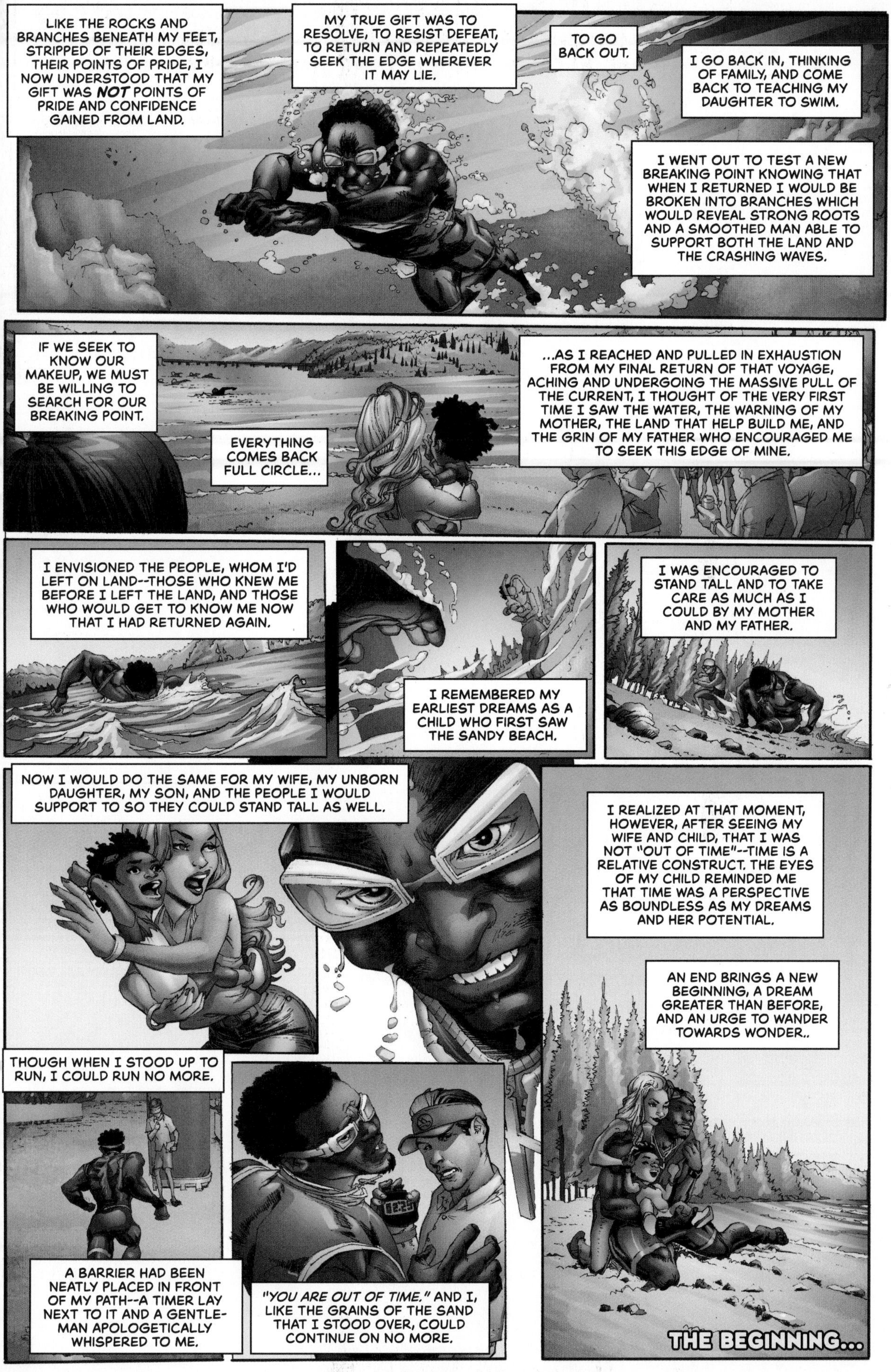
LIKE THE ROCKS AND BRANCHES BENEATH MY FEET, STRIPPED OF THEIR EDGES, THEIR POINTS OF PRIDE, I NOW UNDERSTOOD THAT MY GIFT WAS ***NOT*** POINTS OF PRIDE AND CONFIDENCE GAINED FROM LAND.
MY TRUE GIFT WAS TO RESOLVE, TO RESIST DEFEAT, TO RETURN AND REPEATEDLY SEEK THE EDGE WHEREVER IT MAY LIE.
TO GO BACK OUT.
I GO BACK IN, THINKING OF FAMILY, AND COME BACK TO TEACHING MY DAUGHTER TO SWIM.
I WENT OUT TO TEST A NEW BREAKING POINT KNOWING THAT WHEN I RETURNED I WOULD BE BROKEN INTO BRANCHES WHICH WOULD REVEAL STRONG ROOTS AND A SMOOTHED MAN ABLE TO SUPPORT BOTH THE LAND AND THE CRASHING WAVES.
IF WE SEEK TO KNOW OUR MAKEUP, WE MUST BE WILLING TO SEARCH FOR OUR BREAKING POINT.
EVERYTHING COMES BACK FULL CIRCLE...
...AS I REACHED AND PULLED IN EXHAUSTION FROM MY FINAL RETURN OF THAT VOYAGE, ACHING AND UNDERGOING THE MASSIVE PULL OF THE CURRENT, I THOUGHT OF THE VERY FIRST TIME I SAW THE WATER, THE WARNING OF MY MOTHER, THE LAND THAT HELP BUILD ME, AND THE GRIN OF MY FATHER WHO ENCOURAGED ME TO SEEK THIS EDGE OF MINE.
I ENVISIONED THE PEOPLE, WHOM I'D LEFT ON LAND--THOSE WHO KNEW ME BEFORE I LEFT THE LAND, AND THOSE WHO WOULD GET TO KNOW ME NOW THAT I HAD RETURNED AGAIN.
I REMEMBERED MY EARLIEST DREAMS AS A CHILD WHO FIRST SAW THE SANDY BEACH.
I WAS ENCOURAGED TO STAND TALL AND TO TAKE CARE AS MUCH AS I COULD BY MY MOTHER AND MY FATHER.
NOW I WOULD DO THE SAME FOR MY WIFE, MY UNBORN DAUGHTER, MY SON, AND THE PEOPLE I WOULD SUPPORT TO SO THEY COULD STAND TALL AS WELL.
THOUGH WHEN I STOOD UP TO RUN, I COULD RUN NO MORE.
A BARRIER HAD BEEN NEATLY PLACED IN FRONT OF MY PATH--A TIMER LAY NEXT TO IT AND A GENTLEMAN APOLOGETICALLY WHISPERED TO ME.
"YOU ARE OUT OF TIME." AND I, LIKE THE GRAINS OF THE SAND THAT I STOOD OVER, COULD CONTINUE ON NO MORE.
I REALIZED AT THAT MOMENT, HOWEVER, AFTER SEEING MY WIFE AND CHILD, THAT I WAS NOT "OUT OF TIME"--TIME IS A RELATIVE CONSTRUCT. THE EYES OF MY CHILD REMINDED ME THAT TIME WAS A PERSPECTIVE AS BOUNDLESS AS MY DREAMS AND HER POTENTIAL.
AN END BRINGS A NEW BEGINNING, A DREAM GREATER THAN BEFORE, AND AN URGE TO WANDER TOWARDS WONDER..
THE BEGINNING...

DC REPRESENT!

CHAPTER THIRTEEN
"WHO HIRED THE KID?"

WRITER - KEAH BROWN

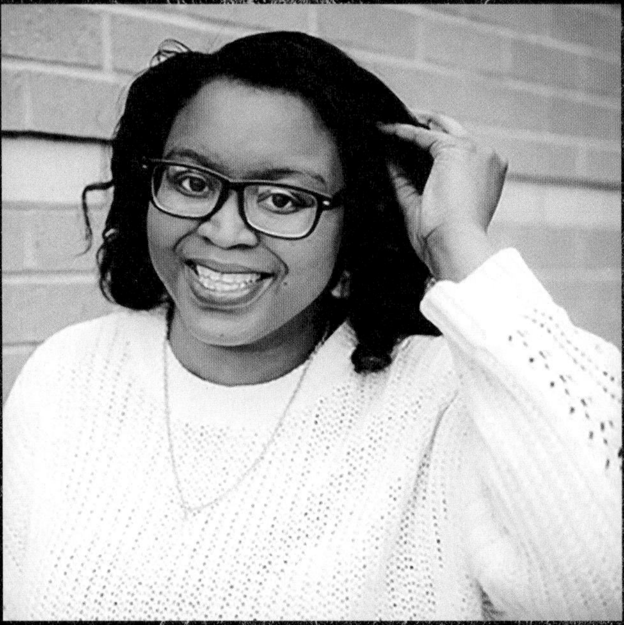

Keah Brown is a journalist, screenwriter, actor, and author. She created the viral hashtag #DisabledAndCute in 2017 and was one of the Root's most influential African Americans of 2018. She is deeply passionate about pop culture, music, film, and TV. Her work can be found in the *New York Times*, *Glamour*, *Marie Claire UK*, and *Harper's Bazaar*, among others. Her debut essay collection, *The Pretty One*, is out now via Atria Books. Her picture book, *Sam's Super Seats,* will be out in 2022 via Kokila Books. You can learn more about her at keahbrown.com.

ARTIST - DON HUDSON
COLORIST - NICK FILARDI
LETTERER - DERON BENNETT

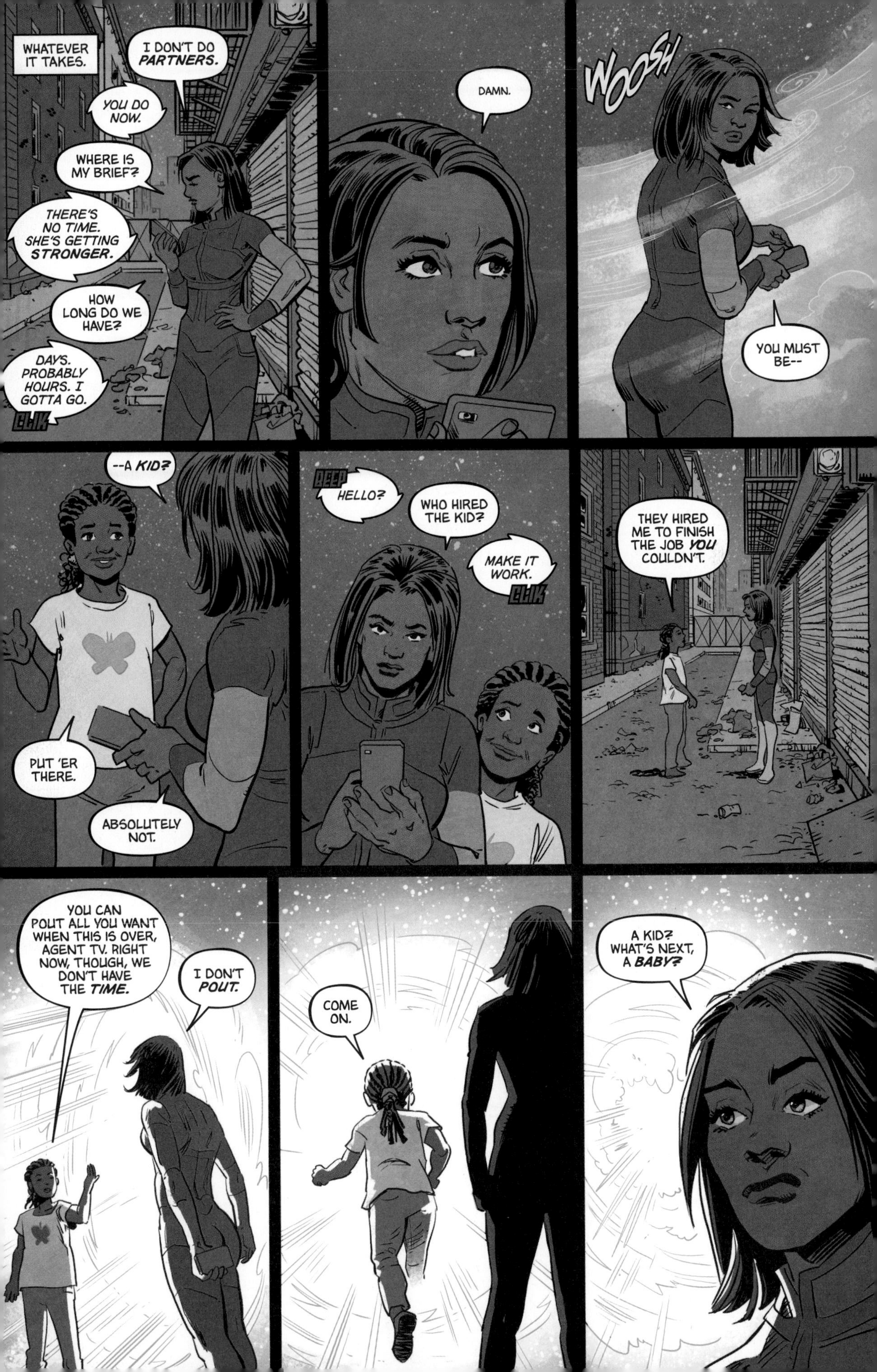
WHATEVER IT TAKES.
I DON'T DO PARTNERS.
YOU DO NOW.
WHERE IS MY BRIEF?
THERE'S NO TIME. SHE'S GETTING STRONGER.
HOW LONG DO WE HAVE?
DAYS. PROBABLY HOURS. I GOTTA GO.
CLIK
DAMN.
WOOSH
YOU MUST BE--
--A KID?
PUT 'ER THERE.
ABSOLUTELY NOT.
BEEP
HELLO?
WHO HIRED THE KID?
MAKE IT WORK.
CLIK
THEY HIRED ME TO FINISH THE JOB YOU COULDN'T.
YOU CAN POUT ALL YOU WANT WHEN THIS IS OVER, AGENT TV. RIGHT NOW, THOUGH, WE DON'T HAVE THE TIME.
I DON'T POUT.
COME ON.
A KID? WHAT'S NEXT, A BABY?

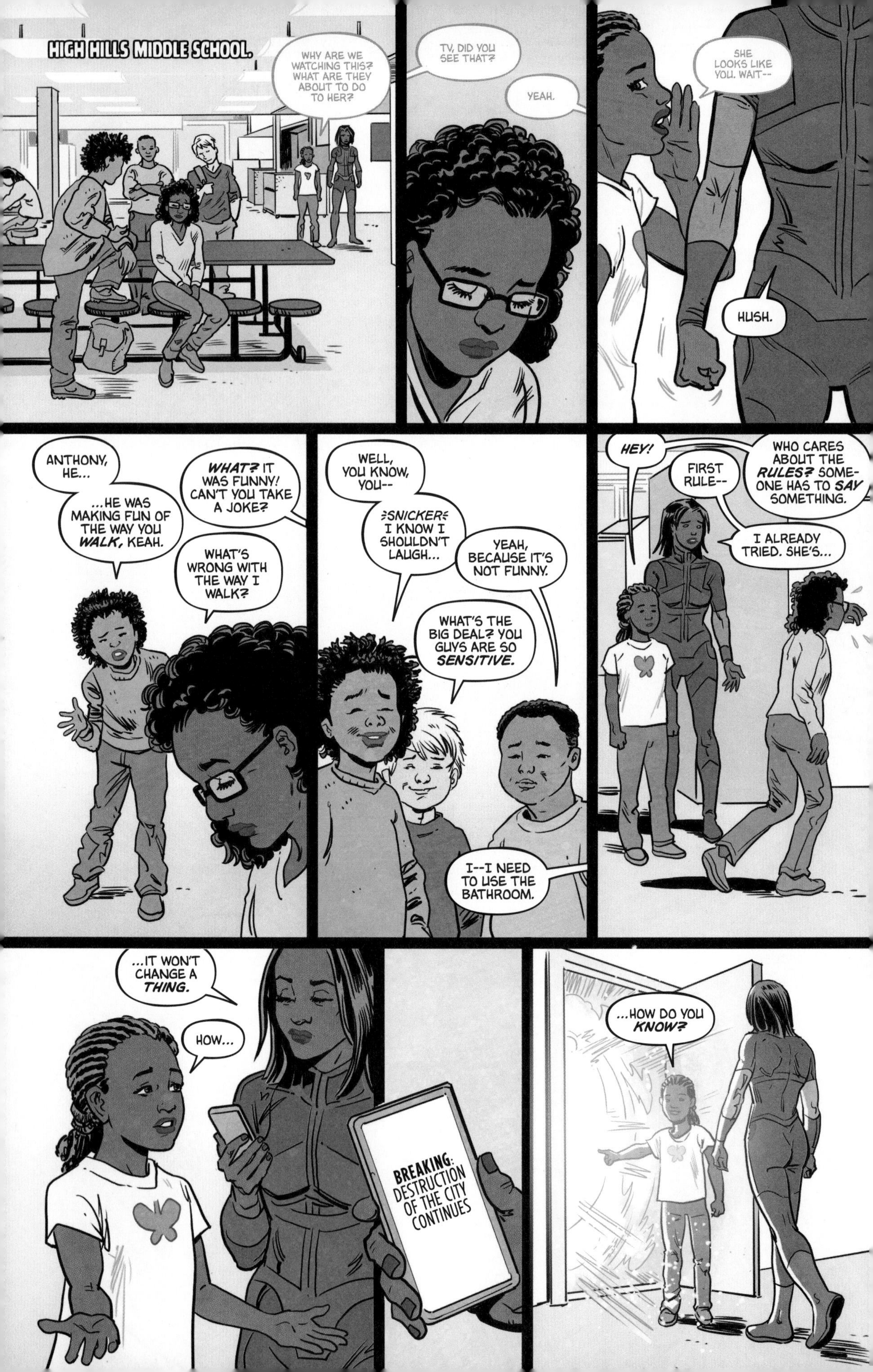
HIGH HILLS MIDDLE SCHOOL.
WHY ARE WE WATCHING THIS? WHAT ARE THEY ABOUT TO DO TO HER?
TV, DID YOU SEE THAT?
YEAH.
SHE LOOKS LIKE YOU. WAIT--
HUSH.
ANTHONY, HE...
...HE WAS MAKING FUN OF THE WAY YOU *WALK,* KEAH.
WHAT? IT WAS FUNNY! CAN'T YOU TAKE A JOKE?
WHAT'S WRONG WITH THE WAY I WALK?
WELL, YOU KNOW, YOU--
SNICKER I KNOW I SHOULDN'T LAUGH...
YEAH, BECAUSE IT'S NOT FUNNY.
WHAT'S THE BIG DEAL? YOU GUYS ARE SO *SENSITIVE.*
I--I NEED TO USE THE BATHROOM.
HEY!
FIRST RULE--
WHO CARES ABOUT THE *RULES?* SOMEONE HAS TO *SAY* SOMETHING.
I ALREADY TRIED. SHE'S...
...IT WON'T CHANGE A *THING.*
HOW...
BREAKING: DESTRUCTION OF THE CITY CONTINUES
...HOW DO YOU *KNOW?*

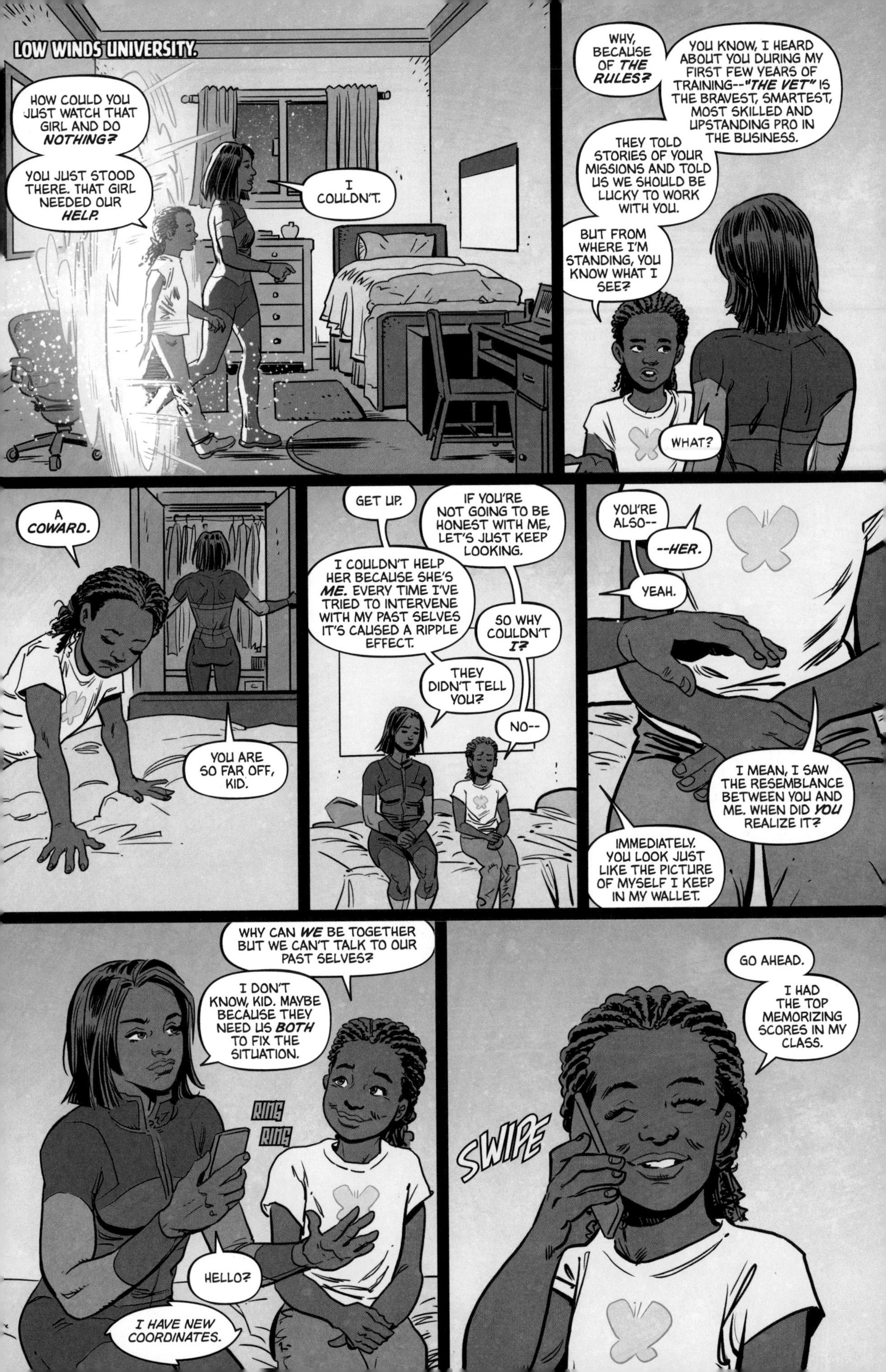
LOW WINDS UNIVERSITY.
HOW COULD YOU JUST WATCH THAT GIRL AND DO NOTHING?
YOU JUST STOOD THERE. THAT GIRL NEEDED OUR HELP.
I COULDN'T.
WHY, BECAUSE OF THE RULES?
YOU KNOW, I HEARD ABOUT YOU DURING MY FIRST FEW YEARS OF TRAINING--"THE VET" IS THE BRAVEST, SMARTEST, MOST SKILLED AND UPSTANDING PRO IN THE BUSINESS.
THEY TOLD STORIES OF YOUR MISSIONS AND TOLD US WE SHOULD BE LUCKY TO WORK WITH YOU.
BUT FROM WHERE I'M STANDING, YOU KNOW WHAT I SEE?
WHAT?
A COWARD.
YOU ARE SO FAR OFF, KID.
GET UP.
IF YOU'RE NOT GOING TO BE HONEST WITH ME, LET'S JUST KEEP LOOKING.
I COULDN'T HELP HER BECAUSE SHE'S ME. EVERY TIME I'VE TRIED TO INTERVENE WITH MY PAST SELVES IT'S CAUSED A RIPPLE EFFECT.
SO WHY COULDN'T I?
THEY DIDN'T TELL YOU?
NO--
YOU'RE ALSO--
--HER.
YEAH.
I MEAN, I SAW THE RESEMBLANCE BETWEEN YOU AND ME. WHEN DID YOU REALIZE IT?
IMMEDIATELY. YOU LOOK JUST LIKE THE PICTURE OF MYSELF I KEEP IN MY WALLET.
WHY CAN WE BE TOGETHER BUT WE CAN'T TALK TO OUR PAST SELVES?
I DON'T KNOW, KID. MAYBE BECAUSE THEY NEED US BOTH TO FIX THE SITUATION.
RING
RING
HELLO?
I HAVE NEW COORDINATES.
SWIPE
GO AHEAD.
I HAD THE TOP MEMORIZING SCORES IN MY CLASS.

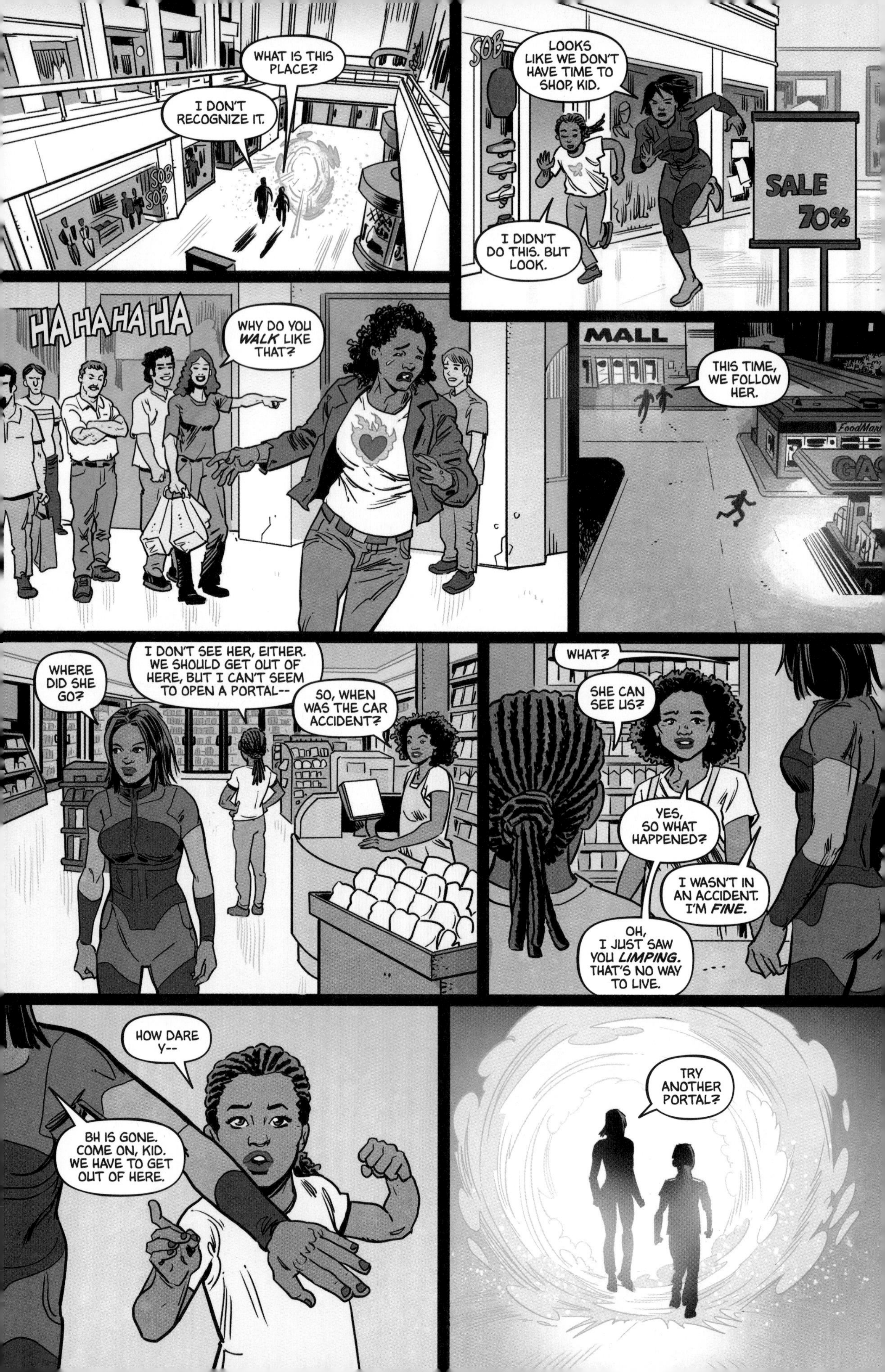
WHAT IS THIS PLACE?
I DON'T RECOGNIZE IT.
SOB SOB
SOB
LOOKS LIKE WE DON'T HAVE TIME TO SHOP, KID.
SALE 70%
I DIDN'T DO THIS. BUT LOOK.
HA HA HA HA
WHY DO YOU WALK LIKE THAT?
MALL
THIS TIME, WE FOLLOW HER.
FoodMart
GAS
WHERE DID SHE GO?
I DON'T SEE HER, EITHER. WE SHOULD GET OUT OF HERE, BUT I CAN'T SEEM TO OPEN A PORTAL--
SO, WHEN WAS THE CAR ACCIDENT?
WHAT?
SHE CAN SEE US?
YES, SO WHAT HAPPENED?
I WASN'T IN AN ACCIDENT. I'M FINE.
OH, I JUST SAW YOU LIMPING. THAT'S NO WAY TO LIVE.
...
HOW DARE Y--
BH IS GONE. COME ON, KID. WE HAVE TO GET OUT OF HERE.
TRY ANOTHER PORTAL?

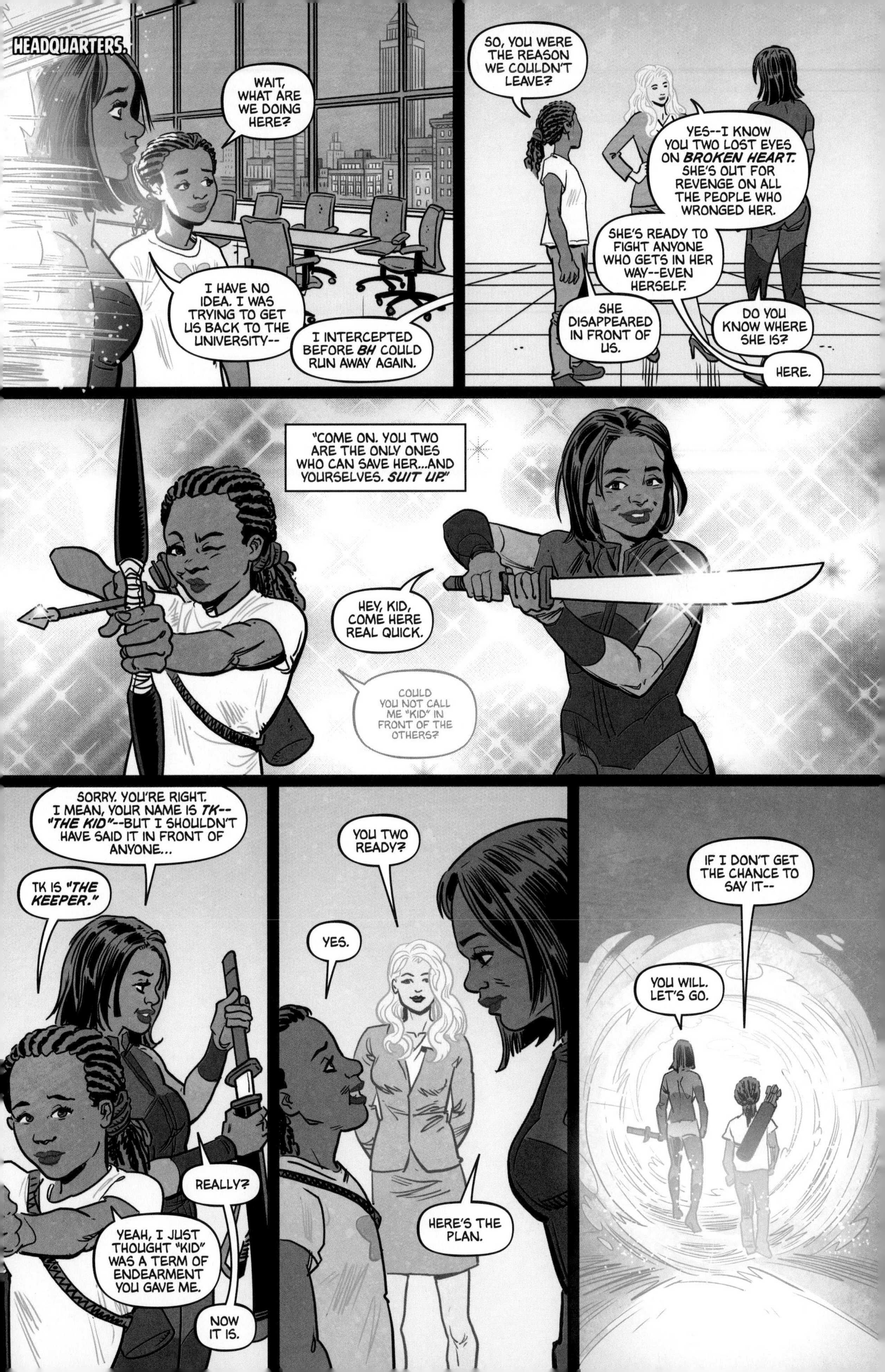
HEADQUARTERS.
WAIT, WHAT ARE WE DOING HERE?
I HAVE NO IDEA. I WAS TRYING TO GET US BACK TO THE UNIVERSITY--
I INTERCEPTED BEFORE BH COULD RUN AWAY AGAIN.
SO, YOU WERE THE REASON WE COULDN'T LEAVE?
YES--I KNOW YOU TWO LOST EYES ON BROKEN HEART. SHE'S OUT FOR REVENGE ON ALL THE PEOPLE WHO WRONGED HER.
SHE'S READY TO FIGHT ANYONE WHO GETS IN HER WAY--EVEN HERSELF.
SHE DISAPPEARED IN FRONT OF US.
DO YOU KNOW WHERE SHE IS?
HERE.
"COME ON. YOU TWO ARE THE ONLY ONES WHO CAN SAVE HER...AND YOURSELVES. SUIT UP."
HEY, KID, COME HERE REAL QUICK.
COULD YOU NOT CALL ME "KID" IN FRONT OF THE OTHERS?
SORRY. YOU'RE RIGHT. I MEAN, YOUR NAME IS TK--"THE KID"--BUT I SHOULDN'T HAVE SAID IT IN FRONT OF ANYONE...
TK IS "THE KEEPER."
REALLY?
YEAH, I JUST THOUGHT "KID" WAS A TERM OF ENDEARMENT YOU GAVE ME.
NOW IT IS.
YOU TWO READY?
YES.
HERE'S THE PLAN.
IF I DON'T GET THE CHANCE TO SAY IT--
YOU WILL. LET'S GO.

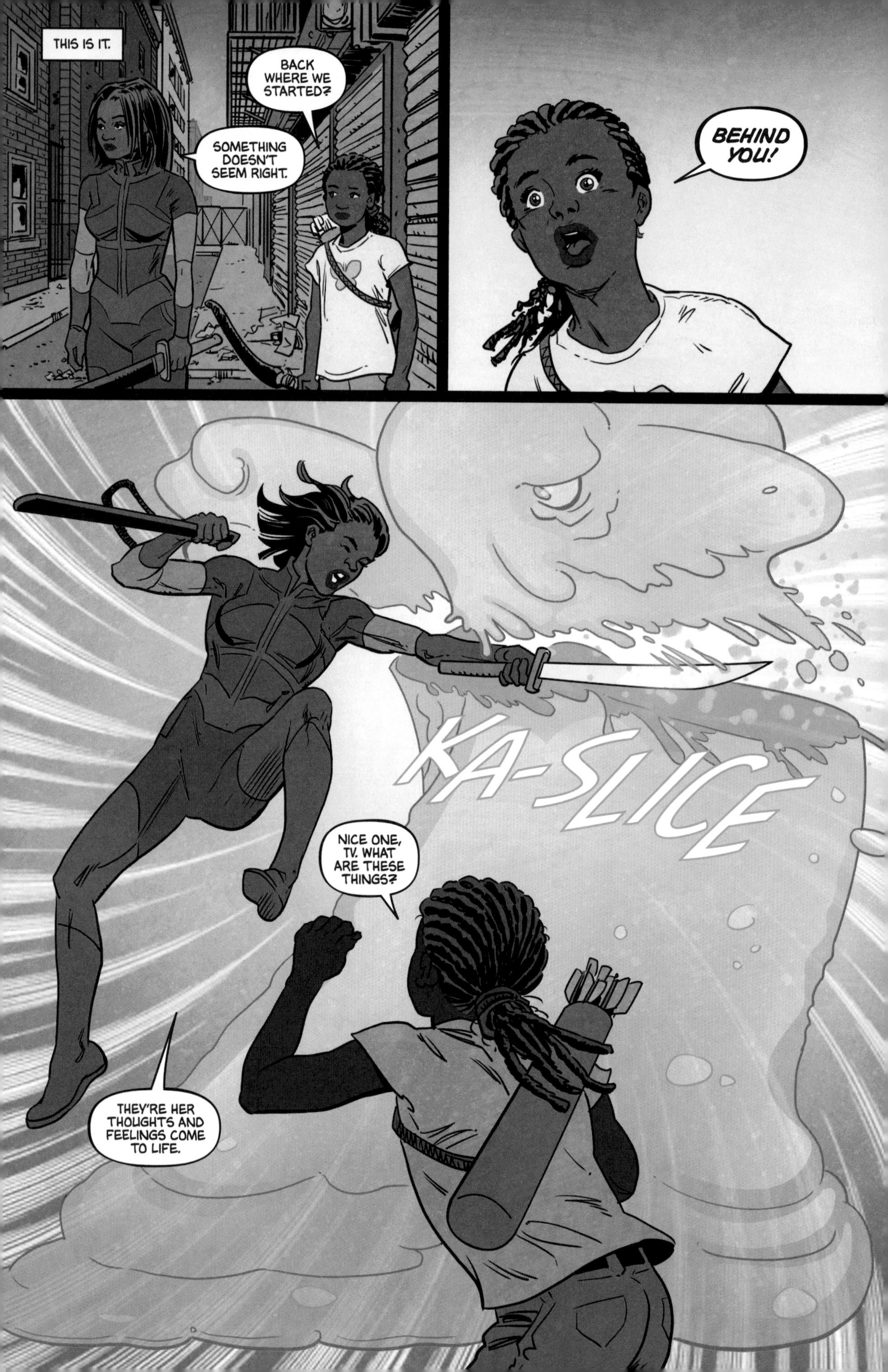
THIS IS IT.
BACK WHERE WE STARTED?
SOMETHING DOESN'T SEEM RIGHT.
BEHIND YOU!
KA-SLICE
NICE ONE, TV. WHAT ARE THESE THINGS?
THEY'RE HER THOUGHTS AND FEELINGS COME TO LIFE.

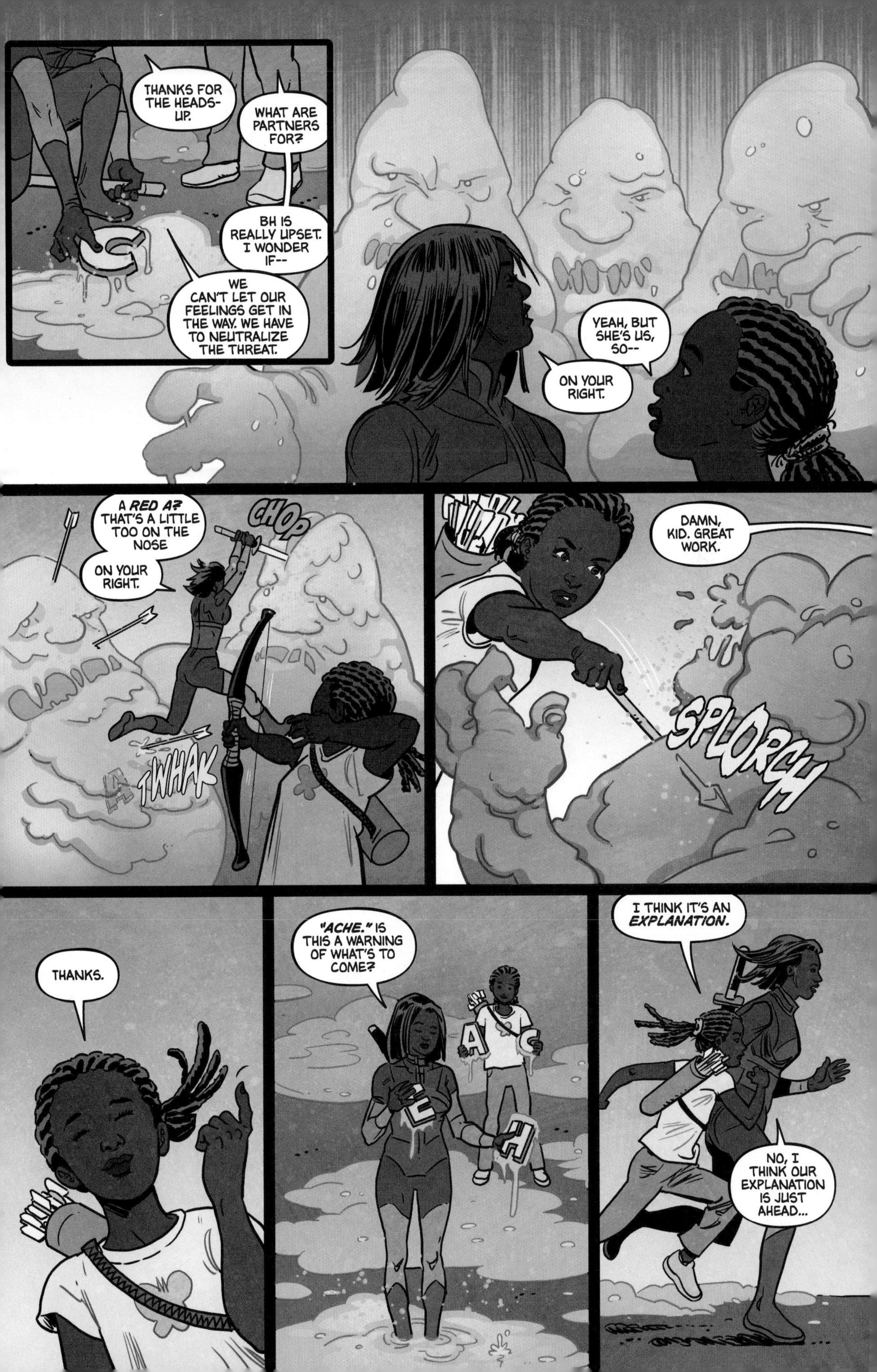
THANKS FOR THE HEADS-UP.
WHAT ARE PARTNERS FOR?
BH IS REALLY UPSET. I WONDER IF--
WE CAN'T LET OUR FEELINGS GET IN THE WAY. WE HAVE TO NEUTRALIZE THE THREAT.
YEAH, BUT SHE'S US, SO--
ON YOUR RIGHT.
A *RED A*? THAT'S A LITTLE TOO ON THE NOSE
ON YOUR RIGHT.
CHOP
TWHAK
DAMN, KID. GREAT WORK.
SPLORCH
THANKS.
"ACHE." IS THIS A WARNING OF WHAT'S TO COME?
I THINK IT'S AN *EXPLANATION*.
NO, I THINK OUR EXPLANATION IS JUST AHEAD...

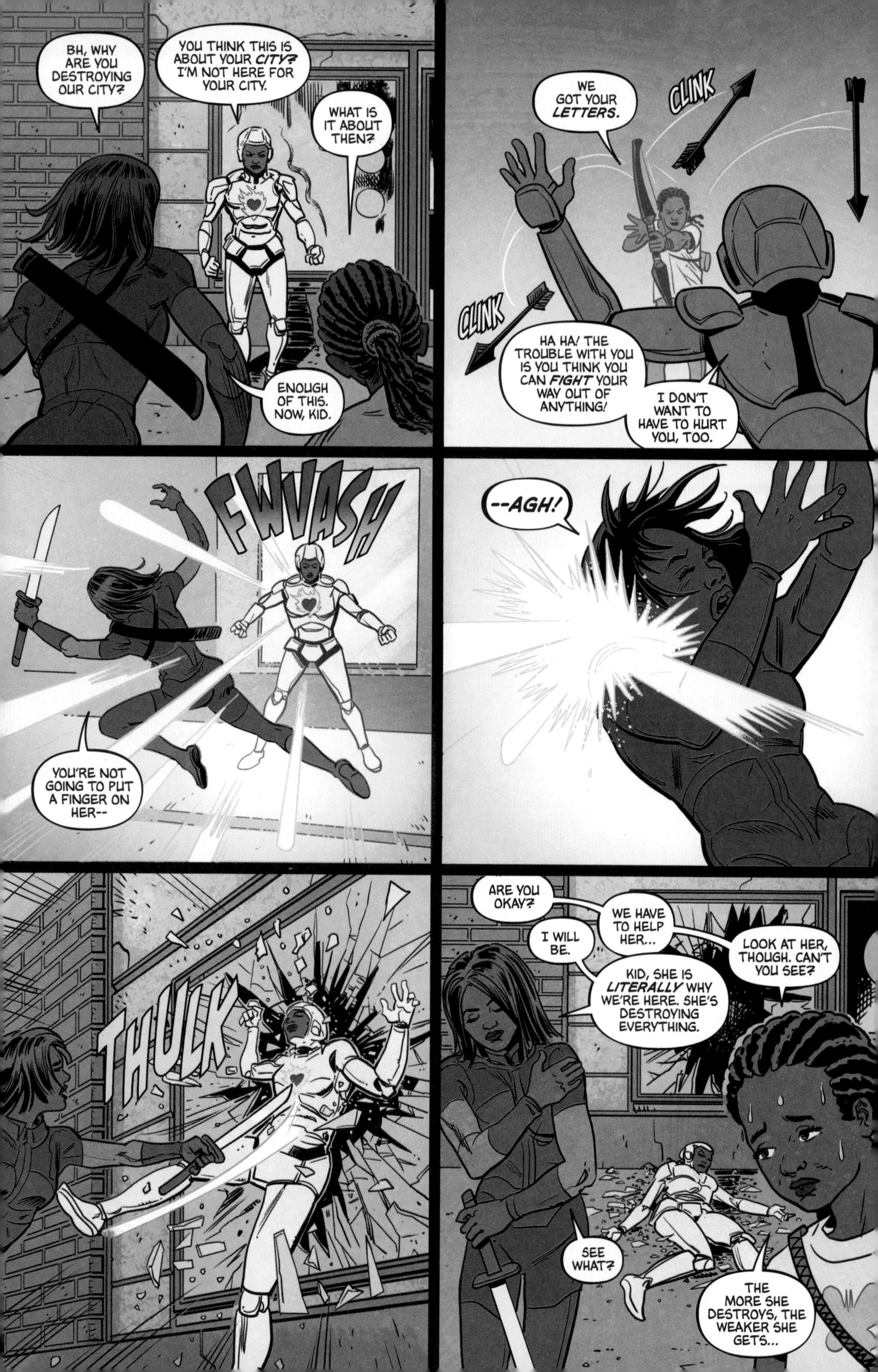
BH, WHY ARE YOU DESTROYING OUR CITY?
YOU THINK THIS IS ABOUT YOUR *CITY?* I'M NOT HERE FOR YOUR CITY.
WHAT IS IT ABOUT THEN?
ENOUGH OF THIS. NOW, KID.
WE GOT YOUR *LETTERS.*
CLINK
CLINK
HA HA! THE TROUBLE WITH YOU IS YOU THINK YOU CAN *FIGHT* YOUR WAY OUT OF ANYTHING!
I DON'T WANT TO HAVE TO HURT YOU, TOO.
FWVASH
YOU'RE NOT GOING TO PUT A FINGER ON HER--
--AGH!
THULK
ARE YOU OKAY?
I WILL BE.
WE HAVE TO HELP HER...
KID, SHE IS *LITERALLY* WHY WE'RE HERE. SHE'S DESTROYING EVERYTHING.
LOOK AT HER, THOUGH. CAN'T YOU SEE?
SEE WHAT?
THE MORE SHE DESTROYS, THE WEAKER SHE GETS...

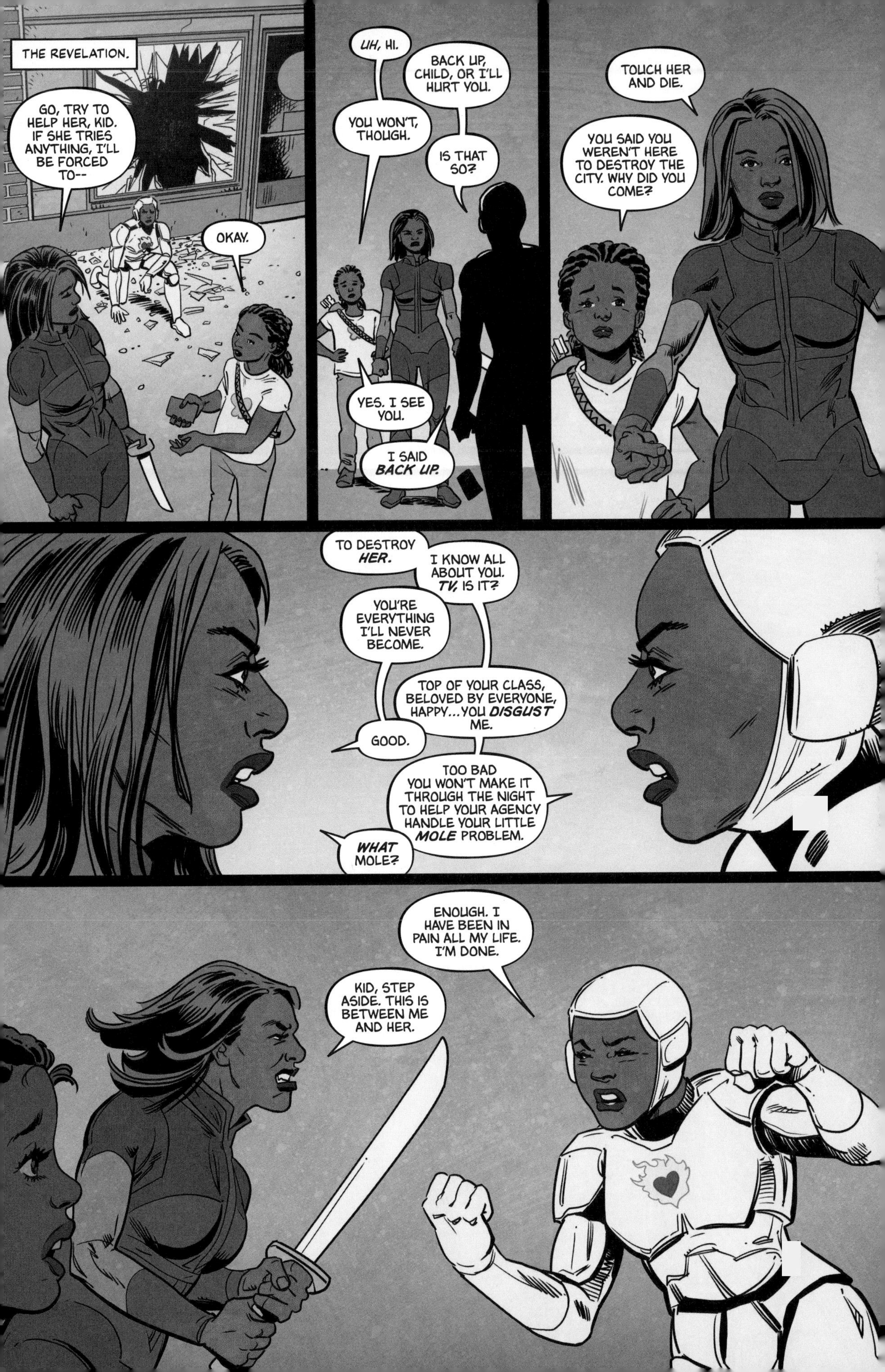
THE REVELATION.
GO, TRY TO HELP HER, KID. IF SHE TRIES ANYTHING, I'LL BE FORCED TO--
OKAY.
UH, HI.
BACK UP, CHILD, OR I'LL HURT YOU.
YOU WON'T, THOUGH.
IS THAT SO?
YES. I SEE YOU.
I SAID BACK UP.
TOUCH HER AND DIE.
YOU SAID YOU WEREN'T HERE TO DESTROY THE CITY. WHY DID YOU COME?
TO DESTROY HER.
I KNOW ALL ABOUT YOU. TV, IS IT?
YOU'RE EVERYTHING I'LL NEVER BECOME.
TOP OF YOUR CLASS, BELOVED BY EVERYONE, HAPPY...YOU DISGUST ME.
GOOD.
TOO BAD YOU WON'T MAKE IT THROUGH THE NIGHT TO HELP YOUR AGENCY HANDLE YOUR LITTLE MOLE PROBLEM.
WHAT MOLE?
ENOUGH. I HAVE BEEN IN PAIN ALL MY LIFE. I'M DONE.
KID, STEP ASIDE. THIS IS BETWEEN ME AND HER.

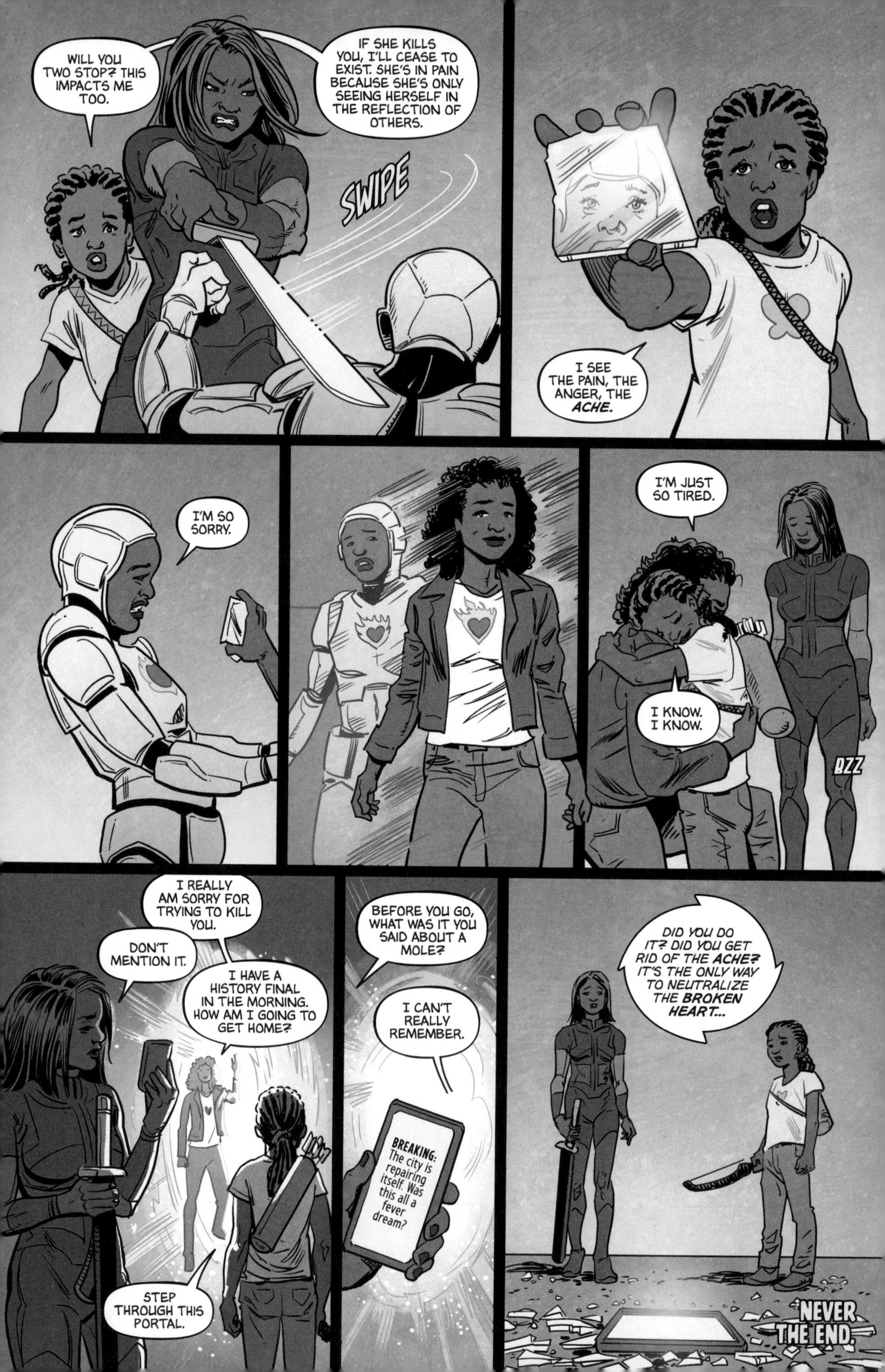
WILL YOU TWO STOP? THIS IMPACTS ME TOO.
IF SHE KILLS YOU, I'LL CEASE TO EXIST. SHE'S IN PAIN BECAUSE SHE'S ONLY SEEING HERSELF IN THE REFLECTION OF OTHERS.
SWIPE
I SEE THE PAIN, THE ANGER, THE ***ACHE.***
I'M SO SORRY.
I'M JUST SO TIRED.
I KNOW. I KNOW.
BZZ
I REALLY AM SORRY FOR TRYING TO KILL YOU.
DON'T MENTION IT.
I HAVE A HISTORY FINAL IN THE MORNING. HOW AM I GOING TO GET HOME?
STEP THROUGH THIS PORTAL.
BEFORE YOU GO, WHAT WAS IT YOU SAID ABOUT A MOLE?
I CAN'T REALLY REMEMBER.
BREAKING: The city is repairing itself. Was this all a fever dream?
*DID YOU DO IT? DID YOU GET RID OF THE **ACHE?** IT'S THE ONLY WAY TO NEUTRALIZE THE **BROKEN HEART...***
NEVER THE END.

REPRESENT!

CHAPTER FOURTEEN
"I'LL CATCH UP"

WRITER - CAMRUS JOHNSON

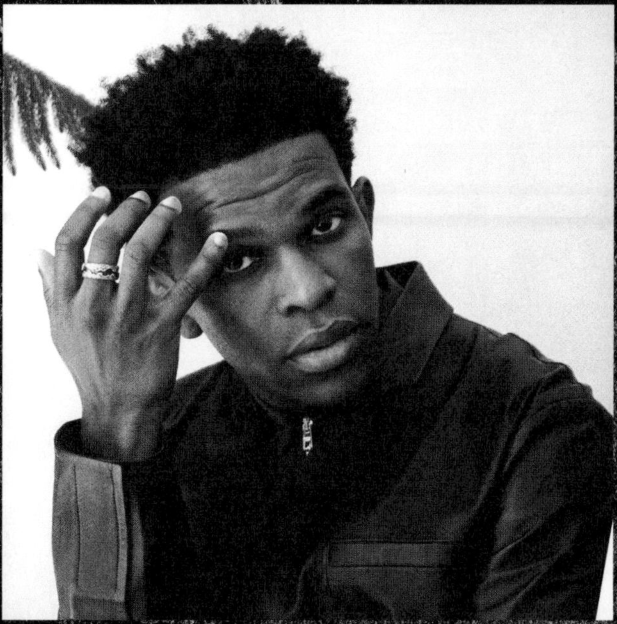

Camrus Johnson is going into season three as the male lead of the CW's *Batwoman*, playing comic book fan-favorite character Luke Fox. His previous animated short film, *Grab My Hand: A Letter to My Dad,* which he wrote, directed, and narrated, has won over 20 awards, including the top jury award at the only two existing Academy Award qualifying children's film festivals in the world. His next animated short, *She Dreams at Sunrise,* makes its world premiere at the 2021 Tribeca Film Festival (as part of the 8:46 Films program), while his first live-action short film, *Blue Bison*, premieres at the deadCenter Film Festival. Camrus's first DC Comics story "Superman Punch" (starring his tv character, Luke Fox), hits shelves in *Batman: Urban Legends* #4, and he also has a feature film and animated series in development.

PENCILS - TONY AKINS
INKS - MORITAT
COLORIST - DEE CUNNIFFE
LETTERER - DERON BENNETT

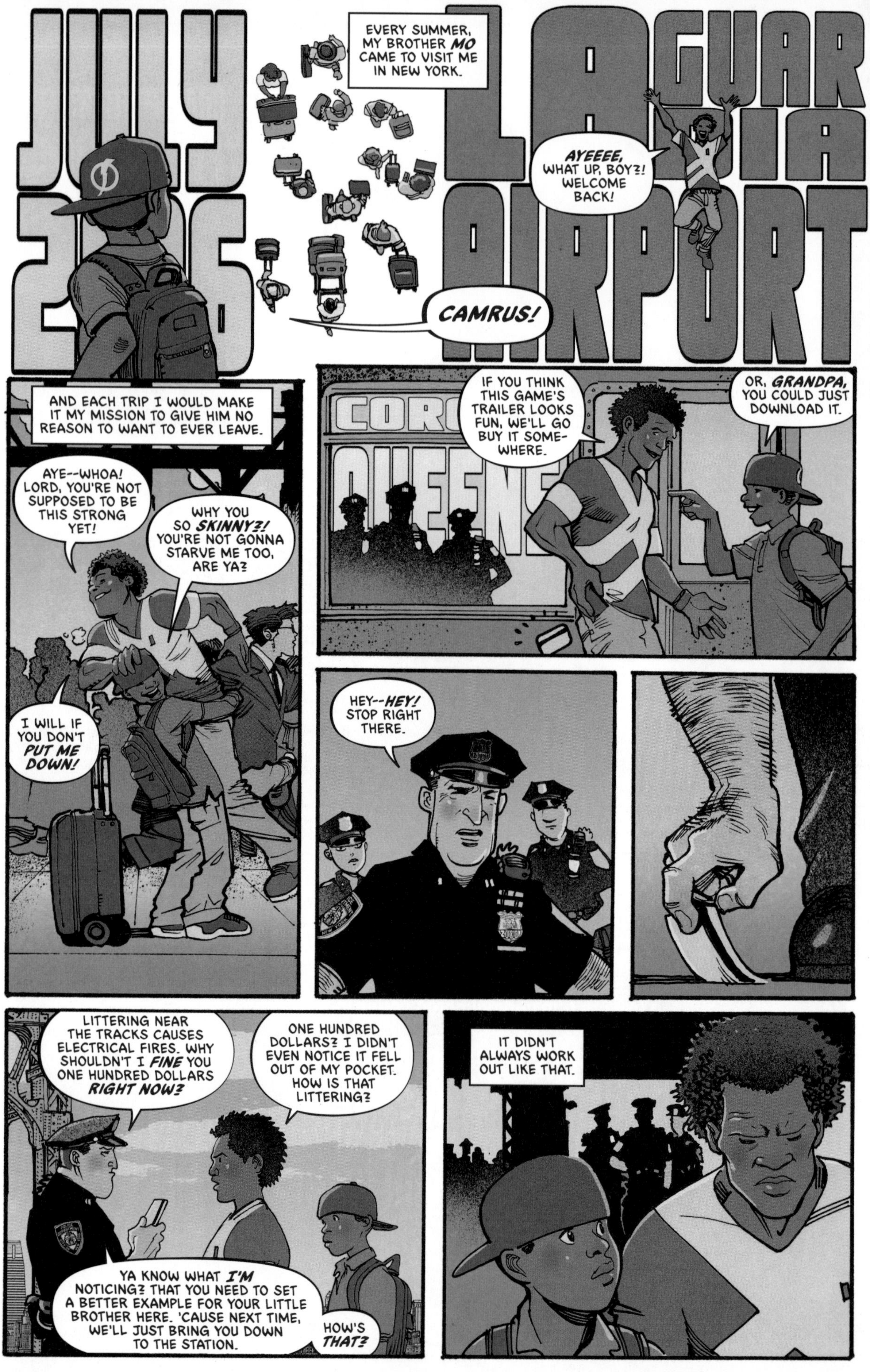

JULY 2006
EVERY SUMMER, MY BROTHER MO CAME TO VISIT ME IN NEW YORK.
LAGUARDIA AIRPORT
AYEEEE, WHAT UP, BOY?! WELCOME BACK!
CAMRUS!
AND EACH TRIP I WOULD MAKE IT MY MISSION TO GIVE HIM NO REASON TO WANT TO EVER LEAVE.
AYE--WHOA! LORD, YOU'RE NOT SUPPOSED TO BE THIS STRONG YET!
WHY YOU SO SKINNY?! YOU'RE NOT GONNA STARVE ME TOO, ARE YA?
I WILL IF YOU DON'T PUT ME DOWN!
CORO
QUEENS
IF YOU THINK THIS GAME'S TRAILER LOOKS FUN, WE'LL GO BUY IT SOMEWHERE.
OR, GRANDPA, YOU COULD JUST DOWNLOAD IT.
HEY--HEY! STOP RIGHT THERE.
LITTERING NEAR THE TRACKS CAUSES ELECTRICAL FIRES. WHY SHOULDN'T I FINE YOU ONE HUNDRED DOLLARS RIGHT NOW?
ONE HUNDRED DOLLARS? I DIDN'T EVEN NOTICE IT FELL OUT OF MY POCKET. HOW IS THAT LITTERING?
YA KNOW WHAT I'M NOTICING? THAT YOU NEED TO SET A BETTER EXAMPLE FOR YOUR LITTLE BROTHER HERE. 'CAUSE NEXT TIME, WE'LL JUST BRING YOU DOWN TO THE STATION.
HOW'S THAT?
IT DIDN'T ALWAYS WORK OUT LIKE THAT.

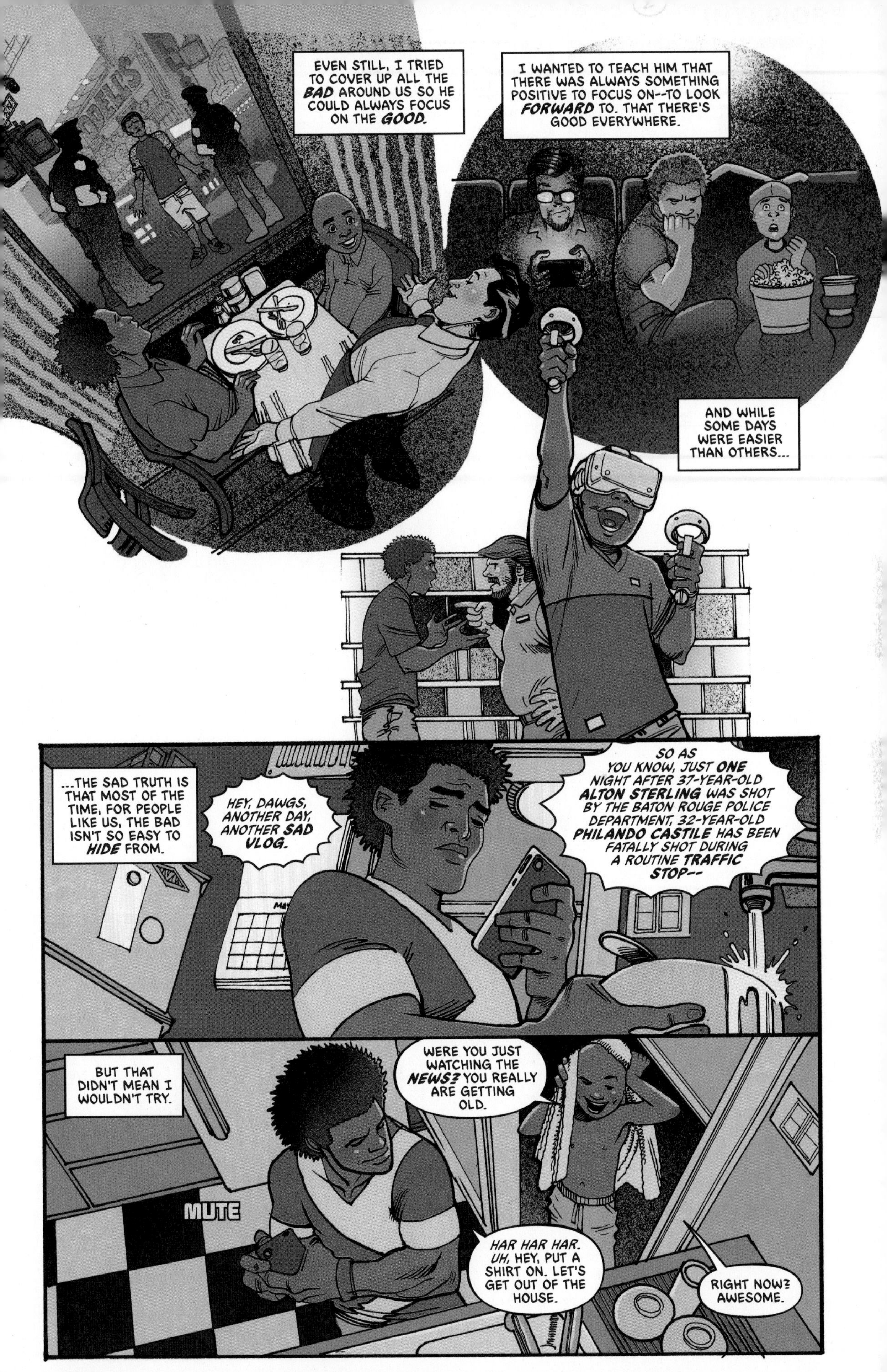
EVEN STILL, I TRIED TO COVER UP ALL THE BAD AROUND US SO HE COULD ALWAYS FOCUS ON THE GOOD.
I WANTED TO TEACH HIM THAT THERE WAS ALWAYS SOMETHING POSITIVE TO FOCUS ON--TO LOOK FORWARD TO. THAT THERE'S GOOD EVERYWHERE.
AND WHILE SOME DAYS WERE EASIER THAN OTHERS...
...THE SAD TRUTH IS THAT MOST OF THE TIME, FOR PEOPLE LIKE US, THE BAD ISN'T SO EASY TO HIDE FROM.
HEY, DAWGS, ANOTHER DAY, ANOTHER SAD VLOG.
SO AS YOU KNOW, JUST ONE NIGHT AFTER 37-YEAR-OLD ALTON STERLING WAS SHOT BY THE BATON ROUGE POLICE DEPARTMENT, 32-YEAR-OLD PHILANDO CASTILE HAS BEEN FATALLY SHOT DURING A ROUTINE TRAFFIC STOP--
BUT THAT DIDN'T MEAN I WOULDN'T TRY.
WERE YOU JUST WATCHING THE NEWS? YOU REALLY ARE GETTING OLD.
MUTE
HAR HAR HAR. UH, HEY, PUT A SHIRT ON. LET'S GET OUT OF THE HOUSE.
RIGHT NOW? AWESOME.

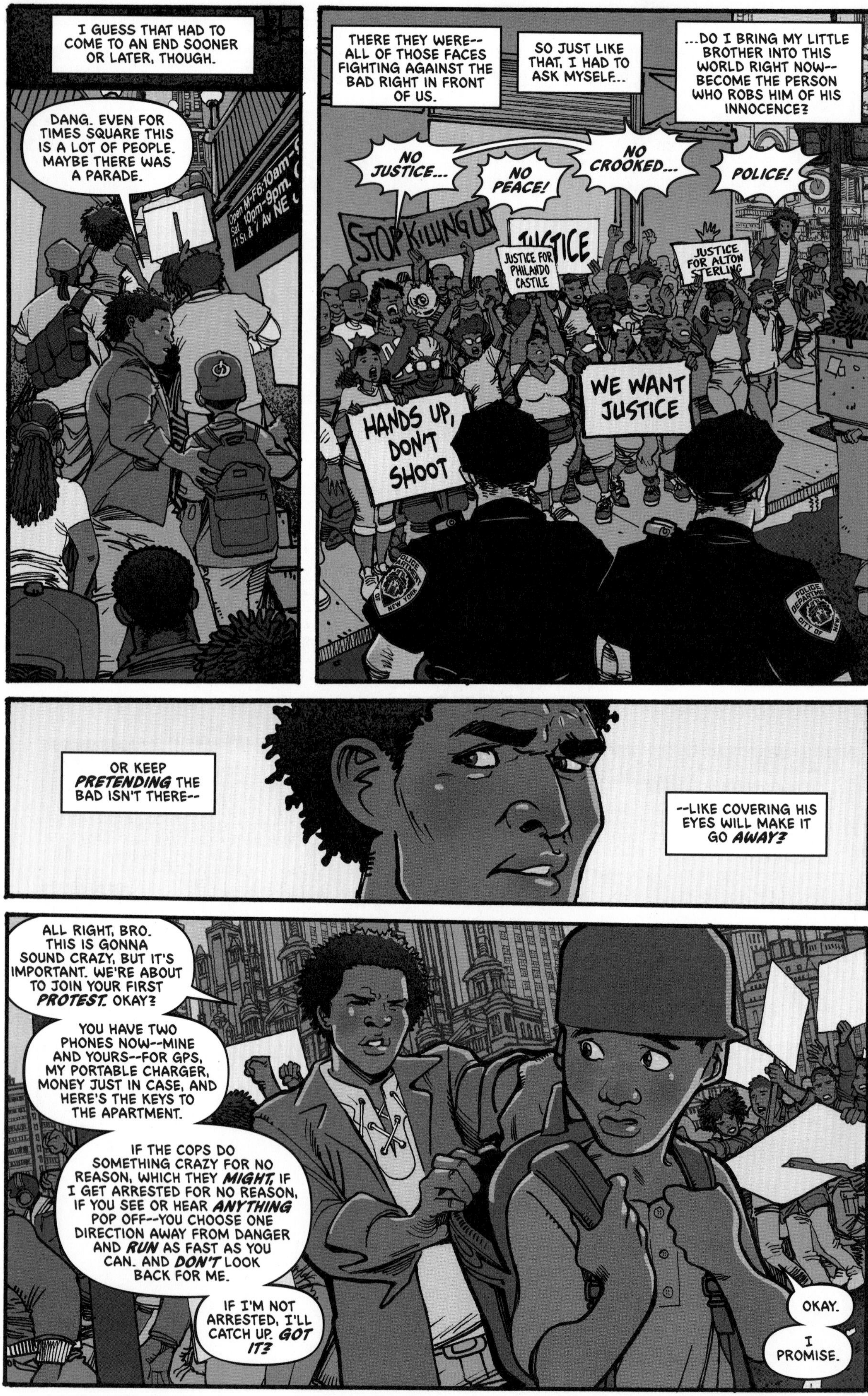
I GUESS THAT HAD TO COME TO AN END SOONER OR LATER, THOUGH.
DANG. EVEN FOR TIMES SQUARE THIS IS A LOT OF PEOPLE. MAYBE THERE WAS A PARADE.
THERE THEY WERE-- ALL OF THOSE FACES FIGHTING AGAINST THE BAD RIGHT IN FRONT OF US.
SO JUST LIKE THAT, I HAD TO ASK MYSELF...
...DO I BRING MY LITTLE BROTHER INTO THIS WORLD RIGHT NOW-- BECOME THE PERSON WHO ROBS HIM OF HIS INNOCENCE?
NO JUSTICE...
NO PEACE!
NO CROOKED...
POLICE!
JUSTICE FOR PHILANDO CASTILE
JUSTICE FOR ALTON STERLING
HANDS UP, DON'T SHOOT
WE WANT JUSTICE
OR KEEP PRETENDING THE BAD ISN'T THERE--
--LIKE COVERING HIS EYES WILL MAKE IT GO AWAY?
ALL RIGHT, BRO. THIS IS GONNA SOUND CRAZY, BUT IT'S IMPORTANT. WE'RE ABOUT TO JOIN YOUR FIRST PROTEST. OKAY?
YOU HAVE TWO PHONES NOW--MINE AND YOURS--FOR GPS, MY PORTABLE CHARGER, MONEY JUST IN CASE, AND HERE'S THE KEYS TO THE APARTMENT.
IF THE COPS DO SOMETHING CRAZY FOR NO REASON, WHICH THEY MIGHT, IF I GET ARRESTED FOR NO REASON, IF YOU SEE OR HEAR ANYTHING POP OFF--YOU CHOOSE ONE DIRECTION AWAY FROM DANGER AND RUN AS FAST AS YOU CAN. AND DON'T LOOK BACK FOR ME.
IF I'M NOT ARRESTED, I'LL CATCH UP. GOT IT?
OKAY.
I PROMISE.

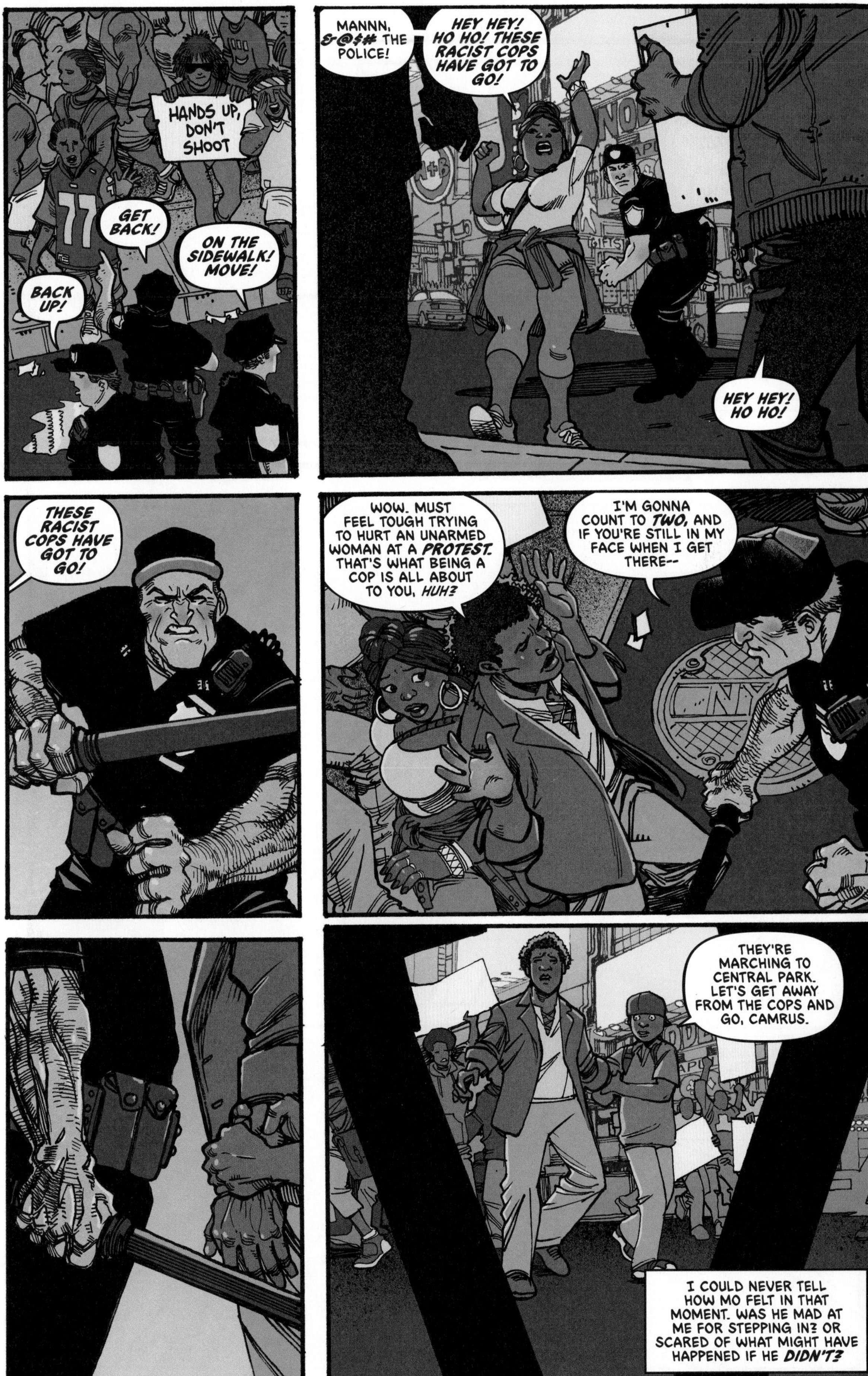
HANDS UP, DON'T SHOOT
GET BACK!
ON THE SIDEWALK! MOVE!
BACK UP!
MANNN, &@$# THE POLICE!
HEY HEY! HO HO! THESE RACIST COPS HAVE GOT TO GO!
HEY HEY! HO HO!
THESE RACIST COPS HAVE GOT TO GO!
WOW. MUST FEEL TOUGH TRYING TO HURT AN UNARMED WOMAN AT A PROTEST. THAT'S WHAT BEING A COP IS ALL ABOUT TO YOU, HUH?
I'M GONNA COUNT TO TWO, AND IF YOU'RE STILL IN MY FACE WHEN I GET THERE--
THEY'RE MARCHING TO CENTRAL PARK. LET'S GET AWAY FROM THE COPS AND GO, CAMRUS.
I COULD NEVER TELL HOW MO FELT IN THAT MOMENT. WAS HE MAD AT ME FOR STEPPING IN? OR SCARED OF WHAT MIGHT HAVE HAPPENED IF HE DIDN'T?

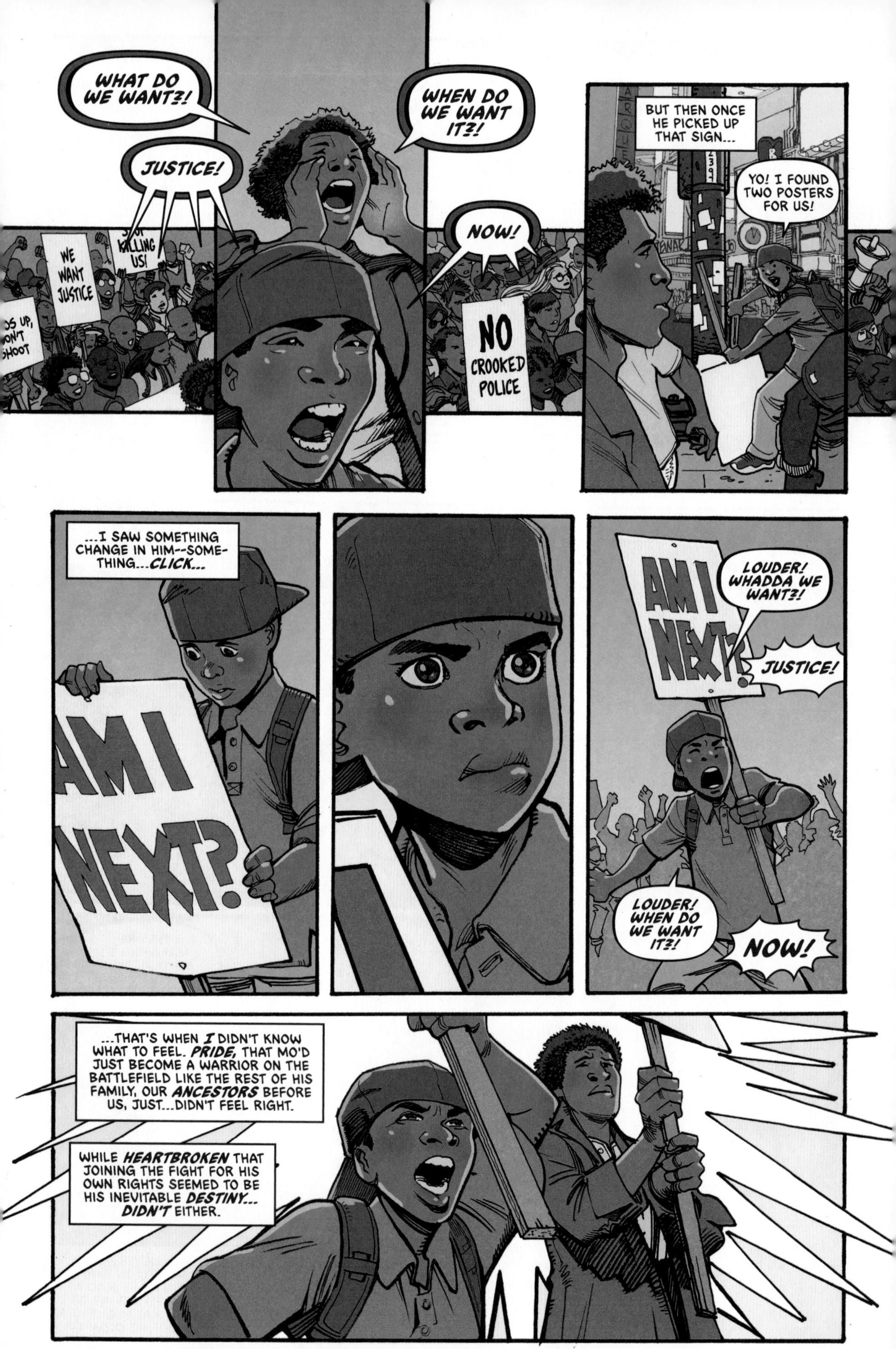
WHAT DO WE WANT?!
JUSTICE!
WHEN DO WE WANT IT?!
NOW!
WE WANT JUSTICE
KILLING US!
NO CROOKED POLICE
BUT THEN ONCE HE PICKED UP THAT SIGN...
YO! I FOUND TWO POSTERS FOR US!
...I SAW SOMETHING CHANGE IN HIM--SOMETHING...CLICK...
AM I NEXT?
AM I NEXT?!
LOUDER! WHADDA WE WANT?!
JUSTICE!
LOUDER! WHEN DO WE WANT IT?!
NOW!
...THAT'S WHEN I DIDN'T KNOW WHAT TO FEEL. PRIDE, THAT MO'D JUST BECOME A WARRIOR ON THE BATTLEFIELD LIKE THE REST OF HIS FAMILY, OUR ANCESTORS BEFORE US, JUST...DIDN'T FEEL RIGHT.
WHILE HEARTBROKEN THAT JOINING THE FIGHT FOR HIS OWN RIGHTS SEEMED TO BE HIS INEVITABLE DESTINY... DIDN'T EITHER.

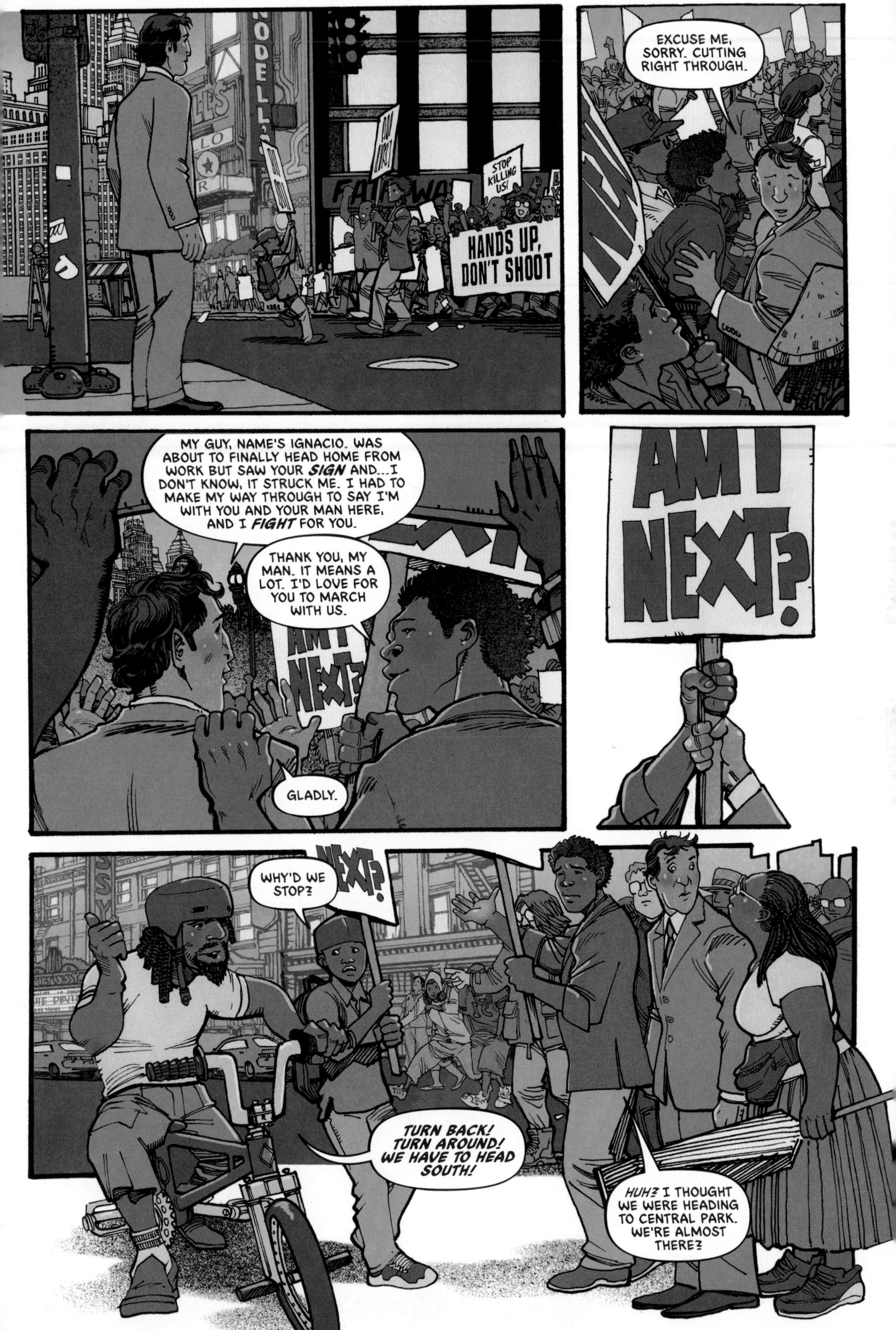

STOP KILLING US!
HANDS UP, DON'T SHOOT
EXCUSE ME, SORRY. CUTTING RIGHT THROUGH.
MY GUY, NAME'S IGNACIO. WAS ABOUT TO FINALLY HEAD HOME FROM WORK BUT SAW YOUR *SIGN* AND... I DON'T KNOW, IT STRUCK ME. I HAD TO MAKE MY WAY THROUGH TO SAY I'M WITH YOU AND YOUR MAN HERE, AND I *FIGHT* FOR YOU.
THANK YOU, MY MAN. IT MEANS A LOT. I'D LOVE FOR YOU TO MARCH WITH US.
GLADLY.
AM I NEXT?
WHY'D WE STOP?
TURN BACK! TURN AROUND! WE HAVE TO HEAD SOUTH!
HUH? I THOUGHT WE WERE HEADING TO CENTRAL PARK. WE'RE ALMOST THERE?

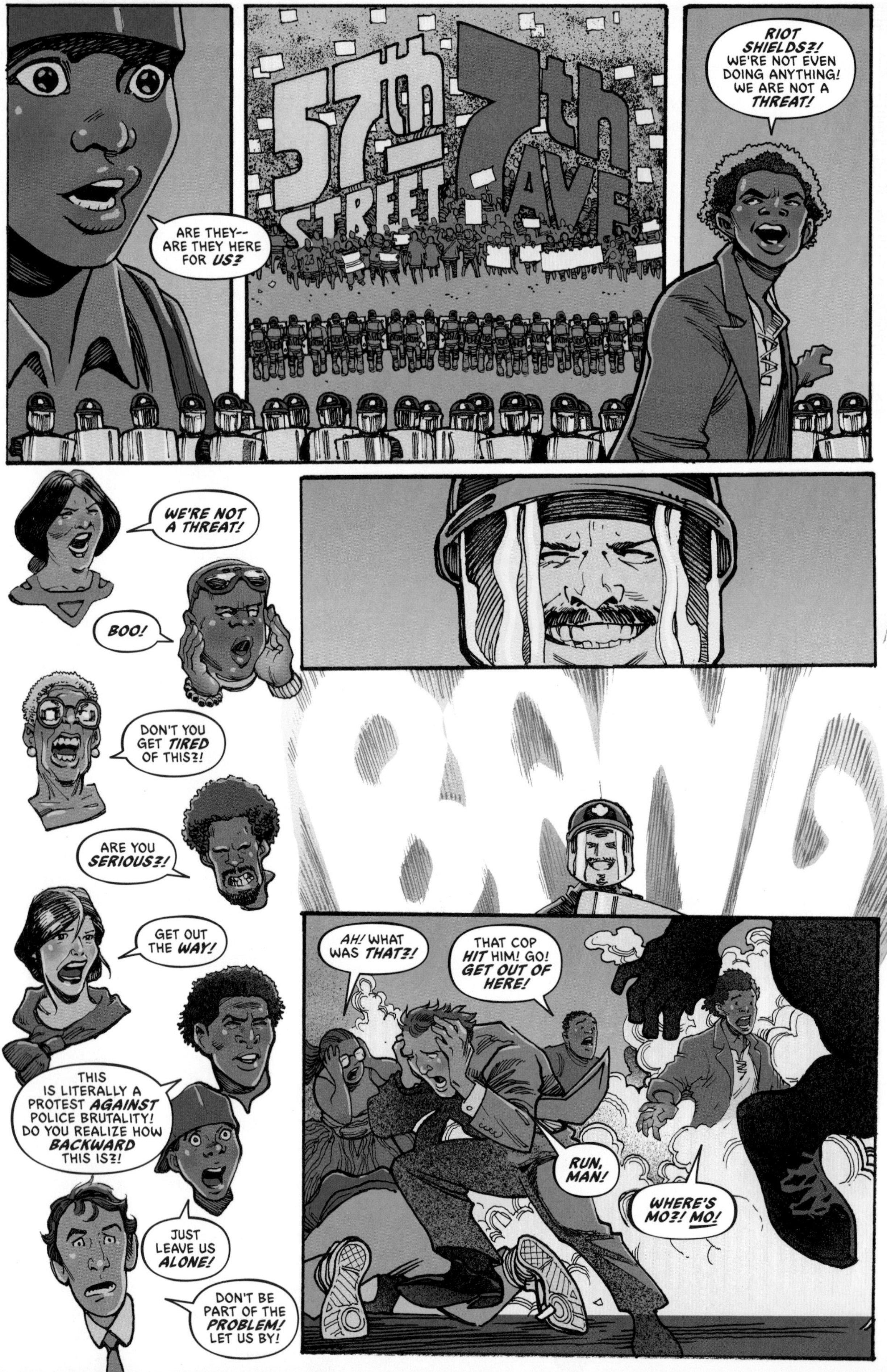
ARE THEY-- ARE THEY HERE FOR US?
57th STREET
7th AVE
RIOT SHIELDS?! WE'RE NOT EVEN DOING ANYTHING! WE ARE NOT A THREAT!
WE'RE NOT A THREAT!
BOO!
DON'T YOU GET TIRED OF THIS?!
ARE YOU SERIOUS?!
GET OUT THE WAY!
THIS IS LITERALLY A PROTEST AGAINST POLICE BRUTALITY! DO YOU REALIZE HOW BACKWARD THIS IS?!
JUST LEAVE US ALONE!
DON'T BE PART OF THE PROBLEM! LET US BY!
AH! WHAT WAS THAT?!
THAT COP HIT HIM! GO! GET OUT OF HERE!
RUN, MAN!
WHERE'S MO?! MO!

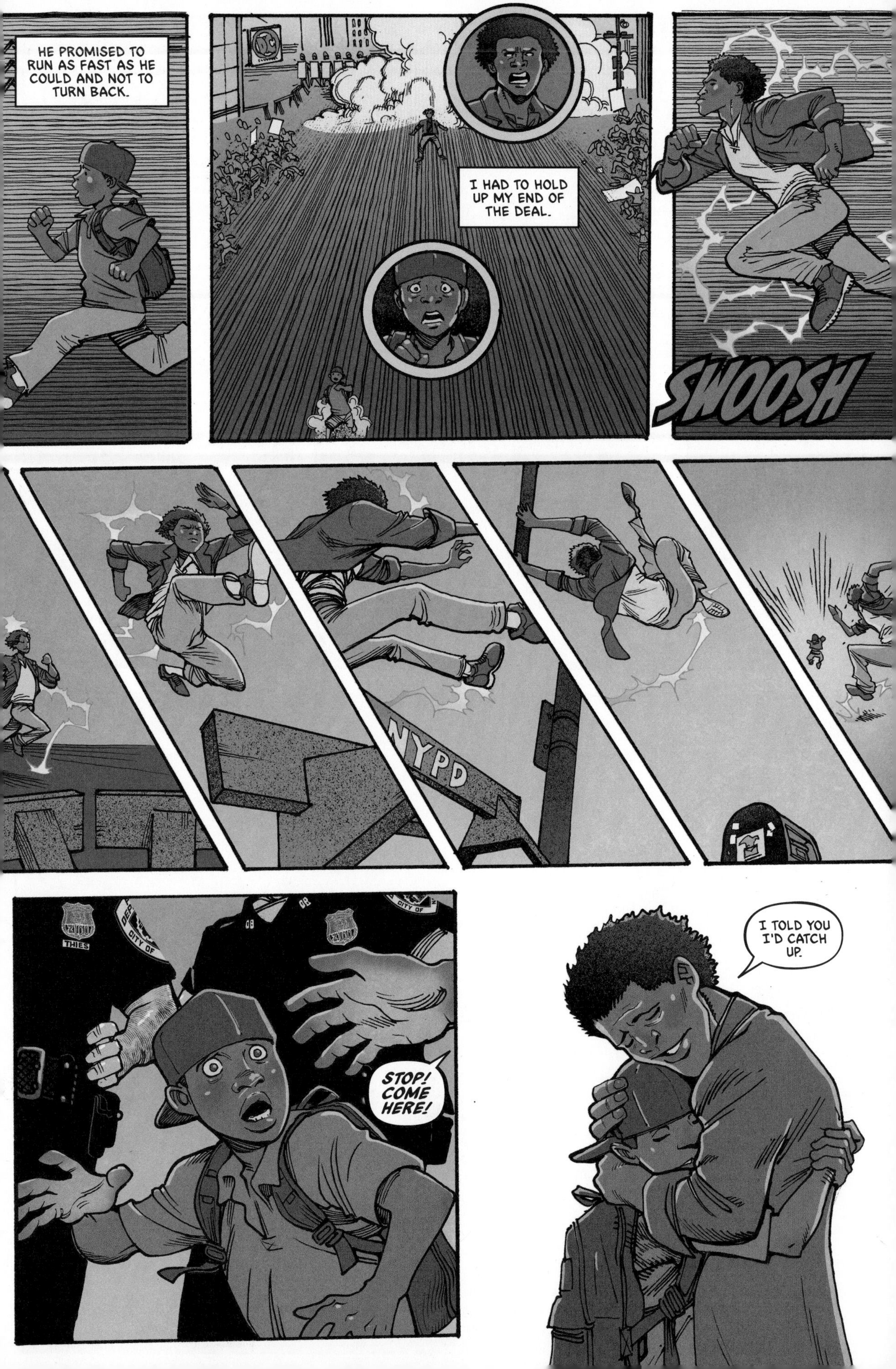
HE PROMISED TO RUN AS FAST AS HE COULD AND NOT TO TURN BACK.
I HAD TO HOLD UP MY END OF THE DEAL.
SWOOSH
NYPD
STOP! COME HERE!
I TOLD YOU I'D CATCH UP.

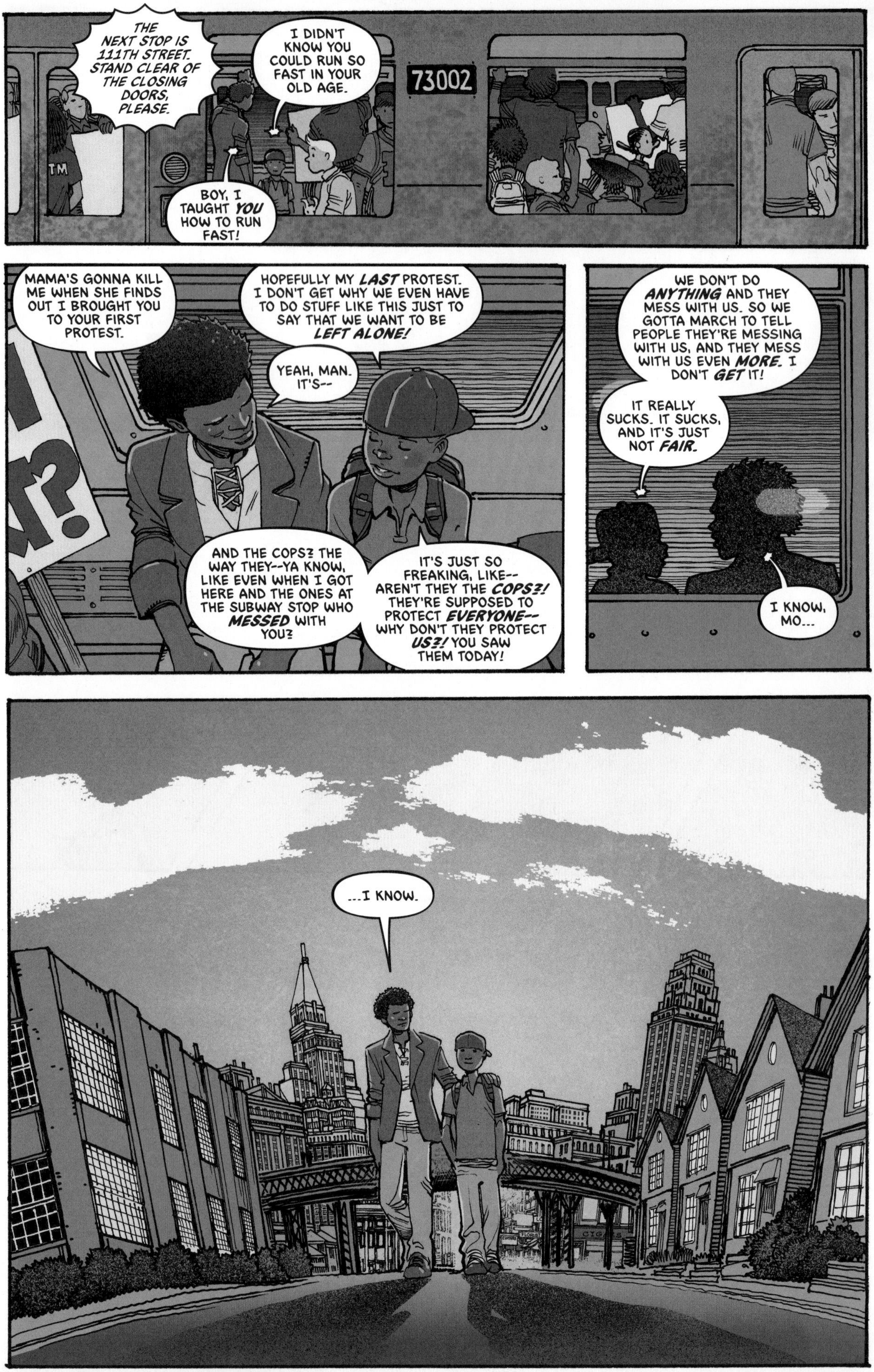
THE NEXT STOP IS 111TH STREET. STAND CLEAR OF THE CLOSING DOORS, PLEASE.
73002
I DIDN'T KNOW YOU COULD RUN SO FAST IN YOUR OLD AGE.
BOY, I TAUGHT *YOU* HOW TO RUN FAST!
MAMA'S GONNA KILL ME WHEN SHE FINDS OUT I BROUGHT YOU TO YOUR FIRST PROTEST.
HOPEFULLY MY *LAST* PROTEST. I DON'T GET WHY WE EVEN HAVE TO DO STUFF LIKE THIS JUST TO SAY THAT WE WANT TO BE *LEFT ALONE!*
YEAH, MAN. IT'S--
AND THE COPS? THE WAY THEY--YA KNOW, LIKE EVEN WHEN I GOT HERE AND THE ONES AT THE SUBWAY STOP WHO *MESSED* WITH YOU?
IT'S JUST SO FREAKING, LIKE--AREN'T THEY THE *COPS?!* THEY'RE SUPPOSED TO PROTECT *EVERYONE--* WHY DON'T THEY PROTECT *US?!* YOU SAW THEM TODAY!
WE DON'T DO *ANYTHING* AND THEY MESS WITH US. SO WE GOTTA MARCH TO TELL PEOPLE THEY'RE MESSING WITH US, AND THEY MESS WITH US EVEN *MORE*. I DON'T *GET* IT!
IT REALLY SUCKS. IT SUCKS, AND IT'S JUST NOT *FAIR*.
I KNOW, MO...
...I KNOW.

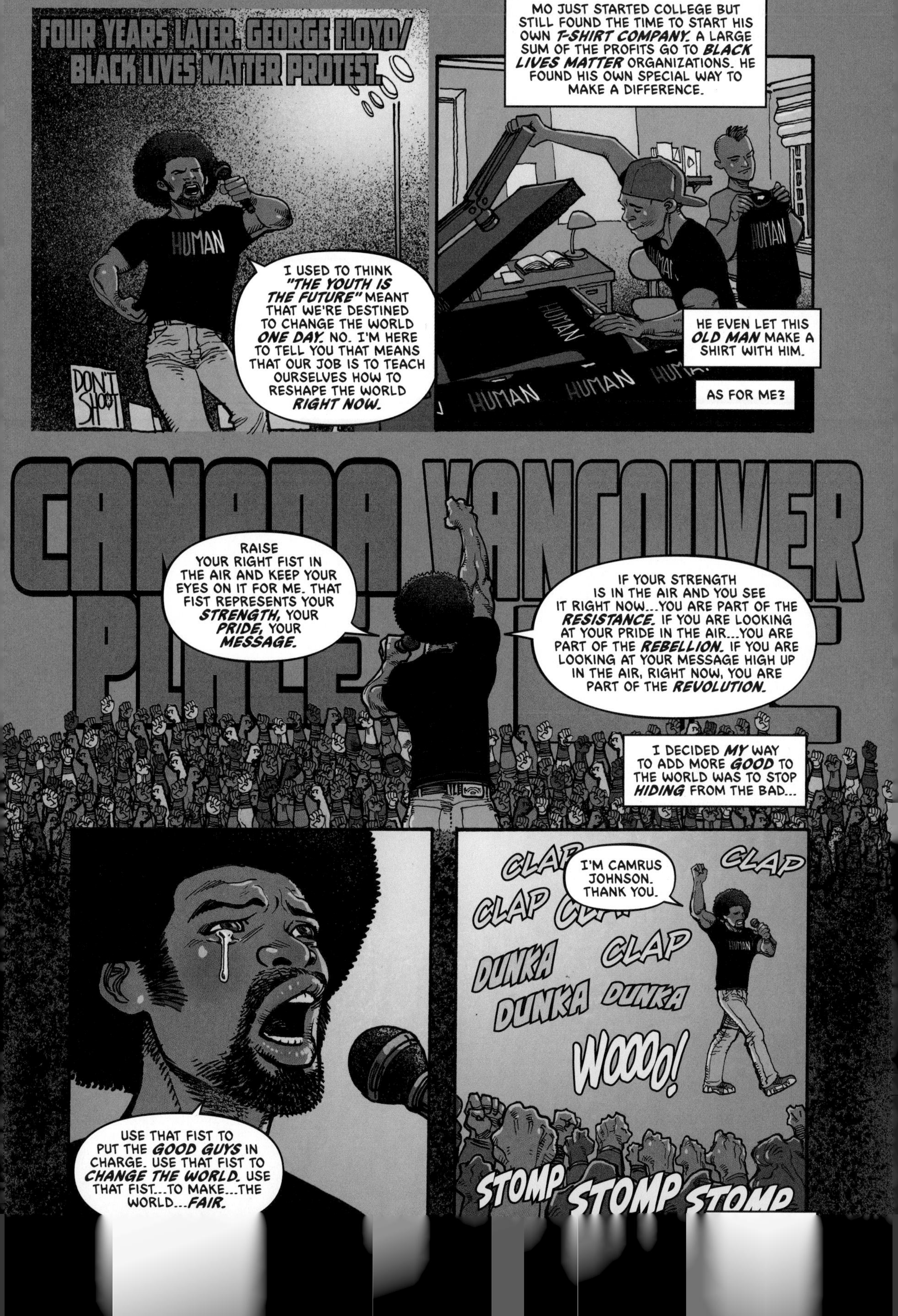
FOUR YEARS LATER. GEORGE FLOYD/ BLACK LIVES MATTER PROTEST.
HUMAN
I USED TO THINK "THE YOUTH IS THE FUTURE" MEANT THAT WE'RE DESTINED TO CHANGE THE WORLD ONE DAY. NO. I'M HERE TO TELL YOU THAT MEANS THAT OUR JOB IS TO TEACH OURSELVES HOW TO RESHAPE THE WORLD RIGHT NOW.
DON'T SHOOT
MO JUST STARTED COLLEGE BUT STILL FOUND THE TIME TO START HIS OWN T-SHIRT COMPANY. A LARGE SUM OF THE PROFITS GO TO BLACK LIVES MATTER ORGANIZATIONS. HE FOUND HIS OWN SPECIAL WAY TO MAKE A DIFFERENCE.
HUMAN
HUMAN
HUMAN HUMAN
HE EVEN LET THIS OLD MAN MAKE A SHIRT WITH HIM.
AS FOR ME?
CANADA VANCOUVER
RAISE YOUR RIGHT FIST IN THE AIR AND KEEP YOUR EYES ON IT FOR ME. THAT FIST REPRESENTS YOUR STRENGTH, YOUR PRIDE, YOUR MESSAGE.
IF YOUR STRENGTH IS IN THE AIR AND YOU SEE IT RIGHT NOW...YOU ARE PART OF THE RESISTANCE. IF YOU ARE LOOKING AT YOUR PRIDE IN THE AIR...YOU ARE PART OF THE REBELLION. IF YOU ARE LOOKING AT YOUR MESSAGE HIGH UP IN THE AIR, RIGHT NOW, YOU ARE PART OF THE REVOLUTION.
I DECIDED MY WAY TO ADD MORE GOOD TO THE WORLD WAS TO STOP HIDING FROM THE BAD...
USE THAT FIST TO PUT THE GOOD GUYS IN CHARGE. USE THAT FIST TO CHANGE THE WORLD. USE THAT FIST...TO MAKE...THE WORLD...FAIR.
CLAP
I'M CAMRUS JOHNSON. THANK YOU.
CLAP
CLAP
CLAP
DUNKA
DUNKA
DUNKA
HUMAN
WOOOO!
STOMP STOMP STOMP

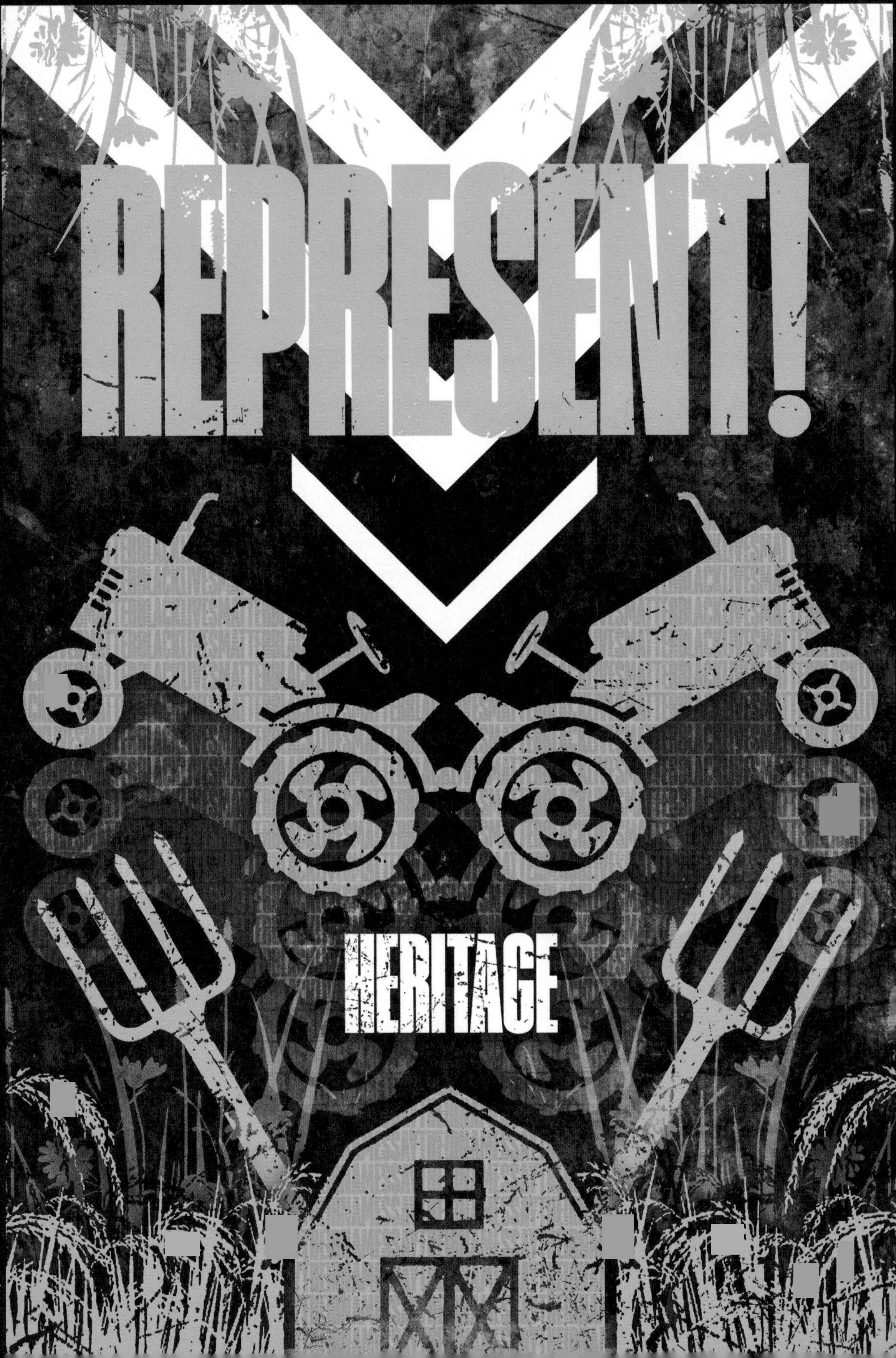
REPRESENT!
HERITAGE

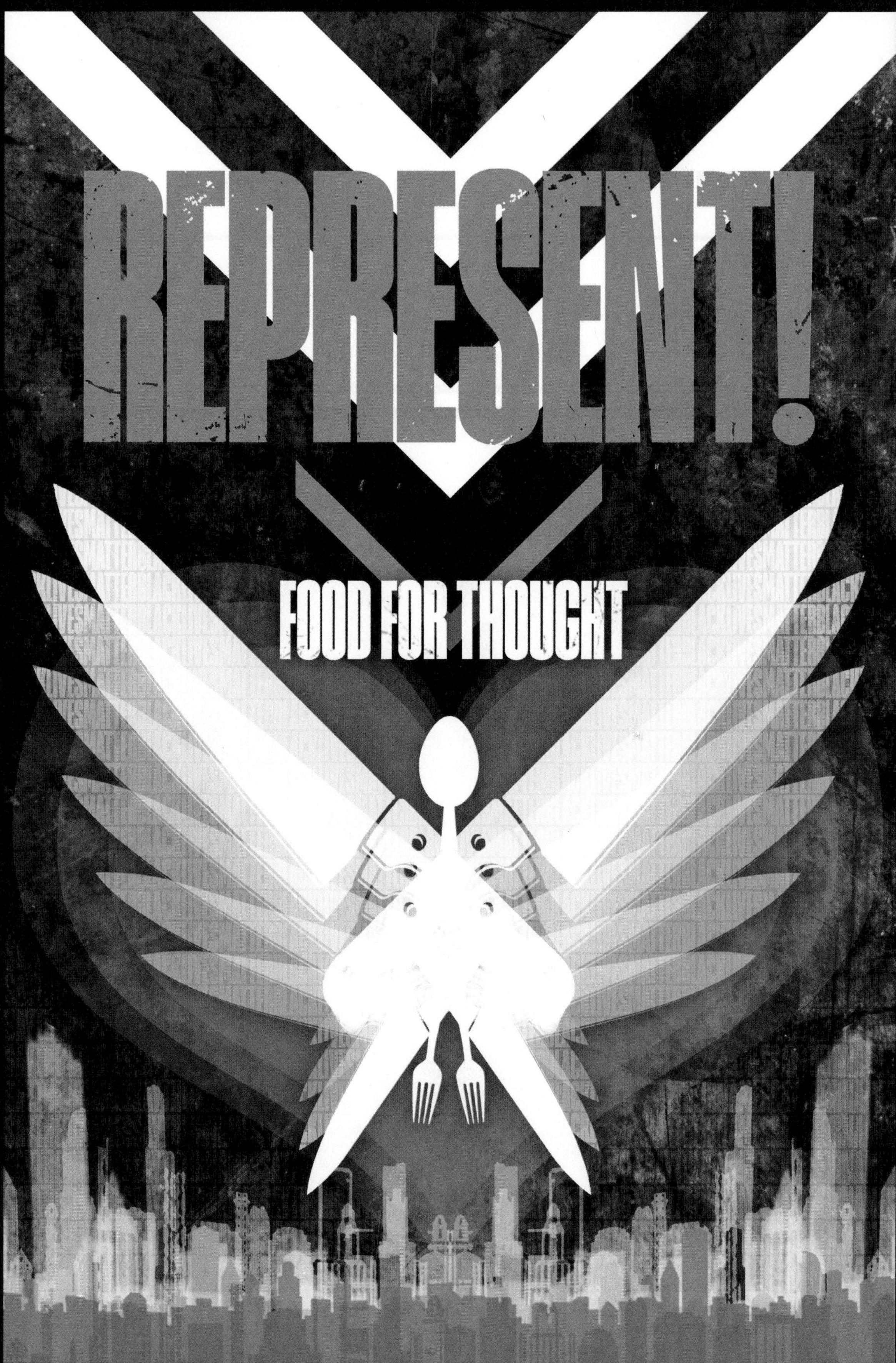
REPRESENT!
FOOD FOR THOUGHT

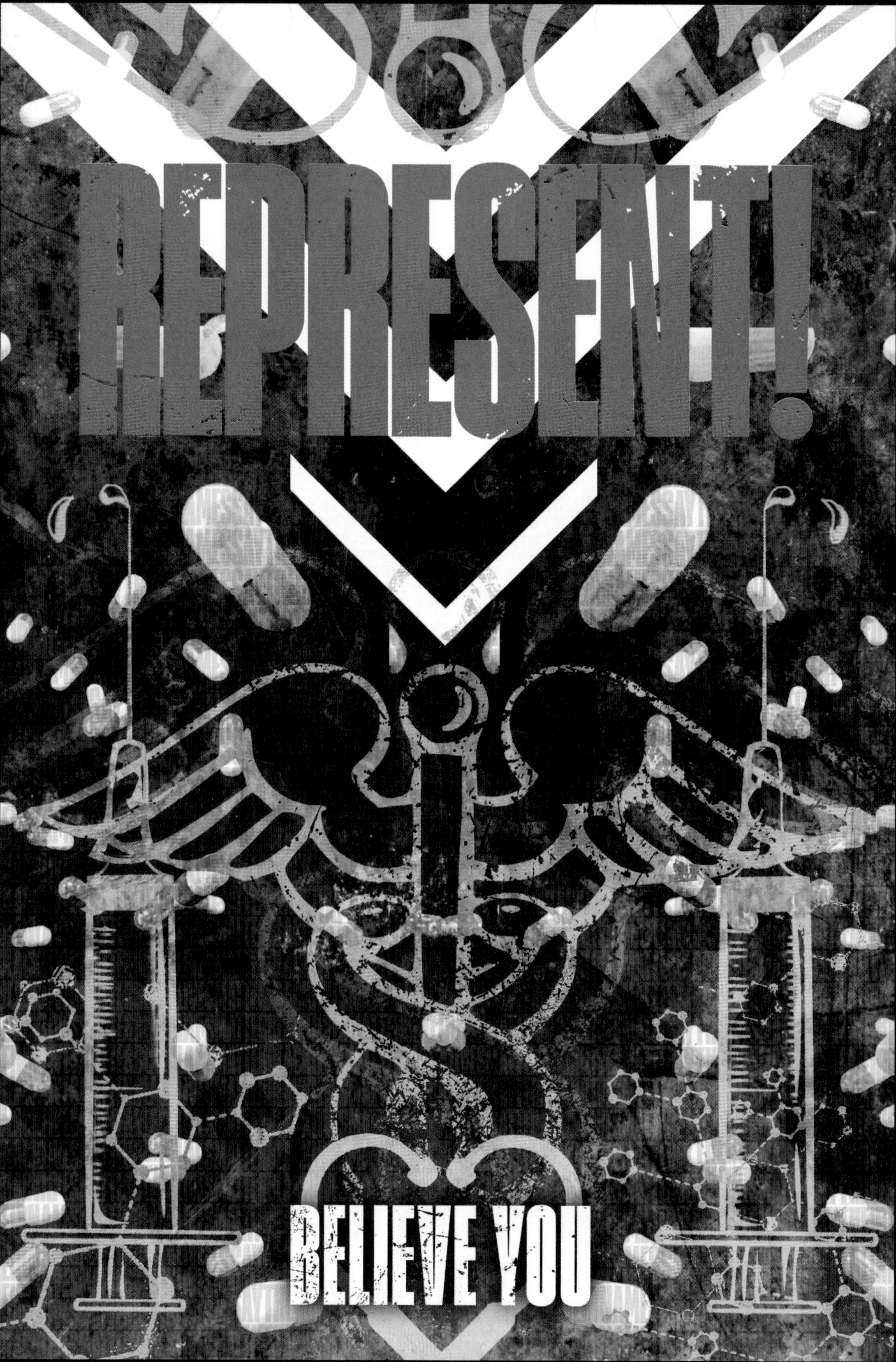
REPRESENT!
BELIEVE YOU

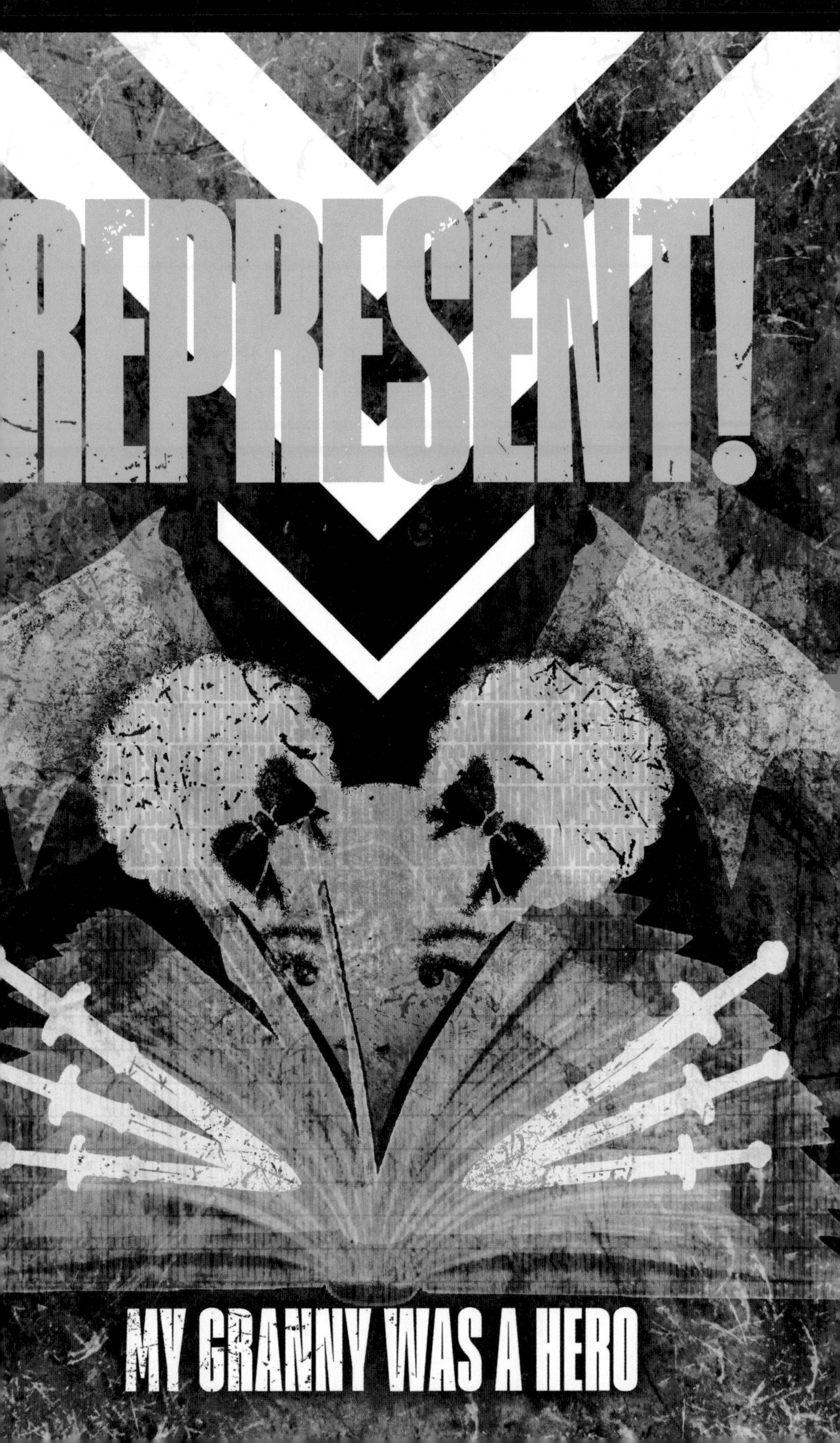
REPRESENT!
MY GRANNY WAS A HERO

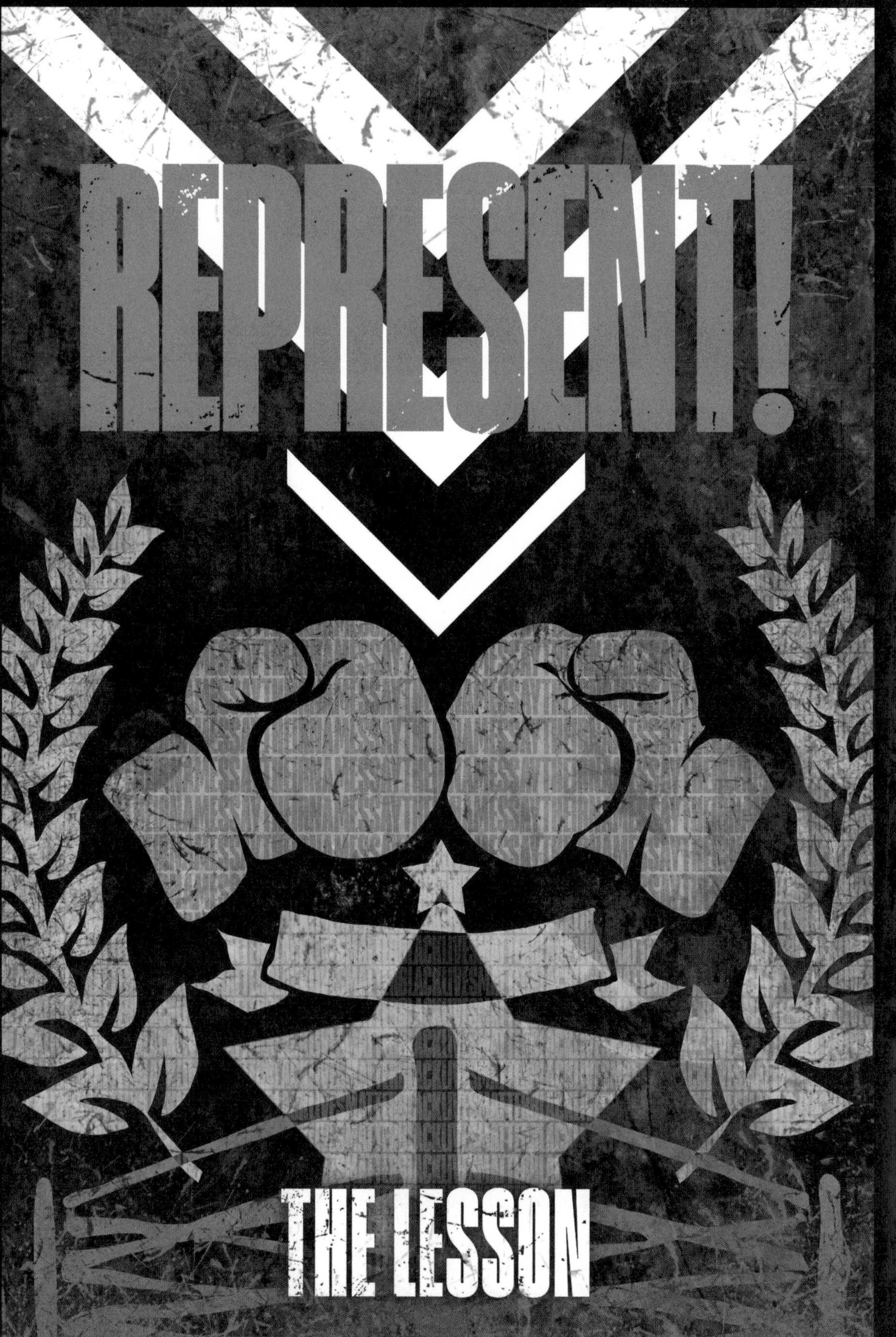
REPRESENT!
THE LESSON

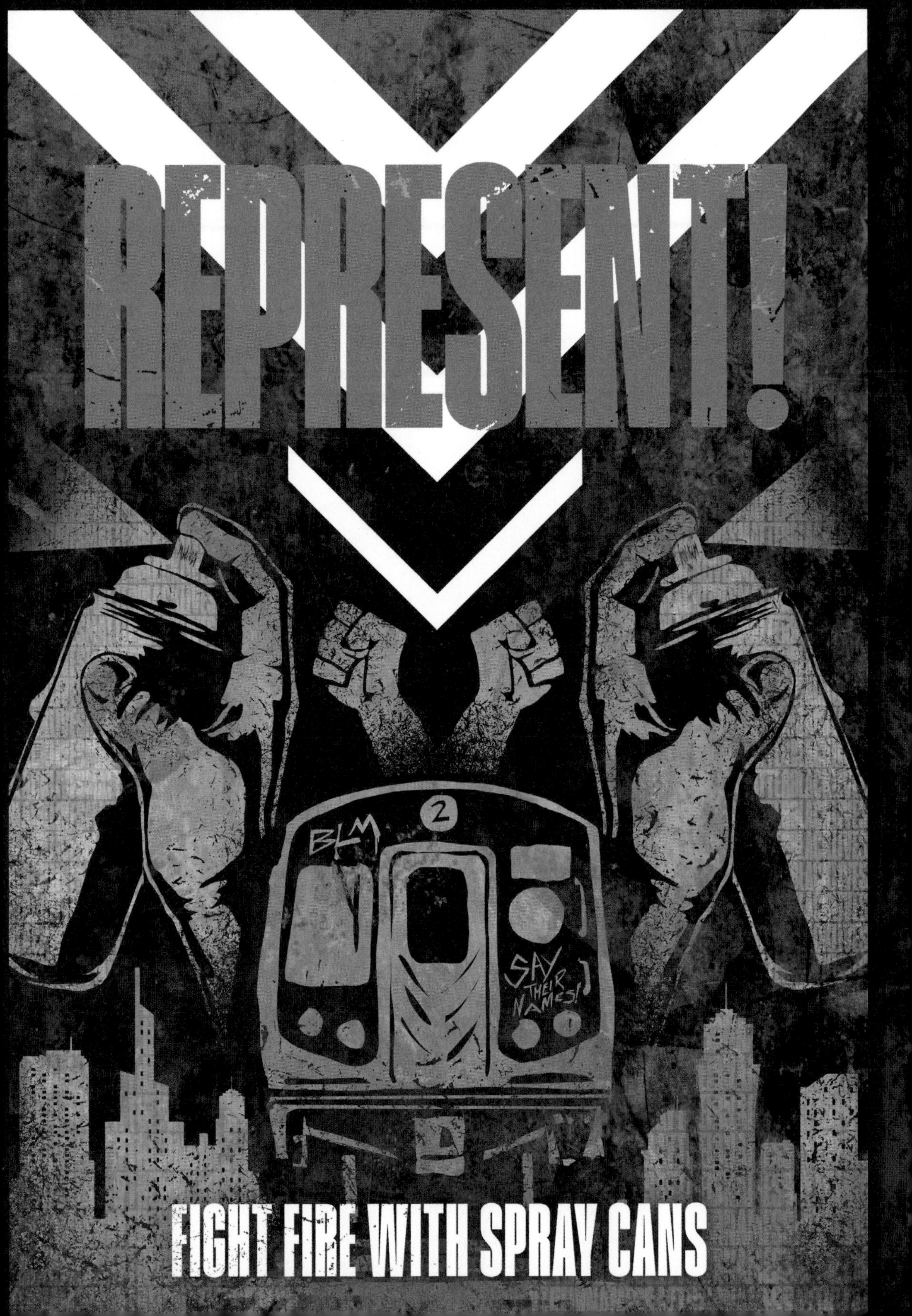
REPRESENT!
BLM
2
SAY THEIR NAMES!
FIGHT FIRE WITH SPRAY CANS

ISSUE #2 "HERITAGE" LAYOUTS BY DOUG BRAITHWAITE

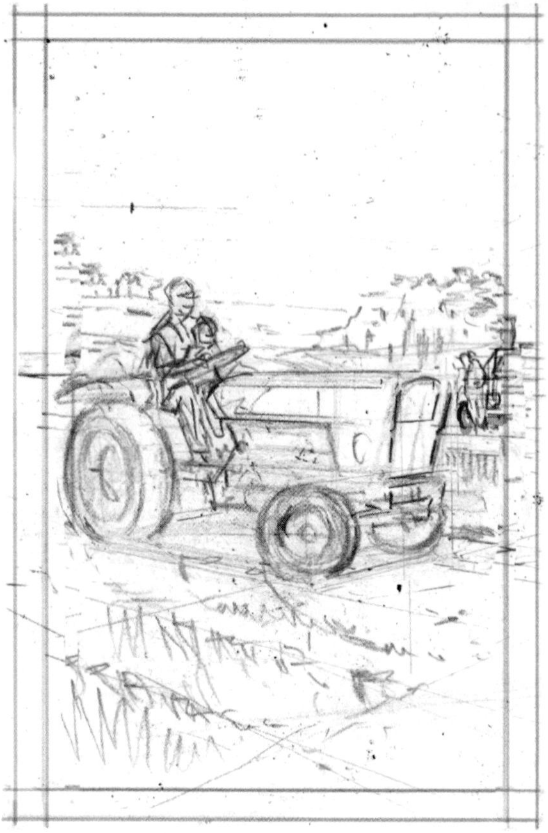

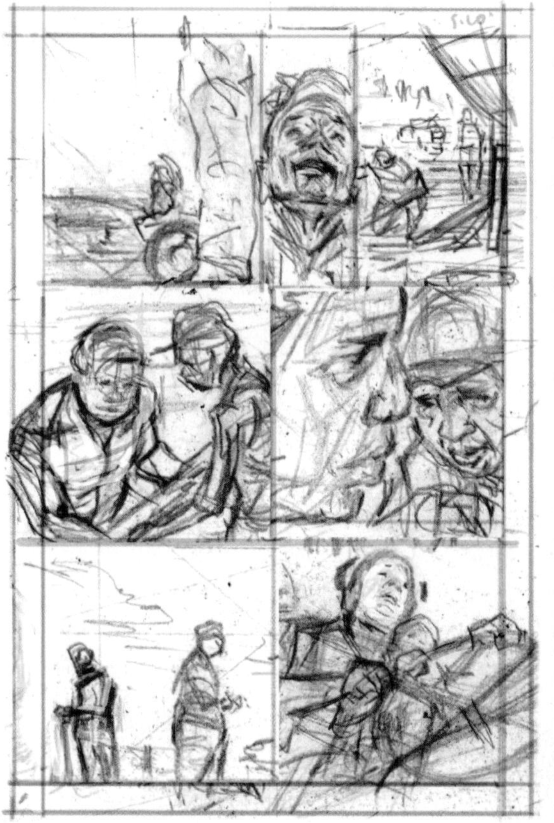

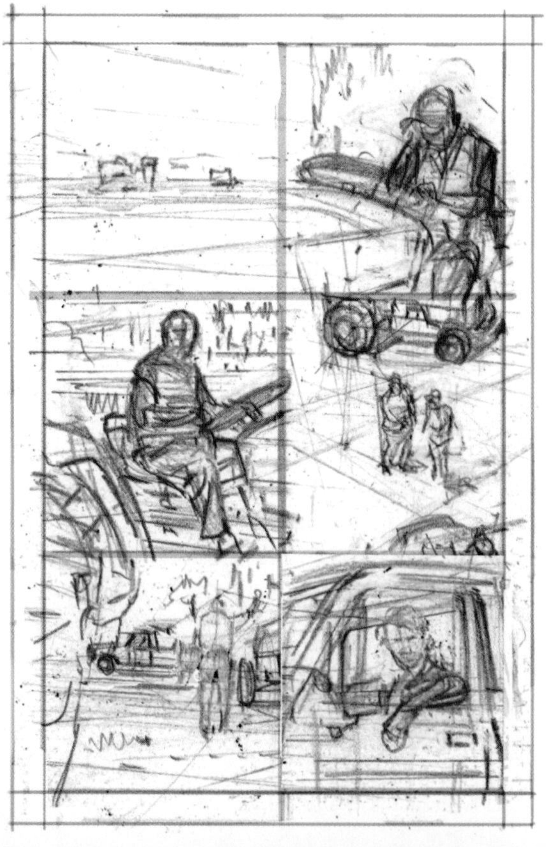

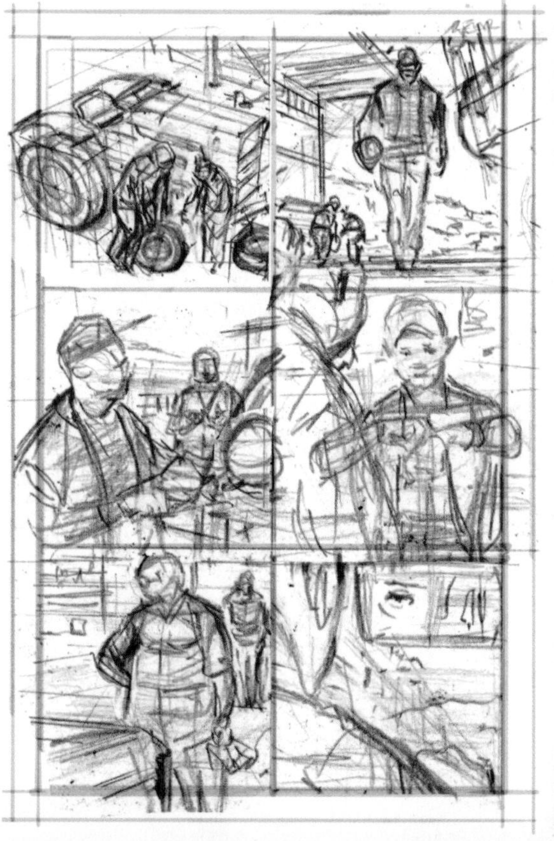

ISSUE #8 "IN DEFENSE OF FREE SPEECH" LAYOUTS BY N. STEVEN HARRIS

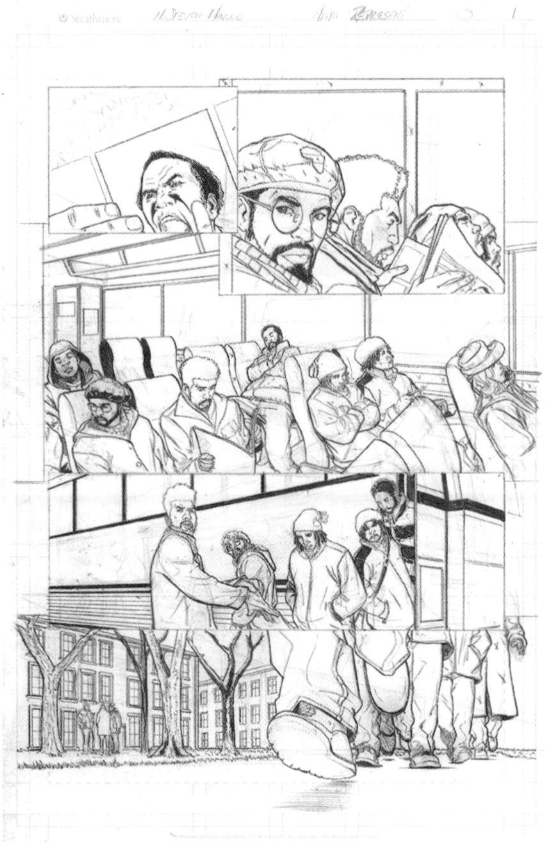

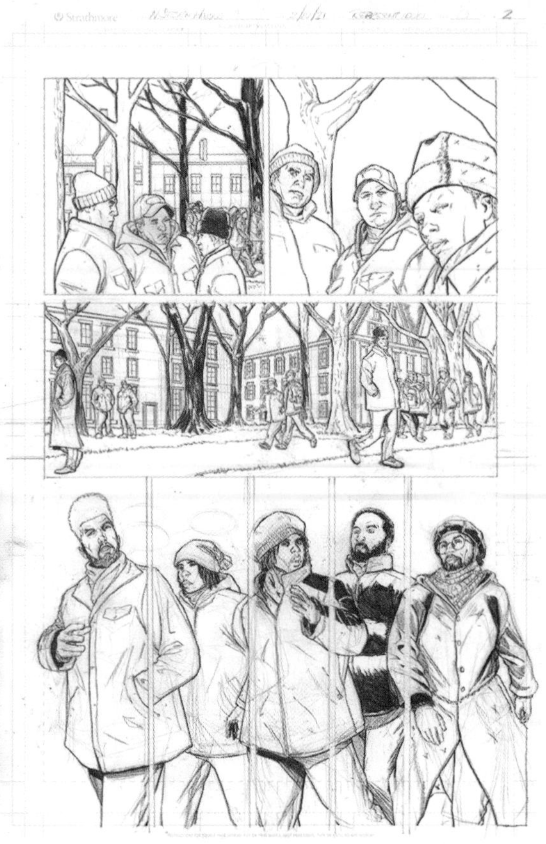

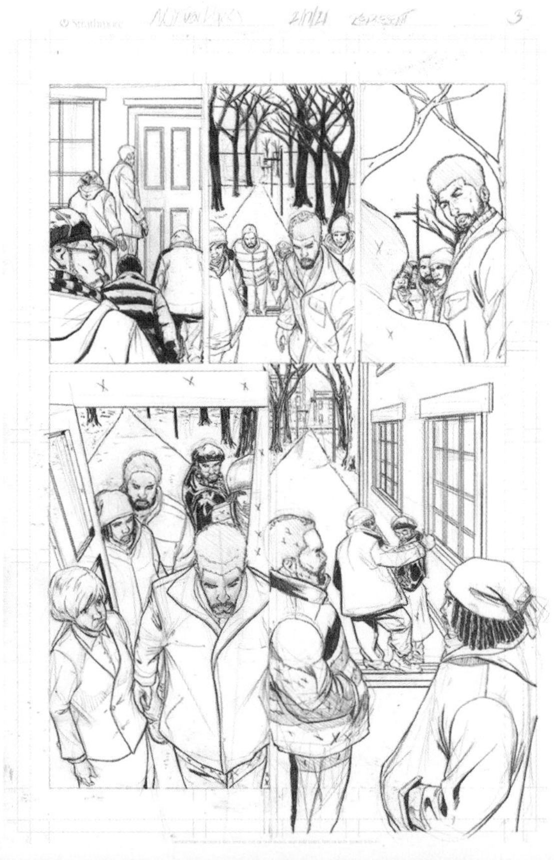

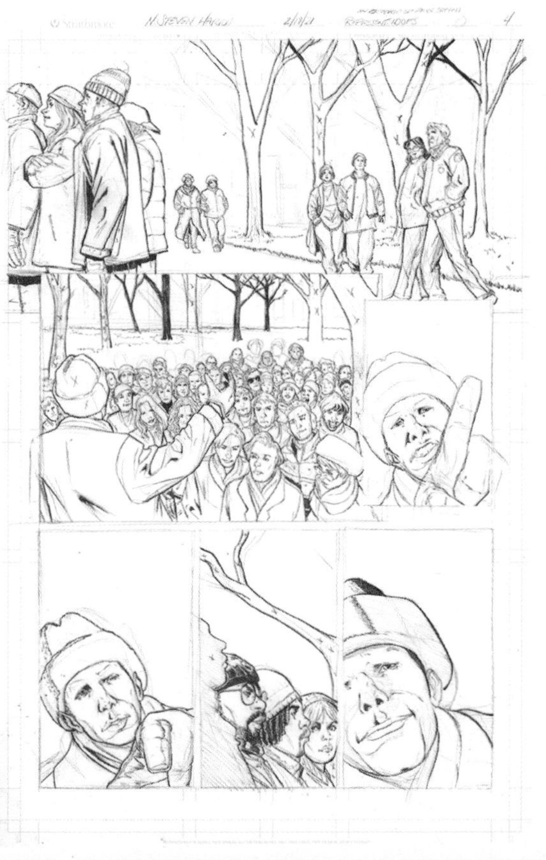

ISSUE #14 "I'LL CATCH UP"

PENCILS BY TONY AKINS

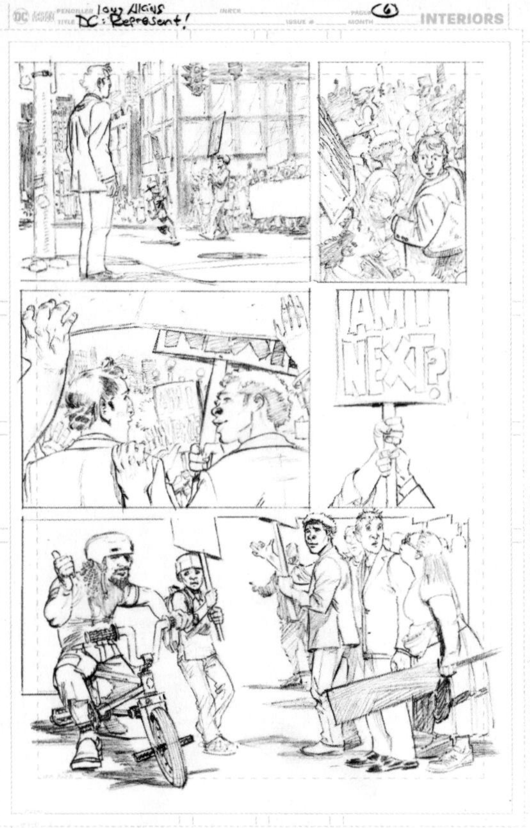

PENCILLER Tony Akins
TITLE DC: Represent!
PAGE# 6
INTERIORS
AM I NEXT?

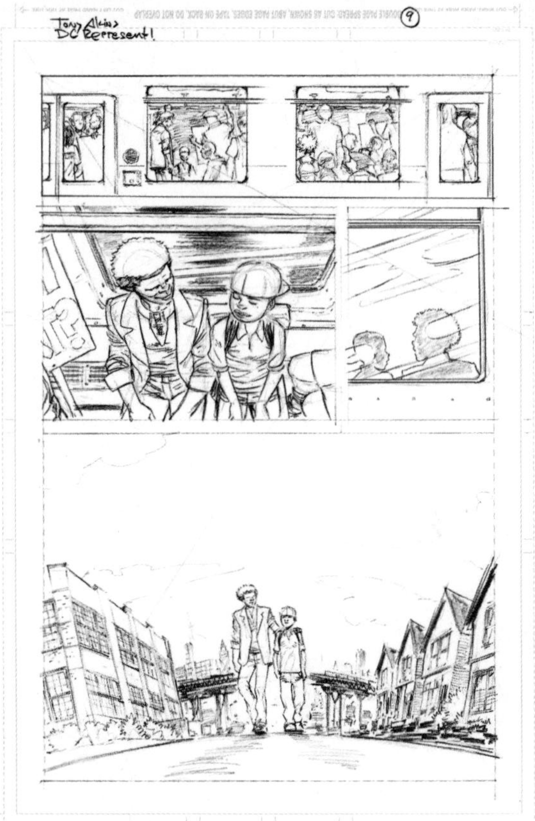

Tony Akins
DC Represent!
9

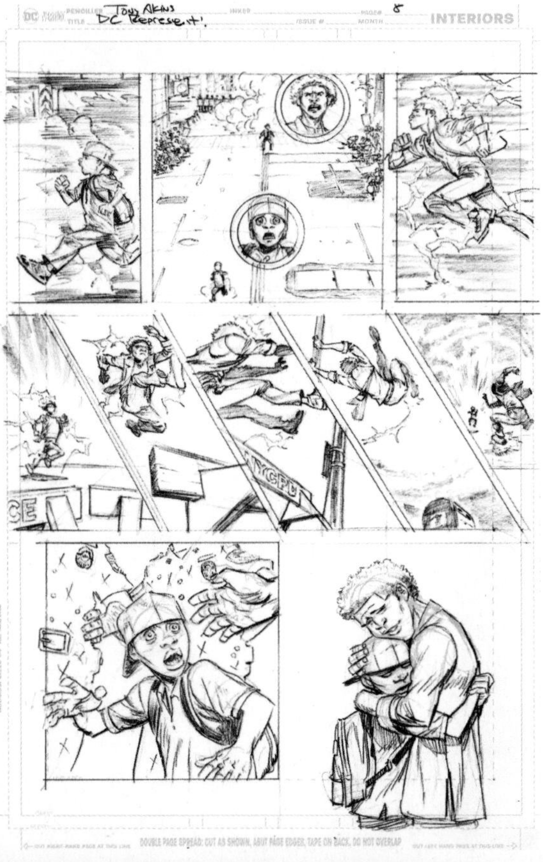

PENCILLER Tony Akins
TITLE DC Represent!
PAGE# 8
INTERIORS

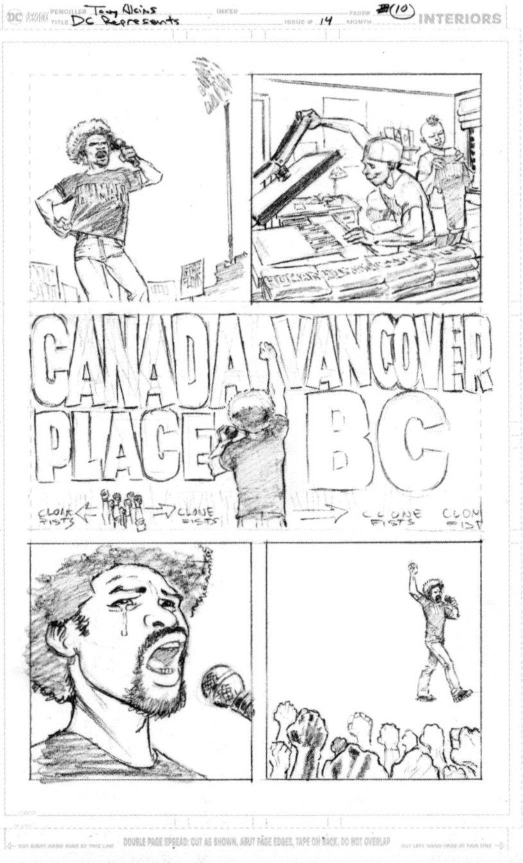

PENCILLER Tony Akins
TITLE DC Represents
ISSUE # 14
PAGE# #10
INTERIORS
CANADA VANCOVER
PLACE BC
CLONE FISTS
CLONE FISTS
CLONE FISTS